Our Man in Charleston

OUR MAN IN CHARLESTON

Britain's Secret Agent in the Civil War South

CHRISTOPHER DICKEY

CROWN PUBLISHERS
NEW YORK

Copyright © 2015 by Christopher Dickey

Published in the United States by Crown Publishers,
an imprint of the Crown Publishing Group,
a division of Penguin Random House LLC, New York.
www.crownpublishing.com

CROWN is a registered trademark, and the Crown colophon
is a trademark of Penguin Random House LLC.

Library of Congress Cataloging-in-Publication Data
Dickey, Christopher.
Our man in Charleston : Britain's secret agent in the Civil War South /
Christopher Dickey. — First edition.
      pages cm
   1. Bunch, Robert, 1820– 2. Diplomats—Great Britain—Biography.
3. Spies—Great Britain—History—19th century. 4. Espionage—Great
Britain—History—19th century. 5. Diplomatic and consular service,
British—United States—History—19th century. 6. Diplomatic and
consular service, British—Confederate States of America. 7. United
States—Foreign relations—Great Britain. 8. Great Britain—Foreign
relations—United States. 9. Confederate States of America—Foreign
relations—Great Britain. 10. Great Britain—Foreign relations—
Confederate States of America. I. Title.
E469.D53 2015
973.7'86092—dc23
[B]

                          2015016637

ISBN 978-0-307-88727-6
eBook ISBN 978-0-307-88729-0

PRINTED IN THE UNITED STATES OF AMERICA

Map: David Lindroth
Title page photograph: © Illustrated London News Ltd/Mary Evans Picture
Library
Title page and part opener art: © Marilyn Volan/Shutterstock
Jacket design: Christopher Brand
Jacket photographs: (figure) Maggie Brodie/Trevillion Images; (tape strip)
Andrew Rich/Getty

10 9 8 7 6 5 4 3 2 1

First Edition

For my grandchildren—
Elise, Calvin, Cecily, and Jason—
learning from the past;
looking to the future

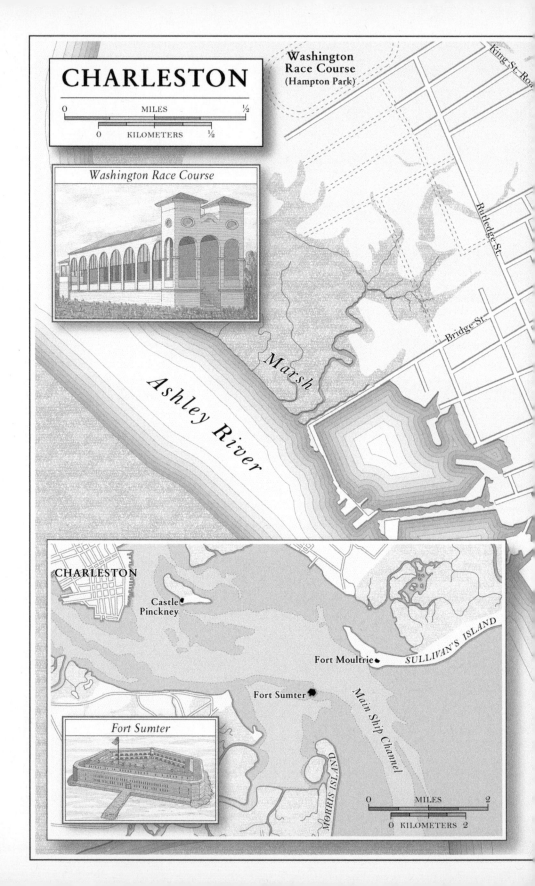

CHARLESTON

MILES 0 ½

KILOMETERS 0 ½

Washington Race Course (Hampton Park)

Washington Race Course

King St. Road

Rutledge St.

Bridge St.

Marsh

Ashley River

CHARLESTON

Castle Pinckney

Fort Moultrie

SULLIVAN'S ISLAND

Fort Sumter

Main Ship Channel

Fort Sumter

MORRIS ISLAND

MILES 0 2

KILOMETERS 0 2

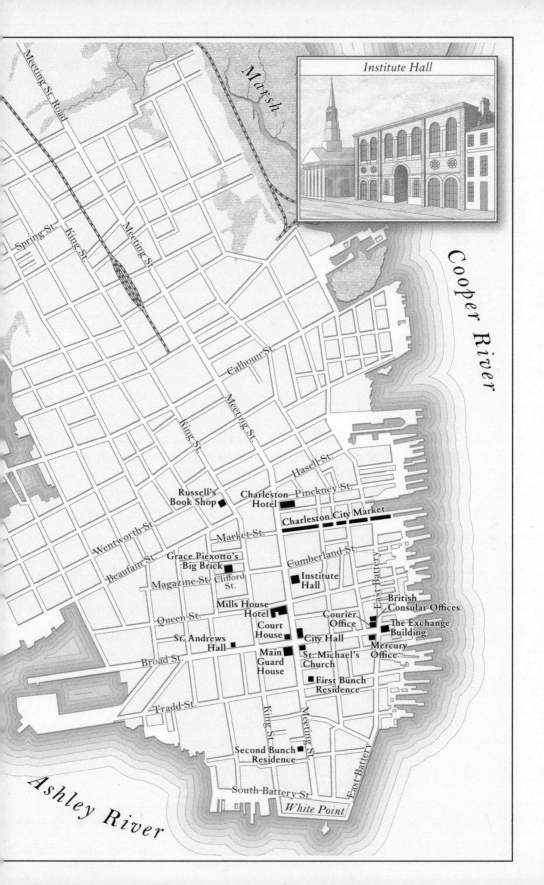

Institute Hall

Marsh

Cooper River

Ashley River

Meeting St. Road

Spring St.

King St.

Meeting St.

Calhoun St.

King St.

Meeting St.

Hasell St.

Russell's Book Shop

Charleston Hotel

Pinckney St.

Charleston City Market

Wentworth St.

Market St.

Beaufain St.

Grace Piexotto's Big Brick

Cumberland St.

East Battery

Magazine St.

Clifford St.

Institute Hall

Mills House Hotel

Courier Office

British Consular Offices

Queen St.

Court House

City Hall

The Exchange Building

St. Andrews Hall

Main Guard House

St. Michael's Church

Mercury Office

Broad St.

First Bunch Residence

Tradd St.

King St.

Meeting St.

Second Bunch Residence

East Battery

South Battery St.

White Point

CONTENTS

"We have seen, at every step, that every defiant movement of Slavery was a stab at its own heart. . . . Its animal ferocity evoked the energy which crushed it."

—*Westminster Review*, London, 1865

———————————

"I must dissemble."

—British Consul Robert Bunch, Charleston, South Carolina, 1856

WILLIAM HOWARD RUSSELL, ON ASSIGNMENT for the *Times* of London to cover the American War Between the States, was up late drinking on the riverboat *Southern Republic* as it cruised with the current on its way down from Montgomery to Mobile. The evening was warm and felt a little lazy that May of 1861. People were talking a lot about fighting as the War of Secession gathered momentum, but, at that point, few were dying. Russell's barroom companions—rich planters and parvenu businessmen—declaimed for hours, whiskey in hand, about Yankees and slaves and the Southern struggle for independence from the North until the air grew heavy with the burning tar of bad cigars, and electric with armchair bravery. "We will never be conquered," one would say. "There is nothing on earth that could make us go back into the Union," another proclaimed. "We will burn every bale of cotton, fire every house, and lay waste every field and homestead before we will yield to the Yankees!"

Captain Timothy Meaher, the boat's owner, was drinking with the rest of them, and he focused his cunning gray eyes on Russell. Meaher figured the foreign journalist might not understand the way folks did things here in America, so close to the old frontier. White men had claimed this land, and white men had brought it civilization, and men like Meaher had made their fortunes here doing whatever needed doing to get ahead. Not so long ago, said the captain, there were a lot of Indians along the river. But the settlers had trapped them on a bluff high above and starved them into surrendering. They were so desperate that, when the white men told them they could leave on boats, the Indians believed them. And once they were on the river, the white men, well, they just shot the hell out of them, Meaher said. Slaughtered hundreds!

Russell was not much impressed. He knew Meaher's type. The captain's blood was Irish, and Russell, who was Irish too, figured it was County Kerry blood. He could tell from Meaher's square jaw and full lips. The captain was rawboned and rough and looked as if he could handle himself in a brawl. He liked to tell tales, and tall ones, and he could be intimidating even when he was having a laugh—maybe especially when he was having a laugh.

The other guests harrumphed their approval and raised their glasses to Meaher's story about pioneer bravado, but Russell knew that the coming fight with the Union Army would be like nothing these men had seen or imagined before. Over the previous decade Russell had made his reputation as a correspondent witnessing the carnage in the Crimea, where the British and the French had fought the Russians. His dispatch about the charge of the Light Brigade had captured the imagination of the world; his descriptions of the grotesque suffering of the sick and wounded soldiers had horrified it. Russell had covered the uprising in India that almost cost Britain the heart of its empire, and he had seen and reported the savagery on all sides. He had slept many times—too many times—on battle-fields where "the air stinks of blood."

What Russell thought about this war in America in May 1861 was that it would be long and savage in the way that only modern warfare could be. Killing would take place on an industrial scale. The South had seceded. The North had declared it would fight to preserve the Union. Tens of thousands of troops were being called up, and histrionic headlines shouted about battles won and lost. But there had been, as yet, nothing more than skirmishes. Even the shelling of Fort Sumter, which had officially started the shooting war a few weeks before, had ended with the surrender of the Federal garrison before anyone was killed. Such "battles" were making for a lot of bourbon-fueled bravado, but they wouldn't decide the conflict.

Russell went out on deck. Beyond the dim glow of the cigars and the crackling flames of pinewood in iron baskets that lit the boat's way down the river, the banks were steep and forested and unwelcoming. Broken branches and other flotsam crowded the muddy water. Torches lit the wharves where the boat would wheel around to take on logs for fuel and a few bales of cotton. At harvest time, later in the year, the decks would be stacked with that white gold. But now only a few wretched slaves watched from the flickering shadows as the boat hands scrambled ashore for the wood that fed the boiler's maw. Sparks flew from the smokestacks. Fireflies, which the Alabamans called "lightning bugs," floated across a landscape otherwise as dark beneath the new moon as the shores of the Styx.

Russell's main worry as he made his way to his cabin that night was that he might be burned alive. The *Southern Republic* was an ostentatious thing, like a four-story hotel perched on a pontoon. The salon alone was a hundred feet long, thirty feet wide, and brightly painted, with staterooms around it like boxes in an opera house beneath a skylight of tinted glass. The boat also boasted offices, card rooms, and barrooms, and atop it all stood the calliope, its organ pipes fed by the engine's steam, its keyboard in the hands of an exiled French musician who alternated between "Dixie" and "La Marseillaise" whenever the *Southern Republic* approached a landing. But for all its pretensions of grandeur, the *Southern Republic*'s structure felt somehow perilous, improvised, and flimsy. The frame was made of resinous pine so raw that the turpentine oozed through the paint. The boat was a pile of kindling that, at the touch of a match, could sputter and flare into an inferno from which there would be no escape.

The wooden beams in Russell's cabin creaked and groaned, while below him the engine throbbed, shaking the whole ship whenever the paddle wheels strained against the current. Russell slept barely at all, and the next morning, as he looked into his shaving mirror, he saw the heavy-jowled face of a forty-one-year-old man who had talked and smoked and drunk way too much the night before and then had slept through breakfast.

Once up on deck, Russell found Captain Meaher in the company of a wealthy planter, and the conversation turned, as it so often did, to slaves. Russell was curious about the different classes of Negroes he saw on the boat. The stewards and maids looked well dressed and well mannered, but some of the hands had a wilder air about them. Could they be from Africa?

Russell knew that, for his British readers and their leaders, this could be—or should be—a critical question. Her Majesty's government could not tolerate the slave trade across the Atlantic. And Russell, as it happened, had just spent several days with Her Majesty's Consul Robert Bunch in Charleston, South Carolina. Lively and indiscreet, indefatigable and thoroughly British, or so he seemed, Bunch had very well-defined views and copious intelligence on the slave-trade question. In fact, it was something of an obsession for him. The consul had been following the horrific commerce for years, and told stories in grim detail about slaves smuggled under the American flag to Cuba and about the Southern firebrands who'd started bringing Negroes by the hundreds to the coasts of the United States. Some of these were people Bunch knew personally and despised, and he had shared much of what he knew with the man from the *Times*. So, yes, Russell was more than a little curious about some of the young slaves he'd seen on the *Southern Republic*.

The planter said he would let Russell in on a little story about Captain Meaher, and Meaher, who was right there, didn't seem to mind listening. Trafficking in slaves from Africa was, as everybody knew, a hanging offense according to Federal law, and it had been so for almost forty years. But times were changing, and as America pushed west—as the South pushed west—opening up new land, there was a hell of a lot of money to be made with slaves farming sugar and cotton. So a group of investors had commissioned a brig to sail from Alabama to the Congo to bring back good, strong human stock. The investors had agreed to pay a certain amount for the vessel and for each head of human cargo if the ship made it and, obviously, a lesser amount if she were seized by the Federal government or lost at sea. Eventually the brig reappeared off the coast of Mobile, and, whether by design or luck, no authorities were waiting to intercept her.

Now, as the planter on the *Southern Republic* continued telling Russell the tale, he made it seem that Captain Meaher had been a shrewd and lucky bystander to the event. At the time he was captain of a riverboat called the *Czar*, which docked alongside the slave brig that evening at dusk. The next morning the sailing vessel was gone, no one knew where, but the human cargo remained, and in the weeks and months that followed, the captain was suddenly rich in fine slaves—enough to let him buy a lot of land and to build the *Southern Republic*. The original investors lost their money, but what recourse did they have? None of them wanted to risk getting hanged for slaving, even if nobody could remember that happening to anyone they'd ever heard of. "Captain Meaher, as an act of grace, gave us a few old niggers but kept the rest for himself," said the planter.

Meaher listened to the tale with a triumphant grin. The truth was well known in those parts: Meaher himself had commissioned the slaving expedition across the Atlantic from start to finish. He'd found the investors among his friends, and he'd had the brig constructed to carry human cargo. It was his to-hell-with-Washington, we'll-do-what-we-damn-well-please project, and he simply wanted to have a little fun with Russell—maybe send a message to those damn British abolitionists.

"Well, now, you think those niggers I have aboard came from Africa? I'll show you." Meaher's eye settled on a boy who looked to be about twelve years old. He was fat and nearly naked, his skin a deep black, his cheeks marked with parallel scars, his chest tattooed, and his white teeth filed to points. Everything about him said he was born and raised and given ritual scars in Africa.

"What's your name?" the captain asked him.

"Bully," said the boy.

"Where were you born?"

"Born in South Carolina, sir."

"There, you see?" said the captain, sure that everyone around him understood the joke. "I've got a lot of these black South Carolina niggers aboard."

"How did he get those marks on his face?" Russell asked.

"Oh, them? Well, it's a way them nigger women has of marking their children to know them."

"And on his chest?"

"Well, really, I do believe them's marks against the smallpox."

"Why are his teeth filed?"

"Ah, there now! You'd never have guessed it: Bully done that himself, for the greater ease of biting victuals."

The Southerners exchanged knowing smiles. The captain and his planter friends finally admitted that they were obliged to bring a few Africans in now and then to make up for those slaves who escaped north to British Canada and to freedom. They understood that the Brits opposed slavery, but they still needed Southern cotton, and they thought London ought to appreciate what was required to keep producing it.

So there it was. These Southerners openly made a joke of their inhumanity and, as they saw it, of Great Britain's long-standing commitment to eradicate the transatlantic slave trade. Russell wondered how the men could be so naïve. Had they ignored fifty years of history? Did they think the Crown could be treated like some venal shopkeeper, willing to accommodate any crime in order to turn a profit? This was just the sort of thing Consul Bunch had predicted Russell might find. The journalist recorded the conversation in his dispatch with very little embellishment. He would let the smug slavers on the *Southern Republic* hang themselves.

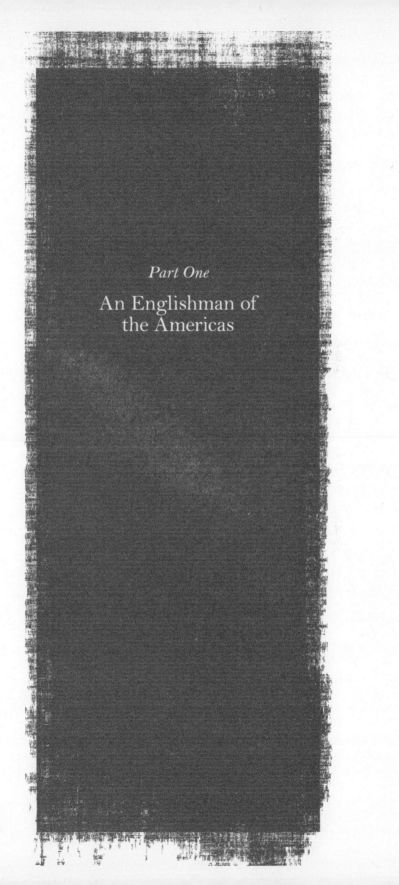

Part One

An Englishman of
the Americas

THE JOURNEY FROM WASHINGTON, D.C., to Charleston, South Carolina, took two days and two nights in 1853, which gave a traveler a lot of time to think, especially if he was with a new bride and about to embark on an ambitious new assignment in a place and culture and clime that he thought both he and she were sure to hate.

Robert Bunch was thirty-two years old and about to assume the office of British consul in Charleston. He was not an imposing figure. He had sharp blue eyes and was slight of build; his hair was thinning; he dressed with little flair and comported himself in a manner, as William Howard Russell noted years later, that was "thoroughly British." Bunch was energetic and perceptive, with an acid wit when he was among those few people he genuinely took into his confidence, and his persistence could be annoying. An ambitious man, he had spent years maneuvering to get posted as Her Majesty's consul *somewhere*, and while serving as the deputy consul in New York City he'd played every angle he could. Finally the Foreign Office put him in Philadelphia, a major American city and a prime assignment, but he'd been there only a matter of weeks when suddenly London decided he should trade places with the consul in Charleston, who'd created an ugly international incident about the treatment of Negro British sailors.

Bunch had to judge whether South Carolina was a post that would bring him advancement or stall his career like a sinking boat in a fetid swamp. A consul's job could be like that of an exalted clerk, or it could be the work of a diplomat. Some of Her Majesty's consuls, over the years, had exercised great authority in other parts of the world, even calling in British warships to enforce British interests. What Bunch wanted was to use his new post as a bridge to a full-fledged position in the diplomatic service as a chargé d'affaires or, in his boldest dreams, a minister to a foreign government. In

Charleston, the array of issues he'd have to deal with, which centered on the problem of slavery, were ones important to London politically and economically—certainly more important than the commercial details he'd been cataloguing in Pennsylvania. And his predecessor in Charleston had made a glorious mess of things. Could Bunch do better? He was tempted to think that he could hardly do worse.

Bunch's predecessor had not even been seen in Charleston for more than a year. George Buckley Mathew had lingered in London most of that time, holed up in the Carlton Club on St. James's Street, because, as he said, his performance of his "duties" in South Carolina had rendered his presence there, "in a social sense, very unpleasant." Many thought it was his performance, period, that had been the problem. Mathew's high opinion of himself was notorious. Contempt for the American "mobocracy" was common currency in the British Foreign Service, and Mathew did little to conceal his disdain. Soon after his appointment to Charleston in 1850, he took copious quantities of strong Madeira wine to the state capital, Columbia, and set about plying the legislators. It was a friendly enough gesture, but behind their backs he called the lawmakers "small fry" and suggested he knew "better than they did what was good for them." The Carolinians, proud to a fault in any case, understood soon enough what his real feelings were. Instead of winning their approval, he earned their opprobrium.

Yet Mathew was of a class, and with the connections, that gave him, in British society, vast leeway to fail. He was as much a soldier, a landowner, and a politician as he was a diplomat. (With unconvincing self-deprecation he called himself "a poor Peelite and West Indian proprietor.") He had been a member of Parliament and governor of the Bahama Islands. He also had the particular backing of the long-serving Foreign Secretary, Lord Palmerston, whose passionate opposition to slavery was characterized by moral righteousness, political wiliness, and commercial ruthlessness. Palmerston believed in the use of Britain's great military power whenever and wherever its flag or its citizens were challenged. And Palmerston had appointed Mathew to Charleston to make a muscular defense of the Crown's interests.

Bunch hated Mathew. He detested his arrogance and his inflated reputation. But at that moment, as he traveled to Charleston to try to set things straight, he himself could not be sure of consistent backing from London. He had no military rank, no political title, no lands to speak of. When Mathew was consul in South Carolina—when he was actually on the ground there—his overbearing personality made him offensive to the provincials, and Bunch certainly could present himself as someone different, younger, more self-effacing, more subtle, more visibly appreciative of the Carolinians' concerns. All that was certain. But there really was no guarantee that Bunch could solve the problems that Her Majesty's government wanted solved. And failure, in his case, unlike Mathew's, could mean the termination of his hopes for a career in diplomacy.

The specific issue Mathew was supposed to have dealt with, and that Bunch was inheriting, was the treatment of black British seamen. Most of them were from the British West Indies, and all of them were free men. Under the laws of South Carolina, if they went ashore or even came into Charleston Harbor, they would be thrown into jail until their ship was about to sail and only then put back on board—that is, if they were lucky. The ostensible reason for all this was the fear that West Indian blacks might have a subversive influence on the local slaves and even incite them to insurrection. White Southerners lived in constant dread that if their servants and laborers were exposed to blacks who had tasted real freedom, they might be inspired to rise up and kill their masters. The fear had grown incalculably worse after the slave uprisings and massacres in French Saint-Domingue, or Haiti, in the late eighteenth century. Then the British had freed all their slaves in the West Indies in the 1830s. The infection of freedom was feared to be contagious. Talk of emancipation was treated in the American South as a kind of disease that might arrive aboard ships. Liberated blacks were seen as carriers of an insurrectionary plague that must be quarantined.

The first Negro Seamen Act was passed in 1822, after a planned slave uprising in Charleston was said to have been inspired and organized by a free person of color originally from the West Indies named Denmark Vesey, who had lived and worked and preached in South Carolina for years. The law was aimed at transient sailors from the North or from other countries. Under the act's provisions, county sheriffs would be obliged to arrest all black seamen, regardless of nationality, until their ships were ready to leave harbor. The captain of the ship would have to pay for the cost of the incarceration, and if he refused to do so, he could be fined and imprisoned, while the black sailors aboard his vessel would be "deemed and taken as absolute slaves, and sold." There was also the risk that the jailed British seamen would be kidnapped by God knows who and sold into slavery God knows where. They were, after all, valuable livestock in the slave markets of the South.

Thirty years later the law was still on the books in South Carolina, it had been replicated in other Southern states, and the issue was a major annoyance for the British. Every time they made port calls in the South, the blacks aboard would be dragged off and thrown into prison, or worse, and the indignation in London grew steadily more intense. When a black stewardess from a British ship was jailed and nearly raped in Alabama, Lord Palmerston denounced the policy as one that had "no parallel in the conduct of any other civilized country."

The feeble Federal government in Washington did not want to intervene for fear that any effort to regulate the treatment of blacks in Southern states, whether they were free or slave, might break the Union apart. So Palmerston gave increasing power to the consuls to deal directly with the state governments. Some took a tactful, fairly conciliatory approach, and with adequate success, as the laws were changed or ceased to be enforced. But in South Carolina, where the people already had a hair-trigger reflex on any slave-related issue,

Mathew, the old military man, repeatedly struck a pose of moral indignation. He wrote formal letters to the governor of South Carolina that were leaked to the press and managed not only to offend local sensibilities but also to outrage Northern commentators who wondered why someone in Her Majesty's service would be dealing with South Carolina as if it were a sovereign state. As Mathew found himself ostracized in Charleston, criticized in Washington, and questioned in London about the path he was pursuing, he only grew more truculent. He started threatening South Carolina politicians with unspecified consequences if they didn't come around on the Negro seamen issue.

In 1850, as it had done before and would afterward, South Carolina was thinking about pulling out of the Union. Mathew seemed to suggest that if Britain did not get what it wanted, it would never back South Carolina's drive toward secession, but, then again, he did not guarantee it would back secession in any case. Eventually everything he asked for in the state, no matter how reasonable, and everything he demanded, no matter how dire the threats that surrounded it, was deemed utterly unacceptable by almost every person of influence in South Carolina. Finally in 1852, after consultations in Washington, Mathew vowed to take the cases of two jailed black British seamen to the United States Supreme Court. This he did against the advice of the Charleston lawyer he'd retained, the redoubtable James L. Petigru, who was one of the most respected attorneys and one of the strongest voices for moderation in a state where indignant rage was as common as yellow fever. Petigru warned Mathew that Carolinians would ignore the Supreme Court if they didn't like its ruling, and if that helped lead to secession, many of them would think that was so much the better. In the meantime Mathew found himself snubbed wherever he turned. His dispatches to London conveyed a growing sense of futility.

By the time the court cases were decided, Mathew had abandoned his post. He left Charleston in October 1852, settled into the Carlton Club, a fifteen-minute walk from the Foreign Office on Downing Street, and set about negotiating a new position for himself. But his patron, Lord Palmerston, was no longer Foreign Secretary, and the Earl of Clarendon, who took over in February 1853, had little use for Mathew's excuses. In a sure sign of displeasure, Foreign Office clerks started questioning the consul's expense accounts. And when Mathew finally did decide to return to the United States in June that year—not to Charleston but to New York and eventually to the consulate in Philadelphia—the Foreign Office refused to pay for his passage.

Intentionally or not, Mathew's tone-deaf handling of what was referred to in correspondence as "the coloured seamen issue" threw into relief the qualities that a man might need to survive as British consul in a place as prone to outrage as Charleston. Any official who hoped to achieve Her Majesty's ends there must be capable of a more delicate touch, with more savoir faire, more social awareness. To live among the slave-owning planters and make inroads into their society, charming them while never forgetting the core interests of the Crown, required a man with a special background and demeanor, and Robert Bayley Bunch had a very unusual pedigree.

Although Bunch seemed on first acquaintance to be thoroughly British, he was, in fact, an Englishman of the Americas, including South America. Bunch's mother was a New Yorker related on her father's side to such notable figures as Elizabeth Ann Bayley Seton (eventually named the first American saint), and on her mother's side to the Barclays, with a family tree that included Tories who had spied for the British during the American Revolution and the War of 1812, then served as the Crown's consuls general in New York City up into the 1850s. These were very well-connected clans deeply embedded in, and intermarried with, the other elite families of New York City, including the Van Cortlandts and the Roosevelts, and they kept very close ties with one another. Indeed, Emma Craig, Bunch's new wife, was also his first cousin: the daughter of his American mother's sister.

Bunch's father, on the other hand, was an English gunrunner, originally based in Jamaica and the Bahamas, who helped finance and arm the great Latin American revolutionary Simón Bolívar. *El Libertador* eventually gave the elder Bunch a large tract of land outside of Bogotá, and Bunch brought in British experts to help him set up the first ironworks in what was then called Nueva Granada.

Robert Bayley Bunch and his younger sister and brother were all born in the United States in the 1820s and baptized at the very heart of the American establishment, in New York City's Trinity Church, where Wall Street meets Broadway. But their mother died when they were still small children, so they grew up in the homes of relatives and, eventually, on the Colombian estate, or *finca*, that belonged to their father. Bunch probably spent some time in school in Britain and later said that he went to Oxford, but he does not appear in the university's lists of graduates.

His first Foreign Service–related jobs were in Colombia, as an unpaid secretary working for the British envoy in Bogotá, then in Peru, before finally heading to New York in 1848 aboard the packet steamer *Trent* to work as the vice consul under Anthony Barclay, one of his cousins. The young deputy's cosmopolitan roots soon recommended him to Lord Henry Bulwer, the British minister to Washington, who entrusted him with several delicate assignments far removed from consular routine. New York City, with its enormous population of immigrants, exiles, and visiting notables was a center of perpetual intrigue, and Bunch learned about those groups and conspiracies that might affect the Crown's interests. He tracked the activities of adventurers plotting to invade Cuba. He appears to have planted stories in the New York press opposing efforts by the tycoon Cornelius Vanderbilt to monopolize the lucrative passage from the Atlantic to the Pacific across Nicaragua. He followed the activities of revolutionaries who fought to unite Italy alongside Giuseppe Garibaldi, who was living on Staten Island at the time. Bunch also watched shipyards where Britain's enemies might have naval vessels built, and he spied on the construction of the racing yacht *America* before it sailed against the Royal Yacht

Club in the fateful competition off the Isle of Wight that became known as the America's Cup race. He was developing his skills as an observer, an ingratiator, a cultivator of useful contacts, and a conversationalist skilled in extracting information. He learned how important it was not only to collect facts, but to calculate the best occasion to use them.

Bunch's private letters to his superiors could be amazingly informal and complicitous, and, given Bunch's record of unusual assignments, by early 1851 he felt he'd earned sufficient credibility to ask a few favors of Lord Henry Bulwer, which would have been quite out of character for another consul, not to mention a deputy consul. In March, Bunch was headed to London for a visit. In a chatty letter to "My Dear Sir Henry," he asked if he could carry some diplomatic correspondence, "any unimportant dispatch for the Foreign Office," so he could get through customs more easily. (This notion of the private ends to which a diplomatic pouch could be used would haunt him years later.) And with purely pro forma modesty, Bunch asked for a personal introduction to the by-then-legendary Foreign Secretary, Lord Palmerston.

Whether Bunch got his wish for a one-on-one with Palmerston is doubtful, but the consul was staying on Pall Mall and could spend as much time as he liked around the Foreign Office, so brief encounters with the Foreign Secretary were possible. Longer meetings with the clerks who ran the place from day to day were imperative. And many of them were involved with an issue that Palmerston viewed with enormous interest and pride.

The biggest single section of the Foreign Office at the time was the Slave Trade Department, staffed by overworked and underpaid "zealots and helots" who devoted themselves to tracking the global commerce in human chattel and, when possible, worked to stop it. For Bunch, these were useful men to know. The issue of slavery and the slave trade—an obsession for some of the most powerful men in London—had been important to the advancement of his early career in Latin America, where treaties for the suppression of the trade were one of Palmerston's major priorities, and in New York City, where slave ships were built and outfitted. The Slave Trade Department required careful and voluminous reporting on these matters, and Bunch already considered himself something of an authority on the subject.

When the British consul in Philadelphia died in early 1853, Bunch applied for his job immediately and got it almost as quickly. But Lord Clarendon, who had become Foreign Secretary following a period of disarray after Palmerston stepped down, decided almost as quickly that he wanted the young operative in Charleston to clean up the string of disasters left behind by Mathew and, finally, to amend or end the abominable Negro Seamen Act.

The posting was a tremendous vote of confidence in the vice consul, but Bunch was at first, if not reluctant, then cautious. "I should very much like to try my hand at the nigger question, and I am, moreover, very anxious to get into a *political* office," he wrote to John Crampton, the old bachelor who had served for years as chargé in Washington and had at last been promoted to minister after Bulwer departed. Bunch's "hankerings," he said, were not after consular work but "diplomacy." To go to live in Charleston, however, was not a happy prospect. The city was virtually uninhabitable in the summer months; it was a very, very small town at any time of year compared to the bustle of New York City or, for that matter, Philadelphia; and, precisely as "a *political* office," an assignment in Charleston was a treacherous one for a British envoy. It was the epicenter of all the contradictions that London, whatever its passions, found difficult to face. England hated slavery but loved the cotton the slaves raised, and British industry depended on it. Defending Britain's political interests while serving its commercial interests required constant delicate diplomacy, even in the most informal settings.

Bunch postponed this trip south as long as he possibly could— months after he first learned of the assignment. "I could not, of course, be required to go to Charleston before the autumn," he wrote in May. "It is almost certain death to one not acclimated to begin there in the summer." Then there had been the matter of his wedding. In October he'd married Emma Craig at a ceremony in New York presided over by an English bishop. The organ had piped "God Save the Queen" as they left the church. They'd honeymooned in Connecticut. And now it was November.

The Bunches' train stopped in Richmond and then in Petersburg, Virginia, which passed for an industrial city in the South, then traveled on to Weldon, North Carolina, on the Roanoke River. Robert and Emma passed through miles and miles of tobacco lands, and now they were starting to see the cotton fields, their picked stalks skeletal in the late-autumn sun. The farms, glimpsed through the sweating windows and the cinders and smoke from the train's engine, looked increasingly inhospitable. Sightings of white people grew rare, and those of slaves began to grow common.

A steamship would ferry the Bunches on an overnight voyage from Wilmington, North Carolina, to Charleston, South Carolina, taking them around the pestilential marshes and inlets—the Low Country, as the Carolinians called it. But still, Bunch could feel the morass closing in on him. What a mess Mathew had created. Why had Bunch agreed to trade Philadelphia for Charleston? The slave question was political, yes. The handling of it was diplomatic, yes— all to the good for one's career, perhaps—but the place, the people, the institution of slavery itself: Bunch looked on it all with loathing and probably with more than a little fear.

The ship plowed through rough seas all night, taking Robert Bunch and his wife to their new home in the middle of a gathering storm.

Chapter 2

WHEN ROBERT AND EMMA BUNCH arrived in Charleston on the morning of November 19, 1853,* the newly minted consul knew that making any progress on the Negro Seamen law would require him to approach the state's slave-owning politicians with sweet reason, or something that sounded like it, and so he would, no matter how much revulsion he felt for them or their institutions.

But ten days after his arrival he sent a frank dispatch to Lord Clarendon. Bunch had been making the rounds of those people he'd been told would be sympathetic to the Crown's views, starting with the distinguished attorney retained by Mathew, James Petigru. But after these first encounters with Charleston society, Bunch cautioned Clarendon, "It is most difficult for anyone not on the spot to form an adequate idea of the extreme sensitiveness and captious irritability of all classes of this community on the subject of Slavery." Even people who were, on other issues, "sensible and well informed," wanted to hear nothing about slavery's "inconveniences, its injustice, or its atrocities." Bunch told Clarendon that for South Carolinians slavery was "the very blood of their veins." Everything they produced or owned depended upon it, and "they become absolutely frantic when any attempt is made to interfere in their 'domestic concerns,' so that they would go to any length, and defy the Federal government, Great Britain, or the world combined, if an alteration in their Legislation were sought by coercion, or were it even threatened."

From a broader perspective, the Negro Seamen Act was just one manifestation of the long-simmering tension slavery had created between Britain and the United States. For decades the slave

---

* The *Charleston Mercury* recorded, as usual, the arrivals of all passengers disembarking at the port, among them "D. Bunch and sister." Accuracy was not the *Mercury*'s strong suit.

question had been tied to one ill-tempered eruption after another between the two nations, and nowhere were all these issues debated with more deadly passion than in South Carolina, a society that prided itself on old money and old values built up like an Attic façade to disguise the ugliness of the structure behind it. That many Carolina aristocrats saw themselves as sons of Britain, and quite a few had been educated there, only made the tensions more fraught. The Carolinians viewed British policies toward slavery as acts of madness or betrayal or both, especially in light of the unique role cotton played in binding their economies uncomfortably together.

In the middle of the nineteenth century, as everyone knew, the key commodity of the British Empire was cotton. The mills of Lancashire that wove cloth from it fed an industry that employed, directly or indirectly, more than a million people. Almost all the raw cotton fiber used to make that cloth was grown and picked by slaves in the American South, and that was a fact that the Crown had managed to live with for decades. So the Southerners had come to expect and even to demand British complacency about their "peculiar institution."

But the Southerners were not content to remain on their properties with their slaves, producing the white gold needed for Britain's mills. Indeed, they could not sit still. Cotton quickly burned out the nutrients in the soil, so land for new plantations constantly had to be cleared and sown, and that sort of work was, purely, slave work. The voracious cotton economy had driven the Americans to expand west into Texas. That led to war with Mexico and the annexation of enormous territories. The internal debate in the United States over what to do with all those vast, newly won lands after 1848 had deepened the bitter divisions between the hungry Southern "slavocracy" and the increasingly industrialized North. And it had raised growing concerns among the British about what seemed to be, quite literally, the boundless ambitions of the United States.

Freebooting American adventurers known as filibusters set out to conquer new territories in the Caribbean and Central America, a region where Great Britain had staked its own claims for territory and influence. Not only did the Americans see a Caribbean empire offering rich new fields for cotton, sugar, and slaves, but the gold rush in California that began in 1849 had made the godforsaken jungles of Panama and the lakes of Nicaragua suddenly vital—and profitable—links between the east and west coasts of the United States. Then there was the problem of Cuba. The American slave-owners wanted it badly so they could have new slave states represented in Congress and build new fortunes. The British were bent on stopping them from getting it.

Behind all this, and intertwined with it, was that one huge and complicated goal that every British government had pursued for almost fifty years: the elimination of the African slave trade. Politicians in London and businessmen in Liverpool could find many ways to rationalize the internal practices of their trading partners abroad; non-interference in another country's internal affairs was—theoretically, at least—a guiding principle of British foreign policy. But there could be no acceptance of a traffic so brutal and so deadly that it loomed in the minds of the British people as nothing less than a holocaust.

The campaign led by devout Christian and anti-slavery politician William Wilberforce to ban the trade in the late eighteenth and early nineteenth centuries had put forth detailed accounts of the gruesome suffering of human cargo on what was called the Middle Passage. There was a triangular trade pattern: Ships departed from Europe with manufactured goods, which were exchanged for kidnapped Africans, who were transported across the Atlantic from Africa as slaves—the Middle Passage. Millions were crammed into the fetid holds of the ships, and hundreds of thousands died. The survivors were then sold in the United States or traded for raw materials, which would be transported back to Europe. Eventually Wilberforce's campaign led both the United Kingdom and the

United States to ban the traffic in 1807.* By then, to oppose the trade was seen as a sign of civilization, to support it an indication of barbarity, even in the American South, which thought, at the time, that the natural growth of the slave population it already had could meet its needs. In the years that followed, the Royal Navy would station a permanent squadron on patrol off the West African coast, then off South America as well, intercepting the vessels of other nations suspected of carrying slaves and, in some cases, risking war to stop them.

Morality and politics were not the only driving forces in this campaign. The Crown's interest in abolishing the trade became commercial as well. After emancipation throughout the British Empire in 1833, the British colonies in the West Indies could not compete with the cheaper, slave-grown coffee and sugar put on the world market by Spanish colonies and Brazil, where slaves bought cheaply in Africa were expendable and worked until they died, only to be replaced by more imports. Over the course of six decades some five thousand British lives would be lost, and the Crown would sacrifice an average of nearly 2 percent of the national income in its crusade to eradicate the African trade.

The United States also stationed warships off the slave coasts of Congo and Benin, but for most of its existence the U.S. Navy's Africa Squadron was not very effective at interdicting the traffic. Over time, the American warships served more to obstruct British enforcement efforts than to support them, since the British were not allowed to board American merchant vessels even if they were strongly suspected of carrying slaves. As a result, ships flying the

---

* The U.S. ban passed in 1807 could not go into effect until 1808 because Article I, Section 9, of the Constitution of the United States, ratified in 1788, had guaranteed the rights of the states to bring in slaves for the next twenty years: "The Migration or Importation of such Persons as any of the States now existing shall think proper to admit, shall not be prohibited by the Congress prior to the Year one thousand eight hundred and eight, but a Tax or duty may be imposed on such Importation, not exceeding ten dollars for each Person."

Stars and Stripes landed hundreds of thousands of African slaves in Brazil and Cuba, even though, technically, the captains and crews were breaking Federal law, and by the 1850s Britain saw American-flagged vessels as the main remaining obstacle to the elimination of the transatlantic traffic. The triangular trade now began in New York. The horrors of the Middle Passage continued.

From Charleston, Robert Bunch could supply the Slave Trade Department in London with a steady stream of dispatches detailing the activities of Americans who wanted to defy Britain's policies in the Atlantic and the Caribbean. And he knew there would be an important audience for them. The British people recognized the fight against the traffic in Africans as one of the great moral crusades of history, and if that crusade could be said to have a chief enforcer, it was Henry John Temple, 3rd Viscount Palmerston, the man who would loom as the single most important figure in Robert Bunch's professional life.

Lord Palmerston was an extraordinary character. An Irish peer somewhat disdained by the English aristocracy, he was notoriously abrasive, parodied as "Lord Pumicestone," on the one hand, but also a politician with an instinct for public opinion who realized more than most of his contemporaries that it was important to understand what the people thought they wanted, that sometimes their lead had to be followed, and that often it could be guided. Not the least of Palmerston's skills was the writing of newspaper editorials, which was a rare talent among his rivals. He also leaked information often and skillfully to the London press.

A facet of Palmerston's character that especially amused and delighted the British public, much to the consternation of the strait-laced Queen Victoria and her husband, Prince Albert, was his utterly unabashed womanizing. He had multiple mistresses who cost him more money than he could afford. He married one of them—his favorite, Emily Cowper—when her husband, Lord Cowper, finally died, and she played no small role advancing young Palmerston's career: her brother was a powerful Whig leader and eventual Prime

Minister, Lord Melbourne. But Palmerston never settled down, and the reputation he earned in his youth as "Lord Cupid" stayed with him even when he was in his seventies—deaf, shortsighted, with wobbly false teeth and dyed hair. He was named as a corespondent in an infamous divorce case when he was seventy-eight.

There was, in a political and military sense, a certain, imposing promiscuity about Palmerston's handling of Britain's affairs as well. As Foreign Secretary, beginning in 1830, he wanted to be everywhere all the time. It's said the term "gunboat diplomacy" was coined to describe his inclination to send warships around the world enforcing his view of international order. He once blockaded Greece to make it pay for a British subject's house that was burned by a mob in Athens (the so-called Don Pacifico Affair).

For more than twenty years, Lord Palmerston had made the fight against the slave trade one of his signature causes—"Palmerston's benevolent crotchet," in the view of his critics—and he exploited it for all it was worth. His passions were first aroused by the enslavement of Greeks by the Ottomans in the 1820s, and throughout his long career he portrayed the fight against slavery as a war that "Christendom" must wage against the forces of darkness. By the early 1830s, when emancipation of the black slaves in Britain's colonies became an important electoral issue, Palmerston embraced it. He looked upon the excuses made by slave owners for their affronts against humanity as both cynical and delusional. "To hear masters of Slaves talk of Slavery," he snorted, one would think "it is the most delightful condition in which a human being can be placed."

Palmerston did not seek to interfere with those foreign countries, including the United States, where slaves were owned. Their vice merely vindicated his view that British civilization was superior. But the "Slave Trade" (he always capitalized the words) he treated as a separate issue, on which there could be no compromise. Britannia ruled the waves and would not let them be used for such an offense against humanity. More than once Lord Palmerston declared that Divine Providence, yes, God Almighty, had smiled on Great Britain because of the tremendous efforts it expended to eliminate the traffic in human beings. He liked to note the "curious coincidence" that "from the time when this country first began to abolish the Slave Trade, followed by abolishing slavery within the dominions of the Crown, and to use its influence for the suppression of the Slave Trade elsewhere, from that period this country has prospered in a degree which it never experienced before."

If societies in transition define themselves most clearly by what they oppose, then Britain in the first half of the nineteenth century, at a time when the middle class was rising and the aristocracy was threatened, found it possible nonetheless to unite in opposition to the horrors of the Middle Passage, and Palmerston played on that theme not only with the people, but with the monarchs.

So deeply felt and universal was the revulsion caused by the slave trade that in 1840 (when Palmerston already was in his second tour as Foreign Secretary) twenty-year-old Prince Albert, the newly married consort of the young Queen Victoria, decided to make his first public speech in London as the new president of the Society for the Extinction of the Slave Trade and for the Civilization of Africa. Albert was not looking for controversy when he accepted the position, but for affirmation, and that is what he got. This fledgling British royal, embarrassed by his thick German accent, carefully wrote out the brief speech in his first language, then laboriously translated it into English with Victoria's help and recited it repeatedly until he had it memorized. On the morning of June 1, he looked out at an audience that seemed to him to number in the thousands. As one of the MPs in attendance wrote, "all the world" crowded into Exeter Hall on the Strand to hear the prince denounce the "atrocious traffic in human beings, at once the desolation of Africa and the blackest stain upon civilized Europe" that was "repugnant to the spirit of Christianity." Sir Robert Peel, leader of the Conservative opposition in Parliament, followed with an emotional description of two slave ships that had closed their hatches during a storm on the high seas, leaving seven hundred slaves belowdecks to die from suffocation.

That morning was, for Albert, and for many who saw him there, an unforgettable moment.

Lord Palmerston was often provocative and sometimes stunningly belligerent. In 1840 he appointed David Turnbull, an ardent abolitionist and former correspondent for the London *Times* who had written a book about the ghastly condition of slaves in Cuba, as Britain's consul-general in Havana. Two years later Turnbull was expelled by Spanish authorities, and they eventually convicted him in absentia for allegedly fomenting a slave rebellion.

In the summer of 1844, during one of the relatively brief periods when Palmerston was in opposition and not in the cabinet, he made a defining speech before Parliament about the subject "which has now, for nearly half a century engaged the attention of the Parliament and people of this country." He noted that almost all the "most eminent and distinguished" men in the country, whatever side of Parliament they sat on, "have exerted the best energies of their minds to put an end to this abominable crime." And then he became very Palmerstonian. Britain had persuaded and in many cases forced other nations to embrace its anti-slave-trade policies. But not all of them observed the terms of their treaties. If they were allowed to get away with this, "we should be making ourselves again partakers in this guilt" and "polluted with this crime."

Palmerston quickly got down to the gritty details, which he said he feared had been forgotten over the course of fifty years, since the debates led by William Wilberforce had roused the nation's conscience. He cited records compiled by Britain's consuls monitoring the slave trade around the world. Two people died for every one who made it to the auction block, he said. They died being marched from the interior of Africa to the coast. They died on the voyage across the Atlantic. If 150,000 Africans were landed in Cuba and Brazil every year, as the consuls there reported, then 300,000 others must have died—again, every year.

Palmerston stood tall before his fellow members of Parliament. In 1844 he was only fifty-nine and in his prime, his frame lanky, his presence enough to still the room. "If all the other crimes which the human race has committed, from the creation down to the present day, were added together in one vast aggregate," he declared, "they would scarcely equal, I am sure they could not exceed, the amount of guilt which has been incurred by mankind, in connection with this diabolical Slave Trade."

Returned to the Foreign Office in the summer of 1846, Palmerston focused his attention on Brazil. He used Secret Service funds to bribe local politicians (including the negotiator of the anti-slave-trade treaty), he subsidized Brazilian newspapers that would print anti-slave-trade material, he hired a network of spies around the Atlantic world, and he vehemently defended the deployment of British naval vessels to intercept the human traffickers. In 1850, following Palmerston's directives, a British gunboat pursued four suspected slavers into the Paranaguá River, scuttled one of the vessels, and burned two in front of a Brazilian fort, which opened fire in a ferocious exchange with the warship. One British sailor was killed and two were wounded, and the squadron backed off for a time, but the Brazilians got the message.

The last slave ship known to land Africans in Brazil was the *Camargo*, whose master was a young rogue named Nathaniel "Lucky Nat" Gordon from a prosperous family in Portland, Maine. He had stolen the vessel from its owner in San Francisco, then sailed to the east coast of Africa for his cargo of five hundred slaves to avoid the British squadron. But a British man-of-war chased him as he neared the Brazilian coast, forcing him to unload the Africans and burn the ship in a frantic rush. Most of the slaves were picked up, and several of the crew were captured. Young Gordon, who had a very slight build, supposedly escaped dressed as woman. And so, ignominiously and definitively, the transatlantic slave trade with Brazil came to an end.

When Lord Palmerston looked back on that achievement years later, he said he regarded it with "the greatest and purest pleasure," and the year 1850—the year he triumphed over Brazil—was also the year he had appointed George Mathew to raise hell in South Carolina.

Then, after a series of political reversals at home in 1851, Palmerston left his post as Foreign Secretary. When he returned to the cabinet in a coalition government at the end of 1852, his old rival among the Whigs, the diminutive John Russell, briefly took the position of Foreign Secretary for himself. Palmerston, somewhat uncomfortably, took the position of Home Secretary. If this was not the end of an era for a very particular style of British foreign policy—Palmerston was destined to become Prime Minister—it certainly seemed an interregnum. Then after a few months Russell, who was the leader in the House of Commons, gave up his hold on the Foreign Office. That opened the way for Palmerston's onetime protégé, longtime ally, and sometime critic, Lord Clarendon, to settle into the dilapidated Downing Street headquarters of British policy around the world.

Clarendon as Foreign Secretary was everything Palmerston was not, and he did not care to be. Clarendon was a cautious diplomat. It's said that Palmerston thought Clarendon weak. But Clarendon had served in two of the most difficult assignments the Crown could give a man in the nineteenth century—minister in civil-war-torn Spain and lord lieutenant in famine-ridden, rebellious Ireland—and he was about to face conflicts around the world, from the Americas to the Black Sea and the heart of India, that tested the mettle of the Empire.

From Robert Bunch's point of view, the stars had aligned in a way he might never have anticipated. Bunch had grown up in the shadow of Lord Palmerston, and he knew he could never be the kind of overbearing, gunboat-summoning figure that Palmerston's George Mathew had aspired to be in South Carolina. Lord Clarendon, on the other hand, was a man who understood subtlety, restraint, calculated duplicity, and relentless persistence.

Twenty years earlier, when Clarendon was still George William Frederick Villiers, before he inherited his title, was a very handsome but not especially accomplished young man. Then, when he was thirty-three years old, Palmerston plucked him out of a dreary post as commissioner of customs and made him the Crown's envoy to Madrid. Villiers for six long years immersed himself in Iberian intrigues, helping to shore up the factions favored by Palmerston in hopes of establishing a relatively liberal monarchy under a child-queen and a temperamental regent. Not the least of Villiers's accomplishments was a treaty committing Spain to end the African slave trade to Cuba, even though it subsequently was ignored. And in good Palmerstonian style, the young envoy's name was linked to some of the most desirable women on the peninsula. The most notable, the Condesa de Montijo, was asked years later if Clarendon might have been the father of her daughter, the Empress Eugénie of France. "The dates don't match," she said.

When Bunch knew Clarendon, the Foreign Secretary's past adventures were amusing anecdotes. But what mattered to the consul was the way the new patron of the Foreign Office would view his work, and he found himself constantly reassured. From Bunch's very first days on his new assignment, he was receiving dispatches written personally by Clarendon offering warm approval of just about everything he did, from his brief visit with his colleague the deputy consul in Wilmington to his discreet diplomatic démarches with the notables of South Carolina.

Even so, Bunch reminded Clarendon often just what he—just what *they*—were up against in this state that was so particular and so peculiar: "She is often alluded to by the press as, 'this fiery little State'—'the chivalric state'; all of which I mention as a proof that she cannot properly be measured by the standard of other sections of this country, which, although Slave-holders, are, at times, open to reason."

Chapter 3

SHORTLY AFTER THE BUNCHES' ARRIVAL in Charleston, they took up residence in a three-story house at 58 Tradd Street. It had been built in the 1730s on the long, narrow road that cut all the way across the little peninsula on which Charleston sits, and it was pleasant enough, with a small garden, and what seemed respectable neighbors.

As Her Majesty's consul set out on his errands each morning, the streets bustled with black laborers and servants, pink-cheeked ladies, rugged Irish and German workmen, and the strapping sons of plantation owners, most of them of English descent. Consul Bunch slipped past them or, tipping his hat, stopped to chat about nothing at all. Bunch was unassuming but amusing, a man well met but easily forgotten. In his demeanor and discourse he had perfected his mask as a perfectly English Englishman looking after obvious English interests.

The purely consular part of a consul's job was never done. George Mathew had left an office on the Central Wharf at the end of Broad Street from which Bunch could keep close watch on the British vessels in the port. The consul was expected to know to the letter the treaty obligations governing commerce and to make sure that local authorities observed them. If there was a problem with a channel in the harbor, or the flame was burning none too brightly in a lighthouse, he would tell the British captains about it and notify London. A consul could estimate the value of a ship's cargo for U.S. customs officials. He represented the interests of all British sailors and citizens when they got into trouble. He notarized documents, embossing them with the lion and unicorn seal. He issued passports to British citizens, and he recorded their marriages, births, and deaths in the wide expanse of territory that fell under his jurisdiction. One of Bunch's colleagues wrote that "With the exception of the administration of the sacrament of baptism and exercising the business of executioner, it would be difficult to say what duties I cannot be called on to perform."

Bunch visited the newspaper offices and the jails, the harbormaster, the postmaster, the Federal prosecutors, and private attorneys. He would keep careful track of transatlantic trade and any impediments to it, from cotton supplies to quarantines (always a big issue on a coast plagued with yellow fever), to legislation by the Federal and state governments and litigation in the courts. His work kept him in constant contact with Carolinians of every stripe. His agreeable mien helped him win the trust of people who had an innate suspicion of outsiders.

A consul supplied the signature on paperwork for British ships entering and leaving the port. He attended formal functions among the ladies and gentlemen of the town, and he dealt with drunken British thugs who wound up in jail, including, occasionally, those accused of murder. But the most important part of Consul Bunch's work would be undertaken in private and, very often, in secret.

Britain posted fourteen consuls in the United States, including seven in slave states, and these men—along with the minister in Washington—comprised the backbone of the system that kept Britain informed about what was happening on the ground. Many of the British consuls in the United States were part-timers who mixed their private business with their unpaid official duties, but Bunch in Charleston in the South and the consul in New York City in the North were salaried professionals. Their business often included quasi-diplomatic functions and always involved the gathering of intelligence—political and military as well as commercial—for Her Majesty's government. The best consuls, and Bunch would soon number among them, sent dispatches to the Foreign Office tracking everything from shifting public sentiment on tariffs to the gritty details of slavery.

Mathew had not left the Charleston consular office in good order, and when Bunch arrived in late November, he discovered that the consulate's only employee was a paragon of Low Country decadence. "Old Davis, my vice consul, has delirium tremens and the pox alternately, as his life fluctuates between the barroom and the brothel," Bunch wrote to John Crampton, the British minister in Washington.* At the same time, Bunch said hopefully, "Nothing can exceed the civility of these good people. Everybody calls, and there are teas and dinners 'looming in the future.'"

But, still, the newlywed Bunches were having a hard time settling in. A city more different from the New York they'd left behind would be hard to imagine. The sun poured down on the sandy avenues. The branches of the live oaks hung heavy with Spanish moss. The grander houses had an elegant simplicity, with wide verandas that sheltered the windows both upstairs and down. Many homes had small gardens filled with lush growth. But when the wind blew, the dust off the streets covered one's clothes and filled one's eyes. Alleys that were homes to the slaves crisscrossed the city. In the markets near the port, amid the sickly scent of decay, Negro vendors sold colorful fruits and the daily catch of mullets and crabs while the butchers threw discarded fat and offal to tribes of lumbering vultures that waited restlessly nearby, protected by law as the winged collectors of refuse.

Bunch quickly found that Charleston society was small, rich, and spoiled. Rice and cotton had made the upper classes as wealthy as any in America, North or South, and the climate had made them, of necessity, an idle aristocracy. For much of the year, when their plantations were plagued by yellow fever and malaria, those Charlestonians who could retire to the mountains, to the outer islands, to the North, or to Europe did so, and, partly as a result, many spent their fortunes elsewhere. The population had been declining slowly for a decade as many people moved west to the new lands of op-

---

* Note that the men who served as envoys in Washington did not have the title "ambassador," which was very rare. They were called "ministers." Great Britain had consuls at Portland, Maine; Boston; New York City; Buffalo; Philadelphia; Chicago; St. Louis; San Francisco; Richmond; Charleston; Savannah; Mobile; New Orleans; and Galveston.

portunity. In 1820 Charleston had been the sixth largest city in the United States. But New Orleans soon surpassed Charleston's port traffic, and many of the old rich, and those who had depended on them, instead of adapting to change took every opportunity to fight it. National power was slipping from their hands, and South Carolinians came to see the Federal government as the enemy, blaming the tariffs it imposed as a reason for their declining fortunes. By the early 1830s Carolinians were claiming they could nullify Federal laws they deemed threatening, and they almost started a war to make that point before President Andrew Jackson—the "American Lion" always ready enough for a fight—forced them to back down. The city's decline continued, and by the time Bunch arrived, the population of Charleston was down to about forty thousand, not one-twentieth the size of New York City. And about half of those Charleston residents were slaves or free men and free women of color.

Visitors remarked that the people of Charleston—the white people from the old families, anyway—were conspicuously tall and handsome. The Charlestonians said, and in some cases it was true, that they were descended from English gentlemen, and long before the phrase "master race" was coined, they saw themselves, literally, as a race of masters. Charleston photographer C. J. Quinby took pictures of many leading lights, and even in his sepia images one can see that most of his subjects had strikingly pale, sometimes almost wolflike, blue eyes. They "live in the open air and work like Trojans at all manly sports, riding hard, hunting, playing at being soldiers," wrote one proud matron.

But a palpable undercurrent of fear and mistrust filled what could seem at first a languorous city with a grating, omnipresent tension. From the first weeks of what eventually became a decade spent in Charleston, Bunch was deeply disturbed by the mixtures of arrogance and fear, cruelty and luxury, piety and hypocrisy that were so deeply ingrained in Southern culture. He tried to look on it all with detached irony, but even in his private letters to his superiors—indeed, even in his official dispatches to London—there were times when the irony, which he could not show publicly, became very bitter indeed on the pages of correspondence marked *private* and *confidential*.

Bunch learned quickly, as anyone learned who spent more than a few days in Charleston, that the Denmark Vesey conspiracy to launch a vast slave uprising in 1822, a rebellion that never actually happened, was a critical moment in the minds of the white people in the city. The fear of the slaves, docile though they seemed, had always lingered in the background. But after the hysterical revelations and allegations that surrounded Vesey's plot, they grew much worse, as if people living in a house they believed might be haunted had discovered, suddenly, that malevolent ghosts really were watching them day and night.

Vesey had been brought from the British West Indies as a young slave, a point often made by those who told the story. He managed to buy his freedom with money won in the lottery in 1799, and for decades he was a popular preacher with slave congregations at Charleston's African Methodist Episcopal Church. White preachers often invoked fire and brimstone to keep the slaves in line, but Vesey used the righteousness of the Old Testament to inspire rebellion. "The city shall be taken, and the women ravished," he would tell his flock, quoting the book of Zechariah. According to the Charleston prosecutors who interrogated him, Vesey meant to seize the arsenal and the ships in the harbor. House servants recruited to the cause allegedly were tasked to murder the governor of South Carolina and other officials in their sleep. Vesey was said to have prepared six infantry companies to roam the streets, slaughtering every white man, woman, and child.

On the night rumored to have been set as the date for the uprising, nothing happened. But after mass arrests, Vesey and thirty of his supposed co-conspirators were tried in secret courts. When he and the others were executed, their bodies were left hanging in the Carolina sun, picked over by crows and the protected vultures day after day until all semblance of humanness was gone. That many of the alleged conspirators were free blacks and others the household slaves for rich and powerful Carolina families made even the most benevolent owners feel threatened and vulnerable, fueling their rage.

And yet the whites of Charleston continued to live surrounded by blacks. "You see, even in the main streets, two or even three of these to every white man, and in the back streets you see no one else," reported a British lieutenant who traveled to Charleston in 1853. You were not supposed to see Negroes on the sidewalk— that was forbidden—but often you did. And you were not supposed to see them at all late at night, but often they were there in the shadows, moving easily enough, because they knew the city better than anyone. Quite a few had been manumitted and lived on their own. (The census had a category for them, f.p.c., for "free person of color.") Others were hired out and did not live with their masters. They met, they talked, and that fact alone convinced many Charlestonians that they might conspire.

In response, the city fathers funded the City Guard, with almost three hundred paid patrolmen, including twenty-five on horseback. It was one of the most efficient police forces in the country, garrisoned in an enormous building on the corner of Meeting and Broad Streets that appeared part fortress, part temple. At the same intersection stood the courthouse, city hall, and St. Michael's Church. These were the military, legal, political, and spiritual bastions of Charleston's slave-owning order, and every night at nine o'clock in the winter and ten in the summer the bells of St. Michael's would peal, followed by the beating of drums at the guardhouse for a full quarter of an hour. The rattling tympani were intended to send blacks running back to their masters and their homes, and the drumbeat became the soundtrack of every evening, ignored by those who did not need to hear it, but a subliminal reminder to all of fear as much as of security. The British consul's new home on Tradd Street was only a block away from the bell tower and the drummer;

the music of martial authority rang loudly through his rooms every night.

The same year that Robert Bunch arrived in Charleston, the English novelist William Makepeace Thackeray passed through town with a small party on a lucrative American lecture tour. The sale of people on the auction block was a common public spectacle, and Thackeray and his friends watched the tableau with mixed feelings. It took place, as always, just outside the elegant Old Exchange building, and about ninety people were on sale that day.

A young British lieutenant remembered the scene emotionally. "The gang was to be sold in families," he wrote. "The Negroes, with their wives and little ones, were standing huddled together in a crowd behind the platform on which each family was exposed for sale in turn, according to a printed program." Many of the slaves "seemed indifferent, and a stout Negress or two looked, occasionally, even defiant; but there were several mothers with their babies at their breasts (and even *black* innocence and helplessness are pretty and interesting) sobbing bitterly." He continued: "The auctioneer explained the conditions of sale to the company, and stated that all the niggers were to be considered sound, unless anything was said to the contrary. There was no degrading exhibition to ascertain physical efficiency, but all the Negroes were in decent clothing. The slaves were arranged in families according to their nearest relationship, and sold in lots at so much a head. The competition was tolerably brisk, and several lots—old men, babies, and all—sold very well. The scene, of course, was most painful, humiliating and degrading. I became quite affected myself, and was obliged to hurry away, for fear of showing what I felt."

These were, precisely, the sights of Charleston that welcomed Bunch and began to change him. The ambitious young consul who had referred so casually to the "nigger question" now found that wherever he walked, and, indeed, wherever he looked, the weight of slavery bore down on him. Bunch had seen plenty of inhumanity and suffering in his life, from the plantations of Peru to the gang-ridden slums of Five Points in New York City. He had seen servants abused countless times in countless ways. But he had never seen or heard anything quite like what he saw and heard in this city to which he had brought his wife and where he hoped to have his children. In this new position with new responsibilities, and in this place, the young consul quickly grew bitter, even desperate. His initial comments on "the civility of these good people" soon gave way to a much darker view.

BUNCH HAD BEEN in touch with members of the South Carolina legislature before his arrival, and, according to the plans he'd worked out with Crampton in Washington and with Clarendon in London, he kept his correspondence and contacts as calm and congenial as possible, although every hour of the day he felt he was dealing with a society almost devoid of sanity. Clarendon had given a speech in Parliament over the summer that recognized South Carolina's concerns about its security and that was intended to help, but Bunch did his best to keep it out of circulation, because sensitivities about British interference ran so high. He was told that even those who thought the Negro Seamen Act was "useless" vowed to oppose any change to it "if the British Consul so much as stirred a finger in the matter, or asked it in the civilest manner as a favor!"

"I have been extremely cautious to avoid the slightest appearance of intemperance in this question," Bunch assured Clarendon. "I have addressed no letters to the governor, no representations to the legislature, and have not even paid a visit to the capital, for fear of my motives being misrepresented. I have not seemed even to *seek* interviews with persons of influence, but have availed myself of such opportunities as were presented by social intercourse, of which there is an abundance of a certain description."

When Bunch met the imposing, white-bearded William Aiken, a former governor and state senator and soon to be a member of the U.S. Congress, Bunch followed the agreed-upon script to the letter, "dwelling especially on our desire to avoid anything like insidious interference with the right of South Carolina to consult her own safety." Bunch said he knew what a "kindly feeling" the Southern states had for Great Britain, and he was sure they wouldn't put laws on their books that would be offensive to her unless they really felt the need, but that need no longer existed. Anyone could see how docile and content the Negro population had become, and how immune to outside agitation, Bunch said, playing to the commonplace hubris of the Charleston elite. Aiken seemed pleased and said the law would be changed, if not during the current session, then the next. Bunch had a similar conversation with Nelson Mitchell, a Charleston attorney who served, at the time, as chairman of the Committee on the Colored Population in the South Carolina House of Representatives. Mitchell claimed he was "very anxious for a change."

These were not the kinds of men Bunch trusted. But one class of people in Charleston seemed "more enlightened and less bigoted" than the rest, Bunch told Clarendon. And at that early date, there's no question he had James L. Petigru in mind. The former state attorney general was an aging bear of a man with long hair, heavy jowls, and penetrating eyes. He was like a paterfamilias to the South Carolina legal community and soon adopted an avuncular, if not paternal, role toward Bunch. Petigru was the man who had codified South Carolina's laws. Many of the state's most notable attorneys and politicians had worked in his law offices. Such was his personal prestige that he could say whatever he wanted and often did, knowing that his opinions would be tolerated even if they went unheeded. He famously said of secession, a notion raised often over cigars and brandy, that "South Carolina is too small for a republic and too large for an insane asylum." But Petigru's Unionist sentiments did not mean that he or any of the other Charleston intellectuals seriously questioned slavery or, if they did, knew how to be done with it.

Another of Bunch's early acquaintances was the Princeton-educated postmaster, Alfred Huger, who was a former state senator and the owner of a large plantation on the Cooper River. Like Petigru, Huger had been an opponent of nullification, a state's supposed right to nullify or declare void within its borders any Federal law or tariff detrimental to its sovereign interests. Huger would stand out as one of the more thoughtful, and conflicted, men in Charleston: a partisan of Union in the heartland of secession; an owner of slaves who despised the institution and feared its effect on society. He was one of many Charlestonians descended from Huguenot refugees who had fled persecution in the Old World, and he felt keenly the painful contradictions of a luxurious society built on the backs of human chattel. Another potential Bunch ally was Huger's brother-in-law, Col. John Harleston Read, owner of Rice Hope Plantation, who eventually became chairman of the House Committee on the Colored Population in the state legislature.

Such men were open to discussion, at least, about the specific problem Bunch had been assigned to fix, and he assured them all that the suggestions he was making privately, socially, in the friendliest possible manner, were no part of any grand plot concocted in London to "advance the interests of emancipation and abolitionism." He had a dry wit that seemed to Carolinians very British, and he could tell tales he'd heard about politicians in Washington and up North. (He was, generally, careful not to tell tales about his British superiors.) Soon the tensions that had greeted him upon his arrival seemed to dissipate.

Already by the end of November Bunch thought his strategy was working. The new governor, John Manning, opened the legislative session in Columbia, the state capital, with a speech that seemed to lay to rest all the bad feelings created by George Mathew. The court cases brought by the previous consul had been decided in South Carolina's favor, said the governor, and "the laws of the State upon this subject [had] been fully vindicated." As a result, the governor added, "the question of modification of them is relieved of all its embarrassment, and may with entire propriety come before you for consideration as a new question."

When Bunch read those words, he could hardly contain his excitement. But the speech got better still. Manning told the legislature that "the course adopted by the British government in the latter stages of the proceeding" had been "entirely proper and respectful," and the legislature should take that into account.

Bunch wrote to Clarendon that he hoped he would be able to report good news soon about changes to the law.

But that didn't happen. The legislature, which met for only a few weeks at the end of each year, adjourned just before Christmas without taking any action on the black-seamen issue. And while Bunch expressed restrained disappointment in his dispatch to Clarendon, he exploded in a private letter to Crampton.

"It is rather hard that we are to dance to the fiddle of this dirty little abortion of an *imperium*," he wrote. Bunch started by describing the defeat of his efforts to amend the seamen's law, then switched abruptly to a description of the scene a day before when a steamboat at the Charleston wharf blew up, sending the boiler on "a voyage of discovery" through the crowds and cotton bales that left thirteen of "the fine and enlightened" people of Charleston dead. Then Bunch concluded by saying, "My wife unites with me in wishing you a merry Xmas."

Already, only weeks into his assignment, Robert Bunch wanted out of Charleston. "You must, of course, be aware that I only look upon this consulate as a *pis aller*," a stopgap, a last resort, he wrote in another note to Crampton. "I hate the U.S. and am most anxious to get away." He started pleading again for a posting in Bogotá, where he had spent much of his youth, where he knew people, where he could take care of his sickly father (and where he could secure his inheritance after his father's recent marriage to a younger woman). But Clarendon wanted Bunch right where he was.

Bunch had not intended to lead a double life when he took the assignment in Charleston, but he quickly realized that he had little choice. He found himself mingling with men and women who held frightful opinions and committed atrocious acts. He wanted them to think him a sympathetic friend, yet in his letters to Crampton and Clarendon marked *private* and *confidential*, and meant for their eyes only, he continued to write of the Carolinians with undisguised loathing.

Chapter 4

D URING THOSE FIRST MONTHS IN Charleston, Robert and Emma Bunch were introduced to the cream of Low Country society, which fancied itself, without apology, an Anglo aristocracy. Rigidly hierarchical and deeply intermarried, it based prestige on the wealth of plantations and the pretensions of bloodlines. Bunch, as Her Majesty's consul, although no aristocrat, was invited into exalted company as an honorary member of the upper crust. He was asked to speak at the Royal Society of St. George, of course, and then to preside. The city was full of more or less benevolent associations that traced their roots to the British Isles and that welcomed Bunch into their precincts. Many of them had grand edifices, such as St. Andrew's Hall on Broad Street, with its dazzling Thomas Sully portrait of the young and voluptuous Queen Victoria. (The Hibernian Hall on Meeting Street, with its Irish roots, was not always such friendly territory for the consul.) The city now boasted two relatively respectable hotels for informal gatherings, the Charleston Hotel and the Mills House, both on Meeting Street. There were endless dinners and balls and soirées. As dreary as the winter weather could be, it was the height of the social season, and that culminated in February during Race Week, when it seemed that all the South, and certainly all of South Carolina's aristocrats, converged on the city to watch their horses compete, to see and be seen by the city's most beautiful belles, and to trade notes on the future of their plantations, their politics, and the American Republic. The Charleston Jockey Club, the most exclusive fraternity in the city, organized the show. And the Jockey Club invited Bunch to attend its functions as well.

It did not take Bunch very long, amid the politicking and the revelry, to discover the darker side of life in Charleston's homes. "The frightful atrocities of slaveholding must be seen to be described," he wrote in a private letter that wound up prominently positioned in the official slave-trade correspondence of the Foreign Office. "My next-door neighbor, a lawyer of the first distinction and a member of the Southern Aristocracy, told me himself that he flogged all his own people—men and women—when they misbehaved. I hear also that he makes them strip, and after telling them that they were to consider it as a great condescension on his part to touch them, gives them a certain number of lashes with a cow-hide. The frightful evil of the system is that it debases the whole tone of society—for the people talk calmly of horrors which would not be mentioned in civilized society. It is literally no more to kill a slave than to shoot a dog."

Bunch sent that letter in the middle of January 1854, a month of cold and storms, when Charleston's rich green tropical allure turned gray and battered and depressing. Flecks of white foam drifted off the whitecaps visible from East Bay Street. Waves crashed against the Charleston Bar, a series of submerged shoals. And a British brig called the *Charlotte* ran up on a reef near the entrance to the harbor. The crew survived, among them a fourteen-year-old black seaman named John Hayes, an apprentice from Barbados, and Bunch knew by then exactly what would happen if the boy didn't get some protection. He'd be thrown into jail "among the outcasts of society" and subjected to the kind of treatment that the young and the weak often suffered in prison. Bunch did not use the indelicate term *rape*, but when he wrote about fearing "an atrocity at which my nature revolted," it was hard to mistake his meaning.

Bunch acted quickly. He sent word to the *Charlotte*'s officers instructing that Hayes be kept away from Charleston. He arranged for the boy to be taken in by the keeper of the lighthouse on Charleston Bar, a few miles from the city near the dilapidated outpost known as Fort Moultrie. For more than two weeks Hayes holed up there with a man kept silent by the friendly, and probably the pecuniary, persuasion of Her Majesty's consul. Finally, Bunch managed to arrange passage for the timorous boy on a British ship about to embark for Liverpool. But to get him aboard, Bunch had to bring Hayes to the city.

Charleston Harbor in midwinter opened onto rough waters, and small steam-powered launches often lurched precariously close to disaster among the waves. As Bunch and Hayes approached the city's wharf, they must have felt relieved that their ordeal was almost over. But waiting for them was one of Charleston's "constables," as Bunch called him, a member of the City Guard who grabbed Hayes as soon as he came ashore.

Bunch stepped in front of the guardsman, demanding that Hayes be released because he was due to leave on the next boat out. The guardsman paid no attention, dragging Hayes toward the jail. Bunch shouted, asserting his authority, only to realize how little he really had. The guardsman was acting in accordance with South Carolina's laws, which Bunch knew at least as well as the constable. Bystanders watched as Her Majesty's consul undiplomatically risked the fatal appearance of impotence. Still, he would not give way, mustering as much imperial authority as he could, invoking the names of his acquaintances among the good and great in South Carolina until, finally, the constable relented. He would not jail Hayes, and he would allow him to leave on the next ship out, but the captain would have to pay a heavy fine.

Bunch, realizing that his bold move to save one young man could imperil his larger goal of changing the Negro Seamen Act, accepted the deal and agreed to pay the fee himself. But he knew he would have to be more careful in the future. And when he wrote to Lord Clarendon, recounting this "flagrant case of extortion" by the constable, he made it clear that he had mentioned nothing about it to the mayor or any other city authorities, not even in private. With the example of George Mathew's failure in mind, he assured the Foreign Secretary that if it proved impossible to change the "abominable injustice of the law of South Carolina," then he didn't want anyone to blame "the indiscreet zeal of Her Majesty's Consul." Clarendon thoroughly approved.

O N KING STREET A FEW blocks away from Robert Bunch's residence was John Russell's bookstore. Its owner bore no relationship to the British Whig politician of the same name, but the shop
did specialize in European writings. This "literary emporium," as
Russell called it, had a large door and plate glass windows looking
out on the lively traffic of the city's main commercial thoroughfare,
and the publications it carried were windows on the world for literate Charlestonians. Over the years it served as an informal salon
for the more liberal element of the population or, at least, the less
secessionist element, like Petigru and his friends.

Mr. Russell, an affable old bachelor, seemed to have little social
life outside the store, but he would order single or multiple copies of
books from abroad, and his shop was just the place to pick up and
peruse reviews such as London's *New Monthly Magazine*. It also carried plenty of Southern publications, including *DeBow's Review* and
John Russell's own *Russell's Magazine*, which many considered the
most literate and reasonable journal in the South.

Conversation in the shop often was animated. In the early 1850s
Charleston's literati would rant for hours about that best-selling author in the Northern states and in Britain, Harriet Beecher Stowe,
and her *Uncle Tom's Cabin*. One of the bards in the group, William J. Grayson, even published a book-length, pro-slavery poem,
which he dedicated to James Petigru, entitled "The Hireling and
the Slave." He intended it as a reply not only to *Uncle Tom* but also
to the British, who seemed to love that book so much. They were ignorant of the benevolent institution that slavery really was, he said,
since a master was committed to care for the slave all his life. Only
"hireling labor" like that of the North or of England created "the
isolated, miserable creature who has no home, no work, no food,
and in whom no one is particularly interested," Grayson went on.

Slavery was Christian; slavery was God's will. If the English wanted to free these people so much, Grayson said, let them buy them!

Bunch, when he chanced to meet such characters at Russell's or elsewhere in his busy day, found ways of offering perfunctory responses. Even with the image still in his mind of his neighbor's slaves stripped, groped, and whipped, he appears to have learned the value of languid silence, at least up to a point. There was little need to argue, he said, in a society where "slavery does seem to blunt a man's moral sense of right and wrong so fearfully."

One of the most cosmopolitan of Bunch's new acquaintances was William Henry Trescot, a lawyer and diplomatic historian just about Bunch's age, who divided his time between Charleston and his plantation deep in the marshes near Beaufort.

When Bunch met him, Trescot had just published his history of American diplomacy during the Revolution. Given that the two men knew many of the same people in New York, Washington, and London, it was not altogether surprising that they got along. Years later, in very difficult times, Bunch would describe Trescot as "a man of talent," an "agreeable companion," and "a particular friend of mine," albeit "a little eccentric." Certainly there was nobody Bunch got to know in Charleston who was better connected.

All Trescot's schooling was in South Carolina's academies. He went to the College of Charleston. He apprenticed with local attorneys. He grew up with the upper classes, sharing jokes, cigars, and probably women. He married well in 1848 to an heiress who brought him a substantial income and a plantation that grew coveted Sea Island cotton. But Trescot was also a man of the world. In 1853, the same year Bunch arrived in Charleston, Trescot returned there from a brief stint as secretary to the American legation in London, where he had gotten to know William Makepeace Thackeray (it seems everybody knew Thackeray), met Whig politician and historian Thomas Babington Macaulay, and interviewed Prince Albert. Once, while being addressed by the venerable Marquess of Lansdowne, who had held high office under Kings George III,

George IV, and William IV and Queen Victoria, Trescot lolled back on a sofa and put his feet up on a table, a gesture of nonchalance that made him quite memorable to a scandalized elite, which is probably what he intended.

William Trescot was that invaluable contact who could introduce Robert Bunch to people he needed to know, inform him about what others were saying, and interpret what it all meant. Although Bunch mentions Trescot only occasionally by name in his correspondence, Trescot, along with Petigru and Huger and Read, clearly was part of that coterie of "better people" in Charleston that Bunch relied on for guidance and intelligence. That they owned slaves and that Trescot, certainly, was a secessionist, did not much matter to Bunch, at least in the early days. The consul's mission at that point was a relatively narrow one and difficult enough as it was. Whatever he thought of his acquaintances in Charleston, he had no illusion that he would change their way of life or their way of thinking.

But some men in Charleston tested the new British consul's self-control to its limits. They were the worst of the worst bigots and secessionists. To say they were firebrands does not do justice to their calculated fanaticism. These extremist pro-slavery politicians were called the "Fire-Eaters," and through Charleston's newspapers their voices eventually became known far and wide.

The most famous was Robert Barnwell Rhett, an angry man full of social and political aspirations he could never quite satisfy. Though born with the surname Smith in little Beaufort, South Carolina, at the beginning of the century with few prospects of wealth or fame, he styled himself an aristocrat and presented himself as heir to the honorable bloodlines of five British colonial governors. In 1837 he and his brothers decided to adopt the name of their great-great-grandfather, Col. William Rhett, who had been the British governor of the Bahamas.

Even in South Carolina politics, Robert Barnwell Rhett stood out as an extremist, and the furious debate over the expansion of slavery that had gripped the nation at the end of the 1840s had given

him a wondrous pretext for his rage. Rhett tried to cast himself in
the mold of his idol and sometime mentor Senator John C. Calhoun,
the great voice of nullification who had taken South Carolina to the
brink of secession and the country to the brink of war in the 1830s
before President Andrew Jackson called his bluff. When Calhoun
died in 1851, the governor named Rhett to fill his seat in the United
States Senate. Rhett, "the lone star of disunion," as some called
him, used his office to call for immediate secession, but he was a
decade too early. Frustrated when his summons went unheeded, he
resigned.

Robert Barnwell Rhett was as pure an ideologue as the South
could find, the very epitome of unreason that Robert Bunch so
detested—because the consul, while he might play his game of
bonhomie with people he despised, did not want to be bored while
he did it. With Rhett and those who followed his line, no appeals
to common humanity or, for that matter, to common sense would
sway their opinions.

Among the elegant patricians of Charleston, Rhett, who was
bald and plain but extremely vain, often came across as an irascible
crank. His politics had nothing to do with the art of compromise,
which is why, for most of his life, political success eluded him. But
the *Charleston Mercury*, owned for many years by Rhett's brilliant
but fatally alcoholic brother-in-law, John A. Stuart, gave Rhett a
platform for his ideas and his anger. Eventually Rhett bought a con-
trolling interest in the paper and gave it to his son to run. Although
the actual circulation of the *Mercury* was only several hundred copies, its articles were picked up and reprinted widely, including in the
New York Times, which used them to show off Southern extremism.

There would be no cajoling or convincing Rhett on the black-
seamen issue. The *Mercury* would be no help to Bunch. When
Rhett was in the state legislature, at the slightest provocation he
would conjure the ghost of Denmark Vesey. He'd claim that the
dread conspiracy of 1822 was the work of free blacks inspired by
alien abolitionists; he'd insist that each Negro sailor walking free

on Charleston's streets, whether from the North or from a foreign country, would be a threat to the city's very existence.

But Bunch could leave Rhett, as he liked to say, to his own devices. Rhett was not really changing anybody's opinion one way or the other in the early 1850s. And while the *Charleston Mercury* was a voice of unreason on almost every issue that concerned Bunch, the *Charleston Courier* under editor Richard Yeadon was a more responsible and balanced newspaper. When Bunch had a message to get out discreetly, a visit to the *Courier* offices or a quiet meeting with Yeadon usually did the trick—and the *Courier*, with only occasional backsliding, supported a revision of the Negro Seamen law.

The editor of a third newspaper in Charleston posed a more complicated problem. Leonidas Spratt was from up-country South Carolina but had married a Charleston woman who had a small town house, ten slaves, and enough money for her husband to buy the struggling *Charleston Standard* in 1853. There, Spratt began a campaign not only to defend slavery, but to glorify it. The young firebrand understood that the elite of what was at once the most revolutionary and the most reactionary city in the South were threatened in more ways and on more fronts than many of them cared to consider. What Grayson, the "bard of the battery," had called "hireling labor" was not just reprehensible; it was an insidious menace to everything the grandees of Charleston held dear. As slaves were taken west to virgin lands, the political and economic complexion of the city was changing. White immigrants from Ireland and Germany were arriving to perform some of the work normally done by slaves or free people of color, and these white employees, simply because they were white, could make demands on the ruling classes that Negroes and mulattoes, slave or free, could never make. By the summer of 1854 the *Standard* was taking a truly radical position intended to shore up the status quo, recommending that the slave trade with Africa be reopened.

The young editor of the *Standard* played to the worst instincts of the Charleston elite, some of whom were appalled, some enthralled, and some both as they listened to his arguments. In the theatrical style of the time, Spratt would push his fingers back through his mane of black hair as his passionate language lured his audience to his cause. He told them that a slave-owning society was different from, and better than, one based on free labor; that this "union of unequal races" ennobled the masters and raised up the blacks to a level of civilization and Christianity that Negroes, inherently inferior beings, otherwise could not attain; that the future of the modern South would require more slaves, not fewer, to work in factories as well as in the fields; and that, above all, there was nothing to apologize for about any aspect of the institution, including and especially the importation of slaves from Africa.

The *New York Times* picked up on Spratt's editorials and mocked them. Spratt responded that the *Times* "failed to come to the moral elevation of our argument," and was making a mistake if it thought that "to be ridiculous is to be defeated." From the Christians of ancient Rome to George Washington, he declared, revolutionaries were always considered ridiculous by the powers they challenged. The *Times* published Spratt's riposte. For an upstart paper in South Carolina, that response was a significant achievement, and Spratt's notoriety began to spread.

Bunch, whose more trusted sources in Charleston told him that Leonidas Spratt was not to be taken seriously, did not bother to report to London the little tempest the *Standard* editor had raised in the *New York Times*, deeming it a distraction. The issues truly complicating Bunch's work on the Negro Seamen law were, he believed, the historical fears of the kind cited by Robert Barnwell Rhett, and resentments of outside interference, which Bunch had heard about even before his arrival. Spratt, intent on glorifying the virtues of slavery, steered away from the dangers of another Denmark Vesey lurking in the shadows.* His critiques of British abolitionist senti-

---

* Spratt would not want to remind anyone that South Carolina, in the last days of the legal slave trade with Africa at the beginning of the century, had

ment were more ironic than they were incendiary. And as sensitive as the issue of the slave trade was to the Foreign Office, in 1854 Spratt's arguments about reviving it seemed mere debating points. Bunch chose to regard this impassioned, relentless polemicist not with alarm but with amusement. The editor of the *Charleston Standard*, Bunch wrote to Crampton, is "personally a decent man, although editorially a jackass."

---

imported forty thousand men, women, and children, and that one of them, known as Gullah Jack, was supposed to have been Vesey's key lieutenant.

Chapter 6

A s race week came to Charleston in February 1854, so did young Governor John Manning, who had said such positive things about Britain to the state legislature in November, apparently to little avail. The atmosphere was festive and friendly, not as wild as Mardi Gras in New Orleans, but neither as reserved as every other week of the year in Charleston. The artist Charles Fraser, who was there, remembered that schools were dismissed, judges adjourned the courts (which had been deserted by the lawyers and witnesses, anyway), clergymen took time off from the pulpit to go watch a favorite horse in a race, and if one couldn't find a doctor anywhere else, one could find him at the track. "The whole week was devoted to the pleasure and the interchange of conviviality," Fraser recalled. "Nor were the ladies unnoticed, for the Race Ball, given by the Jockey Club, was always the most splendid of the season."

Robert Bunch took full advantage of the moment to get to know the new governor. Where George Mathew had fought with the previous occupant of the executive mansion, Bunch flattered and fraternized with Manning. "We have met frequently, both in public and in private," the consul told Lord Clarendon, "and I had the honor last week of entertaining him at dinner. Mr. Manning is a very young man, only 38 years of age; possessing a considerable fortune, and belonging to one of the 'old families' of this State." Amid all the revelry, Manning had suggested to Bunch that he was "much annoyed, and not a little piqued" at the way the legislature had ignored his advice: "Do they think I am going to study the condition of the State for twelve months and urge a certain line of action just so they can disregard my recommendations?" There amid the festive crowds of Race Week, Governor Manning told Bunch that, ten months hence, better changes to the Negro Seamen law could be obtained from the new legislative session than had been hoped for in the last.

"Time alone can show whether he reckons correctly upon the public sentiment," Bunch cautioned in his dispatch to Lord Clarendon. But Bunch felt that Manning was "sincere in his desire to see the law repealed." Still, the year 1854 would be a long one. Charleston was a small town, but the world was becoming a smaller and smaller place, and a conflict in the Middle East began to complicate Robert Bunch's life in ways he never could have predicted. The problem had started over the question of who should hold the keys to some of the major shrines in Jerusalem. The Russians backed their monks, and the French backed theirs; Moscow's demands on the Ottoman sultan, who oversaw the holy city, grew ever more extreme, and fighting had begun along the Ottoman-Russian frontier. Lord Clarendon worried that the Russians might win the conflict and, with that, control of the Bosporus, threatening the Mediterranean sea-and-land route to India. Home Secretary Palmerston, although technically no longer in control of foreign policy, was invited by Clarendon to join the inner cabinet shaping the Crown's response. Soon enough Britain entered the war alongside the French and the Turks. London and Paris often had tense, even hostile, relations, but suddenly those were to be papered over, and Bunch received a circular message from the Foreign Office telling him to work "in perfect harmony" with his French counterpart in Charleston.

It didn't take much prodding from London, in fact, to make Robert Bunch cultivate Count Xavier de Choiseul. The French nobleman, a cousin of King Louis-Philippe, had represented the interests of Paris in Charleston and Savannah for more than two decades. He was very much at home in the Carolinas and, famously, built himself a chateau he called Chanteloup in the mountains south of Asheville, where many Low Country aristocrats escaped the summer heat. De Choiseul was vital to the broad network of contacts

Bunch was building to gather intelligence and exert discreet influence. Bunch told Clarendon that he and de Choiseul already had established relations of "the most friendly character," and the two of them were ready to cooperate "for the advantage of French interests, or annoyance of our common enemy," the Russians.

The United States had declared itself neutral in the Crimean War, but London suspected that the Russians were buying warships or having them built in the major ports of New York and Baltimore and possibly cutting deals in Charleston to acquire them elsewhere. The Foreign Office tasked Bunch to find out more. He confirmed that Russian officers had, indeed, been visiting the other ports and reported that an informant told him that a letter addressed to one of the Russians was waiting at the Charleston post office. He arranged to be tipped off if the Russian showed up, "and I shall not fail to watch his movements should he visit Charleston," he said. But no sinister Muscovite surfaced.

Bunch also found himself drawn to his consular counterpart from Spain, Vincent Antonio de Larrañaga, although the concerns they shared were of a different kind and more closely related to Britain's slavery worries. Both men had followed closely for many years the activities of the freebooting "revolutionaries" from the United States, the so-called *filibusteros* who were bent on conquering (or, as they put it, liberating) Cuba.

When Bunch was vice consul in New York City, a would-be savior of the Cuban people, Narciso López, had organized an ill-fated invasion of the island. He and his men landed on Cuban soil in 1850, only to find that the oppressed Cuban people did not rise up to support them. In fact, the invaders had to flee for their lives. A year later, López and his band of *yanquis* tried once again. This time the Spanish governor-general had López garroted in front of the Morro Castle in Havana. The governor also had forty Americans and a handful of other fighters summarily shot. Anti-Cuban riots broke out in New Orleans, and the whole of America seemed to see

López and his men as martyrs. But, of course, the British didn't feel that way at all. When Bunch heard the news, he sent a particularly cynical note to Crampton. "Is not the execution of those fifty-two pirates too delicious?"

In Charleston, at the direction of his government, Larrañaga had followed the López affair when it looked as if the *filibusteros* might try to base their operations out of South Carolina. And now he and Bunch watched as, once again, the issue of Cuba began to loom large in the American and especially in the Southern mind.

IN APRIL 1854 it was Charleston's turn to host the annual Southern Commercial Convention, an economic and political meeting of delegations from thirteen slaveholding states. Amid the dinners, the ball, the regatta, the fireworks displays, and what Bunch considered "puerile pronunciamentos," there were only a few points on which all delegates agreed: they needed to build more railroads. (Bunch told Clarendon he doubted that would happen: "I have no confidence in the energy of the Southern people."); there should be a committee of American notables appointed to mediate the Crimean conflict (to this gross implausibility Bunch merely added an exclamation point); and, "the acquisition of the Island of Cuba is an object sincerely to be desired by the Southern States."

By June the Cuban issue loomed as a very real problem for both London and Madrid. Many in the United States, and not only the South, were convinced that the British government had put so much pressure on Spain about its Cuban colony and the slave trade that soon the island would not only emancipate its vast numbers of blacks, but also begin to arm them. This "Africanization of Cuba" scare was used to whip up anger at Britain and fear of Cuba and to argue that if the Americans didn't move first to acquire the island, they'd have a renegade black regime on their doorstep inspiring rebellions all over the South.

Bunch had official confirmation from the legation in Washington denying that Britain had the slightest intention of "Africanizing" Cuba. But he convinced almost no one, because, in fact, the British *had* put enormous pressure on Spain and Cuba to move toward emancipation, hoping that such measures would end the slave trade. And, in a wonderfully cynical move, London let Madrid know that if the Spaniards and Cubans did not cooperate, then they could hardly depend on British support if some crazy Americans annexed their island.

Now there was a new governor-general in Havana, the abolitionist soldier and author Juan de la Pezuela, and in Madrid for a few months Federico de Roncali, whose wife Bunch had once escorted through the streets of New York City, served as prime minister of Spain. Change was in the wind.

In May 1854 all Cuban slaveholders were ordered to appear before local authorities to register their property. Since many if not most of the slaves were straight from Africa, their importation had been in point of fact illegal for thirty years, and now the captain general was saying that all those without proper papers would be freed. The effect would be de facto emancipation on a massive scale. But de la Pezuela went one step further: free mulattoes and blacks were to be armed to help protect Cuba from invasion.

A former governor of Mississippi, John A. Quitman, who had backed the López expedition, was pulling together a new force, and the powerful senior senator for Louisiana, John Slidell, was fighting to get the neutrality laws of the United States repealed so that the Federal government would quit interfering with America's freelance conquerors. Senator Russell Mallory of Florida introduced a resolution warning there was "a settled design to throw Cuba ultimately into the hands of its Negro population." A young freshman senator from Louisiana, Judah P. Benjamin, introduced similar resolutions.

Bunch wrote to Clarendon with undisguised frustration. News of these developments put him in an impossible position. "I have exhausted my arguments and nearly my patience in the endeavors to persuade those who have spoken to me on the subject that Great Britain is not engrossed in plotting the destruction of the American Union [and] the abolition of slavery within its limits," he wrote. "But I believe that words are thrown away; for every paper teems with repeated accusations; and I can see from the manner of my friends that they doubt, if not my sincerity, at any rate the correctness of my information."

The consul warned that the British game with Cuba might provoke exactly the kind of American adventurism it meant to deter. "The citizens of North and South Carolina have taken no active part in the buccaneering movement," he wrote, but the registration of slaves and the plan to raise black regiments had created "huge excitement" and "induced some of the quietest people to declare that, if it be true, the Southern States will be forced to invade Cuba," not so much to punish Spain but "as a measure of self-preservation."

"This cry, I may be permitted to remark, is always on the lips of a Carolinian when he is about to justify an outrage connected with Slavery."

President Franklin Pierce had issued a proclamation that reiterated the U.S. government's opposition to the kind of unauthorized expeditions that had already been mounted against Cuba and Mexico. The U.S. Neutrality Act of 1818 had made it a felony to recruit Americans on U.S. territory to fight in foreign wars. But Bunch had seen enough to advise London that Pierce was not able, even if he was willing, to keep these people on a leash.

"It is the precarious chance of success," he wrote, "and not the President's proclamation, which keeps down, for the present, the lawless marauders who swarm in the cities of this Union, and in the semi-civilized regions of the West; particularly on the banks of the Mississippi.

"There exist whole bands, or regiments, of would-be buccaneers," said Bunch, "thoroughly armed and equipped; deadly marksmen; under perfect control; having pass-words and signs of recognition, who are willing to pour down, at a moment's notice, upon the Island of Cuba, whenever they may deem themselves sufficiently powerful." That moment hadn't come yet, but "they are acquiring strength every day; and, when ready, they will not be stopped by Proclamations, nor by the efforts, even if honestly exerted, of the civil and military officers of the United States. They will have with them, that which, in this country, is more powerful than treaties or than law, and often sets both at defiance; I mean, Public Opinion."

But Bunch's biggest immediate concern was rejection of the proposed amendment to the damned Negro Seamen law: "A Member of the Senate stated a few days ago to me that if it were proved that Great Britain had anything to do with the measures of the Governor of Cuba, it would be useless even to introduce a proposal for change." A few days later Bunch told Crampton that his fears were being realized, and the revisions to the Negro Seamen law were in deep trouble.

In June, Clarendon sent Bunch a dispatch telling the consul he had "the full authority to state that Her Majesty's Government are totally ignorant of any plan for the 'Africanization of Cuba,'" and that the sole objective of Britain's "remonstrances and interventions" with the Spanish government was "to prevent the importation of Negroes from Africa."

This was the message Bunch had conveyed in every way he could imagine. Now he had the explicit backing of the Foreign Office, giving him a clear diplomatic assignment. But it was not this declaration that finally eased the tensions in the South; it was a change in Havana. Governor-General de la Pezuela was replaced by one of his hard-bitten predecessors, José Gutiérrez de la Concha, and the old policies returned, allowing the great landowners to pay lip service to the law banning the importation of Africans with no risk that they'd actually have to comply.

· · ·

AS THE STIFLING summer heat settled onto the Carolinas, most of those who could leave for cooler climes were doing so. In late June of that first year of Robert Bunch's posting in South Carolina, he and Emma took off to join their in-laws, the Van Cortlandts, on their large estate in Yonkers, New York.* Bunch liked it there, surrounded by familiar wealth, and the Bunches stayed as long as they could. In New York and Philadelphia they could visit with their old friends and also meet with some of their new acquaintances from South Carolina. Bunch was continuing his careful diplomacy to get the Negro Seamen law repealed and lobbying with those who might have some influence, including Governor John Manning's brother-in-law, John S. Preston. (The two men were both married to daughters of Wade Hampton, the richest planter in South Carolina.)

It wasn't until October that Bunch headed back to South Carolina. By then Emma was quite visibly pregnant. For better or worse, the Bunches would begin their family in Charleston.

WHEN GOVERNOR MANNING opened the new session of the legislature in late November, he suggested in his speech, as he had promised he would, that the time had come for the Negro Seamen law to be amended. He didn't say how, and Bunch, in his report to Clarendon, made excuses for his valuable friend. It had been, said Bunch, a difficult year and a disastrous summer for South Carolina as storms and floods devastated the coast, destroying the rice and Sea Island cotton plantations, while a widespread epidemic of "a very malignant fever during many weeks put a stop to labor and paralyzed trade." The state was facing an economic depression. So, as Bunch explained, Manning did have a lot on his mind. Bunch said he'd been assured by "persons of great weight" that the seamen

---

* The Van Cortlandt manor house still stands in the middle of a public park in Yonkers, where a man in Colonial garb guides schoolchildren through rooms filled with period antiques.

law would be amended, but strong currents opposed change. "One step too much will lose all that we have endeavored to gain."

In the end, the bill was passed in the state senate by a substantial majority and sailed through the House Committee on Colored Populations, thanks to its chairman, John Harleston Read (the brother-in-law of Charleston postmaster Alfred Huger), whom Bunch had cultivated successfully, it seemed. But then the bill stalled on the House floor. The legislative session closed for the year. The bill died. And Bunch wondered whether all his efforts to court the South Carolina grandees had been for naught. "It is impossible for conciliation or generosity to be carried further," he told Lord Clarendon. Britain's position had been reasonable and right, but "that is of little assistance in an encounter with a bigotry and a fanaticism unparalleled, I hope, in any other section of the civilized world."

Even John Harleston Read surprised Bunch as the legislature closed up shop for the year. His committee reported that it had examined a proposal for the revival of the slave trade with Africa. The ceaseless pro-slavery shouting of Leonidas Spratt and his handful of fellow radicals was having an effect.

The committee report noted that since 1807 the trade with Africa had been declared illegal and since 1819 was declared piracy, punishable by death. For a whole host of reasons, Southerners had supported those measures. But times had changed, and the committee members were "decidedly of the opinion that the re-establishment of the trade under the sanction of law and commercial regulation would confer a blessing on the African Race."

Of course, there would be major advantages for the white race, as well: in the committee's view imported Africans would help develop "new and extensive slave territories" and bring "wealth and political strength to the slaveholding States." But there would also be drawbacks: the price of slaves in the United States would plummet, and "this reduction would reduce the profits to be found in rearing slaves." If that happened, then Virginia and Maryland and other border states where slaves were bred might lose interest in the institution, "and thus bring the cordon of free states closer and closer 'round us," as if emancipation were a noose threatening the South. So, the committee took no action, but the members made their sentiments clear.

Bunch sent a clipping about the report to the Slave Trade Department at the Foreign Office and to Clarendon, drawing ironic attention to the committee's opinion that the trade in slaves "would confer a blessing on the African Race."

"This enlightened proposal," Bunch told Clarendon, "may serve as an additional proof of the popular feeling in this State on the subject of Slavery in general." In a separate, private note to John Crampton, Bunch wrote that there was no chance that this "absurd proposition" would lead to any practical result.

Fifteen months later Bunch would feel very different.

Chapter 7

THROUGH THE WINTER OF 1854–1855 the denizens of John Russell's bookshop could read, battle by battle, the vivid accounts of the Crimean War published in the *Times* of London. Its correspondent, who also happened to be named Russell—William Howard Russell—applauded the British soldiers' phenomenal bravery and exposed the British high command's inexcusable incompetence. In the chill Carolina afternoons that December, with light flooding in through the windows of the bookshop, the men of Charleston read and discussed Russell's account of a disastrous charge into the mouths of Russian cannons: "At ten minutes past eleven, our Light Cavalry Brigade advanced. . . . At thirty-five minutes past eleven, not a British soldier, except the dead and dying, was left in front of those bloody Muscovite guns."

Queen Victoria's soldiers had gotten used to fighting "little wars" all over the globe, many of them simultaneously. But this was a big one, and Britain had to redeploy resources from around the world. As its warships gathered in the Black Sea around Sebastopol, the waters around the mouth of the Congo River and the Bight of Benin were neglected, and any lapse of surveillance and enforcement was exploited. The slave traffic between Africa and Cuba once again began to increase dramatically, to the point where Parliament began to question whether the Royal Navy's Africa Squadron was worth the fortune expended on it each year. One of its former commanders told the House of Commons, "Experience has proven the present system to be futile."

The dispatches arriving at the Slave Trade Department meanwhile showed that the Americans and their flag continued to play a growing role in the deadly commerce between Africa and Cuba. A typically detailed report from the consul in Havana in October 1854 traced the movements of one Don José Egea, who was traveling to

New York City to purchase a schooner "capable of bringing over 500 slaves from Africa." The intelligence gathered on him gave the address of the offices he planned to visit and the precise coordinates where he was supposed to anchor near the mouth of the Congo River. The Foreign Office's man in Havana said he hoped that officers of the U.S. government could be found "who will know that it is necessary to observe the greatest secrecy and discretion so as to trace Mr. Egea and watch his progress, in order to pounce upon the expedition at the moment of its completion."

Lord Palmerston, languishing at the Home Office but always in close touch with Lord Clarendon, found these sorts of communications infuriating. The intelligence was there; the enforcement was not. "In Cuba, when our consul sends proofs to the Captain General that a cargo of slaves has been landed at such a time and place, and calls upon him to punish the offenders, the Captain General says he will make inquiries, and after a certain time he reports that he has made inquiries, and is unable to trace any proof that a landing has been effected; and when he is requested to search certain plantations to which it is suspected the slaves have been removed, he replies that he has not the power to do so." As for the Americans, the fact that so much of this trade took place on ships flying their colors was, purely and simply, the "prostitution of their flag."

Then word leaked that three U.S. envoys in Europe—Pierre Soulé, the minister in Madrid (a very "*peculiar* man," as Crampton called him, with emphasis); James Buchanan, the envoy to London (widely known as "Buck" or "Old Buck"); and John Y. Mason, the minister to Paris—had all come together at what was supposed to be a secret meeting in the seaside resort of Ostend, Belgium. The "manifesto" that emerged called for the purchase of Cuba or, failing that, the use of force to seize it. Still, the British, struggling as they were in the mud of the Crimea, could do little to respond except to lodge diplomatic protests.

As these tensions and frustrations rose, Robert Bunch, wise

to the ways of the society around him and of the bureaucracy he served—and now the father of a baby girl—tried to keep his head down. But other consuls were not so prudent.

The army in the Crimea cried out for volunteers, and Bunch's old bête noir, Col. George Mathew, now in Philadelphia, wrote to the Foreign Office suggesting it should give consuls the authority to buy tickets to Britain for American doctors and others who wanted to volunteer for service in the Crimea. John Crampton, in Washington, didn't like this idea at all. The closer he looked at the would-be cannon fodder Mathew was lining up, the less savory the project appeared. Many supposed volunteers were simply looking for a quick buck in a faltering American economy. Crampton checked with his lawyers, who told him that any arrangement that recruited anyone on U.S. soil for the war against Russia was not only illegal but would be breaking the same neutrality law that was used by the Federal government, when it chose, to try to stop the filibusters in the Caribbean.

Still, Crampton hoped to please London. He tried to find a way to fund volunteers headed for the Crimea, using money from his Secret Service account. He corresponded confidentially with several agents, usually by special messenger because he didn't trust the mails, and they set up a network that would encourage Americans to go to Canada, then enlist. Old Anthony Barclay—Bunch's cousin, who was the consul in New York—got dragged into the recruitment conspiracy. (He would later claim it was his clerk in his back-alley office who made all the decisions, that he knew nothing about them.) Soon the whole scheme had leaked to the press and suddenly became part of a widening crisis.

Complicating U.S.-British relations still further, the American adventurer William Walker had taken an armed gang to Nicaragua, thrown his weight behind one of the political factions, and was emerging as a *yanqui* dictator in the heart of Central America. Newspapers called him "the grey-eyed man of destiny," as in "Manifest Destiny." Many admirers in the United States saw Walker striking a blow for their country, for slavery, and against the Crown, which presumed to limit their territorial ambitions.

Not for the first time, and certainly not for the last, Minister Crampton and his consuls came to believe that American politicians were stirring up war fever to help pull together the increasingly divided "united" states that were unable to resolve their bitter differences over slavery. Crampton was particularly suspicious of the new Republican Party that had grown out of the Free Soil Party, and of its leader, Senator William Seward of New York. These men saw "a foreign war," as Crampton wrote, "being the great cure for the black disease which is now tearing the vitals of the Union."

All this talk of violent conflict with Great Britain, month after month, grated on Bunch's nerves in Charleston, threatened his family's interests in the North (where Emma owned some properties), and threw into his face the contradictions of his position. He could not say what he felt nor dare to feel what he said. "Really, the temptation to speak one's mind to somebody is irresistible," he wrote. "As the tyrant in the melodrama says, whilst biting his gauntlet, 'But I must dissemble'—so I am forced to wear the smile of indifference."

IN LONDON, LORD Palmerston was now Prime Minister. It had taken him a lifetime to reach the top position—he was seventy-one years old—but he was still remarkably fit, despite the hair dye and false teeth, and he still showed the kind of energy and determination that the British hungered for after a long year and a half sunk in the Crimean mire. Palmerston's well-known force of personality, his almost insouciant imperialism, and his promiscuous use of British arms brought confidence to the home front and encouragement to the war front. His decision to keep Clarendon as Foreign Secretary also lent the new administration an air of confident continuity.

As Palmerston focused his energies on the war against the Russians, the truculent Americans seemed like little more than a nuisance, and he pondered ways to strike back at them, if necessary, on the cheap. In a hasty but revealing note to Lord Clarendon, Palmerston called the Americans "mere swaggering bullies." If they "should push matters to extremities, we should be quite able to meet them," he scrawled. Were they afraid of a huge slave insurrection? Then Britain could perfectly well give them one. "We have a deeply piercing blow to strike at their Southern States if ever we should be at war with them," wrote Palmerston. "Freedom to the Slaves proclaimed by a British force landed in the South would shake the Union to its base."

ROBERT AND EMMA and little Helen Bunch were now well established in Charleston society. Such were the interlocking kinships among the Mannings and the Hamptons, the Blakes and the Rutledges, the Allstons, the Chesnuts, the Pinckneys, and others that acceptance in one circle could lead to acceptance in many. Bunch was invited to dinners and Emma to teas, where she listened as closely to the opinions of the ladies as Robert did to those of the men. But even as the young consul's many personal connections helped keep him informed, they also made it hard for him to reconcile the elite that he cultivated with the slavery he hated. The discrepancy between the sentiments he expressed to his government and the sentiments he expressed in Charleston society grew wider by the day. The smile of indifference became his habitual expression.

Most problematic of all was Bunch's relationship with Daniel Blake, who owned as many slaves or more than anyone else on the Eastern seaboard. When Bunch first met him, Blake was recently widowed. Then Emma's younger sister, Helen Craig, came to visit Charleston, and Blake fell for her. Within a year they were married. Helen was thirty, and, like Emma, she was petite with dark hair, thin lips, and intelligent, worldly eyes. Blake was fifty-three but, at the time, looked younger. He was almost gaunt and had the mien of an ascetic country preacher, which shouldn't have been surprising, since he was almost as famous for his piety as he was for his fortune.

Blake was from an old Anglo-American family that had lived in South Carolina since the seventeenth century yet never lost entirely its connection to Great Britain. He was born in England and educated at Cambridge. But he was as deeply embedded in the slave economy of the South as anyone alive. His properties included huge rice and cotton plantations in South Carolina. The main one was called, simply, Board House. And he had a summer retreat called The Meadows that covered almost eight thousand acres near the Count de Choiseul's relatively modest "chateau" in the North Carolina mountains.

Blake came to think of Bunch as a close member of his family and eventually named his new bride's firstborn son Robert Bunch Blake, suggesting that the never-very-pious consul had put on enough religious airs to become the boy's godfather. Certainly Cousin Helen had played the card of piety. In the little town of Hendersonville, North Carolina, near The Meadows a church was erected in the name of both Helen and Daniel Blake. But neither of the Craig women, Emma Bunch nor Helen Blake, was inclined to hold her tongue, and neither one of them accepted entirely the self-satisfied "slavocracy" around them. Even after the war had begun, when one of Blake's sons by his first marriage was serving as a Confederate officer, Helen remained an outspoken Unionist.

For Bunch, the passion of these women so close to him eventually became a serious problem, but he could hardly fail to sympathize in private. In 1855 and 1856, even as Helen's wedding approached, Bunch took a morbid fascination in the runaway-slave advertisements carried by the local papers, which marked such a contrast with the holier-than-holy posture of planters like Blake. Bunch sent the clippings off to Crampton almost randomly:

STATE OF NORTH CAROLINA, Sampson County: Whereas D.W. Cromartie has this day made oath before us, John R. Ezzell and George W. Atkins aforesaid, that his Negro girl, ROSE, absconded from his service sometime in the month of June last, and is lurking about in the neighborhood of South River, or Cape Fear, committing acts of depredation and felony contrary to law. In consideration of which the said girl is hereby commanded to come forward and deliver herself up immediately, otherwise we hereby authorize any person to kill said girl without any fear of punishment. . . . Said girl is about 18 years old, of black complexion and about five feet high." Then there is an addendum from Cromartie: "I will pay Twenty-Five Dollars reward for the delivery of said girl, ROSE, to me in Clinton, either dead or alive, and a further reward of One Hundred Dollars for sufficient proof to convict any white person of harboring her.

FOR ALL ROBERT BUNCH'S growing cynicism and fatalism about the slave society he inhabited, he remained relentless in pursuit of a resolution to the Negro Seamen law. And despite the many setbacks, Lord Clarendon continued to praise Bunch's handling of the issue: "I feel certain that no effort on your part has been wanting." Then, over the course of the spring, much to Bunch's surprise, the new governor of the state gave him hope that the law might yet be changed.

The consul's initial report on the election of Gen. James Hopkins Adams had not been optimistic. He was from "the interior of the state" and is "little known in Charleston," Bunch told Clarendon. He portrayed Adams, essentially, as a yokel and did not expect him to support the kind of humane recommendations Governor Manning had approved. But when Adams visited Charleston in early March 1855, Bunch quickly arranged to meet him and propose "in a temperate and friendly manner," as he had done with so many others so many times, the need to change a law that was a problem for Britain and was no longer required for the safety of South Carolina. Adams, far from resisting the arguments, said he was "fully impressed with the importance of the subject" and said he felt that public attitudes about it were changing. He wouldn't commit on the issue, but he did ask Bunch to write him a formal letter about it.

This was a touchy proposal. Formal letters written by Consul Mathew had paved the way to diplomatic disaster. Bunch told Clarendon he thought it was worth doing, but only if the text of the letter was approved by Clarendon himself. Then, in June, Adams invited Bunch up to his Live Oak Plantation on the Congaree River near Columbia, where he seemed to be "conciliatory in the highest degree." Bunch read the Clarendon-approved draft letter aloud to the governor, adding that he, the British consul, would take personal responsibility for changing anything in the text approved by the Foreign Secretary that Adams thought might "excite an unpleasant feeling." He also told the governor that the letter was meant for his "information and guidance," not for public consumption. Adams agreed to keep it private and said there wasn't a word in it he'd want to change.

Bunch was as pleased as he was surprised by the whole encounter, which seemed to be the beginning of the end of the Negro Seamen Act. "General Adams has always been known as one of the leaders of the high Slavery Party, uniformly opposed to any negotiation on the subject of this obnoxious law," Bunch reported to Clarendon. To have won out over this man's prejudices was, Bunch suggested, a "triumph."

Indeed, Bunch apparently felt so relieved that he spent an extra two days at Adams's plantation, allowing himself to endure the hospitality of the master and his slaves.

IN THE CRIMEA, Sebastopol had fallen in September 1855, and by early 1856 Lord Clarendon was in France personally negotiating the Treaty of Paris that would bring the war to an end. The parties then followed up with a declaration respecting maritime law that seemed, at the time, to have very little to do with South Carolina or Consul Bunch's mission there. The signatories of the declaration were all the great powers of Europe: the United Kingdom, France, Russia, Sardinia (which controlled much of Italy), Austria, Turkey (the Ottoman Empire), and Prussia. These were followed in rapid succession by forty-eight other countries but not, as it happened, the United States, which seemed, at just that moment, intent once again upon picking a fight with the British Empire.

President Franklin Pierce had devoted the first three thousand words of his eleven-thousand-word State of the Union address to grievances against Great Britain, from its claims on Belize and the Mosquito Coast in Central America to the recruiting of troops for the Crimea and border disputes with Canada in the Pacific Northwest. It all just confirmed Bunch's generally gloomy assessment of Anglo-American relations. The consul said he was watching "anxiously out to windwards for an approaching squall."

Bunch started to make the rounds of his Charleston contacts to test their sentiments. His message for each of them was the same: "You and nine-tenths of the respectable people of South Carolina look upon a war between the United States and Great Britain as a chimera—a bugbear to control an election—but an impossibility in fact." The sooner they got over that idea, the better, Bunch told them. They should be doing everything they could to calm the waters and encourage peace, because war was a very real possibility.

"My friends really seemed greatly alarmed and equally astonished," Bunch wrote to Crampton. "To them a war, or even a rupture, could be ruinous—the cotton and rice crop of last season are not paid for, and of course they would have no orders for the next."

At a dinner party in Charleston, Bunch found himself up against a Mr. William Watts Sherman of the New York banking firm of Duncan, Sherman, & Company, "a finicking specimen of the money-changer turned dandy, pert, presumptuous, and a parvenu."

At the end of the meal, the ladies rose and left, and Sherman turned on Bunch. "What do you say to the Central America question?"

The matter was fraught with complex hostilities as London and Washington tried to negotiate a new treaty recognizing each other's interests in Nicaragua, or not. Bunch intended his reply to end the conversation. "Really, Mr. Sherman, I do not think it is a question to talk about at all just now."

But Sherman kept at it. "I presume you have read the correspondence between the two governments," he said. "I have no hesitation in saying that the question is a vastly more complicated one than *you* suppose." Sherman talked about his exalted position in finance and his close friendship with Secretary of State William L. Marcy, which enabled him to say that the government of the United States would never budge from the position it had taken opposing British claims to a protectorate on the Mosquito Coast that would give it effective control over any effort to build a trans-isthmus canal. Bunch repeated more or less what he'd said to his friends, with "perfect good humor and with the sweetest smiles," essentially: "You may look on this as a ploy to win your elections, but Great Britain is not going to back down, and you could get yourself into a war."

"Lord Clarendon is pettifogging," said Sherman, suggesting that the Foreign Secretary was just quibbling about little details.

"Lord Clarendon can bear that imputation with Christian fortitude," said Bunch. "When such a term is applied to the behavior of England, it has the merit of novelty and would have to be supported by some stronger evidence than your word, Mr. Sherman, for even the American public to believe it."

Bunch's blood was up. In the days that followed, encouraged by Crampton, he tried to create a wider campaign of information and persuasion that would show Charlestonians and Southerners generally that Britain should not be trifled with. He wrote to William Mure, who'd been the British consul in New Orleans for decades. Bunch presented himself in the letter as acting on Crampton's behalf because Crampton was so busy. What he probably could not say was that Crampton, under pressure because of the Crimean recruiting scandal, was increasingly paranoid about his communications being monitored. The minister in Washington apparently thought he might get a letter to Bunch in Charleston unopened, but not as far as Mure in New Orleans. In any case, Bunch told Crampton he wasn't too optimistic about Mure's response: "M is a touchy sort of customer and *might* object to the appearance of my giving him instructions."

"There is, in Mr. Crampton's opinion, little doubt that the Administration at Washington is bent upon *mischief*," Bunch told Mure. So the plan was to create as much pressure on the government in Washington as possible by appealing to the cotton interests. "You and I have been selected," Bunch wrote, "to create such an alarm amongst our most influential dealers in cotton as, without passing the bounds of prudence or of truth, and without exposing ourselves to a charge of indiscretion, may serve to show the stirrers up of strife that a power can be found, within their own territory, stronger than they, against which it is useless to strive."

Mure demurred. He had no time, no budget, no taste for it: if his role were found out, the effect would be disastrous. And he knew that whether this information was from Crampton or not, Crampton had already gotten himself into enough trouble.

Chapter 8

IN THE END, THERE WAS no new Anglo-American war. Despite the diplomatic chill in the air, the squall never came ashore. Instead, President Pierce's bellicosity was partly assuaged by attacking the British diplomats involved in the Crimean recruiting scandal. Late in the spring of 1856, months after the Treaty of Paris had ended the Crimean War, George Mathew and Anthony Barclay both had their consular accreditations—their "exequaturs," in diplomatic language—taken away. Mathew went on to new assignments in Europe and then in Mexico. Barclay retired to Savannah with his very wealthy wife, a Georgia heiress who owned considerable properties and many slaves.

John Crampton was expelled from the Washington legation. He returned to England to receive a knighthood and a new European assignment from his appreciative government. The ostensible cause for his removal was his violation of the Neutrality Act because of his recruiting for the Crimea, but the *New York Times* made another, in some respects, more interesting connection. It reported that Crampton was "dismissed" by the Americans only three days after he had handed over to the State Department a damning report on the slaving activities of ships under the U.S. flag off the coast of Angola.

Inside the United States, passions in the debate over the expansion of slavery in the territories had grown so violent that nobody could predict what course they might take from day to day, whether at home or abroad. Charles Sumner, the tall, handsome, and refined Republican senator from Massachusetts, had many friends in London society and politics and had been a major source for much of Crampton's intelligence about the inner workings of the U.S. Senate. He was a ferocious opponent of slavery, the slave trade, and the South, whose leading men he spoke about with savage contempt. On a stifling day in the spring of 1856 he addressed a packed Senate chamber about the critical question of whether "bleeding Kansas" should be admitted to the Union as a slave state or a free one. Then he focused his attention on the absent Senator Andrew Butler from South Carolina, personally insulting his reputation and that of the state in as many creative ways as he could imagine. Two days later, after the Senate had adjourned in the afternoon and Sumner was sitting at his desk signing envelopes so he could use his franking privilege to mail his speech all over the country, a congressman from South Carolina, a cousin of Butler's named Preston Brooks, walked up to Sumner and laid into him with his gold-tipped cane. He beat the senator from Massachusetts senseless and shattered the cane.

In Charleston, according to Bunch, the incident got mixed reviews. "The mob, always the majority, like it, and the gentlemen do not." But people were taking up collections to buy Brooks silver teapots as trophies—and new gold-headed canes, of course. *"Vive la république!"* Bunch concluded.

With Crampton gone and unrest so obvious, Clarendon authorized Bunch to report "from time to time on all matters of interest occurring in the United States." This was an extraordinary vote of confidence in the would-be diplomat. Suddenly the Charleston consul was filing official reports to the Foreign Secretary almost as if he were the minister in Washington, D.C., and he wrote long dispatches about the upcoming American elections of 1856.

The Democratic Party, as Bunch wrote, had nominated the former U.S. minister to London, James Buchanan, who looked set to win against the new Republican Party, the Know-Nothings, and a few lesser contenders. Bunch reported on "the frightful state of civil war which has broken out in the Territories of Kansas and Nebraska," and on what he interpreted as the surprising acceptance of its horrors by the man on the street. Abolitionists were burning down towns and capturing villages. So were the pro-slavery factions. The U.S. marshal and four of his men were killed arresting rioters. Several people, including two women, had been massacred when a hotel was burned in Lawrence, Kansas. "Were the matter of less fearful significance, it would be almost ludicrous to observe how little alarm or indignation these outrages appear to excite," Bunch wrote. "The principal cause is doubtless the recklessness of the American character, and the aggressive propensities of the people. From every quarter persons are flocking toward the disturbed districts, all anxious to fight."

The raw, barbaric emotions of the mob were easy for British gentlemen to sneer at (often they attributed them to the large number of Irish immigrants in the United States), but however that might be, violence was a given in American society. In the 1840s, after Charles Dickens toured the United States, he linked the American inclination to bloodshed with the barbarity of slavery. It was no surprise, he said, that in a country where humans were branded, whipped, and maimed, where men "learn to write with pens of red-hot iron on the human face," they grew to be bullies and, "carrying cowards' weapons hidden in their breast, will shoot men down and stab them" when they quarrel. Every day as Bunch walked the streets in South Carolina, he had cause to remember those lines.

Chapter 9

THE BUSINESS OF SELLING SLAVES had been changing in Charleston. It was no longer as picturesque as it had been when William Makepeace Thackeray first visited. In 1856, the city decided the auctions near the Old Exchange and Custom House were out of hand, and the various slave brokers started opening up their own showrooms, with pens outside to hold the chattel. Probably this was a relief for Bunch, who had had to pass the auction block almost daily as he performed his duties around town. But it also signaled a shift in the dynamics of the market. Slave auctions were too big, and the action too important, to be conducted on the street.

In financial terms, slaves in the South had become the stuff that dreams were made of. More than land, cotton, rice, or sugar, owning slaves came to be considered the standard measure of prosperity, the safest investment, and the most profitable commodity for speculation. "This alliance between Negroes and cotton, we will venture to say, is now the *strongest power* in the world," wrote James De Bow, editor of the widely read *De Bow's Review* in New Orleans, "and the peace and welfare of Christendom absolutely depend upon the strength and security of it."

A pro-slavery crusade that could no longer be ignored was taking shape in the South, its centerpiece the fight to reopen the trade with Africa. One of the most passionate and persuasive advocates was William Yancey of Alabama. He could move an audience to tears, then beyond tears to calls for secession. The Virginian Edmund Ruffin, a soil expert and agrarian ideologue with piercing blue eyes and a mane of shoulder-length gray hair, was the grand old man of the movement, while Robert Barnwell Rhett and his *Charleston Mercury* competed with Leonidas Spratt and his *Standard* to keep the fires of the slave trade and secession burning brightly in Charleston.

The newly changed atmosphere in South Carolina made Bunch's life and work harder than ever. In December 1855 Spratt had put himself directly in Bunch's path on the question of the Negro Seamen law. Earlier, Governor Adams, to the surprise of many but not, of course, Bunch, had spoken out in favor of amendments to the law during his address to the legislature, and much of the phrasing he used was picked up verbatim from the letter Bunch had written and Clarendon approved for Adams's "information and guidance." Adams had concluded, "I do not think that our safety requires a law of such unrelenting and indiscriminate severity. The remedy is worse than the disease it seeks to cure."

Spratt did not bother with such common sense. "Our greatest objection to the changes is in the fact that it will be a concession to anti-slavery sentiment," Spratt wrote. "Foreign States"—meaning Britain, of course—"contend that there is a natural right in the Negro to a state of freedom, and they have navies to prevent his introduction to our country as a slave. We contend that slavery is a natural condition of the Negro."

Once again, to Bunch's dismay and frustration, the amendments to the law failed to pass.

By the end of 1856, Bunch had reinforced Clarendon's confidence in him with his dispatches on Kansas and the American elections. He had also visited London and, doubtless, met with the Foreign Secretary, although when they talked and what they talked about is not revealed in their official or their unofficial correspondence.

What is clear is that Bunch's scope of action, necessarily, was growing broader. The explosive atmosphere around the issues of slavery and the slave trade, and the bellicose eruptions of hostility between the United States and Britain, heightened the need at the Foreign Office for more and better information from the United States and increased Foreign Office reliance on its man in Charleston. Bunch remained interested in getting the Negro Seamen law changed, hopeless though that seemed, but he began to focus more of his attention on bigger issues.

He did not need to look far afield. South Carolina's politics were fraught with surprises that had national and international implications. As the 1856 legislative session opened, Governor Adams gave an address that left even Bunch at a loss for words. Not only did the formerly hospitable master of Live Oak Plantation say nothing at all about the changes to the Negro Seamen law that he and Bunch had discussed at such length and that he'd endorsed in such carefully cribbed language the year before, but now he attacked the British Empire as a hostile competitor with South Carolina's interests and reached a conclusion, after citing some surprising statistics and employing rather original economic logic, that set his state and, indeed, the whole South on a collision course with the United Kingdom.

The amount of cotton being produced outside the American South, especially in British possessions, "should open our eyes to our true policy," said Adams. The idea that only African slaves can successfully grow cotton "is an entire mistake." Peasants and "coolies" in India and other British dominions—Adams called them "free slaves"—were producing "more than the entire crop of the United States in 1820." Adams cited a report from U.S. Secretary of State Marcy showing that in 1855 the United States had shipped roughly 679 million pounds of cotton to Great Britain, while the East Indies, Egypt, and Brazil had shipped it 202 million pounds.

Yes, the South still supplied almost 80 percent of England's cotton, but the trend was going against it, and Adams claimed that this was all part of a British plot to free the slaves. "Whenever England and the Continent can procure their supply of the raw material elsewhere than from us, and the cotton States are limited to the home market, then will our doom be sealed," Adams declared. "Destroy the value of slave labor, and emancipation follows inevitably," he said. His oddly twisted conclusion: "To maintain our present position, we must have cheap labor also. This can be obtained in but one way—by re-opening the African slave trade."

Then a few days later came a development that, in other circumstances, might have been a matter for celebration at the Bunch house and on Downing Street. Bunch wrote to Clarendon on the day after Christmas: "It is with great satisfaction that I have the honor of reporting to Your Lordship that the Legislature of South Carolina has passed an Act for the modification and amendment of the Law for the imprisonment of free persons of color arriving within the limits of the state."

Col. John Harleston Read had reintroduced the same bill that was defeated at the last minute the year before, and at a crucial moment in the debate *Charleston Courier* editor Richard Yeadon, who was a member of the House, spoke up and carried the day. "At nine p.m. on the last night of the session, the act was ratified by both houses," Bunch reported. Then he added, "The governor, perhaps fortunately in the present instance, has no veto power in this State."

After three years, Bunch's work on the Negro Seamen law had paid off, and it was a well-earned victory for Her Majesty's consul. His core mission had been accomplished. But the constant flow of anti-British vitriol and, now, Adams's amazing speech linking hatred for London with a call to reopen the Middle Passage, gave Bunch and his reporting a new purpose.

The South was headed toward a confrontation not only with the North but with Great Britain. Bunch had no doubt about that, even if others failed to see it.

Once again, his friends assured him that Adams was not to be taken seriously, that he was leaving office, anyway, since his term was up, and that he was really just a laughingstock. But Bunch wasn't so sure. The man might be a fool and his ideas, as Bunch wrote, "anomalous," but they could no longer be dismissed. The hideous traffic in African slaves to Cuba was growing. Tens of thousands were being landed there each year. Traffic in slaves to the Southern United States would be next if, indeed, it had not already begun. And should that happen, Bunch knew that he and his countrymen could be set against the Americans in a fight that was sure to be fiercely waged on both sides.

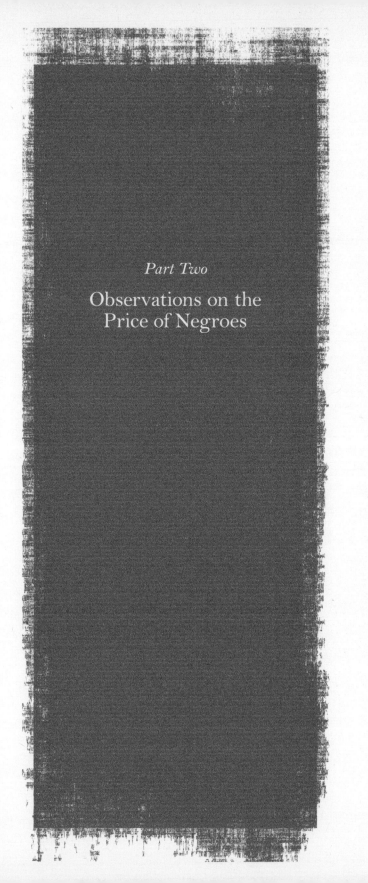

Part Two

Observations on the
Price of Negroes

I N THE FIRST WEEK OF March 1857 Robert Bunch wrote a confidential dispatch from Charleston that he hoped would have a profound effect on the views of Lord Clarendon and, if it could be gotten to him, of Prime Minister Palmerston. This was not one of Bunch's acid glosses on current events; it was much more like a policy paper, and even if Bunch had never written another letter to the Crown, Dispatch No. 10, March 4, 1857, was a defining document. Forwarded without enclosures via a Royal Mail steamer from Boston, it was received at the Foreign Office in London some twenty days later. It was addressed directly to the Earl of Clarendon, and it bore the heading "Increase in the value of Negroes: scarcity of Labor in the Cotton fields: probable results."

"So very remarkable a rise has of late taken place in the price of Negroes," wrote Bunch on the opening page, "that I am desirous of calling Your Lordship's attention to the subject." Bunch was firmly confident as he laid out the sums and percentages, the antecedents and the consequences. Within "the last few years" the price of an able-bodied man had gone from $800 to $1,500, a woman from $600 to $1,400. The cause was simple: slaves were needed to pick cotton, and cotton production had increased about 3,000 percent in the first half of the century, while the population of slaves increased only 150 percent, according to Bunch. The natural growth of slave populations was inadequate and, Bunch wrote, could not begin to make up the difference. The effect was perfectly predictable: to meet the demand for cotton, the South would be forced to reopen the slave trade with Africa. "Such is the evil which is rapidly developing," wrote the Charleston consul.

Eventually, Bunch predicted in Dispatch No. 10, the economic arithmetic would prevail over all other objections. The idea of reopening the trade was widely discussed and often denounced, but "it will grow in favor as the necessity for fresh laborers becomes more pressing. When this time shall arrive, England will be placed in a position of some difficulty." On the one hand, Bunch reminded Clarendon, England depended on the South for four-fifths of her raw cotton. On the other, "She will find that it is only to be obtained at the price of the renewal of a trade which is opposed by the universal sentiment of the British People and by every feeling of humanity; by a reversal, in fact, of a policy to which she is so fully committed that retrogression could only be attended with disgrace."

Bunch, with careful political calculation, was taking the speech of Governor James Adams and the diatribes of Leonidas Spratt and turning them against the Southern slavers. "The remedy, I believe the only one, cannot fail to occur at once to Your Lordship, viz, the disentanglement of the English Manufactures from the thrall of the American Cotton-grower; the production of the raw material in some quarters of the Globe where it can be grown without the attendant horrors of Slavery. It is not for me to do more than to suggest the subject to Your Lordship, whose attention, I doubt not, has been already directed to it. But I venture to do so with the more earnestness that I believe the impending evil to be of great magnitude, and that, so far as my humble judgment goes, we have the cure in our own hands, thanks to the magnificent resources of Africa, of the East, and probably of the West Indies."

Bunch signed Dispatch No. 10 knowing it might be slow to take effect in London if, indeed, it had any effect at all. But he returned to the theme often in the years that followed, writing with contempt about the catastrophe his Charleston acquaintances were bringing upon themselves and concern about the risks that they might pose to British interests. From 1857 onward, he hammered home the same point again and again, playing a role out of all proportion to his nominal position. But, then, that is what he had been looking to do all of his career.

When Bunch wrote his observations on the price of Negroes, he was using the same laws of supply and demand as those leading the pro-slave-trade crusade. But almost as Bunch wrote, supply and demand were giving way rapidly to speculation that defied economic reason and that would lend new urgency to the debate.

A financial panic in the fall of 1857 had devastating consequences for the industrial North, where so much capital was in factories and equities. To the extent that the South was affected, it was because of the decline in Northern markets, but by and large the South escaped the worst effects of the panic because its money was not in stocks and bonds. Its money was in land and slaves. "The peculiar institution," according to one speculator among many, was "decidedly the most profitable and safe investment in the whole country." There was a feverish desire to buy slaves to the limit of possible credit and in the spirit of speculation. This was a bubble market in human beings.

The majority of Southerners, however, were deeply uneasy with the idea of importing Africans en masse, even though De Bow, Yancey, Spratt, and Rhett worked overtime to convince them that doing so would be all for the good of the Negro, too. The strongest objections came from Virginia and Maryland, where much of the soil was worn out and it was understood that slave breeding and slave raising had become profitable industries for some of the masters. If the market were opened up to African imports, the value of those locally produced human assets would plunge. Pro-slave-trade crusaders countered that huge numbers of Africans were needed to revive old lands as well as to open new ones, increasing production and profits everywhere. For example, in factories, which the South so far had been slow to build, African slaves would be docile workers and wouldn't threaten the status quo the way white laborers frequently did in the North. "The smoke of the steam engine should begin to float over the cotton fields, and the hum of spindles and the click of looms make music on all our mountain streams," mused an editorialist in the New Orleans *Times-Picayune*.

Slaves became so valuable that nobody could afford to let them go, and the cherished notion among genteel planters that they would try to keep slave families together rather than auction off members separately became mere pretense. As a matter of economic self-preservation, emancipation was unthinkable for the South's elites. If slavery were abolished, they'd be bankrupt, pure and simple. A large slave owner and man of fortune spoke "with all the fervor of a capitalist menaced by a set of Red Republicans," wrote one British reporter touring the South. (Jefferson Davis would later say bluntly that the slave-owning states would secede "to save ourselves from a revolution" that threatened to make "property in slaves so insecure as to be comparatively worthless.")

With prices so high for legal slaves, the temptation to import illegal ones from Africa finally was more than some planters could resist, and, thanks to the Cuban traffic, the infrastructure for the revival of the trade already was in place. Ships with oversize water tanks, special hidden decks, cages, and shackles, many of them outfitted in New York, operated extensively between West Africa and the West Indies.

In his Dispatch No. 10, Bunch had warned that the Crown would find itself in an untenable situation if the South seceded and reopened the slave trade with Africa, and he had recommended that other sources of cotton be opened, exploited, and developed by Great Britain. This was not a new idea. Indeed, the British search for alternative supplies of cotton had been at the center of Governor Adams's bizarre oration. It had been talked about in the British government, in British journals, and also in American ones for many years. But it was hard for the merchants and factory owners of Lancashire to break free from their addiction to the cotton produced by the slave-owning Southern market. The prices were attractive, the networks were well established and highly profitable, and nobody wanted to turn his back on a good return. So Bunch had made the case, in the coolest language possible, that the moral dilemma posed by the renewal of the African slave trade would soon be trumped by the convenience of commerce with the South.

. . .

IN WASHINGTON, D.C., a new minister, Lord Napier, arrived from London. He was about the same age as Bunch but had all the natural advantages of money and political connections in Britain that Bunch had to spend so much time cobbling together. Napier's father, an old friend of Palmerston, had died trying to open up China to British trade in the 1830s, and the young Napier had been under Palmerston's wing ever since. Even from the United States he felt comfortable giving the Foreign Office his own opinions about dealing with the Chinese and the latest British military campaign fighting its way toward Peking.

Napier was considered quite handsome, with long hair and bedroom eyes and a manner at once so casual and enthusiastic that his innate arrogance was seen as good humor. Women loved him, and influential senators—most notably William Seward—became great fans. But Lord Clarendon was not overjoyed with his reporting. From London's perspective, Napier seemed to have fallen in line very quickly with the American view of Manifest Destiny in Central America. Certainly he downplayed concerns about the slave trade to Cuba ("I think the account of the *profits realized* in the traffic, as estimated by the British Authorities in Cuba, must be overrated"), but Clarendon believed his men in Havana and Charleston. Only months after the elegant young minister had taken over the Washington legation, Clarendon named a second envoy to deal with the whole Central America mess.

In the months after Clarendon received Bunch's Dispatch No. 10—and also dispatchers from other consuls informing him that the slave trade to Cuba conducted under the U.S. flag was burgeoning—the Foreign Secretary kept insisting that Napier follow up on the matter. Napier responded dutifully: "Your Lordship's wishes about the slave trade shall be attended to." But they rarely were.

American politicians playing on rampant jingoism had turned the issue into a matter of national sovereignty: it wasn't really about slaves; it was about the question of whether the Royal Navy should be allowed to search American ships. Even Northerners such as Seward jumped on the bandwagon, raving against England and shrieking for war at the slightest hint of a provocation. American naval vessels in the Africa Squadron of the United States, which were supposed to be capturing slavers, actually spent much of their time trying to prevent the British from interfering with any ships that flew the Stars and Stripes, even if those vessels stank of the slave trade. There were several standoffs at sea and episodes of hysteria in the press and in Congress.

It wasn't until a year after Bunch had sent his Dispatch No. 10 that Napier paid a visit to the office of the cosmopolitan senator from Louisiana, Judah P. Benjamin, a wealthy litigator famous for his soft manner and enigmatic smile, to ask his views on the slave trade. One of the ploys being used by politicians in the Louisiana legislature to get around Federal laws against trafficking Africans was to legalize the importation of "apprentices," who would be, no one doubted, slaves in all but name. But Benjamin reassured Napier that even if the "apprentice" measure passed in Louisiana, it would be crushed in Congress. "The whole North will rise against the revival of the Trade under any disguise," said Benjamin, "and the middle and Western slave states would take the same side to preserve the value of their breeding Negroes and maintain the Union."

Napier was only mildly relieved by this prediction. It had taken him a while, but he had begun to reach the same conclusions that Bunch had reached the year before about the inevitable reopening of the slave trade. And while Senator Benjamin might have been right about the current state of public feeling on the subject, it didn't look as if that would last long. South Carolina, Alabama, Louisiana, and Texas claimed to be desperate for new cheap labor. "If they cannot get Negroes in the Union, they will break the Union and get Negroes as an independent federation," Napier concluded. "I do not believe that the existing political structure can last long."

The message to London finally was coming out of the legation in

Washington in the same register as it had come out of the consulate in Charleston, and even President James Buchanan had begun to see the threat posed by the slave-trade issue. He finally ordered American warships to crack down on the Cuba traffic that had been protected by the U.S. flag, and soon captured slavers were bringing to American shores the inhuman savagery of the Middle Passage for anyone to see, if anyone cared to look.

Chapter 11

THERE, RIGHT IN CHARLESTON HARBOR, was the horror that the South did not want to imagine—a slave ship. Vomit and urine and feces and blood had seeped deep into the raw wood of the sunless, slapped-together slave decks in the hold, staining them indelibly with filth. Cockroaches by the millions seethed among the boards, and clouds of fleas and gnats rose up from them. The stench that came from this vessel wasn't the smell of a ship full of cattle and horses, but that peculiar smell that surrounds humans, and only humans who are very afraid and very sick or dying or dead. And in late August 1858, when the water in Charleston Harbor was as still and flat and thick as oil, and the air was stifling hot and heavy, that hideous odor issued from the brig called the *Echo* captured off the coast of Cuba a few days before.

Because it was the summer, the season of disease, many of Charleston's better-off residents had left the city. Robert and Emma Bunch and their daughter, Helen, were back in New York on annual leave. But for those Charlestonians who remained behind, the spectacle of the *Echo* and its Africans was a disgusting but almost irresistible novelty. Because the transatlantic slave trade had been banned for fifty years, many people had never beheld such a ship before. "You will see by this morning's *Mercury* that we have a slaver in our harbor," one distinguished Charlestonian wrote to a friend. "She has on board about 300 naked native Negroes, sixty of them women. Every one of whom is in the family way. Everybody is talking about them. The yellow fever ... and every other subject have faded before this. There is really and truly an excitement among these cold, stolid Charlestonians."

That the *Echo* had been captured at all was the result of a dawning awareness by the U.S. government of something that Robert Bunch had been explaining to the Foreign Office in London for years: the fleets of slave ships flying the American flag, supported by moneymen in New York, and incited and abetted by fire-eaters such as Rhett and Spratt, posed a growing threat to the authority of Washington and to the Union itself. The slave traffic was growing fast. Something had to be done before the momentum became unstoppable. So, quietly and against stubborn bureaucratic resistance, President Buchanan had ordered American warships to step up their anti-slaving patrols off the coast of Cuba as well as the coast of West Africa. And the *Echo* was their first prize.

The story of the *Echo*'s capture, as told in the Charleston newspapers, began at dawn on Saturday, August 21, 1858, when the USS *Dolphin* pulled out of the Cuban port of Sagua La Grande, about 150 miles east of Havana. The *Dolphin* was a brig-of-war, and she had been on desultory anti-slaving missions off the coasts of Brazil and Africa from the time she'd first been commissioned more than twenty years before. With two square-rigged masts and six 32-pound guns she was, despite her age, quick and deadly by the standards of the time, but she'd seen little action.

Now, through the course of the morning, the *Dolphin*'s crew could see far ahead of them the twin masts of another brig. They didn't pay much attention. The stranger wasn't a very big ship and looked like the kind of boat used for coastal trade among the maze of islets and keys off the north shore of Cuba. But by around one in the afternoon, the *Dolphin* had pulled closer. Its commander, Lt. J. N. Maffitt, was about as shrewd a skipper as could be found in the U.S. Navy at the time, and he knew right away that this ship looked too light in the water for a coastal trader. The *Dolphin* picked up speed. The strange brig started to take evasive action, hauling in some of its canvas and tacking hard to starboard with the celerity and efficiency that is possible only when a ship is manned by a large and well-trained crew. Coastal traders didn't normally have those kinds of men on board.

Maffit decided to play a little game with his quarry. He ran up the British flag, so the strange brig could see the colors clearly. The British could not board an American vessel without provoking an international incident, which is why so many slavers flew the Stars and Stripes whenever they thought they might be challenged by one of Her Majesty's ships. At first the stranger showed no colors at all, but after hours of giving chase, Maffitt fired a shot close under her stern. The stranger ran up the American flag. She had fallen into the trap. Maffitt took down the British ensign and ran up the American one. Still the stranger struggled to get away. Maffitt fired again, this time under the ship's bow. The stranger hauled down her sails, struck her American colors, and threw them into the sea.

The armed boarding party from the *Dolphin* noticed that the name of the ship, *Echo*, was painted on a slab of wood nailed to the stern, but the original name, *Putnam*, was still visible, a ghost image of white painted over in black. "We found her a brig of 320 tons, filled with Africans," one of the *Dolphin*'s officers wrote to a friend later that week. "The appearance was most revolting; never can I forget it. There were 328 negroes crowded together between decks." They were crammed in, half crouched and so closely packed that only the tops of their heads were clearly visible, and the stench was almost unbearable. "The poor wretches looked half starved, and some of them were mere skeletons," wrote the officer. The sails and other fittings of the ship were American. Many of the crew were American. The captain, a Mr. Townsend, was from Boston.

Some 455 Africans had been taken on board the *Echo* near Kabinda on the African coast. More than 100 perished during the weeks at sea and were thrown overboard. ("The shark of the Atlantic is still, as he has ever been, the partner of the slave trader," wrote a British editorialist.) It took the U.S. Navy prize crew six days to sail the *Echo* to Charleston Harbor, the most important American port within reach of the fetid vessel. By then, another eight captives had died. And they just kept dying.

Within hours of the *Echo*'s arrival, Charlestonians were debating what to do with the human cargo. Even if the Negro Seamen Act had still been in full effect, there was no precedent for the arrival of Africans under these circumstances, and there was no jail in the city that could hold them. In the *Charleston Daily Courier* the next morning, a correspondent writing under the name "Curtius" argued that the only "humane" thing to do would be to make slaves of the African prisoners and train them to perform useful occupations in South Carolina. But, of course, the Northern states would condemn such an action, he wrote, and the Federal government would never allow it.

In the event, Federal officials decided to hold the Africans at a massive fort called Sumter, which had been under construction for years near the entrance to the harbor and still was not quite finished. The *Echo* was brought in and anchored near the Custom House. The town's notables had to charter their own transportation to get a look at the Africans themselves.

"The gentlemen, representing a great variety of interests, were much gratified at the spectacle presented by these savages, who appeared in fine spirit and entertained their visitors with a display of their abilities in dancing and singing," wrote the correspondent for the *Charleston Mercury*. The dancing was a grim ritual, in fact, that belonged to no particular culture in Africa, but to the trade in captives. Once a day at most, the people packed into the ship's hold would be brought on deck to get some air. Those who were dead or dying were identified and thrown into the sea. Food was forced down the throats of those who refused to eat. Sometimes the captain and, rarely, some of the other officers took their pick of the women. And there on the shifting deck, someone would beat a drum "to dance the slaves," to give them a little exercise. Those who refused were whipped. Then they were herded below again into their floating hell.

"Their dances resembled in great degree the popular burlesque of the Shaking Quaker," wrote the correspondent for the *Mercury*. "In their singing they preserve good time, but their voices are rather sharp and shrill." The writer, with sneering irony, compared them to opera virtuosos. "The whole exhibition was exceedingly interesting and novel, in which the Negroes seemed to take great delight," he said. "Very few are left in the hospital, and those manifest anxiety to get out. The ailments with which they are afflicted are readily yielding to medical treatment, and the general health of the gang has much improved."

This was a lie, of course. Yellow fever was raging in Charleston at the time, and Fort Sumter was not immune. The Africans also "ate freely the shell-fish which collected around the fort, and died rapidly," wrote a doctor assigned to care for them. "Their condition on leaving the brig *Echo* was painful and disgusting in the extreme. They had been huddled together closer than cattle, and slept at night in as close contact as spoons when packed together. Privation of every kind, coupled with disease, had reduced all of them to the merest skeletons, and to such a state of desuetude and debility that on entering the fort they could not so much as step over a small beam, one foot high, in the doorway, but were compelled to sit on it and balance themselves over. It is impossible for you to imagine their sad and distressed condition."

A week after the *Echo* first arrived in Charleston Harbor, its manifest horrors had begun to sink in. The *Mercury* might paint a picture of happy savages desperate to stay in the United States, but the *Courier* seized on the evident atrocities committed aboard the ship to justify its position against revival of the slave trade. It is "inhuman and brutalizing, and we would not stain our national flag, or our Southern escutcheon, by re-opening it." Bringing new Africans to the South would "heathenize" the "now civilized and Christian slaves" already there, said the *Charleston Courier* editorial. It would brutalize the owners, breaking down ties between servants and masters; it would fill Northern pockets with more money, since that is where the capital would come from for the trade; it would anger the Northern tier of slave-owning, slave-rearing states and would have a ruinous effect on the price of the slaves now in their owners' hands. "The very agitation of the question is calculated to distract and divide the South," the editorialist wrote. It would "alienate friends and strengthen enemies" and "precipitate the downfall of the Republic."

"God forbid that the slave trade should ever again be prosecuted under the flag of the Union or the flag of the South," proclaimed the *Charleston Daily Courier*.

The U.S. marshal at Charleston, who had been vocal in his support for reopening the slave trade with Africa, felt different after watching over some of its victims for three weeks at Fort Sumter. "Thirty-five died while in my custody," he wrote to a friend, "and at one time I supposed that one hundred would have fallen a sacrifice to the cruelties to which the poor creatures had been subjected on board the slaver. I wish that everyone in South Carolina who is in favor of the re-opening of the slave trade could have seen what I have been compelled to witness. . . . It seems to me that I can never forget it."

But for those who viewed the slave trade as the key to the South's economic future and the symbol of slavery's righteousness and rectitude, even the spectacle of atrocity presented by the *Echo* was unavailing.

F OR A FEW WEEKS, COVERAGE of the *Echo* case played across the pages of the Northern and the Southern press. Senator William Seward, exploiting the moment, called for ten new war steamers to be commissioned for patrol duty on the African and American coasts to suppress the outrageous traffic being conducted under the American flag. But advocates of the slave trade claimed that the arrest of the *Echo*'s crew was an affront to their beloved South and her institutions—what one Mississippi paper called "the assault of fanatical and unscrupulous enemies who are bent upon her destruction."

Fear was, as always, a current beneath the tide of anger. The old security worries behind the Negro Seamen Act surged back into the public debate as concerns grew that the example of these Africans in the harbor might somehow inspire the long dreaded "servile in-surrection." A correspondent calling himself "Conservative" wrote to the *Charleston Daily Courier* that the city's slaves were talking among themselves and wondering why the Africans were protected from slavery and whether they had "powerful friends." Although Charleston's slaves generally were docile, Conservative wrote, they might become "unsettled in their notions." And the spectacle of the ship's crew under arrest had had an especially dangerous impact. "On Saturday last, right through the public streets, handcuffed and followed by a rabble of Negroes, were fifteen white men marched, under a guard of officers, from the landing on the wharf to the jail ... and that, too, with the knowledge (not only of those who followed, but of the sixteen thousand other Negroes of our popula-tion), that they were so manacled and so marched for the reason only that they have been engaged in the trade in slaves—a thing which is done daily in our streets."

Consul Bunch occasionally noted in his correspondence that the "better class" of people in Charleston, like Richard Yeadon at the

Charleston Courier, opposed the slave trade. But Bunch believed, after almost five years in South Carolina, that the political momentum lay with the relentless minority manipulating a feckless majority. The fire-eaters pushed day after day to reopen the trade or, failing that, to use the issue as the critical wedge between North and South.

Bunch's first reports on the *Echo* case at the end of August and in September were written from New York, but the dispatches were timely and accurate, thanks to telegraph communications with South Carolina. By September 14 Bunch was even guardedly optimistic about the way the Federal government had handled the case. President Buchanan had sent the U.S. Navy's steam frigate *Niagara*, which had just won fame for laying the first transatlantic telegraph cable, to take the captured Africans to Liberia. There, under the auspices of the American Colonization Society, they were to be clothed, fed, and educated for one year. The captain and crew of the *Echo* were under arrest, and it looked as if they would be tried in Federal court in Columbia, the capital of South Carolina, before the end of the year. "I feel much pleasure in directing Your Lordship's attention to the evidence of respect for the Law," Bunch wrote, meaning Federal law.

For the Africans themselves, however, there was no happy ending. By the time those who survived Fort Sumter reached Liberia, another seventy-one had died on board the *Niagara*. The American agent charged with caring for them was furious at what he had seen and wrote to a friend in Britain that the Christian nations of the world had to unite to stop the trade. "Some new mode must also be introduced for the trial of those found on the slavers," he wrote, "probably by trying them at once and swinging them up to the yard-arm."

Bunch was inclined to share that sentiment as it became obvious that South Carolina was not a place where justice could be had. The apparent American respect for the law that Bunch praised in September all but disappeared by late November, when the proceedings against the captain and crew of the *Echo* got under way. The whole affair had taken a "very remarkable" turn, Bunch reported in an official dispatch. The lead attorney for the defendants was none other than Leonidas Spratt, who "has made himself very conspicuous by his advocacy . . . of a revival of the Slave Trade." And despite the overwhelming evidence against the captain and crew, the grand jury, in what Bunch called "a monstrous piece of absurdity," refused to indict. In his confidential correspondence with London, Bunch was flabbergasted: "That the offense with which the men were charged was committed, and by them, no one professed for a moment to doubt. They were taken in the very act, and every witness was present who could affirm their guilt. There was, therefore, no loophole through which the grand jury could escape. And yet, such is the force of public sentiment, that they refused to allow a trial to take place."

JUST THREE DAYS after the abortive end of the *Echo* case, Bunch had another irresistible chance to show that forces were at work intent on reopening the slave trade, breaking apart the Union, or both. A slaver had been caught unloading hundreds of Africans on Jekyll Island off the coast of Georgia. Bunch dashed off a letter to the Earl of Malmesbury, who had replaced Lord Clarendon as Foreign Secretary after a short-lived Conservative government was formed earlier in the year. Georgia was, to be sure, another consul's territory, but such was the nature of this slave-trade case, said Bunch, that "I am, nevertheless, emboldened to offer a few remarks upon it."

The Charleston consul was looking not only to further his own views but to undermine those of Edmund Molyneux, the Savannah consul, who had held that position since 1831. Molyneux had no aspirations as a diplomat. Like many British consuls at the time he did not get a salary, only reimbursement for a few expenses, and he used his position to further his personal business ventures.

Molyneux, by the 1850s, had married a rich widow and was well established as part of Savannah's elite. He moved easily among the self-appointed aristocracy in the Low Country, and during the summer he decamped to his estate in the North Carolina highlands among the Blakes, the de Choiseuls, and other gentry escaping the pestilential heat on the coast. Molyneux owned many slaves, and he quietly, consistently ignored the British government's abolitionist sentiments as he bought and sold the humans who made up a large part of his fortune. As one might expect, Molyneux's reporting on other slavers and slaveholders was, at best, passionless and perfunctory. So Robert Bunch, ever a mix of moralist and careerist, decided to step in.

"It appears to be almost beyond doubt," he wrote to Lord Malmesbury, "that a Cargo of Africans has been landed within the last few days on the Coast of Georgia, from a Schooner called the *Wanderer*." Bunch knew the boat. It was a fast, luxurious craft that sailed under the burgee of the New York Yacht Club, with lines similar to those of the *America*, which Bunch had spied on under construction when he was vice consul in New York years before. Her captain and his companions wore the club's buttons, and the yacht "availed herself of the privileges and immunities accorded to vessels of her class to disarm suspicion and carry out the nefarious purposes of her reputed owner."

The *Wanderer* ostensibly belonged to Captain William C. Corrie, but Bunch did not believe that was the case. Rumor had it that she belonged to "a notorious Slave Trader in Savannah." (In fact, she was owned by Charles A. L. Lamar, one of that city's most prominent young businessmen, who moved in very much the same circles as Molyneux.)

"It is not my intention," said Bunch, "to report to Your Lordship the details of the supposed landing of these Africans, of their being carried past the very City of Savannah, of the lukewarm action of the United States' Authorities, or of the horrors of the voyage, which caused, as I learn, the death of 101 Negroes out of 471. These particulars will, doubtless, be supplied by Her Majesty's Consul at Savannah." (Bunch was making sure that if such details went missing from Molyneux's dispatches, London would know about it.) But Corrie, the man being billed as the *Wanderer*'s owner, represented almost everything Bunch hated in American life, and he could barely contain himself as he sketched a portrait of him for Malmesbury.

"Mr., or as he styles himself, Captain Corrie is a South Carolinian by birth; his father was a Scotchman, who earned a precarious livelihood in Charleston by mending the wheels of the rough plantation carts of the country." The son had followed the Army of the United States as a sutler during the Seminole War in Florida in the 1830s but afterward settled down in Washington, "where his occupation has been what is called 'lobbying,' that is, bribing members of Congress to vote for the payment of pecuniary claims upon the government of the United States. His business appears to have prospered; indeed, there are several notorious instances of his success. His influence at the Capital is very great; I was assured not long ago by one of the Members from this State that he had more power than all the South Carolina Delegation put together. Personally, he is a vulgar, swaggering fellow, addicted to drink, habitually boasting of this power in Congress, and fond of specifying the exact sum for which each member is to be purchased.

"Such being his antecedents, I need hardly add that he is capable of Slave Trading or any other villainy."

Bunch reported "with much regret" that in Charleston "the general feeling is one of delight" on hearing the news of the *Wanderer*'s voyage: "in the first place, at the outwitting of the United States' authorities, and, in the second, at the success of this importation of fresh laborers into the Southern Country." As Bunch saw it, the Americans, and especially the Southerners, had no respect for law. The grand jury's refusal to indict the captain and crew of the *Echo* in Columbia a few days before had been proof of that. But there was more: "The Legislature of this State passed yesterday a joint resolution calling upon the President of the United States to abrogate the 8th Article of the Treaty of Washington, which stipulates an American Squadron on the Coast of Africa." If the fire-eating Carolinians could not yet force an overturning of the slave-trade ban, they would do everything they could to weaken its enforcement.

AFTER THE *Wanderer* offloaded its surviving cargo on Jekyll Island that night in December 1858, it did not take Federal officials long to catch up with the yacht and impound it. They also arrested the brains and money behind the operation, the Savannah businessman Charles A. L. Lamar, on a steamer transporting 170 of the Africans up the Savannah River. Under Federal statutes, the *Wanderer*'s crew might have been convicted of piracy and hanged, but they knew—as everybody knew—that they never really had much to fear from the courts.

Lamar, the thirty-four-year-old heir to a banking fortune, was a friend of Leonidas Spratt and Robert Barnwell Rhett and the other fire-eaters, and one of those who had grown tired of waiting for the repeal of laws against importing slaves from Africa. Lamar saw himself as an unassailable Southern aristocrat, and eventually he used the trial of his men to score political points against the Federal government. One evening he sprung the skipper of the ship from jail so the two of them could join friends for a night on the town, and when the government put the seized *Wanderer* on the auction block in Savannah, the young Georgian with a blazing red mustache showed up front and center, brandishing his gold-tipped cane, announcing to the crowd that the ship had been taken from him unjustly and that no one should bid against him. The Savannah jailer raised his hand and bid four thousand dollars. Lamar was furious. He bid four thousand and one. The terrified auctioneer hammered down the sale. Then, amid cheers from the crowd, Lamar punched the jailer and knocked him to the ground.

The courts eventually handed Lamar a minimal sentence for his escapade liberating the *Wanderer*'s skipper. But Lamar's adventures had been about more than profiteering, after all. He knew the slave-trade issue could hasten the breakup of the whole United States, and he figured he was ready for that. "I can whip the Government any time they make the issue, unless they raise a few additional regiments."

Bunch understood Lamar's game only too well. All the British consuls were supposed to keep punctilious records about any activity connected with the transatlantic slave trade. But with the exception of Edward Mortimer Archibald in New York, none devoted so much time and attention to the reporting as Robert Bunch did, and none understood better or explained more carefully the issue's implications for the future of the United States and its relations with the United Kingdom. At that moment, in any case, it was as if Bunch could see the future. The ferocious arrogance of the slavers would tear apart the Union and very likely destroy the South as well.

IN JANUARY 1859, the British squadron off the African coast seized a ship called the *Brothers*. "She had an American Register on board and hoisted the American flag, and was fully equipped for the Slave Trade," as Bunch notified the Foreign Office. The Royal Navy delivered the captain and crew of the *Brothers* to Charleston in January 1859 to be put on trial under U.S. law, but, again, the South Carolina grand jury refused to indict. Indeed, the court treated the Federal statutes as a joke. "At present the people of the State do not seem to see the facts in so serious a light," Bunch wrote in one of his most prescient dispatches. "They are rather amused at the idea of embarrassing the Federal Government, and perhaps, in a lesser degree, of annoying Great Britain, but they will awake from their delusion to find the Democratic Party broken up and the whole power of the Country thrown into the hands of the 'Republicans'....

When this shall happen, the days of Slavery are numbered. . . . The prestige and power of Slave holders will be gone, never to return."

The Charleston consul would do what he could to make sure that that prestige and power were broken, at least in the minds of Britain's leaders, but that job was growing more difficult.

Lord Palmerston was back as Prime Minister, but he had not brought Clarendon with him to the Foreign Office, and it was said that Queen Victoria herself was disappointed. "We would have felt so sure with Lord Clarendon," she wrote. Bunch almost certainly shared that sentiment. In the Palmerston government that took office in June 1859, the post of Foreign Secretary went to former Prime Minister Lord John Russell, who kept his diplomats, and especially his consuls, at arm's length.

Palmerston and Russell had been maneuvering around each other for many years. In 1845, when the diminutive Lord John succeeded Palmerston's brother-in-law Lord Melbourne as head of the Whig Party and became Prime Minister, he and other Whig grandees tried to keep Palmerston out of the cabinet. Russell, at the time, was respected as the heir to a Whig lineage that dated back far into the previous century. His features were fine, his eyes kind, and his mouth generous. But he was not an inspiring figure. "Men might think Lord John taciturn, angular, abrupt, tenacious, and dogmatic," wrote one biographer, who then hastened to add that, nonetheless, "it was impossible not to recognize his honesty, public spirit, pluck in the presence of difficulty, and high interpretation of the claims of public duty." In fact, Russell and the other hereditary leaders of the Whigs were never a match for Palmerston. Again and again, even when declared politically extinct, the aged "Lord Cupid" would come roaring back onto the scene as, indeed, he had done once again that summer of 1859. Now Russell was essentially a Prime Minister in waiting, and that wait might be a long one.

Clarendon was not totally out of the picture. He played the part of the candid friend to Palmerston's government behind the scenes, and he had an important family connection to one of the key members of the cabinet. Clarendon's brilliant and beautiful sister, Maria Theresa, was married to the journalist and statesman Sir George Cornewall Lewis, who would serve in the new Palmerston government as Chancellor of the Exchequer and, at an absolutely critical moment, as Secretary of War.

But where Robert Bunch had the ear of the Foreign Secretary himself when Clarendon was in office and had managed to continue cordial communications with the relatively taciturn Earl of Malmesbury, now the Charleston consul found himself increasingly shunted off to the permanent bureaucrats of the Foreign Office, those quibblers over protocol and expense reports, such as Permanent Under-Secretary Edmund Hammond.

Bunch needed someone to talk to.

Chapter 13

"OLD BUCK," PRESIDENT BUCHANAN, decided to send a spy to the South. In the summer of 1859, after many months of news about the *Wanderer* affair, reports kept surfacing about Africans being smuggled ashore in different corners of the Republic. Senator Stephen Douglas of Illinois claimed there had been fifteen thousand of them landed in recent years. The British were concerned and angry. Buchanan hoped the capture of the *Echo* would show he meant to honor his government's obligations to fight the African trade, but the outcome of the court case had been a disgrace. Buchanan's secretary of state, Lewis Cass, told Lord Napier in Washington that the slave trade was discussed in the cabinet, that at least one steamer would be sent to the African coast for interdiction, and that "every effort would be made to substitute steam power for the present old-fashioned sailing vessels." But if the secret slave trade between the Southern states and Africa really was as big as Senator Douglas said, then President Buchanan needed to know. And if it was not, he needed to be able to say so with real conviction. This was a domestic political issue now. The fire-eaters and their sympathizers had used the *Wanderer* expeditions to flout Federal law. Buchanan understood perfectly well that these heirs of nullification and partisans of disunion wanted to challenge the office of the president, the leadership of the Democratic Party, and him personally.

So in early September 1859, Buchanan's secretary of the interior, Jacob Thompson, hired Benjamin F. Slocumb to travel through the South and see what he could find out. When the slow-talking Mississippian told folks he wanted to buy Africans, they believed him. He spoke with a drawl, and he might say he'd "heard tell these Africans was cheaper than home-bred stock." He might say he was just curious and was always in the market for good workers. Whatever his technique, he'd coax out the information he needed.

Slocumb traveled from Washington down to Wilmington,

North Carolina, where he saw no sign of Africans. Then he went on to Charleston, where he met with "a gentleman somewhat prominent as an advocate of the African slave trade." Slocumb didn't offer up a name in his subsequent report, but the man most likely to fit that description at that time of year would have been the ever-loquacious Leonidas Spratt. The source confided to Slocumb that all the reports of Africans landing on American shores were "mere fabrications," apart from those about the *Wanderer*. The Spratt-like source also told Slocumb that a swindler from New York had been down to Charleston a few weeks earlier and nearly convinced people to put up money for African slaves to be landed at Beaufort, several miles south of the city. But the swindler had been found out and "given a cold bath." Slocumb wrote that "there are doubtless men in Charleston, as in New York and Boston, ready to engage in the African slave trade, but they are few and are generally deterred from active operations by fear of incurring the penalties of the law." Since the penalties were never imposed, it's not clear why Buchanan's spy thought they were so dissuasive.

Slocumb seems not to have heard about the *Jehossee*, a suspected slaver that had sailed from Charleston just before he got there. And probably he could not have known about the activities in Mobile of Captain Timothy Meaher, builder of the *Southern Republic*, who was just beginning to plot a voyage to Africa in the fall of 1859. In any case, Slocumb never mentioned them in his report, which left the impression with the Buchanan administration that the *Wanderer* was an isolated incident.

ROBERT BUNCH WAS in New York when Buchanan's spy passed through Charleston. From an estate called The Grange he kept filing his various dispatches directly to the Foreign Office and expecting direct responses, just as he'd been doing for most of the decade. Bunch missed the kind of personal praise and attention he'd gotten from Lord Clarendon. Lord Russell was a model of formality, but

Bunch's routine was pretty much the same. And then, suddenly, it wasn't.

There was a new minister in Washington, Richard Bickerton Pemell Lyons, and he was in a cold rage. The senior diplomat found it utterly unacceptable that a mere consul, which is what he considered Bunch to be at the time, would presume to leave the minister in Washington out of the loop on any sensitive matter. And no question was as sensitive as slavery.

In the particular case that prompted Lyons's fury, Bunch had asked for instructions from Lord John Russell about how to proceed in the case of a recent detention of two British citizens. Lyons had already written to Bunch twice about the case with instructions to hire legal counsel, but Bunch ignored him and wrote to Lord John Russell directly. Lyons told Bunch bluntly that this was "neither regular in point of form, nor courteous to me," which Bunch understood was British understatement that cut as deep as a steel blade. Clearly the new minister was concerned about the reaction in the Foreign Office, not only on the part of Lord Russell, whom he did not know well, but on the part of men such as Under-Secretary Hammond, who could make or break an envoy they ceased to respect. They could nibble away at his budget. They could spread rumors and insinuations, whispering hints of contempt into the ears of the Foreign Secretary and even the Prime Minister. No, this sort of insubordination from a consul in South Carolina—who happened to be in New York!—simply would not do. Lyons called Bunch down so sharply, with both a letter and a telegram demanding immediate responses, that the consul was left sounding breathless even in his correspondence. Bunch wrote to Lyons that he was "deeply mortified at the rebuke," the worst he could remember in eighteen years of official service.

It is not surprising that Lyons was sensitive. At the age of forty-two and unmarried, he had seen a lot of the world, but for many years it took little notice of him. Most of his younger life he lived in the shadow of his father, Admiral Edmund Lyons, a naval officer and diplomat who eventually rose to command the Royal Navy's Mediterranean Fleet during the later stages of the Crimean War. When Richard Lyons was only twelve, he'd gone to sea as a midshipman on a forty-six-gun frigate under his father's command. But unlike his hale and hearty younger brother, Edmund, who was his father's favorite as well as his namesake, Richard was shy, not very athletic, and prone to seasickness. After a miserable time cruising the Black Sea and the Mediterranean in 1829, Richard eventually returned to land and took his degree at Oxford, then followed his father to the legation in Athens, where the elder Lyons, who had forged a close friendship with the Greek king, was the British envoy. When, later, the old man returned to active duty in the Royal Navy, Richard remained behind in Athens, languishing year after year until he became the oldest attaché in the service. Only when he threatened to quit altogether was he accredited to the Court of Tuscany with residence in Rome. And finally, in the tumult of Italian politics, Richard Lyons got a chance to show what he could do. He won the release of two Britons who'd been taken prisoner amid the revolutionary intrigues in southern Italy, and he found himself suddenly a star at London, regarded no longer as a lowly functionary but as a troubleshooter extraordinaire. In the resolutely class-conscious Foreign Office it probably helped, as well, that, with his father's death in 1858, Richard succeeded to the peerage. As Lord Lyons, in the late spring of 1859 he replaced the out-of-step Napier in Washington.

President Buchanan was not pleased with the change. When Old Buck had been the American minister to the Court of St. James's, he'd gotten acquainted with most of the leading politicians and diplomats in Great Britain, and he knew that, lord or no lord, Lyons was not one of them. Buchanan wanted "a first-rate man whose character is known to this country." And a dispatch from the American legation in London only underscored the new envoy's unimpressiveness. Lyons was "sensible," it said, "unobtrusive," and "short." Lyons is supposed to have had such a horror of scenes that it was said (perhaps apocryphally) that he put up with the same breakfast every morning for many years rather than risk upsetting his valet.

But none of those self-effacing characteristics restrained Lyons's anger at Bunch, and his insecurities probably heightened his ire. Lyons had spent his career immersed in European diplomacy, politics, and intrigues. He knew next to nothing about the United States. When he arrived in Washington, in a nation rapidly heading toward a war between North and South, he had never even heard of the Mason-Dixon Line, which demarcated the slave and free states. In what passed for social life in the grim village that was Washington, D.C., Napier had been a star. Lyons was a drudge. If, with his new title as minister, he couldn't command the respect of the consul in Charleston—and if he let London see that—then this sudden upturn in his career could come to a quick and ignominious end.

Bunch knew all this, and he showed only grudging contrition. He had *never* been in the habit of communicating with the minister in Washington until after his work was done and reported directly to the Foreign Office, he told Lyons. He had conducted delicate negotiations; he had delivered sensitive diplomatic messages to the South Carolina governor; and although he informed the various ministers in Washington of these activities only after the fact, and privately, he had entertained very good relations with all of them. Or so he said.

Lyons noted drily that "the relations between the Consulates and this Mission appear to be very undefined and somewhat anomalous. I doubt whether the ordinary rules can be applied strictly in the U.S., where each separate state is in most respects independent of the Federal Government."

Since Bunch was in New York that summer, as usual, Lyons decided it was time for a face-to-face meeting in Washington when Bunch headed back to Charleston. Lyons politely suggested "a short visit, at any time which best suited you," and promised "I should have a room at your disposal." Lyons said he didn't want to inconvenience Bunch. Bunch said it was "no sort of inconvenience," and he made arrangements to visit Washington at the end of the first week in November but not, in the end, without a little complaining. "The land journey is tiresome and troublesome," he wrote, "especially when one is encumbered by children and servants, to say nothing of baggage." He would leave Emma and Helen with friends in Baltimore and make the side trip to Washington himself, he said. But before the two men could meet, events began to overtake them.

O N OCTOBER 16, 1859, the abolitionist zealot John Brown attacked the Federal arsenal at Harpers Ferry, Virginia, aiming
to launch, at last, the long-feared "servile insurrection" that would
sweep through the South. Brown's plan, as such, was an utter failure. But he ignited the smoldering anger on both sides of the slavery
issue like a bellows pumping flames out of white-hot coals.

Lyons at first hugely underestimated the impact the Brown raid
was likely to have. "The Harper's Ferry Affair has turned out absurd enough," he wrote to the Richmond consul a few days after
the incident, and he advised London that the American public was
"absorbed by a foolish affair." But Bunch saw the furor around John
Brown as the cataclysm it was. News of the "extraordinary servile insurrection," often wildly exaggerated, had caused "unprec-
edented excitement in all the Southern country," as South Carolina
papers reported. "I anticipate a disagreeable winter at my post,"
Bunch wrote to Lyons while en route to Washington. "There is
much trouble brewing for us all."

Lyons, by then, had begun to realize that, new as he was to
Washington, to the United States, and to the ways of the South,
he needed Bunch's intimate expertise. And Bunch knew that Lyons
knew. He sent him a steady stream of private letters and clippings
as well as dispatches to be duly forwarded to London.

In the aftermath of Harpers Ferry, there was an immediate
problem for the Crown's interests. A great many Britons had been
involved with John Brown. So had several of the politicians from
the North who had been very good friends to the British legation.
Indeed, if anyone cared to look, the John Brown plot could be portrayed as a conspiracy by John Bull.

Jefferson Davis of Mississippi, a former U.S. secretary of war
and now one of the most powerful senators on the Hill, was among

those who saw multiple signs of British complicity. "I believe a conspiracy has been formed," said Davis, and if English abolitionists weren't behind it, there was no question that some were part of it. It seemed the British had even sent an expert in guerrilla warfare to train John Brown's men in Kansas.

What Davis did not know was that Her Majesty's consul in Charleston was one of that guerrilla fighter's most sincere admirers.

HUGH FORBES WAS the kind of character who erupts in America's headlines, then disappears from its histories as if he never had a life outside his brief moment of fame in the press. But Forbes, even as soldiers of fortune go, was pretty extraordinary. In the words of British historian George Macaulay Trevelyan, "He was what is called 'an original.'"

Forbes came from a prosperous family and entered Oxford when he was fifteen. He received a commission in Britain's famous Coldstream Guards and after about twenty years of service tried to settle down with his second wife, a beautiful Italian, to a comfortable life in Tuscany. But Forbes at forty was restless, and so, everywhere he looked, was Italy. In early 1848 Forbes joined the revolution and went to fight by the side of Giuseppe Garibaldi.

At first the Italian wasn't sure what to make of this "eccentric Briton." Forbes was lean and grizzled and instead of a uniform wore a light summer suit and a white stovepipe hat more appropriate for a gentleman strolling in Hyde Park than for a soldier on the battlefield. But while many of Garibaldi's red-shirted partisans melted away into the countryside on the long, harrowing march from Rome through the mountains to the Adriatic coast in 1849, Forbes marched and fought. The Italian commander, watching the column snaking through the hills, could always see in the distance that pale suit, that stovepipe hat. Later, Garibaldi remembered Forbes as a "most courageous and honorable soldier."

When the Austrians captured Forbes, the British government

took a keen interest in his release. This may have been because of his connections in London; the fraternity of the Coldstream Guards was no negligible thing. But the most important reason why Her Majesty's government pushed hard to liberate Hugh Forbes in 1849 was that then–Foreign Secretary Palmerston could not bear to see any Briton in the hands of those Europeans he considered lesser beings. "The Austrians are really the greatest brutes that ever called themselves by the undeserved names of civilized men," Palmerston wrote to his envoy in Vienna.

When Forbes got out, he made his way to New York City, and for a few months Garibaldi joined him there. The father of Italian unification worked in a candle factory on Staten Island, then went back to sea as a merchant captain. Forbes stayed behind. He found such employment as he could: he taught fencing; he worked as a journalist and translator for Horace Greeley's *Tribune*; and he ran a little paper of his own, *The European*, promoting the ideals of revolution and liberty among the immigrants of New York. He seems to have been constantly short of money and often in despair.

In those years, from 1848 to 1852, Bunch was serving as the British vice consul and acting consul in New York City, and he certainly would have heard of Forbes. He may even have known him. When he wrote about Forbes in his private letters to Lyons and in formal dispatches to the Foreign Office, he endorsed many of the freedom fighter's views so enthusiastically that it's hard to imagine the two had never crossed paths in the days before Forbes got involved with John Brown.

In 1855 Hugh Forbes published his *Manual for the Patriotic Volunteer on Active Service in Regular and Irregular War*, a practical guide to insurgency whose basic principles were as solid as anything penned a century later by Che Guevara. But it made Forbes no money, which is what he needed. By 1857, down and out and often drunk, Forbes was living in a slum apartment next to a whorehouse on Delancey Street.

Another English journalist working for Horace Greeley, James

Redpath, arranged for Forbes to meet Brown, whose fame as a righteous, sword-wielding zealot in Kansas had begun to grow after he and his sons carried out a massacre at the town of Osawatomie. Brown might have had what one newspaper called "the craftiness of partial insanity," but with help from his British friend Redpath he was winning the respect of—and collecting money from—some of the most important anti-slavery figures in the United States. They extolled his commitment to freedom; they claimed to admire his sacrifice. Sometimes they shipped him guns. What he needed most, however, was someone who could show him how to use those weapons more effectively, someone like Hugh Forbes.

The British veteran of the Italian wars had mixed feelings. Forbes despised slavery—no question about that. But this "Captain Brown," as he styled himself, was no Garibaldi. His Kansas exploit was about chaotic ambushes, mobs, and murder in the night. Brown's strategic thinking seemed delusional. It depended on what God told him and little else. "Enthusiasm is a very fine thing in its peculiar way," Forbes wrote in his guerrilla manual, "but it cannot be constantly depended upon."

Then again, the cause was good, the money was good, and Forbes imagined he would be a general in a great war against human bondage. When Forbes showed up in Iowa at Brown's base camp to start his job, however, he discovered to his dismay that almost nobody was there. Most of the guns donated by support committees proved to be useless. The violence in Kansas had begun to subside, making Brown's claims to be raising a militia for self-defense less credible to his backers. And the notions Brown started putting forth about starting a slave rebellion in the South sounded, to Forbes, completely and fatally flawed.

Brown's plan, if it could be called that, lacked sufficient fighting men, it lacked direct communications with the slaves in Virginia, and by attacking a U.S. arsenal, it would provoke a direct test of arms with the Federal military, which would be unwinnable.

So Forbes came up with a plan of his own: small bands of guerril-las operating along the border with the slave states would raid into them, helping the slaves escape in large numbers and undermining the value of slaves generally, because they quickly would be seen as unreliable and potentially dangerous property. John Brown would have none of that strategy. God knew better.

Forbes started trying to warn Brown's backers about what the zealot with the icy blue eyes was planning in Virginia. He hoped that either they would cancel the project altogether or they would put him in charge of a more sensible guerrilla strategy. But several knew already of the dangerous plan for an uprising and immedi-ately saw Forbes as a threat. When he demanded the money owed him, they deemed him an extortionist. Those who didn't know about the Virginia plot thought Forbes, not Brown, was the one who was crazy. And one Northerner in particular had a significant investment in making sure Forbes appeared crazy.

IN THE SPRING of 1858, Senator William Seward of New York had just about quit denying that he wanted to be president. Nobody had believed him, anyway. He was the voice of the free-labor North, the moral and political leader of the fast-growing Republican Party. Good money said that he stood to be the next commander in chief of the increasingly divided United States.

Then a sere man with a stovepipe hat came knocking at Seward's door in Washington. "The person who called himself Forbes was a stranger to me," Seward told investigators two years later. "He came to my house and asked to see me. I saw him alone." That much probably was true, although much of Seward's account was evasive. "All kinds of erratic and strange persons call on me with all manner of strange communications and applications," Seward said. "He was one of them, and it passed out of my memory without leav-ing attached to it the least idea of any importance." The story that

Forbes told him, Seward said, was "very incoherent, very erratic," and seemed to be the product of "an unsound or very disturbed mind."

Normally William Seward was amusing, theatrical, interested in everything. He hunched forward when he talked as if his "keen eyes were seeking for an adversary." But by his own account, that night he remained silent. Smoke curled up from his cigar, and he let Forbes ramble on about being "a revolutionist in Italy in the year 1848, or about that period," as Seward recalled. "He was a foreigner, either an Englishman or a Scotchman, I do not know which." Seward remembered that Forbes showed him "a strange and absurd book, as I thought, giving the art of exciting or getting up military revolutions." And then Forbes talked about John Brown, and what a bad man he was, and he talked about Kansas, which is when Seward cut him off. "I never give advice about Kansas," the senator told Forbes. And the conversation ended. Or so the senator said when he was questioned about it.

Seward insisted that Forbes told him nothing at all about John Brown's plan to launch a slave uprising in the South, although why Forbes would have spared Seward this information when he was spreading it around to so many others is not clear. Forbes wrote afterward of the meeting, "I went fully into the whole matter in all its bearings." Probably Forbes *did* tell Seward about the plot for an uprising, but that did not mean Seward endorsed it. He was far too cautious for that. The consequences could have been fatal, politically and literally, given the vindictive spirit of the times.

Faced with the threat of Forbes's revelations, several conspirators behind Brown pushed back their planned launch of the slave uprising to the winter and then well into the following year. They hoped that Hugh Forbes would look more like a lunatic than ever when his predictions failed to materialize. And once the raid on Harpers Ferry took place, the rest would be history.

· · ·

"NOTHING COULD BETTER prove Old Brown's unfitness for the part he undertook to play than the reckless manner in which he compromised all his friends by preserving their correspondence instead of destroying it," the *New York Herald* informed its readers at the end of October 1859, when John Brown's trial began. "He had a carpet bag stuffed full of letters from leading men in the North and West; and, in addition to that, his house was strewn with documents."

Hugh Forbes loomed large in that scattered archive. His texts soon filled the columns of newspapers all over the United States and Europe. And in Forbes—or at least in the Forbes documents— Robert Bunch found an ally.

"Amongst the papers seized by the authorities of Virginia after the late outbreak at Harper's Ferry, there is said to have been found a 'Report,' addressed by one Hugh Forbes, an Englishman, to the Secretary of the British and Foreign Anti-Slavery Society in London upon the subject of slavery in the U.S.," Bunch scrawled in a letter marked *private* that he sent directly to Lord Russell, the Foreign Secretary, after duly asking Lyons's permission. Indeed, Bunch was sending not one but two copies of the clipping to London, almost as if he were the proud author. "I consider it both an interesting and correct statement of the rise and progress of the pro-slavery feeling in the South of this Republic, of its present dangerous condition, and of its probable future," Bunch wrote. "It is possible that I may view Mr. Forbes's opinions with too partial an eye, as they are, in almost every respect, the same which I have submitted to Her Majesty's Government at various periods during my residence in South Carolina, but notwithstanding this risk, I have thought it advisable to communicate the papers to Your Lordship."

The Forbes letter to the Anti-Slavery Society in London, written in February 1858 at about the same time Forbes was knocking on the doors of Brown's backers in New England and Washington, is not in the least deranged or erratic. It is straightforward, passionate, and unreserved in a way that Robert Bunch obviously appreciated.

For starters, Forbes set out to demolish the notion that slave owners and slave advocates were open to sweet reason on humanitarian or economic grounds. "Slavery in the United States is a political question," he wrote. "All other matters sink into insignificance beside it. It may actually be termed the only permanent question, since it absorbs all others. Not merely does it regard America, but it affects the well-being of all mankind; and if its partisans be not checked in their course, they will scatter desolation and blood over this continent to acquire land of which to make slave territory, and will plunge the world into war to sustain the piratical Slave Trade."

The author of the *Manual for the Patriotic Volunteer* explained in his letter to London that the American government was controlled by the Senate and the Senate controlled by Democrats whose only criterion for office was "How is he on slavery?" The abolitionists were weak and the anti-slavery forces in the Senate divided and unreliable, he said. "As to Seward, of New York (the pet of the *Tribune*), he is a thorough party wire-puller and manager; and, notwithstanding his suavity of manner and speech, is the least reliable of them all."

"Where will all this lead to?" Forbes asked. "If not impeded by practical measures, the pro-slavery political managers, North and South, will continue their encroachments on liberty." Driven by the Democratic Party, the United States "will grasp islands in the West Indies, and slices of Mexico and Central America wherein to plant and to perpetuate slavery—it will reopen the slave trade (the poor whites are already swallowing the bait in the shape of a promise of a slave each)—it will re-enslave the free men of color (the project is already canvassed)—it will make the United States become the great slavery propagandist power of the world, and consequently the mortal enemy of every oppressed people which may struggle to throw off the yoke of despotism." It will be especially "antagonistic to England, which is the great anti-slavery power," wrote Forbes. "Neither the intrigues of corrupt, unreliable stump orators and political wire-pullers, nor the tricks of cheating speculators, nor the sighing and preaching of amiable philanthropists, deficient in energy and resolution, will arrest the onward march of slavery."

If Bunch had ever met Forbes when he was consul in New York or during those long sojourns up North escaping the summer pestilence in Charleston, he did not say so in his surviving correspondence. Perhaps he just liked what he read. It was such a clear synopsis of his own views, there was almost no point with which he disagreed, and by sending the clippings to Lyons even before his visit to Washington, Bunch was giving the new minister in the capital of the United States a crash course in the hard political truths of slavery in America.

But for Bunch to embrace Forbes's radical views virtually as his own in official correspondence, sending them with enthusiastic endorsement directly to Lord Russell in London, suggests something more than mere admiration. Why would Bunch, so cautious in so many ways, want to identify himself wholeheartedly with a man seen by much of the world as an eccentric, drunken reprobate? Perhaps he did know Forbes and knew his worth, and, if that was the case, perhaps he thought it wiser not to put that fact in writing. He'd gone quite far enough. In Charleston it would cost him his life if he were linked to a fellow Briton who advocated guerrilla war to free the slaves.

CONVERSATION DURING BUNCH'S overnight at the British legation on Sunday, November 6, must have covered quite a bit of ground. Certainly it changed radically the tone in the relationship with Lord Lyons. The new minister wrote to Bunch a few days later to tell him he hoped "whenever you come North again, you will not forget that I shall always have real pleasure in seeing you here."

What had they talked about? Inevitably there would have been stories shared, cautiously at first, about colleagues in the Foreign

Office Maybe they reminisced about Old Bulwer, who was in ill health in Constantinople, and Crampton, who'd been made ambassador to Moscow, where the old bachelor's name was being connected to that of a beautiful opera singer. The two might compare impressions, discreetly, of the elegant Clarendon and stiff little Lord John Russell. Perhaps they groaned a bit if one or the other of them mentioned Hammond. Certainly Lyons and Bunch talked about the John Brown affair. The old man had been tried already and convicted, his bravery inspiring his partisans and discomfiting his enemies. "If it is deemed necessary that I shall forfeit my life for the furtherance of the ends of justice," Brown told the judge who sentenced him to hang, "and mingle my blood farther with the blood of my children and the blood of millions in this slave country whose rights are disregarded by wicked, cruel, and unjust enactments, I say let it be done."

Lyons and Bunch, pondering such a figure, would have had a chance to test each other's real views on slavery. When Lyons's father had been the minister in Athens years before, he'd maneuvered to stop Greek ships trafficking slaves off the Barbary Coast, and Lord Lyons could find no excuse for the institution wherever it existed, but he had little direct contact with slavery as it was practiced in America. Bunch, for his part, had no end of rough stories to tell about the Southerners, their servants, their victims, abuses, arrogance, duplicity, and the dangers they could pose to British interests. Maybe Lyons had expected, after exchanges with Napier, that he would have to deal with another apologist for Manifest Destiny. Maybe he had heard about the Savannah consul, Molyneux, and wondered if this Charleston consul, too, was a slave owner. But, no, here was this younger colleague who could easily, concisely, amusingly present the whole dreadful political show in America, making observations on the price of Negroes and explaining the way the political parties were fracturing and reforming and how all this was driving the South not only toward secession but toward a reopening of the slave trade across the Middle Passage, which was something that the Crown—indeed, that the Queen and her Consort—could never abide.

By the time Robert Bunch ended his visit with Lord Lyons at the legation in Washington on Monday, November 7, it appears that he and the new minister had reached a meeting of the minds and forged the beginning of an alliance that would play a vital role in London's decision making during the next three critical years.

Their dispatches would go to Lord John Russell, but their main target would be Lord Palmerston. They knew they did not need to convince either man about the evils of the slave trade as an abstraction or as a historical problem. What they had to do, and would do again and again, and in many different ways, was to remind Russell and Palmerston that the slave trade holocaust was here and now in the Congo and Cuba, and coming soon to what would be called the Confederate States of America.

Part Three

Quasi-War

Wᴏ HEN BUNCH GOT BACK TO Charleston on November 10, 1859, he started tracking the post–Harpers Ferry panic in the South like a sailor watching the mercury plunge in a barometer. There was "a feeling of uneasiness, and even of terror in this community and state," said Bunch. And for a consul leading a double life among the slave owners he denounced so often and so unequivocally in his secret correspondence, that unease must have been profound. One intercepted dispatch could cost him his position and even his life.

"I do not exaggerate in designating the present state of affairs in the Southern country as a reign of terror," Bunch wrote to Lord John Russell in early December. "Persons are torn away from their residences and pursuits, sometimes 'tarred and feathered,' 'ridden upon rails,' or cruelly whipped; letters are opened at the post offices; discussion upon slavery is entirely prohibited under penalty of expulsion, with or without violence, from the country. The northern merchants and 'travelers' are leaving in great numbers." In another dispatch, Bunch wrote that "on the part of individuals the sense of danger is evinced by the purchase of fire-arms, especially of revolver pistols, of which very large numbers have been sold during the last month."

Bunch was sending a constant stream of letters marked *private* and *confidential* to his new ally in Washington, Lord Lyons, and Lyons, summarizing and reinforcing, was using those in his own correspondence with Lord John Russell.

On December 6 Lyons warned the Foreign Secretary that the U.S. government was not going to address the slave-trade issue any more than it had done already by stepping up some of its naval patrols. Buchanan already had gone out ahead of public opinion, said Lyons, although in the South legalizing the slave trade "has many avowed advocates." Indeed, "the state of feeling at this moment in the South upon the whole question of Slavery is shocking," Lyons warned. "The Harper's Ferry Affair seems to have excited Southern passions to an indescribable degree." The dissolution of the Union is just one measure that was being talked about, said Lyons: "There are plans for the re-enslavement of all the emancipated Negroes, for the purging of the South of all Whites suspected of abolition tendencies."

Because the mails had become so insecure, Lyons gave Bunch a version of diplomatic code to use for sensitive correspondence, and on Christmas Eve the consul could not join Emma and Helen for the celebrations until he had finished laboring over a little pad full of crisscrossed alphabets. "There seems a prospect—I think a remote one—of trouble in the neighborhood," Bunch wrote in his usual, functional longhand. But that was not really what he wanted to say. The characters changed to seemingly random sequences of Greek letters and symbols in groups of four:

uβm8 oιdκ fxdπ uΔea
oδχα φxzg τηΥg qκΨΘ . . .

The cipher continued for a page and a half. What it said, decoded, was: "Six companies of infantry are ready to march at a moment's notice to Kingstree . . . to repress Negroes. Revenue cutter is searching all country boats, and the [powder] magazine here is guarded."

Charleston had revived a volunteer force called the "Fire Guard": two companies of infantry and a squadron of cavalry that turned out whenever there was a fire in the night in case it might be the result of a riot or an uprising. Bunch sent clippings back to London about the creation in Charleston of a "Committee of Safety" with branches in several wards of the city "to aid in the detection, arrest, and proper treatment of Abolition sympathizers and emissaries whose presence may be prejudicial to the public peace." Bunch wrote beneath the clipping: *"Comité de Salut Publique,"* alluding to the murderous political gangs of the French Revolution.

Even Bunch's long, painstaking work on the narrow issue of the

Negro Seamen Act was now in danger. "Two idiots in the S.C. Legislature brought in bills to restore the old law of 1835," he wrote to
Lord Lyons. "They were submitted to the 'Committee upon Colored Populations' of which my friend Mr. Read is the chairman,"
and "he writes that he fears the worst, as he gets no support even
from the Charleston Delegation."

FROM WASHINGTON, LYONS also warned Lord Russell that the old,
draconian law might be reinstated, but he believed that Her Majesty's man in Charleston could handle the situation: "I trust Mr.
Bunch, the Consul in South Carolina, may succeed in preventing
the infamous colored-seamen law from passing. He has had great
experience of such matters and has shown on previous occasions
great tact and judgment in the management of them."

Bunch wrote that his friend Read in the state legislature had
suggested to "my excellent old ally" Alfred Huger that expressions
of support from Charleston merchants might help prevent the return to the old ways of dealing with black sailors. So Bunch prepared memos to the South Carolina House and Senate signed by
the president of the Chamber of Commerce and leading businessmen saying they liked the law just the way it was and didn't want it
changed. "Of course, I do not appear," Bunch explained to Lyons.
"Mr. Huger (the Post Master) manages it all."

Bunch was shrewd, but that did not mean he wasn't very worried. "Under ordinary circumstances, I should have no fears,"
Bunch told Lyons, "but when people go stark, staring mad, and one
cannot get at them to put on straight-waistcoats [straitjackets], one
should be prepared for a good deal of damage."

Lord Russell, legalistic as ever, was sure the South Carolina law
would be unconstitutional and suggested that a test case could be
taken to the U.S. Supreme Court, apparently ignoring the disastrous results of George Mathew's attempt to do that many years
before. Lord Lyons, drawing on Bunch's advice, tried to kill that

idea. As Bunch had pointed out, the Supreme Court as then consti-
tuted was completely pro-slavery. The explosive Dred Scott decision
in 1857, which required free-soil states to return escaped slaves to
their owners and declared that no blacks could be citizens or enjoy
any citizen's rights, provided ample proof of the Court's views. It
was "a direct misinterpretation of the law" and a flagrant "prostitution of judicial integrity," said Bunch. The bottom line: the Crown
would have to rely on Bunch's diplomacy. And, indeed, when the
South Carolina legislature finally adjourned, Bunch had won once
again. The law—the one that Bunch had written, to all intents and
purposes—would stay in force.

Lyons, studying up on his history, probably heard from Northerners in Washington such as Senator Seward that the South's rage
would blow out in 1860 just as it had during the nullification and
secession crisis almost thirty years before. So Lyons asked Britain's
man in Charleston to compare anti-Union sentiment then and now.

This was the holiday season, and as Bunch wrote he was interrupted several times by fellow Britons showing up at his residence
in "various stages of decadence" and by the venerable French consul, the Count de Choiseul. But Her Majesty's man in Charleston
gave long and careful consideration to the question posed by the
new minister in Washington, and to his own feelings about those
United States, where he had such deep roots and for which he felt
such complex emotions:

"That the dislike to the Union now existing in the Southern
Country is more intense than it has been at any former period is,
I think, unquestionable," Bunch wrote. Even during the secession
movement of 1832, to which "the venerated Jackson, familiarly
known as 'Old Hickory,' put so decided a stop," the state of South
Carolina and the South generally were pretty equally divided into
Union and Disunion parties. "Now, scarcely a voice is raised in
favor of the Union—everybody, including those who were the most
energetic Union Men in 1832, is in favor of immediate separation if
the South fails to secure from the present Congress some effective

guarantee, not only against attacks à la John Brown . . . but against any interference at all with Slavery on the part of the Free States. I think, therefore, that I can safely assure Your Lordship that the feeling against the Union, *just now*, is stronger and more widely spread than it has ever been before."

But Bunch allowed himself a bit of wishful thinking. He did not believe the Union would disintegrate immediately, he said, and clearly hoped that it would last a good long time. "A great Republic like this—the evolution of a great thought—of a great experiment, is not to be broken to pieces by one, or half a dozen blows," he wrote. "It has immense vitality and will, in my humble judgment, stand a good deal more knocking about than it has yet had. Besides which, are the South prepared to organize a government which shall take its place? Why, I do not believe that any three Southern States could be found to agree upon any one simple point, except perhaps that every man has an inalienable right to 'wallop his own nigger.'" That, said Bunch, would be a poor foundation for the building of a new empire.

"My own belief is that we shall see, before long, a reaction at the North," said Bunch. "There is, as Your Lordship will have seen, a substratum of conservative common sense at the bottom of the American character which, although covered and concealed by the fantastic folly of the masses, still exists to be counted upon when the need arises. So soon as that is dug down to, in other words, so soon as people are really persuaded that the Union is in danger, we shall see a great change."

Bunch was not being sentimental. He said he liked American-style democracy about as much as he liked sour wine, but, "I own to a sneaking kindness for our American off-shoot, and I should see with regret the application of the pruning-knife" that would shear away large parts of it. "Full of faults as the system is . . . it has much to do yet for the good of mankind. Once divided, the prestige is gone." If one or two states could break away, and the principle of secession were accepted, "where will the practice stop?"

Chapter 16

THAT SAME DECEMBER OF 1859, Senator William Seward arrived back in the United States spoiling for a fight. A fateful political season was beginning. He had been away for almost eight months, but now he was the man of the hour. Even his political rivals, those who thought his positions too radical to win, thought he would certainly be chosen the Republican candidate for the presidency at the party's national convention in Chicago in May 1860.

Seward's political momentum had been growing in the North, he had become the "black Republican" symbol of all that was hated by the South. The previous fall, in October 1858, he had given a speech in Rochester, New York, that effectively, albeit informally, launched his candidacy for the nation's top office and also sounded like a thinly veiled declaration of war. As the crowd greeted him with intense applause, he spread his slightly bowed legs and thrust his hands deeply into his pockets, almost like a gunslinger. He looked around at the audience. "Are you in earnest?" he asked. People didn't know how to react. They fell silent for a moment. "Are you in earnest?" Seward demanded again. And the crowd erupted in applause. Now he had them.

The United States had been built on "two radically different political systems; the one resting on the basis of servile or slave labor, the other on the basis of voluntary labor of freemen," Seward said. There should be no mistaking the fact that this was "an irrepressible conflict between opposing and enduring forces, and it means that the United States must and will, sooner or later, become entirely either a slaveholding nation, or entirely a free-labor nation." The showdown between North and South was very near at hand. Seward was vague about the means that would decide the conflict, and he could be conciliatory about short-term measures to keep the peace, but those details were the fine print. The headlines as people understood them declared that the death match was coming.

Seward had summed that up in a phrase, "irrepressible conflict," and there was no question which side he was on.

Then, in May 1859, seven months after the Rochester speech and a year before the national convention, Seward left on a grand tour across the Atlantic.

The band played "Hail to the Chief" as hundreds of supporters joined the senator from New York aboard the steamer *Josephine* for the ride across the harbor to the ocean liner *Ariel*. A brass cannon fired a salute; men waved their hats and handkerchiefs. "The sky is bright, the sun is auspicious, all the indications promise a pleasant and prosperous voyage," Seward told the crowd of friends and dignitaries gathered around him. Another boat full of supporters, this one from Brooklyn, pulled alongside, and Seward gave them a fabulously disingenuous speech: "I had hoped, as I had thought, that I could pass out of the country in silence, to suck strength, health, vigor, and knowledge in foreign lands, unattended, unnoticed, if not unknown." Seward told them that he believed "the great questions of justice and humanity before the American people are destined to be decided, and that they may be safely left to your hand, even if the instructor"—that is, Seward—"never returns." The New York crowd, of course, went wild.

London, when Seward arrived, was a bit more reserved. The reputation that preceded him, which he did little to dispel, was of a party hack who, to win votes, liked to rattle a saber—especially in the direction of the United Kingdom. Although Europe's dignitaries received Seward on the assumption he was likely to be the next president of the United States, he was such a divisive figure that many wondered how many states would remain in the Union over which he might preside.

Seward's friend Lord Napier had prepared the way for him with introductions to all the major players in Britain. State etiquette prevented Queen Victoria from receiving Seward at court, so she arranged a private meeting. Lord Palmerston and Lord Russell were busy just then forging the centrist alliance that would retake the government in the name of their new Liberal Party. Still, they made time for Seward: Palmerston entertained him at his home in Picadilly; Russell invited him to his country estate, Pembroke Lodge. Seward was thoroughly pleased, but he did recognize that, in some respects, he was out of place. "I would not be an aristocrat here—I could not be a plebeian," he said.

His time in England, largely because of his Yankee bluster and obliviousness to British sensibilities, was one long series of misunderstandings. Even taking into account the way British views of Seward changed over the next few years, coloring memories of his visit, he seems to have spread ill will among people who might have been expected to support him. He traveled to the Lake District to pay homage to Harriet Martineau, a woman whose understanding of the United States and commitment to social reform were well known on both sides of the Atlantic. But when he told her he had supported the violent diatribes in the United States against the Royal Navy's Africa Squadron stopping slavers that flew the American flag, because "the more noise there is about war, the less probable war becomes," she not only found the argument unconvincing, but was "aghast."

This bellicosity toward Britain was something Seward put on and took off in America like the caricatured masks of a frown and a smile in Greek drama. One year he was talking about the inevitability of Canada breaking away from the Crown to join the United States; the next, after traveling north of the border, he decided that Canada would be a great independent nation in its own right. And this notion that talking about war would stop a war—especially with the United Kingdom—was something neither the British aristocrats nor the plebes cared to indulge. Palmerston, looking back on his encounters with Seward in London, called him a "vaporing, blustering, ignorant man" whose sheer egotism could make him a threat.

The Seward voyage of discovery did not end with his two months in Britain. It went on for almost six months more. One reason was that Seward's political advisors were afraid he'd destroy his chances for the presidency if he were rolling around Washington and New York like a loose cannon on a fragile ship. "All of our discreet friends unite in sending me out of the country to spend the recess of Congress," he wrote to his associate George Patterson the month before he boarded the *Ariel*, and Patterson, a seasoned New York politician, agreed. "You had better be absent a few months," he wrote back. "Everything looks well now for 1860, and as no mistake will be made next winter, I feel as if the thing was pretty much finished."

Another reason for the trip was Seward's inclination to wanderlust. He had an omnivorous appetite for experience. He had been to Europe as a young man in the 1830s; he would go back as an old man on an around-the-world voyage in the 1870s. And there was the question of Harpers Ferry. Many of Seward's critics, especially in the South, believed he had timed his absence so as not to be implicated in John Brown's activities. (Although Seward and Jefferson Davis were personal friends, Davis and Senator James Mason of Virginia grilled him about Brown and about Hugh Forbes not long after he got back from his travels. But they never were able to build a case against him.)

For the apostle of "irrepressible conflict," one of the most important reasons for this long sojourn in Europe and the Middle East in 1859 was anticipation of the crisis he might have to address as president. The United States was very possibly on the eve of Armageddon: the first war fought with the horrifying firepower of the full-blown Industrial Revolution. This would be a struggle vitally dependent on decisions made, goods bought, arms shipped, and bonds sold across the Atlantic. Economic power would be hugely important, and alternative supplies of cotton—from Egypt, for instance—might make up the difference if Southern cotton were cut off. So, clumsy as Seward was when he met with prime ministers, pashas, the pope, and an emperor, he hoped to explore likely alliances and alternative markets. "I came to Europe in 1859," he said later, "to study the strength and disposition of the nations with whom we had important questions, and in a possible contingency, might have critical ones."

But there were many times in the months and years to come when the calculations he made based on that study took the United States and Britain toward war, with Her Majesty's consul in South Carolina right in the middle of the crisis.

Chapter 17

WITH THE APPROACH OF THE American elections came, too, the whole host of evils that Robert Bunch had predicted. Lord Lyons wrote privately and frequently to Lord Russell, raising the points their man in Charleston had touched upon so often. Russell had broached, for instance, the question of the American diplomat in London, George Dallas, attending an international conference to be held on the slave trade. Lyons said he feared that President Buchanan "will not dare to let Mr. Dallas take a part." Both Buchanan and Secretary of State Lewis Cass had grown "irritable" on this subject, he said. "The fact is that the country is becoming more and more divided into an absolute anti-slavery and an absolute pro-slavery Party," Lyons explained, and Buchanan's Democratic Party "does not like to have even the Slave Trade with Africa denounced. On the contrary, the success of their struggle for superiority in the Senate depends upon their getting new states admitted into the Union as slave states, and they are happy to think that they must import slaves in order to have enough to send into those states."

In Charleston, enthusiasm for a reopening of the Middle Passage continued to grow. The slaver *Jehossee*, named for an island on the South Carolina coast, had sailed out of Charleston the previous year. Everybody had known what she was up to. Her owner, Hugh Vincent, had helped outfit and supply the *Wanderer*. But nobody in the city had lifted a finger against her. In fact, many were proud of her.

Once the *Jehossee* arrived off the African coast, however, she didn't fare so well. The British sloop-of-war *Falcon* stopped her, boarded her, and discovered that the slave deck was laid. The *Falcon*'s officers didn't want to take any chances. Probably they knew of the embarrassing revelations about officers of the British squadron who had fallen for American bonhomie aboard the *Wanderer*. In any event, the *Falcon*'s officers treated the men aboard the *Jehossee* as criminals. They strip-searched the crew and kept them prisoner aboard the vessel. The American ship's captain, stranded on the African shore, busied himself writing letters trying to get the American commander of the U.S. Africa Squadron to intervene on his behalf: "Now, Sir—I look to you for that *protection* and *redress* that is due to *American Citizens* and their *Insulted Flag*." But the commodore, it seemed, was nowhere to be found. So Vincent, the *Jehossee*'s owner in Charleston, brought a lawsuit against the British, as if they were the criminals and his *Jehossee* was perfectly innocent. "The infernal impudence of these brutes is a little too much," Bunch wrote to Lyons in April 1860. All winter long people had been "bragging and hurraying" about the *Jehossee* and its mission. To demand compensation from Britain for her capture "passes even Slave Trading impudence."

Then word reached the United States that Queen Victoria's eldest son, Edward Albert, the Prince of Wales, might well be paying a visit to North America. Bunch dreaded the idea that the heir apparent might come to Charleston. He said he worried about the health issues in the summer. He didn't want the prince dying of yellow jack on his watch. But, more important, he didn't want the prince implicated in slavery in any way. Mere politesse—a cup of tea delivered by a servant—could suggest complicity. Wales could not ride down the street without passing hundreds of slaves, and he would be feted by the same Charleston "aristocrats" who had applauded the *Wanderer* and defended the *Jehossee*. Probably a part of Bunch also thought so much attention focused on the British royal could focus too much on his consul in South Carolina's claustrophobic community. Bunch survived by playing on ambiguities and deceptions that might be stripped away if he had to host the son of the Queen. Bunch did not want to have to make too many explanations to the prince about the slaveholders' impudence, or to the slaveholders about the Crown's vehement views. But he did want to see the royal visit. So Bunch began maneuvering to get himself up to Canada or New York to catch a glimpse of the eighteen-year-old royal scion and connect there with the entourage from London, some of whom Bunch knew personally from earlier assignments in Latin America and New York.

Lyons was receptive to the idea. He had been in the United States almost a year but still hadn't quite gotten his footing in Washington. The John Brown affair had blindsided him at first, and, like a visitor following an orderly through an asylum, he'd relied on Bunch to help him steer his way through the madness that followed Harpers Ferry. He had been shocked to find that the Crown's "remonstrances concerning the Slave Trade" counted for less and less with the "irritable" Buchanan. But, of course, Bunch had warned him that would be the case.

One day in April, Lord Lyons met President Buchanan out walking in Washington. As the president and the minister took in the spring weather, Buchanan said it had always been his great ambition to be able to say at the end of his administration that he had left no question with Great Britain unsettled, that for the first time since the Revolution "*the docket was clear.*"

Buchanan's concern at that moment was in the faraway Pacific Northwest, where an errant pig belonging to an American farmer had provoked a confrontation over who owned the little island of San Juan next to the Canadian city of Vancouver. Federal troops had occupied it in the firm belief that possession was nine-tenths of the law, and Lyons's conversation with the president among the spring blossoms shows how easily, almost casually, American politicians continued to toy with the idea of military action against Great Britain in order to appease political sentiments at home. "I hope that a matter of such small real importance won't be allowed to cause a war between two great nations," Buchanan told Lyons. "But the people of the West Coast are becoming very excited, and I really don't know what to do. Can you help me on this? I am sure if you put your wits to it, you can come up with an amicable settlement."

Lyons did not even raise the question of the slave trade in that meeting, even though it was still very much on "the docket."

LORD LYONS LEARNED very quickly that of all the British consuls in the United States there were only three whose information and judgment were consistently reliable. One was Robert Bunch in Charleston, the epicenter of secessionism. One was William Mure in New Orleans, the gut, the *ventre*, of the American heartland. And one was Edward Mortimer Archibald in New York City, which was, in its way, the center of the world. Archibald, a Canadian-born attorney, had replaced Anthony Barclay as the British consul after the Crimean recruitment scandal in 1857, and he reported on the slave trade with almost as much dedication as Bunch. Near the South Street docks he could pick up plenty of intelligence about the brigs being outfitted for the African journey, and for good measure he also put a ship broker in Havana on his payroll as a secret agent.

There was no question that the traffic between Africa and Cuba remained heavy. Despite the Buchanan administration's stepped-up efforts at enforcement and the many dark clouds on the political horizon in the United States, the trade appeared to be increasing, money for the U.S. Africa Squadron was drying up, and the Buchanan administration didn't want to ask Congress for more, lest the slave-trade debate add more fuel to the fires of secession (which was, of course, precisely what the fire-eaters wanted).

All the while, the price of Negroes kept rising as the marketplace bet that the cotton-growing South would be able to keep its slaves even if it stayed in the Union. And if the South seceded, of course the slaves would be more valuable than ever as cotton cultivation and the peculiar institution would push west and down into Central America. The temptation to bring African slaves back to the United States kept growing—and also the temptation to sell into slavery any black man of any nationality, free or not, British citizen or not.

Lyons, who supposedly feared embarrassing his valet about his breakfast and saw more of his servants' shoes than their faces, took to visiting the U.S. Senate and House chambers, where the atmosphere was charged with as much dangerous electricity as a summer thunderstorm. He tried to talk to all the key players but instinctively gravitated toward the Northerners, and the more he moved among them, the more suspicious the Southerners grew of his motives. The *Charleston Evening News* went on record warning Lyons that "if civil and sectional war should be the issue of the present controversy, England will have herself to blame." England, said the *Evening News*, "was the nurse and foster-parent of that sentiment of Negro-equality which may yet shake the foundations of her fabric manufacturing industry." Southerners missed few opportunities to remind Britain of its dependence on their cotton exports.

One day the blustery Senator Louis Wigfall from Texas was holding forth on the Senate floor. He was tall and imposing, and some compared his eyes to those of a tiger, they were so intense and unsettling. He was in the middle of answering questions about his rambling oration on the Homestead Act, when suddenly he shifted his gaze and called the attention of visitors in the Senate gallery to a sofa in the Senate chamber. William Seward, the "embodiment" of the Republican Party, as Wigfall put it, sat there—right there in the Senate—"conferring" with Lord Lyons. Wigfall, who had a reputation as a bully, didn't need to huff and puff about some international English-Yankee abolitionist conspiracy. The Senate was still investigating the John Brown affair; Seward had been questioned, and from the moment the commission went to work, it had been looking for a conspiracy that stretched across the Atlantic. The investigation hadn't come to any conclusions, but it is precisely under such circumstances that a well-timed implication draws more blood than tedious explication.

Lyons looked up, shocked when he heard his name, and quickly left the chamber "a good deal embarrassed." As soon as Bunch read a report of what had happened, he dashed off a note to Lyons. Senator Wigfall may have been elected from Texas, Bunch wrote, but, in truth, he was "from and of South Carolina." He is "a drunken blackguard. He is what is called a Southern 'fire-eater,' has fought one or two duels, and also killed a man named Bird in cold blood." Then Bunch added with his usual acidic irony, "He has richly deserved his place in the U.S. Senate."

IN THAT SPRING of 1860 it seemed the whole national crisis was "from and of South Carolina," and it was just about to reach its climax there as the convention of the national Democratic Party came to Charleston.

For many years the party, which liked to call itself "The Democracy," as if it were the be-all and end-all on the subject, prided itself on being a political organization that embraced all parts of the nation, North and South, East and West. To achieve that goal it had become the party of conciliation and accommodation, especially on the issue of slavery. But all that was coming to an end. The party's efforts to split the difference between Northern and Southern views with the Kansas-Nebraska Act of 1854 and the notion, called "popular sovereignty," that the people of a territory could choose whether the territory would enter the Union as a free state or a slave one, failed horribly. The Act destroyed an earlier compromise, in place since 1820, that barred slavery north of latitude 36°30' except in the state of Missouri; and the result, as settlers and squatters had poured into Kansas, had been the torrents of blood and terror exploited by the likes of John Brown.

At the Charleston convention, the Southern fire-eaters planned to make their stand against Senator Stephen Douglas, the slippery author of the Kansas-Nebraska Act, who had ceded the nomination to Buchanan in 1856—with Buchanan vowing not to seek a second term—and who now wanted the White House, at last, for

himself. The Southerners hated Douglas. In fact, they hated compromise. They intended to block his nomination at the convention,
or walk out, or both. Several of them wanted not only to divide the
party, but also to split the nation in two like a half-rotted log, and
one of the issues they planned to use as a wedge was the question
of the African slave trade. If the Democratic Party could be torn
asunder, then the anti-slavery Republicans would carry the much
more populous North and write off the demands of the South. That
would lead to an exodus of the slaveholding states, and that would
be the end of the Union.

The scenario was clear. Bunch had predicted it more than a year
before in his letter to the Foreign Office about the contemptuous
way the courts in South Carolina had thrown out the Federal case
against the slave ship *Brothers*: "They will awake from their delusion
to find the Democratic Party broken up and the whole power of the
Country thrown into the hands of the 'Republicans.' When this
shall happen, the days of Slavery are numbered. It may still exist in
that comparatively narrow strip of territory in which a pestilential
climate renders black labor necessary, but the prestige and power of
Slaveholders will be gone, never to return."

Now the first act of that drama was about to play out just a few
blocks up Meeting Street.

Chapter 18

IN A CRUDE FRESCO ABOVE the stage of Charleston's Institute Hall three "highly colored but very improperly dressed females" presented themselves to the thousands of Democratic delegates searching for their places among the wood-bottomed chairs or but-tonholing one another in the aisles. One of the neoclassical nymphs "seems to be contemplating matters and things in general," ob-served Murat Halstead, a sharp, sarcastic political reporter from Cincinnati. "Another is mixing colors with the apparent intention of painting something." And the third, ah, the third was "pointing, with what seems to be a common bowie-knife, to a globe," where the continent outlined most conspicuously was marked *Africa*.

The national Democratic convention in Charleston was under way at last. Charleston was filling up with the thousands of drunks and blackguards from The Democracy, and Bunch warned Lyons what to expect from "the dreadful convention which is hanging over us." He used the billboard language of brawling prizefights to make his point: "That 'battle, murder, and certain death,' will form a portion of the 'platform,' no one seems to doubt." But Bunch, who desperately wanted to be ringside, would be flat on his back during much of the big event. His head ached; his throat burned. The damp air of the city in early May did him no good at all.

BUNCH WROTE THAT many of those who came to the convention did so because they wanted to claim, "I was of those who fought at Charleston." Between 2,000 and 2,500 people, including hundreds of delegates and their many hangers-on, descended upon the city. And while hotelkeepers and bar owners actually were disappointed in the numbers, most of the other locals were relieved. "The good people of Charleston have been tormented for many weeks with visions of burglaries, shootings in the market-places, and the other

amenities which distinguish the workings of American institutions,"
Bunch reported. "But we have re-inforced our police—arrested several perfectly innocent persons on no charge whatever—talked a
good deal about what we will do to offenders, and are now standing
in a watchful attitude, fully satisfied with ourselves generally and
individually."

Bunch said he'd "purchased a long and very stout steel bolt for
my street door," which previously had been undefended. Probably
it was a good investment. Since 1856 Bunch's home and office had
been in an elegant if relatively simple three-story house on Meeting Street near Smith's Lane. The promenade on the Battery was
just a couple of blocks away. The convention at Institute Hall, the
Douglas headquarters at Hibernia Hall, and both the major hotels,
the Charleston and the Mills House, also were on Meeting. In fact,
most of the new arrivals attending the convention didn't know any
other street in the city, except, perhaps, Beresford Alley, where
they could visit Grace Piexotto's famous house of prostitution, just
a block and a half from the convention. So they wandered up and
down, and the drinking just kept getting heavier, the carousing and
the confrontations more chaotic. As the newspaperman Halstead
concluded one of his dispatches, "I hear, as I write, a company of
brawlers in the street making night hideous."

The political culture of the time considered it unseemly for the
leading candidates to attend a convention, so Douglas stayed away
from Charleston. And the radical Southerners in attendance did not
so much have a candidate as a cause. But there was no question
that among them William Lowndes Yancey of Alabama reigned as
"the prince of the fire-eaters." At a time when fame spread mainly
in print, there often was a disconnect between reputation and appearance, and so it was with the mild-mannered Yancey, who came
across in person as quite bland. "He is a compact, middle-sized man,
straight-limbed, with a square-built head and face, and an eye full
of expression," wrote Halstead. "No one would be likely to point
him out in a group of gentlemen as the redoubtable Yancey, who

proposes, according to common report, to precipitate the Cotton States into a revolution, dissolve the Union, and build up a Southern empire." The Douglasites accused him of being a "disunionist," but that epithet would hardly frighten Yancey or his Southern friends. Indeed, they were likely to wear it as a badge of honor. "I very much doubt whether the Douglas men have a leader competent to cope with him in the coming fight," Halstead reported. "It is quite clear that while the North may be strongest in voters here, and the most noisy, the South will have the intellect and the pluck to make its points."

There in the big hall in Charleston, under the gaze of the nymph with the bowie knife pointing at Africa, Halstead also noticed a man he'd met before, seated at a round table covered with books, newspapers, and writing materials. This politician had long, thin, white hair "through which the top of his head blushes like the shell of a boiled lobster." His face was red, too, "the color being that produced by good health and good living joined to a florid temperament. His features are well cut, and the expression is that of a thoughtful, hard-working, resolute man of the world. He is a New Yorker by birth but has made a princely fortune at the New Orleans bar. He is not a very eloquent man in the Senate, but his ability is unquestioned," and he was, unquestionably, President Buchanan's man, or, as most people thought, Buchanan was his.

"The name of the gentleman is John Slidell," wrote Halstead. "His special mission is to see that Stephen A. Douglas is not nominated for the Presidency. If I am not much mistaken, he just now manipulated a few of the Northeastern men with such marvelous art that they will presently find they are exceedingly anxious to defeat the nomination of Douglas, and they will believe that they arrived at that conclusion coming uppermost in their minds in their own way." Slidell "is a matchless wire-worker," wrote Halstead, and the news of this puppet-master's approach "causes a flutter. His appearance here means war to the knife."

Slidell knew how to count noses, and the numbers had been

clear to him from the start. As Bunch explained in a note to Lyons and in a formal dispatch to Lord Russell in London, the arithmetic of the convention was simple: there were 303 delegates, of whom 183 were sent by eighteen free states and 120 by fifteen slaveholding states. To win the nomination for the presidency, a candidate—and Douglas was *the* candidate—would have to get 202, a two-thirds majority. But passage of the party platform required only a simple majority of 152. The nose-counters like Slidell knew that Douglas could get his platform—and probably would—but he could not get the nomination. So there was an air of chaotic inevitability about the whole show. Douglas would be defeated, but then what?

Over the course of forty years The Democracy had become the party for a nation of immigrants and westward-moving settlers and also for the South with its slaves. The coalition portrayed itself as an alliance of outsiders, a majority of minorities: the relatively poor newcomers in Eastern cities, the men of the North West (which was what we'd call the Midwest today), and the people of the South dominated by the money and mind-set of the slave-owning planters. Since the days of Andrew Jackson that populist sense of being outliers fighting against a bigger system and violent enemies, whether abolitionists or nativist Know-Nothings, Whigs or Republicans, was summed up by the phrase "unterrified Democracy."

Bunch found the term vaguely risible and told Lyons that he planned, that first weekend of the convention, to hold a big "unterrified Democracy" party, but by Thursday he was confined to bed by his violent cold and sore throat. It was probably just as well. Nobody felt much like celebrating at that point. By Friday, April 27, four days after the convention began, the two sides of The Democracy were establishing once and for all that on the questions most important to them they had almost nothing in common.

Rain poured down outside the window of Bunch's bedroom, clattering on the roof. U.S. District Attorney James Conner, one of Bunch's friends and frequent allies trying to fight the slave trade, came by to offer a detailed picture of what had gone on at the convention that morning. Competing platforms had been presented, and it looked as if the Southern one would be rejected by the Douglas majority, and some or all of the Southern delegates would walk out. "Altogether, there seems to be every prospect of a very pretty quarrel," Bunch wrote from his bed.

In the convention hall that afternoon, when Halstead looked up from amid his piles of writing paper and pencils sharpened at both ends, he saw that many of the ladies in the gallery had missed their meal during the recess. The South Carolina beauties had splendid eyes and hair, "with fine profiles and bright countenances," and "the ladies are a great feature of the Convention," he wrote, while "the delegates are desperately gallant." But because of the sudden heavy downpour the women in the gallery had been more or less trapped. "There were hundreds of ladies in the hall without umbrellas in hand or carriages at command," Halstead noted, and there was no way they would brave the storm in their new dresses and elegant bonnets. "The atmosphere of the hall was already damp and chilly—and their fine feathers are drooping." Even when the rains let up, they did not dare leave, because everyone knew what was coming, or, better said, who was coming.

Yancey was coming.

The fire-eaters had done their work well. Two of the five new resolutions they proposed for the platform had barely eked out a majority in committee, but they had passed, and they played hell with the convention. Their ostensible purpose: to make the Federal government the ally of slavery, and more. The Federal government was supposed to be the slaver's enforcer, and not just in the existing United States, where runaways to the North had to be returned to the South, but in its territories, where nothing could be done to impair the right to own slaves, and, yes, even "on the high seas," where the Federal government should be duty bound "to protect, when necessary, the rights of persons and property."

No one failed to understand the meaning of that line about protecting property on the high seas. As a delegate from Massachusetts pointed out, it was put in the platform to open the way for the African slave trade, and no amount of dissembling could change that fact. The unthinkable had been made official. The Northern Democrats knew it would be political suicide to go into the election with those planks in their platform. But the fire-eaters insisted. They said it was a matter of principle, a matter of the U.S. Constitution.

"Mr. Yancey is a very mild and gentlemanly man, always wearing a genuinely good-humored smile and looking as if nothing in the world could disturb the equanimity of his spirits," reported Halstead.

Yancey rose to speak. Institute Hall thundered with applause.

If the Democrats had been defeated in elections in the North, said Yancey, it was because they had given up the moral high ground, "which must be taken on the subject in order to defend the South—namely, that slavery was right." Yancey "traced the history of Northern aggression and Southern concession as he understood it" and argued that the time had come for the party to take a clear "constitutional" position. "He pronounced false all charges that the State of Alabama, himself, or his colleagues were in favor of a dissolution of the Union *per se*." But he told the Northern Democrats they had to go home and tell their voters that failure to back this platform and win at the ballot boxes in November would mean "the dissolution of the Union."

The crowd applauded again and again, galvanized by Yancey's electroshock logic and its secessionist implications. The wilted ladies in the balconies flushed pink with emotion even as the daylight faded outside the windows and the gaslights were lit. This had been the speech of the convention, and the scene, as Halstead saw it, was unforgettable. "The crowded hall, the flashing lights, the deep solicitude felt in every word, the importance of the issues pending, all combined to make up a spectacle of extraordinary interest, and something of splendor."

The critical votes came two days later, on Monday, April 30, one week after the convention began. The last-minute maneuvers by the

Douglas men were over. Many of the hangers-on from the North had left, and the galleries were full of Charlestonians whose sympathies were entirely with the fire-eaters, egging them on. Suddenly an elderly gentleman on the floor called the chair's attention so he could ask "a privileged question." The gentlemen in the galleries were spitting tobacco juice onto the delegates below, he said. The gentlemen of the gallery were "respectfully requested not to use the heads of the gentlemen below them for spittoons."

There was not one ballot, but several. The Douglas platform was adopted, the Southern platform was rejected, and the Southern states began, first, to withdraw their votes, and then their entire delegations, from the convention. At a critical moment, just as one of the speakers pleaded desperately with the delegates not to destroy the Democratic Party, but to pause at the brink of the precipice and look into the abyss below, Yancey caught Halstead's eye. "He was smiling as a bridegroom," Halstead remembered.

Bunch was still sick. "I have crawled out today for a little air and news and am writing a brief line from the Club to say that the Convention has broken up," he told Lyons. "Seven states having seceded, and four others are deliberating." There was "an immense deal of excitement" as "our fire-eaters consider the Union at an end." That night serenades and processions were planned. "My friends around me are drinking 'Death to the Union,' and blood and thunder generally," Bunch wrote.

On that same night of April 30, Halstead the newspaperman strolled from the convention hall down toward the Battery. The moon "silvered the live oaks along Meeting Street, and made the plastered fronts of the old houses gleam like marble." Halstead was not sympathetic to slavery or to the South. He was a Republican, in fact—a Seward man, no less. But he was caught up in the moment. It was eleven o'clock, going on midnight, but the town was still full of people hurrying around, "looking excited and solicitous," or talking and laughing on street corners. The Mills House Hotel and the hall next door, where the Douglasites had congregated, looked dark and deserted. But at the courthouse at the corner of Meeting and Broad a throng was listening to Lucius Q. C. Lamar, a famous cousin of the Lamar who owned the *Wanderer*. Then Yancey spoke again, in his typical gentlemanly way, saying he was saving his strength for the meeting in the morning. He left it to Charles E. Hooker, a South Carolinian who'd moved to Mississippi, to set the night ablaze with what Halstead called "a flaming, fire-eating harangue." Then the crowd moved down to the offices of the *Charleston Mercury*, the fire-eaters' favorite newspaper, and called out for Robert Barnwell Rhett Jr., the old radical's hardworking son, to cheer him on as he raced the next edition into print on the historic evening.

"There was a Fourth of July feeling in Charleston last night," Halstead wrote the next day. "There was no mistaking the public sentiment of the city. It was overwhelmingly and enthusiastically in favor of the seceders. In all her history Charleston had never enjoyed herself so hugely."

"Considerable excitement prevails here," Bunch wrote to Lyons that afternoon, confirming the schism in the convention. "The South evidently thinks that it has done a very clever thing, but that is a way the South has."

The next day, on May 2, after those left in the original convention had voted fifty times, they still could not manage to nominate Douglas. The chair had ruled that the two-thirds rule still applied, and the nominee had to have that proportion of the votes based on the numbers of the original convention: 202 of 303. Douglas got 150, 150½, 151, and once he got 152 votes, but there were never enough. So the old convention adjourned to Baltimore; the new, Southern convention adjourned to Richmond; and the whole process dragged on into June. Eventually the Democrats fielded three candidates while the Republicans put forth only one. The first part of Bunch's prediction from the year before had come true: "The Democratic Party broken up and the whole power of the Country thrown into the hands of the 'Republicans.'" It was, Bunch wrote to Lyons, "a frightful fiasco."

Chapter 19

MRS. BUNCH WAS OFFERING A post-convention tea at the residence, and her husband was upstairs, rushing, as usual, to send off several dispatches. She had invited a few of their friends from the better class of people in Charleston and some of the notables from the Democratic Party. Among them was the former U.S. attorney general Caleb Cushing, who had presided over the debacle. "I will try to get something out of him—i.e., if there be anything to get, which I doubt," Mr. Bunch scrawled in a quick note to Lord Lyons. But the consul's main concern that afternoon was to wrap up two formal reports to London. It was vital that the Foreign Office understand the implications of what was happening, and his dispatches were more urgent than ever.

The first, "Slave Trade No. 3," looked at the judgment handed down in the trial of the detestable William C. Corrie, lobbyist and yachtsman, who'd presented himself as the owner of the yacht *Wanderer* in 1858. Federal judge A. G. Magrath had rewritten the law from the bench in a way that could set a precedent for the Union if it held together or, more likely, for whatever agglomeration of Southern states emerged from secession. Magrath's "very novel view of the law" held "that the offense of carrying off and bringing to the United States a Negro or Mulatto, *who had been a slave in Africa*, does not amount to piracy under that law, which, in Judge Magrath's opinion, is only applicable to the case of kidnapping, or bringing away by force, a Negro or Mulatto who was a free man when he was so kidnapped!" (Bunch could not resist the exclamation point, even in this formal communication.) Since nearly all the captives bought from the barracoons of West Africa already had been enslaved, this reasoning could open the door wide to the African trade as far as American, or at least Southern, courts were concerned.

Maybe Bunch was working too hard and too fast and still feeling sick, or maybe his quiet fury about Corrie and his disdain for the Democrats got the better of him, but his second dispatch that afternoon, written over the sound of teacups and saucers clinking and a soft hum of polite conversations, took a very strident turn. After duly sketching for Lord Russell the basic issues and the breakup of the Democratic Party, Bunch wrote a long concluding paragraph giving his opinion of what it all meant: The election of a Republican president probably would be a good thing for relations with Great Britain, since the Democratic Party, "which is by nature both insolent and aggressive" had never missed a chance to pick a fight with Britain. Her Majesty's government had showed dignified restraint, "but I have never doubted that the time would come when we should be compelled to vindicate our honor by a war."

Perhaps after the tea that afternoon, or maybe after he woke up the next morning—but in any case after there was no way to call the dispatches back—Bunch started to have some serious second thoughts about that last paragraph. Lord Russell was not Lord Lyons. Lord Russell was not Lord Clarendon. And Lord Russell was not the bellicose Lord Palmerston. Lord Russell was extremely interested in formalities and not very interested in the opinion of consuls. For Bunch to instruct Lord Russell on the vindication of British honor by means of war was the kind of mistake that could turn the Foreign Secretary against him and stop the Foreign Office from paying any attention at all. And if Lyons got the idea that Bunch was drawing attention to himself at Lyons's expense, that could be the end of their vital alliance.

Desperately, Bunch shot off a scrawled note to Lyons saying he "earnestly" hoped Lyons agreed with him. Three days after that, as his unasked-for opinions about defending British honor were wending their way across the Atlantic, Bunch wrote to Lyons again with more second-guessing about that last dispatch. "I am sometimes afraid that I shall get the character at home of being a person too bitterly prejudiced against democratic institutions to render my opinion worth the taking. *Mais, quoi faire?* . . . How am I to praise, or even to hold my tongue, when everything around me is in direct opposition to all I love and respect?"

Bunch had spent a decade dissembling—biting his glove like the villain in a play, as he once put it. The job wasn't getting any easier, and it was getting decidedly more dangerous in a land of lynch law and assassins. The vigilantes, the guards, the informers, the detectives—all continued to multiply. Bunch should have encrypted his message, but he had grown annoyed with the laborious process. He had wanted to express himself clearly, passionately, and he couldn't do that in code. Blocks of four Greek characters were barely adequate for conveying basic facts, let alone intense emotions. But what if those unencrypted letters were intercepted? He knew from his friend Postmaster Alfred Huger just how insecure the mails could be.

Bunch's family had become a worry, too. His sister-in-law Helen, apparently confident she was invulnerable as the wife of Daniel Blake, as the mistress of Board House and The Meadows plantations, and as the pious founder of a church in the up-country attended by the finest people from Charleston and Savannah, made no secret of her Union sympathy. Inevitably that reflected on her sister, Emma, and on Bunch, as well. And then there was little Helen, their daughter. She was five years old, just the age when bits of conversation overheard in private may be repeated by a child without guile and without malice but with hugely embarrassing consequences.

If any of those men at Bunch's club drinking "Death to the Union" and blood and thunder generally knew how bitterly he opposed the expansion of slavery, if any of the men and women invited to his wife's tea had any inkling that he believed a Republican victory desirable and had so advised his government, these were the kinds of things that could make life unbearable in Charleston. This was not 1852, when George Mathew had been snubbed for his offenses. These days people were shot. And at the same time Bunch had to ask himself what recompense he got for his analysis and his opinion and his years of service in this place. If Lyons were offended, if Russell were incensed, Bunch would be all alone trying to protect himself and his family from the dangers closing in upon them.

Chapter 20

A T JUST ABOUT THE SAME time as the fire-eaters at the Charleston convention were pushing the idea that the Federal government (or maybe a future Confederate government) should protect "persons and property on the high seas"—meaning, slave property from Africa—a U.S. Navy cruiser patrolling the Cuban coast came across a beautiful but suspicious ship.

Consul William Mure in New Orleans wrote up a succinct report for Lord Russell: "Intelligence has been received here, from Key West, of the capture of a slaver named the *Wildfire* by the Steam Ship *Mohawk*, which was commanded by Lieut. Tunis Augustus MacDonough Craven of the U.S. Navy." The slaver was a three-masted barque designed along the lines of a clipper, 128 feet long, and very fast. More than five hundred Africans were still alive on board, "three fourths of whom appear to be children." When Craven boarded the clipper, he was horrified. Amid the heat and stench of the slave deck there was "scarcely space to die in."

The *Mohawk* towed the *Wildfire* to Key West, where a primitive barracks was thrown up to house the Africans, and thirty-four U.S. soldiers were assigned to guard them "for the purpose of preventing any attempt at kidnapping."

BEFORE THE END of May two more slavers, the *William* and the *Bogota*, were brought to Key West. (The *Bogota* was captured by the same Lt. J. N. Maffitt who had caught the *Echo* using the same false-flag tactics.) By then the African population in the makeshift barracks was up to more than fourteen hundred, many of them fatally ill. Almost three hundred eventually were buried at a place called Higgs Beach, and, as with the *Echo*, more died on the trip back to Africa than had died on their first voyage across the Middle

Passage. But Old Buck's navy was, at last, making a real show of its dedication to the fight against the African slave trade.

President Buchanan had a carefully hedged political strategy behind this new campaign to capture slavers. On the one hand, he wanted to ease relations with Britain—to "clear the docket" at last on this difficult issue—and his actions were more or less in line with what Lord Russell had been demanding. On the other, he saw the potential reopening of the slave trade to the United States as a threat to the old-money planters who supported him and who certainly did not want to see their stock of slaves devalued. In a message to Congress in December 1859 Buchanan had warned against "the introduction of wild, heathen, and ignorant barbarians among the sober, orderly, and quiet slaves whose ancestors have been on the soil for generations."

But what really was central to Buchanan's thinking was the notion that if Cuba were annexed, then a number of problems might be solved. This had been an obsession of his for years, even before the Ostend Manifesto in 1854 called for the United States to buy Cuba from Spain, or declare war if Spain refused. And as a means to that end of annexation, he believed that the more slavers that were captured, the harder it would be for the Cubans to sustain their sugar-based economy by working expendable Africans to death, and the less Spain would be inclined to hang on to the island. Once Cuba was part of the United States, a moral good would be achieved: the last major market for African slaves in the civilized world would be closed. But the practical political benefit would accrue to the existing slave owners among Old Buck's constituents. With the acquisition of Cuba, the South, by dividing the island, would get at least two more slaveholding states with four senators. Southern dominance would be restored in the U.S. Senate. That outcome, or its imminent possibility, would in turn isolate the fire-eaters trying to tear the Union apart.

All this was going on while Buchanan's party was falling apart.

He might have thought that the constellation of issues he assembled around the rescue of the Africans and the acquisition of Cuba could pull The Democracy back together. Or perhaps he thought this strategy could pull the *nation* back together. He could see as well as anyone that secession loomed and, with it, the likelihood of civil war. He did not want to become the last president of the these United States. He needed a masterstroke to protect his nation and his legacy. But that was not to be.

On May 9, 1860, at the convention center known as the Wigwam in Chicago, the Republican Party nominated Abraham Lincoln as its candidate for president, leaving William Seward stunned and not a little bitter. He had played the cards of abolition and irrepressible conflict too often; he had spent too much time in Europe and the Levant; his overconfident team had been, purely and simply, outmaneuvered on the convention floor.

The Southern Democrats had proposed reopening and protecting the African slave trade, and the issue had been part of the platform package that split the party in Charleston. The Republicans in Chicago, in contrast, put an unequivocal plank in their platform: "We brand the recent reopening of the African slave trade, under the cover of our national flag, aided by perversions of judicial power, as a crime against humanity, a burning shame to our country and age; and we call upon Congress to take prompt and efficient measures for the total and final suppression of that execrable traffic." No wonder Robert Bunch was so inclined to favor the Republicans. Even he could not have written a more powerful statement of Britain's desires regarding that "execrable traffic." On this issue, at least, the battle lines were clearly drawn, and Bunch believed there should be no question which side Her Majesty's government would favor.

ROBERT BUNCH WAS DYING TO get out of Charleston, the epi-center of Southern madness, but he tried to sound lighthearted about it in his letters. Life in the city was as flat as ditch-water compared to Champagne, he told Lyons. "Heat and mosquitoes reign supreme," he said. "Our fashionables are 'going, going, gone,' and so we of the baser sort can tarry no longer." The yellow fever scares were mounting—nobody had forgotten the raging epidemic of 1858 when more than seven hundred people died, which was more than ever before in the history of the city. Trade was at an end; ships were no longer coming into port; a quarantine was in force but employed measures Bunch thought "absurd." Ships from the Bahamas were on the list of banned vessels, he noted, but his family had owned property there for 150 years, and he knew it to be a much healthier place than Charleston. Any place seemed healthier than Charleston. Where was the fever coming from? In South Carolina people said it originated in Havana. In Havana people said it came from Siam. The connection to mosquitoes was not understood at all.

Meanwhile the secessionist ranting of the Charlestonians was almost impossible to bear. After months of listening to his supposed friends complain about the supposed British abuse of the supposedly innocent captain and crew of the *Jehossee*, the South Carolina slaver captured off the coast of Africa was brought at last into Charleston Harbor. Even Bunch had begun to wonder if the British had gone too far, but now the evidence was clear. "I am glad the slave deck was laid," he said.

The Charleston consul's mind was already up North, where Lord Lyons had agreed to make him his private secretary during the impending and rather impetuous visit of the eighteen-year-old Prince of Wales to Canada and the United States. It promised to be quite a royal spectacle and a great opportunity for Bunch to connect with influential old acquaintances while deepening his ties to Lyons. It had the potential to improve dramatically relations between the Union and the Crown, or sour them fatally. So Bunch wanted everything in his Charleston office to be in order before he set off. He stayed up late to work in the relatively cool hours after midnight, but it was still eighty degrees, "and the mosquitoes," as he told Lyons, "knowing that my hands are occupied, have been basely piercing my ankles and legs as high as they can get." Bunch remembered a colleague in Bogotá who was attacked by so many of the insects that he killed about twenty of them and dropped them into his dispatch to explain why the handwriting was so bad and smeared by smashed bugs.

A NOTION HAD developed in Washington with Buchanan, and in London with Russell and Palmerston, that the problem of the slave trade was, like yellow fever, something that came from Havana, and that if the Cuban connection to Africa could be broken, the Atlantic slave trade would simply come to an end. The secret mission of slow-talking Mr. Benjamin Slocumb through the South the summer before, looking to buy Africans fresh off the boat, and failing, was part of Buchanan's effort to prove that thesis and to refute claims by the likes of Stephen Douglas that as many as fifteen thousand Africans had been imported to the United States.

Robert Bunch never tried to argue that huge numbers of Africans already had been landed. He argued, and Lyons believed, that the risk would come in the near future for the economic reasons he'd laid out in his Dispatch No. 10, commenting on the price of Negroes in 1857, and for the political ones that were a constant refrain in Southern politics. From this point of view, the interest in the huge volume of Cuban slave traffic conducted in defiance of supposed Spanish law and treaty obligations had very specific relevance. If, somehow, the Cuban trade were cut off, as it almost had been during the "Africanization" initiatives of 1854, then it was far from certain that all this criminal traffic would end. Rather, it would be displaced. And precisely because it was a criminal enterprise, based on enormous illicit profits, it would go where it could find the most welcoming markets. Those, most likely, would be in the American South—especially an independent confederation of Southern states that had very little respect for any central government authority anywhere.

The reporting to the Slave Trade Department of the Foreign Office in the summer of 1860 made it perfectly clear that the size of the criminal traffic in African slaves to Cuba remained very large, and dispatches continued to flow in suggesting that, contrary to Slocumb's findings, the efforts to reopen the African trade with the Southern states were very much alive if not, indeed, flourishing.

In July 1860, Consul Edward Mortimer Archibald in New York forwarded to the Slave Trade Department a published list of twenty-six slavers fitted out in American ports or sailing under the American flag known to have landed an estimated 13,000 Africans in Cuba over the previous couple of years. The same clipping showed that the British squadron had captured six slavers under the American flag from mid-1858 to the late spring of 1860, while U.S. warships had captured four: the *Putnam* (aka *Echo*), the *Wildfire*, the *William*, and the *Bogota*. It noted that "but one cargo landed in the United States—the yacht *Wanderer*." But several other dispatches coming into the Slave Trade Department from New Orleans, Galveston, and Mobile told Lord Russell, if he cared to believe it, that Africans landed on American shores with clandestine, continuous regularity.

Despite all the controversy that the British and American naval squadrons generated, neither seemed to be making a serious dent in the trade, nor serving as much of a deterrent. When Lord Russell saw the list of the twenty-six slavers, he fired off a note to Lyons in Washington: "It appears to H.M.G. that two such powers as G.B. and the U.S. ought to be able to prevent the landing of two-thirds or three-fourths of these cargoes, and thus cause the dealers to abandon the traffic." He proposed that the British and American warships might travel in pairs. But in any case he said he wanted Lyons to tell Buchanan and Secretary of State Lewis Cass that "it is incumbent on the U.S. to take measures of their own which if vigorously pursued may in two or three years extirpate a traffic condemned many years ago by the legislation of the Republic and repugnant to every feeling of humanity."

THE *ROGER B. TANEY* was one of Timothy Meaher's huge, creaking constructs made of kindling-like wood painted to resemble a floating palace. He named the riverboat after the Supreme Court chief justice who declared in the Dred Scott decision that slaves were not citizens and had no rights anywhere in the United States. Like Meaher's other paddle wheelers, the *Roger B. Taney* plied the Alabama River between Mobile and Montgomery, with Meaher frequently serving as captain and as host. Then one night in 1859, amid all the talk of Africans landing and American warships patrolling, the usual bourbon-fed bluster got especially heated.

A New Yorker on board thought that people-smugglers ought to be executed. Federal law said they were pirates. "Hanging the worst of them will scare the rest off," he proclaimed.

Captain Meaher turned his cold stare on this Yankee know-it-all. "Nonsense!" he said. "They'll hang nobody—they'll scare nobody."

A Mr. Ayer from back East, renowned for his sarsaparilla and cathartic pills ("the best family medicine for sick headache, constipation, dyspepsia, and liver troubles"), figured it was well nigh impossible to introduce Africans anywhere in the United States: There were too many customs men, and now the British and Americans were cruising the coasts of Africa and Cuba. There were some French and Portuguese warships, too. It couldn't be done. Mr. Matthews, a planter from Louisiana, begged to differ. It was very feasible, he said, and he ought to know; there were a whole lot of Africans landing in his state in the dark of night.

Tempers rose. The talk got hotter, and somebody put a hundred dollars on the table. Suddenly everybody wanted in on the action, putting up money for and against the possibility that someone somewhere would get a confirmed shipment of African slaves into the country, until, suddenly, Meaher trumped them all. "A thousand dollars says that inside two years I myself can bring a ship full of niggers right into Mobile Bay under the officers' noses," he said. And so he did.

In March 1860, the schooner *Clotilda* set out from Mobile under the command of Meaher's good friend William Foster, who had built her four years earlier. She was much smaller than most slave ships. She didn't expect to load more than 150 Africans, whereas the yacht *Wanderer* had carried 500, and some slavers crammed 1,000 people into those hidden decks with "scarcely enough space to die in." But even with 100 slaves, the likely profit would still be huge, when they could be bought for $100 a head and sold for $1,500.

Many years later, Foster dictated an account of the voyage that, like many reminiscences of old men, might have been compressed or distorted with time. But it gives a vivid sense of an amateur slaver's encounter with Africa.

The *Clotilda* had a hard voyage out. She hit a gale off Bermuda that lasted nine days, carrying overboard just about everything on her deck, including boats and davits, ripping off half the steering wheel, and splitting the rudder into three pieces. Close calls with Portuguese warships frightened the mates and crew, and Foster had to promise to double their wages to avert a mutiny. After putting in for repairs at the Cape Verde Islands, due west of what is now Senegal, the *Clotilda* set off for Whydah, or Ouidah, in what is now Benin. The surf was too heavy for Foster to land in one of his own boats, but the locals had no problem paddling out in sixty-foot canoes manned by twenty men that "darted through the waves like fish." Onshore, an interpreter arranged for Foster to be carried in a covered hammock to meet "the Prince" in Whydah.

The spectacle that Foster beheld fascinated and repulsed him.

The prince weighed a good 250 pounds, and all his court bowed down when he approached. Inside a walled compound, the trees, the ground, and everything else seemed to be covered by snakes. Among them moved worshippers with serpents winding around their necks and waists. The prince was hospitable, sharing a drink with Foster, but there were times during the eight days of negotiation when Foster wondered if he would ever be allowed to leave.

Finally the price was set at $100 apiece. "We went to the warehouse where they had in confinement four thousand captives in a state of nudity," Foster recalled. "They gave me liberty to select one hundred and twenty-five as mine." The prince's people offered to brand them, but Foster emphatically said no to that. The next day the slaves had to be taken through the heavy surf to be loaded, and about seventy-five had gotten on board when a lookout on the *Clotilda* spotted two steamers approaching. The crew panicked and wanted to try to escape to shore, but the surf was too rough for their boats. Foster finally managed to keep them aboard, and to load another thirty-five slaves, but he had to leave the last fifteen on the beach as the *Clotilda* raced to outdistance the approaching warships. She had another run-in with a Portuguese cruiser near Cape Verde, then narrowly missed hitting a sunken ship near the Bahamas that would have sunk her as well. When, finally, on July 9, 1860, the *Clotilda* entered Lake Pontchartrain, Foster expected to find Meaher, but the captain was nowhere to be seen. Foster had to take a carriage into Mobile, get the money to pay the still-restive crew, and hire a tug to tow the *Clotilda* upriver. The Africans were hidden in a canebrake. Foster burned the schooner to the waterline. He sank the hull. And the legend of the *Clotilda* began to grow.

On August 9 the British consul assigned to Mobile, Charles Tulin (a feckless bureaucrat who was summering in Pennsylvania and trying desperately to get reassigned somewhere else in the world), reported an item he'd seen in a Philadelphia newspaper:

Slaves landed in Alabama. New Orleans, July 10—The Schooner *Clotilda* with 124 Africans on board, arrived at Mobile Bay today. A steamboat immediately took the Negroes up the river.

Later the same day, after hearing from the deputy consul in Mobile, Tulin sent a clarification to Lord Russell: "Mr. Labuzan informs me that although the transaction is wrapped in mystery, the statement appears to bear some truth and that newly imported African Negroes have been landed in some place up the Alabama River.

"As some time ago it was reported that many of the slaves landed at Key West in Florida from captured vessels had been kidnapped and carried away into the country, but reported as dead, I should not be at all surprised if the Negroes landed in the Alabama River were those kidnapped at Key West."

FOSTER NEVER IDENTIFIED the two steamers spotted through the lookout's spyglass, the ones that panicked the crew and forced the *Clotilda* to leave behind on the Whydah beach slaves that had cost him $1,500 and could have made him fifteen times that much. But they may have been the two American warships, the *Mohican* and the *San Jacinto*, that were patrolling the Slave Coast more aggressively that summer than ever before. President Buchanan had ordered Secretary of the Navy Isaac Toucey to crack down on the trade, and the secretary blasted Commodore William Inman, who seemed to think the purpose of his Africa Squadron was to spend as much time as possible on the Portuguese island of Madeira, famous for its clement weather and fortified wines. Finally, the squadron moved into action.

Toucey sent explicit orders to watch out for a ship called the *Erie* that had cleared Havana bound for Africa earlier in the year and looked almost certain to be a slaver. Everything about her was incriminating, including and especially the captain, the notorious Nathaniel "Lucky Nat" Gordon.

On August 8, about fifty miles from the mouth of the Congo River, the *Mohican* and the *San Jacinto*, patrolling together, spotted two suspect ships traveling in opposite directions.

One was the *Erie*, and the *Mohican* gave chase. Gordon saw the *Mohican* coming after him: she had steam, she had sail, and she was closing in fast. But even with his spyglass Gordon couldn't make out her nationality. The *Mohican* showed no flag at all. The rules of engagement did not require her to do so until she sent out a boarding party. Thinking she must be a British warship, Gordon hoisted the American colors. And then so did the *Mohican*. She had him.

The U.S. Navy prize crew put aboard the *Erie* sailed it to Luanda on the African coast to offload the Spanish crew, then to Monrovia to offload the Africans, then to the United States to put Gordon and his mates on trial. One of the Navy officers was a young midshipman named Henry Davis Todd, who was at least as terrified as he was disgusted by the Africans on board. At first he did not want to let them up on deck, and when they came, he felt he could hardly breathe for the stench. Some of the Africans had stuffed bits of corncob or cotton up their noses to ward it off. But worst of all for Todd was that he could not figure out how to load them again in the hold. At that point "Lucky Nat" Gordon stepped forward. He showed the Navy officers how "by spreading the limbs of the creatures apart and sitting them so close together that even a foot could not be put upon the deck" he had managed to cram more than six hundred aboard. It was nothing personal, as the saying goes; it was just business.

On the U.S. Navy's screw-propeller-driven *San Jacinto*, Captain Thomas Aloysius Dornin, sixty years old, Irish born, Virginia bred, serving in the U.S. Navy from the age of fifteen, including an around-the-world voyage with the South Seas Exploring Expedition under Charles Wilkes, set his sights on the brig *Storm King*. After three hours Dornin pulled alongside her. She flew no flag, but two carved versions of Old Glory graced her stern. The *San Jacinto* called on her to identify herself. "*No entiendo*," came the reply. Once the officers and men from the *San Jacinto* clambered aboard, however, there was no doubt what sort of ship this *Storm King* was.

The *San Jacinto* became famous the following year in another connection. But those aboard her that day in August 1860 would always remember what they had found aboard the *Storm King*. "It was impossible to look on and not have our feelings of humanity touched," wrote one of the officers. "It was a brutal sight," he said, but it was not an unusual one: "130 women, 160 men, 68 female children, 261 boys, altogether 619 Negroes."

Such stories had begun to appear so regularly in public, reinforcing the reporting of Bunch and Lyons in private, that for anyone outside the South, it seemed impossible that such a commerce could be countenanced. But Bunch knew that, just as the zealots of secession had ignored the horrors of the *Echo* when it was right in front of their faces, they would find reasons to ignore or explain away the atrocities carried out on ships like the *Erie* and the *Storm King*. And the plethora of such stories risked making the revelations seem banal. News of the capture of the two ships was slow to reach the United States, in any case. An anonymous dispatch from one of the officers aboard the *San Jacinto* was published in the *New York Times* on September 28. But by then the imagination of the American public was consumed almost entirely by the visit of the teenage heir to the British throne.

Chapter 22

CONSUL BUNCH HAD GOTTEN HIS first wish. When the eighteen-year-old Prince of Wales toured North America in the late summer of 1860, Lord Lyons accompanied him, and Robert Bunch accompanied Lord Lyons as his private secretary (although not part of the official entourage). And Bunch had gotten his second wish, as well. The prince would not be coming to South Carolina.

The royal party traveled through Canada, where the reception was rapturous, which was to be expected. And then they crossed into the United States at Detroit, where the reception was, if anything, even more enthusiastic. And that was a bit of a surprise. But this was the American way—to love the "lion" of the moment—and this adolescent nicknamed "Bertie" certainly qualified as a star in the eyes of the American public. If the trip continued to go well, Lyons and Bunch hoped it might smooth the very rough relations between the United States and the United Kingdom.

Lyons had been assigned the task of stage-managing the whole show, and he came up with the novel idea that Edward Albert should be known during his American sojourn as "Baron Renfrew," one of the heir apparent's lesser titles, as if that would enable him and his retinue to travel incognito. But the Renfrew ruse soon became something of a joke. Journalists followed the royal ramblings everywhere. There was no press secretary on the trip, but Bunch was just the kind of person reporters might turn to for bits of information and insights. The journalists soon exhausted their metaphors for the "seas" and "torrents" and "throngs" and "hives" of Americans who turned out to cheer the prince. Editorialists, trying to strike a more sober tone, called the tour and the public reaction across the North a sign of the mutual respect the two countries now had for each other. In fact, it was more a matter of romance than respect. But so far, so good.

The problem, as Bunch had cautioned, was the South. No part

of the country felt a greater romantic attachment to British royalty. Bertie might not have been much to look at, but for the self-styled cavaliers of Virginia and the aristocrats of the Carolinas, he embodied the heritage of chivalry to which they aspired. That Bertie's father had campaigned against slavery and the slave trade, that the British Crown colony of Canada was refuge to thousands of runaway slaves—none of that really mattered to Southerners who'd grown up reading Sir Walter Scott and hoped to get a glimpse of real British royalty.

But, of course, the issue of slavery mattered quite a bit to Lyons and Bunch, as well as to many others in the prince's party, and the original agenda that Lyons laid out for "Baron Renfrew" did not include a single Southern state. The official reason for snubbing Dixie was, as Bunch suggested, concern about the health of the heir apparent. But the bigger problem, of course, was preventing any hint that by visiting the South, Wales was approving its peculiar institution.

Only at the last minute, under considerable pressure from the Federal government in Washington, did Lyons add an overnight trip to Richmond, Virginia. Many of the traveling press did not make the journey and relied on secondhand, anonymous accounts from those few who were there. The picture was not a pretty one, and the spin (perhaps by Bunch) was entirely negative. In Richmond, it seemed, the locals were offensive. The sheets on the prince's bed supposedly were dirtied before he arrived by rubes fondling the fine fabric. Protocols and etiquette were ignored, and a mob jostled the monarch-to-be so badly at one appearance that he had to leave by a back door. The British press picked up on the "rudeness" in Richmond, contrasting it repeatedly with the warm and respectful reception everywhere else, which was to say, in the North. Later, the *Richmond Times-Dispatch* refuted the accusations one by one, but in London the unsavory impression of Southern behavior remained.

The way the prince snubbed Dixie might have been taken as a sign of British reticence. But secession fever was growing in the South and, with it, wildly unrealistic notions of its ties to the Old

Country. By then, Southerners were not inclined to heed any omen that did not justify their belief that Britain would back their bid for independence.

A few months earlier, in February, Consul Bunch was an honored guest at the Charleston Jockey Club's annual dinner, the culmination of Race Week. Amid all the pronouncements about equine bloodlines and gentlemanly bonhomie, Bunch was, of course, called on to make a toast.

"I think we are all familiar with the encouragement Her Majesty gives to the Turf at home and abroad," he said. "At home, we have the Queen's Plates and Cups. Her Majesty attends Ascot, and during that week her hospitality at Windsor is well known. Abroad, the Queen has given Plates to be run for in two colonies at least, Canada and Australia, and, gentlemen, without intending to be unkind, or to taunt you with your misfortunes, I cannot help calling your attention to the great loss you yourselves have suffered by ceasing to be a Colonial dependency of Great Britain, as I am sure that if you had continued to be so, the Queen would have had great pleasure in sending you some Plates, too."

Bunch was just joking, trying "to raise a laugh after dinner," as he put it. But to his amazement, the men of the Jockey Club, some of the richest and most influential in the state and in the country, took him at his word. The applause was long and loud. "After I had finished," he informed Lyons, "several members came to congratulate me, declaring that I was quite right in condoling with them upon their loss, that they were great fools for ever leaving Great Britain, and proposing that the Queen should be requested to 'annex the South.'"

All this happened after dinner over brandy, Bunch told Lyons, but "it was ten minutes after dinner," so nobody was that drunk, "and several people have today alluded to the subject and declared that they should consider, if not annexation, at any rate, a close alliance with Great Britain, and a remodeling of their democratic form of government, the greatest of blessings.

"The fact is that this community, at least, is thoroughly disgusted with the present state of affairs and would go to *very great lengths* to remedy them."

Many in the South were convinced that their economic bonds to Britain would trump all other questions, and Bunch often reminded London of that delusion. As he informed Lord Russell, the Southerners "count upon three things: Cotton, Slave Labor, and Free Trade." They were convinced that the first could be produced nowhere else in the world as well as in the South, and that slaves were essential to do that. Cotton, they thought, would "secure to them not only immediate recognition from abroad, but even an armed intervention in their behalf" if the U.S. government decided to fight at all. Free trade would then make the South a more intimate partner of Britain than of the Northern United States, or so they believed.

Senators were wearing pistols on the floor of Congress that summer, flushed with the wet heat of Washington and a pervasive sense that the great duel was about to begin. The hysteria created by John Brown still raged throughout the slaveholding states almost a year after the raid itself. (The acting British consul in Mobile seemed to think a full-fledged rebellion was under way deep in the heart of Alabama.) But the investigation into Brown's conspiracy had come to seem almost irrelevant, and likely counterproductive, in the face of the coming war. Jefferson Davis had convened the investigating commission saying, "I believe a conspiracy has been formed," and that it reached across the Atlantic. But now he concluded that Brown's raid at Harpers Ferry was "simply the act of lawless ruffians." The wiser Southerners understood that it wouldn't do to antagonize the Crown in the months to come.

WHEN THE PRINCE of Wales arrived in New York City on October 11, he received, according to a correspondent for the London *Times*, "such an ovation as has seldom been offered to any monarch in ancient or modern times." "Renfrew" and his party had traveled across New Jersey by train, and at Perth Amboy they boarded the revenue cutter *Harriet Lane*, named after the bachelor President Buchanan's niece and hostess, for the final leg of their journey to what, even then, was called the "Empire City." Gen. Winfield Scott, the great hero of the Mexican War and the commander of the U.S. Army, received them. New York dignitaries crowded the deck. Lord Lyons hovered near the royal, while Bunch faded into the background and, one can surmise, spent some of his time talking to reporters.

Robert Bunch, who knew New York City well, had been worried from the first moment he heard of the planned visit. The Irish could be a particular problem, and as for the mayor and his cronies, they were "common scoundrels," Bunch warned. He had watched the operations of the city's rival political machines up close when he was deputy consul there. He was back in New York every year, surrounded by talk of Mayor Fernando Wood's violence and corruption, which were extraordinary even by the standards of the time. Wood was a man not just of the street but of the gangs. His great supporters were the Dead Rabbits and others in the slums around Five Points. In 1857, rival police forces—the incredibly venal Municipals loyal to Wood, and the Metropolitans, more or less loyal to his Republican rivals—fought pitched battles against each other while they let the infamous mobs run wild. "It would be taken as a very poor compliment were the Prince turned over to the civilities of such a set of blackguards as the New York City Fathers are," said Bunch.

Bunch's reservations about the likely scene in New York City were echoed in several American papers, including the *New York Herald*, and were duly picked up by the British press to such an extent that the correspondent of the London *Times* eventually complained about the "constant succession of coarse articles" that depicted New Yorkers as "little better than a horde of savages" and conjured visions of the prince in an open coach "tossed like a little boat upon the surges of a violent, irrepressible, rough, half-drunken mob, all trying to shake hands with him and clamber into the carriage at once."

But now, here was the prince, and here was Bunch, and here were many unsavory city fathers, and all were slowly but steadily approaching Manhattan. As soon as the *Harriet Lane* left the docks in New Jersey, the royal party sat down to an opulent luncheon of oyster soup, meat and game dishes cooked with a great deal of lard and truffles, plus a variety of meringues, charlottes, and cakes for dessert. There were also ample libations, and the young prince was keeping pace with the best of them. An English reporter writing for the *New York World* thought he looked "decidedly rickety—shaky on the legs" but "didn't put it in the paper, thinking doing so would be in bad taste."

It was nearly two o'clock before the city came into view: a long, low, interminable mass of redbrick houses; the skyline was dominated in those days not by buildings but by the masts of the many tall ships in the harbor. As the steamer came into sight of the wharf, the guns from the shore batteries fired off a salute, shrouding the waterfront in clouds of white smoke. Slowly the prince and his party aboard the ship began to make out the dense swarms of people on the shore: they were on the tops of walls and peering out of windows, climbing up the masts and yardarms of the ships, clinging to the branches of trees, all seemingly in motion, waving hats and handkerchiefs, cheering and clapping, creating what one correspondent remembered as a "hoarse, undulating roar" as they greeted the British royal. Flags and banners were strung above the road, handkerchiefs fluttered like a vast fringe above the crowd, and hats flew into the air amid shouts of "Welcome to New York!" and, yes, "God save the Queen!"

The slave traders of New York, whose offices were only a few blocks away from the prince's parade up Broadway, did not stop their business for the royal reception. That same week a notorious broker of slave ships for the Cuba trade, John A. Machado, sent a bark called the *Mary Francis* on its way to Africa. And on October 10, 1860, the day before the prince sailed from Perth Amboy to Manhattan, the American gunship *San Jacinto* went after the hermaphrodite brig *Bonita* off the west coast of Africa in what became the "longest successful chase of a laden slaver ever made by an American cruiser." The *Bonita*, like the *Wanderer* and the *Clotilda*, was relatively small and very fast, but she was heavy with 622 Africans crammed on board. After more than three hours, the *San Jacinto* steamed close enough to fire warning shots just behind the *Bonita*'s stern, and she came around. The mostly Spanish crew went on board the *San Jacinto* and were sent for trial to New York.

But all the slave-trade news breaking with metronomic regularity in the pages of the *New York Times* and forwarded punctually to the Slave Trade Department did nothing to diminish the excitement around the royal spectacle.

It wasn't the disaster that Bunch had expected, but, then, neither was the bonhomie meant to last.

IN ALBANY A few days later, William Seward was probably drunk at the dinner for the Prince of Wales and his entourage. He'd been out campaigning in Michigan—campaigning for Lincoln, which wasn't easy for a proud, defeated man like Seward. He'd smoke his cigars and drink his whiskey, and he'd do his gunslinger stance on stage, his hands deep in his pockets. "Are you in *earnest?*" He'd soak up the applause like a dog being stroked. And then he'd tell his listeners what he believed and what they wanted to believe. At one point Seward said that, sure enough, Canada would be part of the United States one day. He'd said such things before, but this was not, certainly, the wisest thing to be quoted saying when you are about to have dinner with the Prince of Wales and his party. When Seward arrived at the home of New York governor Edward Morgan that October evening, everyone there had read his remark, and the air was thick with suspicion. Not a good time for another drink, but probably, for Seward, an irrepressible time.

Seward spied the Duke of Newcastle, a former Secretary of War, who was hard not to recognize with his full red beard and face redder still. They'd met the year before on Seward's goodwill European tour and had had a perfectly civil conversation. But, of course, then everyone had thought Seward would be the next president. Even so, Seward figured he knew these people. He had met Queen Victoria and her husband, Prince Albert. He had been received at the homes of Lord Russell and Lord Palmerston. He knew their inclinations and their concerns, and he understood that they would not want to intervene in an American war on the side of slavery, although some of them—Seward had no doubt about it—might hope the Union would break apart quietly. This, Seward assured Newcastle, would not be the case. The Union would fight secession, and, moreover, if it had to, it would fight any power that supported secession.

William Seward, as he had done so often before, seemed to play with the notion of war as if it were a parlor game, as if Britain could be insulted publicly and then he could just wink and nod and turn away. A flabbergasted, furious Newcastle remembered Seward telling him that "he would make use of insults to England to secure his position in the States, and that I must not suppose that he meant war. On the contrary, he did not wish war with England, and he was confident we should not go to war with the States."

This war-no-war game of Seward's by this time was all too familiar territory to British diplomats and consuls. Maybe after a decade of threatened conflagrations over Central America, over recruiting soldiers for the Crimea, over that pig on San Juan Island, and, yes, over supposed British insults to the American flags that, in fact, protected notorious slave ships, the rabble-rousers really did think they could threaten war against the greatest naval power on earth with impunity. But they were striking poses very close to the edge of an abyss. Palmerston would not want to support the slave-owning South, yet if he was goaded too often by Yankee truculence, he might very well turn on the North, and the Union would be finished. That was one reason Bunch, helped by Lyons, kept up the steady drumbeat of reports about the pro-slave-trade crusade of Spratt and Rhett and others. The fire-eaters' insistence on reopening the commerce in human beings straight from Africa would stick in Palmerston's craw and perhaps make him pause before lashing out at a Northern incendiary such as Seward.

In any case, at the precise moment of the Prince of Wales's visit in 1860, during that dinner in Albany on the last leg of Bertie's happy sojourn in North America, war between the United States and Britain seemed a remote possibility. Nobody but Seward appeared to be thinking about it, just then, much less talking about it. To use such language at a dinner for the prince was highly inappropriate. But Seward, it seemed, just could not help himself, and that did not bode well.

Chapter 23

"TODAY IS TO DECIDE THE question of Lincoln or no Lincoln," Robert Bunch wrote to Lord Lyons on November 6, Election Day, 1860. The Charleston consul was still in New York, perhaps fearful, as he said, of the fevers that continued to rage along the South Carolina coast, perhaps fearful of the fever in the minds of the men there, or, maybe, just tired of the predictable insanity of it all. "My people are stark staring mad, and in the present temper I should be surprised at nothing they might do," he said. But if anyone knew what was coming, Bunch did.

The results of the election reached Charleston four days after the vote. People poured out of their homes and offices clamoring for immediate secession, calling for the creation of a great Southern Confederacy. A huge red flag waved above Broad Street with a yellow palmetto on it, the symbol of South Carolina, and a lone star, for independence. Judge A. G. Magrath, who had handed down the infamous decisions in the *Wanderer* case and the *Brothers* case, declared that the Federal court over which he presided could no longer sit, because the Federal government no longer had jurisdiction in his country.

Bunch did not think there would be a lot of challenges to British interests at first. Quite the contrary: "I suppose the line will be for the South to love us very much." Even so, he suggested, somewhat to Lyons's dismay, that "it might be well for us to have a ship of war, of small draught of water, in our neighborhood during these troubles." If South Carolina tried to impose new duties or other restrictions on British vessels, that would be an issue for Her Majesty's government, and, "I should be greatly aided by the presence of one of H.M.'s ships." He might also have been thinking of his personal safety.

By the time Bunch wrote directly to Lord Russell in London

on November 10, Charleston was thoroughly inflamed with rebellious sentiment. "A state of things has arisen since the election of Mr. Lincoln very nearly akin to a Revolution," Bunch said, probably knowing how little Russell liked that word. Bunch hoped South Carolina would at least wait until the Republicans committed some outright act of aggression "before it commits itself to a course which cannot fail to result in its humiliation and disgrace," but he thought it just as likely that the state would provoke the Federal government and leave it with no choice but to respond with force. "The violent agitation which has prevailed throughout the State of South Carolina during the last fortnight," wrote Bunch, "seems to increase day by day in intensity." In South Carolina and Georgia hundreds volunteered to be "Minute Men," ready, like the legendary militias of the American Revolution, to fight at a moment's notice. Mobs descended on anyone accused of "uttering abolition sentiments." Edmund Ruffin, Virginia's grand old man of secession, arrived in Charleston to celebrate. Leonidas Spratt, irrepressible, addressed a crowd of hundreds at the Charleston Hotel.

A couple of days later Bunch followed up with another "brief summary" to Lord Russell about "the feeling of hatred to the North, which has been steadily growing ever since it became evident that the rule and power of the South were rapidly vanishing before the superior population, wealth, industry, and enlightenment of the Free States."

The people of South Carolina and other slave states, Bunch said, had convinced themselves that their very lives were at risk if they remained part of the Union. Many would acknowledge that Lincoln's election was fair, but with their fears of "servile insurrection" constantly fanned by what they read of William Seward and other Republicans, "they contend that the question is no longer [of] one's logic, but of existence, and that the instinct of self-preservation renders it impossible for them to recognize a Ruler whom they believe to be pledged to their destruction." Bunch understood their concerns and wanted to make sure Lord Russell did, as well. But just as soon as Bunch was back on the ground in South Carolina, he continued using the issue of slavery and the slave trade to undermine the Southerners' cause.

The outgoing governor of South Carolina, William H. Gist, sent a message to the legislature as it began its session in late November that gave Bunch a perfect chance to illustrate the sentiments that prevailed. He dissected the address word by word. Gist talked about encouraging direct trade with Britain and Europe, cutting New York out of the picture. But that was "nothing particularly new," and there was no mention of where the "enterprise and capital" might come from to make that happen. Bunch knew there wasn't any. Gist wanted to roll back even those very limited rights that black men and women might hope for. In Charleston, particularly, free blacks worked in small commerce and in crafts, and slaves often were hired out by their masters to do skilled labor—or they earned their own money and paid their masters a share. Gist wanted to do away with all that, in a "system of slavery," Bunch wrote, that was meant "to keep the man of color, for all time and to all purposes, as a hewer of wood and drawer of water, without rights as a human being and without the power of raising himself in the social scale by ability, industry, or good conduct." The threat and the promise of secession were bringing out all that was worst in Southern thinking.

Then there was the matter of the Federal forts in Charleston Harbor, Moultrie and Sumter, which Gist said would have to be surrendered by the Federal government, even as he called on the people of South Carolina to take up arms. Bunch underlined several passages in red pencil, including one toward the end of the message, where Gist said that if the forts were not surrendered, it would mean a fight to the death. Hyperbole was helping to drive the country toward war, and Gist gave a fine example of it. South Carolina, he said, would "infinitely prefer annihilation to disgrace."

Bunch's final word on Gist's message: "I have no hesitation in saying that, in the present excited condition of the public mind, an opportunity for the shedding of blood would be eagerly welcomed."

What Bunch did not say, but certainly knew, is that he was always just one discovered dispatch away from the risk that the blood shed would be his. Long ago Crampton had thought the mails were not secure enough to get a dispatch to William Mure in New Orleans. And though Bunch could take some comfort in the security of the diplomatic pouch, he could never be sure of the lengths to which his paranoid neighbors might go as war drew nearer. Over the years Bunch had known of white men beaten, tarred and feathered, and ridden on rails. He had written dispatches about all that. Now the public mood was still more dangerous. The mob was looking for people to hate, and there was no hatred as intense as what the mob felt when it felt betrayed.

Bunch had never set out to portray himself as a brave man, and probably he was not. He never had been or tried to be a soldier. The greatest risks he took as part of his consular duties through most of the Charleston years had been the rescue now and then of a black British subject unfairly thrown into one of the prisons of the Carolinas. He had guarded his tongue as best he could, and he had built a life of relative creature comfort by ignoring in public and even among his in-laws the abuses of a system he attacked constantly in his official dispatches and private and confidential letters. But in a society whose leaders talked of preferring annihilation to disgrace—*annihilation*, what a word!—the madness he had half-joked about in the past truly had taken over. Irony could no longer protect Robert Bunch from what lay ahead.

T HE SOUTHERNERS NEEDED TO DECIDE who were their enemies and who were their friends. The enthusiastic secessionists brandishing the Palmetto Flag wanted fervently to believe that
Great Britain would be more than a friend—that it would be their
ally. Many assumed it had to be their ally because of the cotton
question. But now that South Carolina was about to declare itself
an independent republic, as everyone knew, the leaders of secession
needed more than assumptions about British behavior; they needed
assurances. Which is how it came to pass that in early December
Charleston's most famous fire-eater, Robert Barnwell Rhett, paid a
visit to Bunch's home to talk about "commercial relations."

Not since 1852, before his resignation from the U.S. Senate, had
Rhett held such sway with the citizens of South Carolina. When
moderation remained the watchword through the middle of the decade, the fire-eater rhetoric of Rhett and his sons had fallen from
favor, and the radical banner passed to more original firebrands,
such as Leonidas Spratt, or those with stronger backing to the West,
such as William Yancey. But with the tympani of war growing ever
louder, subscriptions to the *Charleston Mercury* rose, and Rhett's
scorched-earth exhortations were echoed on the lips of many of
his Southern countrymen. He could see for himself a role, now, as
a great statesman of the South, perhaps the president of what he
called "a great Slaveholding Confederacy." But unlike the "coop-
erationists" throughout the South, who believed a united front of
Southern states was necessary for secession to succeed, Rhett figured prominently among those who called for "separate action"—if
one powerful state took the lead, other states would soon follow.
He and his allies would consult with prominent figures from other
states, but they put South Carolina at the head of the charge. The
Secession Convention scheduled in Columbia in just a few weeks

would spell the beginning of the end of the Union and the true beginning of Robert Barnwell Rhett's new nation.

So when Rhett knocked on Consul Bunch's door to ask about commercial relations between the South and Britain, he was not asking theoretical questions.

How hard it must have been for Bunch to open that door. With the possible exception of Leonidas Spratt, there was no prominent figure in Carolina politics for whom Bunch felt more distaste than Rhett, the thin-lipped, thin-skinned "Mr. Smith" who affected an aristocratic British heritage.

Rhett's hunger for nullification and secession were avowed and abiding, but his family organ, the *Charleston Mercury*, had been less than enthusiastic about the pivotal issue of the slave trade with Africa. Rhett's old-money supporters were among those didn't want to see their expensive human livestock devalued by cheap African imports, and Rhett had thought there were other paths to secession that might work better. Now that the path was wide open, Bunch wanted to test Rhett's mettle on the question he thought could and should kill the future of the Confederacy while it was still in the cradle.

When the initial pleasantries were over, the conversation started as if it were almost a discussion of technicalities, with Rhett the self-important statesman condescending to Bunch the mere consular officer. Rhett asked Bunch how he thought Britain would act if ships arrived in its ports that came from the seceding states but that did not have clearances from the customs collectors of the Federal government—assuming, of course, the Federal government didn't object to their sailing and wasn't going to "coerce the Seceders back into the Union."

"Is that what you believe will happen, Senator?"

"The course most likely to be pursued by the President is that he will not acknowledge the right of a State to secede as an abstract question, but, practically, he will not interfere with it for doing so."

Robert Bunch, Her Majesty's consul in Charleston, South Carolina, around 1860. The original was published as a *carte de visite* by Quinby & Co., which had a branch on King Street. From the collection of the Charleston Historical Society

Charleston, South Carolina, in January 1861. Militia are marching down Broad Street. The Palmetto flag flies about the Exchange. Fort Moultrie and Fort Sumter lie at the mouth of the harbor. This and other images from *Harper's Weekly* courtesy American Library in Paris

Engraved detail of a portrait that Thomas Sully painted of Queen Victoria in 1838 when she was eighteen years old and had recently ascended the throne. He gave an original full-length version of this painting to Charleston's St. Andrew's Hall where, over the years, the monarch gazed down on cotillions and, finally, the birth of the Confederacy. © National Portrait Gallery, London

George William Frederick Villiers, 4th Earl of Clarendon, who was Foreign Secretary during Robert Bunch's early years in Charleston and one of his key supporters. This portrait was published somewhat earlier, in 1847.
© National Portrait Gallery, London

Henry John Temple, 3rd Viscount Palmerston, as he appeared in 1857, during his first term as Prime Minister. He made the fight against the African slave trade one of his great causes.
© National Portrait Gallery, London

Foreign Secretary John Russell, 1st Earl Russell, in 1861 as the American Civil War began. © National Portrait Gallery, London

Overleaf: William Makepeace Thackeray's traveling companion, Eyre Crowe, sketched a slave sale near the Exchange in Charleston in 1853 and published this engraving in 1854. A British soldier, George Ranken, was there as well, and wrote about the sale afterward: "The scene, of course, was most painful, humiliating, and degrading. I became quite affected myself, and was obliged to hurry away, for fear of showing what I felt." From the collection of the New York Public Library

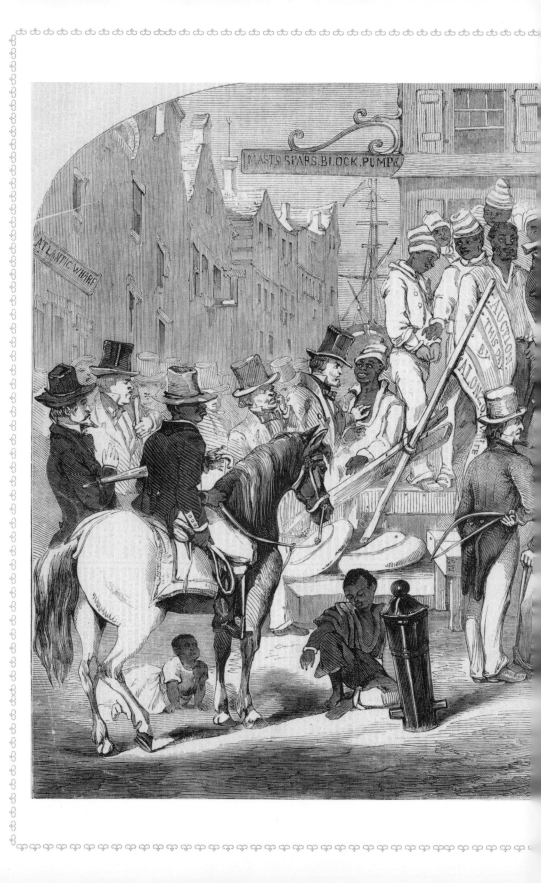

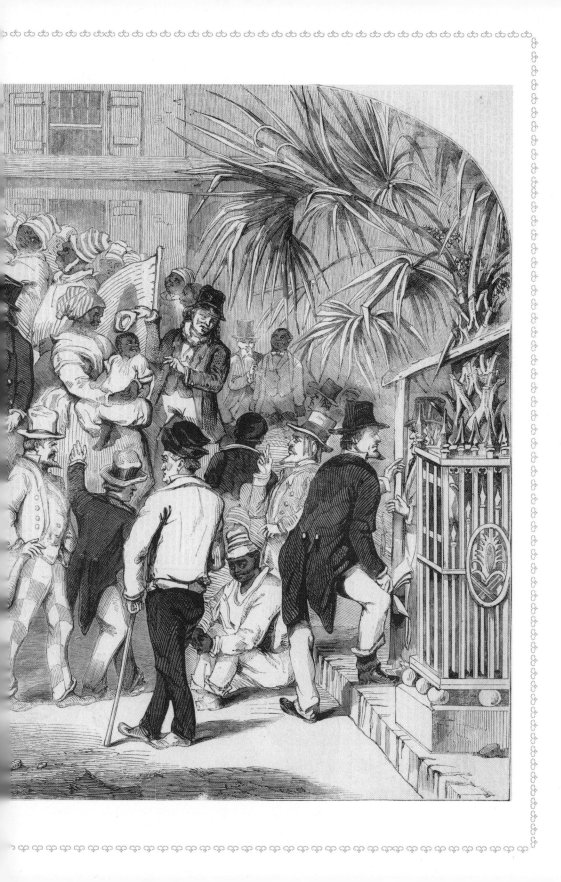

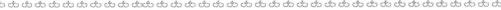

Left: Consul Bunch admired British adventurer Hugh Forbes, who fought alongside Garibaldi in Italy, penned a manual on guerrilla warfare, and tried to train John Brown's insurrectionists. Forbes's betrayal of Brown tainted his reputation, but his report to the British Anti-Slavery Society matched Bunch's dispatches point by point. Library of Congress *Right:* William Seward soon after he became Lincoln's Secretary of State in April 1861, the month in which the Civil War began. Seward would become Bunch's nemesis, unaware that he and Bunch shared the same loathing for the slavocracy. *Harper's Weekly*

The yacht *Wanderer,* built along the lines of the great racing and pleasure vessels of the time, was used to bring some four hundred African captives to Georgia in 1858, breaking—and eventually defying—federal law. More than one hundred other captives on the ship had died during the voyage. *Harper's Weekly*

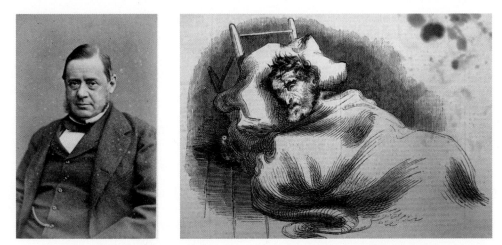

Left: Richard Bickerton Pemell Lyons, Lord Lyons, who served as Her Majesty's minister to Washington from 1859 to 1865, before and during the Civil War. Lyons defended his consul when Seward's spies accused Bunch of Confederate sympathies. This photograph was taken in the 1870s during Lyons's long tenure as the British ambassador to France. © National Portrait Gallery, London
Right: The abolitionist John Brown, wounded and a prisoner, after his attack on the federal arsenal at Harpers Ferry, Virginia, in October 1859. *Harper's Weekly*

Delegates to the Democratic Convention leaving the Charleston Hotel on the morning of April 23, 1860, to attend the opening ceremonies. The breakup of the Democratic Party that followed a few days later, which Bunch had predicted more than one year before, effectively handed the election to "the Black Republicans" and made the secession of South Carolina and several other slaveholding states inevitable. Bunch called it "a frightful fiasco." *Harper's Weekly*

William Howard Russell, correspondent for the London *Times*. He had covered the Crimean War and the Indian uprising, and his global reputation preceded him. His honest coverage of the North and the South during the first year of the war earned him the hatred of both sides. After a long dinner party hosted by Bunch, Russell was fed up with what he saw as Southern arrogance. "You won't mind it when you get as accustomed to this sort of thing as I am," Bunch told him. © National Portrait Gallery, London

The interior of Fort Sumter during the bombardment that began the war in April 1861. When the Union forces surrendered on April 13, Bunch wrote, "So far as I can learn, not one soul has been hurt on either side, which after 33 hours bombarding is a little curious. But we live in curious times." *Harper's Weekly*

"Indeed? And the customhouses and forts?" Bunch was asking the questions now.

"He will surrender them upon receiving official word that the State has left the Union. Under these circumstances," Rhett continued, "foreign nations would be at perfect liberty to consider the secession as an accomplished fact and to use their own discretion as to recognizing or making treaties with the new state."

"Senator," said Bunch, "I am not in possession of the sentiments of Her Majesty's government upon such a subject, and so I cannot really pronounce any opinion about it." But, of course, Bunch went on and did pronounce an opinion he hoped would draw Rhett out. "To my mind," he said, "a great deal will depend upon the views of secession taken by the president and by Congress, which will in great measure serve as a guide for foreign nations." Suggesting these matters would be up to Washington to decide was a direct provocation, and it worked.

Rhett quickly came to the point. He expected the cotton states to form a Confederacy within the next sixty days, and he wanted to make it clear that "the wishes and hopes of the Southern states centered in England"; that they would prefer an alliance with her to one with any other power; that they would be her best customer; that free trade would form an integral portion of this scheme of government, with import duties of nominal amount and "direct communication by steam between the Southern and British ports."

Rhett had come to believe, along with many of his cohorts, that recognition from foreign powers—the more quickly, the better— was essential to the survival of any incipient Confederacy. And so in his conversation with Bunch he was not shy as he tried to hit every point of possible leverage. "I hope," he continued, "that with Great Britain dependent upon the South for cotton and the South upon her for manufactured goods and shipping, an interchange of commodities would lead to an unrestricted intercourse of the most friendly character."

Bunch knew this script by heart. He had heard it at the Jockey Club, at the St. George's, in the grandstands at the races, in the drawing rooms of polite society, and in the market stalls near the port. This was the boilerplate of secession, and to a seceder's way of thinking, its logic was ineluctable. All Bunch had to do was raise an eyebrow or remain silent for an extra second, and Rhett would just keep going, saying more, perhaps, than he should.

"Now, I'm not obscuring the fact that the feeling of the British public is against the system of slavery," Rhett went on, "but I don't see any reason at all why this sentiment should stand in the way of commercial advantages. Great Britain trades with Brazil, which is a slaveholding country, and Great Britain is, moreover, the largest customer of the Southern states for the productions of slave labor."

Bunch sat back and listened, smiling, perhaps, enigmatically. With all the finesse he could muster, he started moving Rhett toward the critical issue.

"Let me be explicit," said Bunch. "I have no authority to speak on behalf of Her Majesty's government, so any remarks I might make here would be strictly my own. We're talking about this as friends, you and I, nothing more. But as far as I can judge, there seems to be no reason why your ideas shouldn't be carried into practice. Great Britain has a great interest in the success of free trade and is a firm believer in its benefits. If the South wants to carry out this idea and perhaps open its coastal trade to British ships, I think that such a movement would be perfectly acceptable to the British people.

"As for the question of domestic slavery," Bunch continued, throwing plenty of chum into the water before he set the hook, "I really see no reason to expect the British public to interfere with it, since it's a matter with which they have no direct concern. Of course, they could wish that their own example might influence the South in its judgment of the moral wrong of such a system of labor, but beyond this, they're not likely to go. But—there is one point you haven't touched on, and it appears to me to offer a difficulty of considerable magnitude. I would really like to have your opinion about it."

Perhaps Rhett was expecting this moment. Certainly he should have been.

"I am talking," said Bunch, "about the African slave trade, which Great Britain views with horror and which, as far as I've been informed, is likely to be tolerated if not encouraged by the new Confederation. In my own personal opinion, Great Britain would require from that Body some very distinct assurance of a satisfactory nature on this subject before she could be brought to enter cordially into communication with this Confederation."

The old fire-eater bristled. Probably he sensed a trap. But Robert Barnwell Rhett was not a man to hold back on a matter of principle, and he was not going to hide his true feelings from this impudent British consul. Suddenly the conversation became a declamation.

"No Southern State or Confederacy will ever be brought to negotiate upon such a subject," said Rhett. "To prohibit the Slave Trade would be virtually to admit that the institution of slavery is an evil and a wrong, instead of, as the South believes, a blessing to the African Race and a system of labor appointed of God."

AFTER HIS TALK with the great fire-eater, Bunch sent a brief word to Lyons, just to make sure he took notice: "I think that Your Lordship will be interested in the account of Mr. Rhett's pow-wow with me, and I trust that you will concur with me in the impression that Lord J. Russell ought to know of it."

Indeed, when Bunch sent a confidential dispatch detailing the conversation, the Foreign Secretary did take notice, and so did Prime Minister Palmerston. Bunch had read him well. A cryptic, hand-scrawled note interleaved in the bound consular dispatches from the end of December 1860 addresses the Bunch letter directly. It is signed, simply, *P* and makes clear once again where the British government generally, and Palmerston individually, drew the red line on slavery. "The example of Brazil and of Spain and of Portugal shew that an engagement to abolish Slave Trade is not incompatible as Mr. Rhett asserts it to be with the maintenance of slavery within the territory of a state."

The South might keep its slaves as it tried to woo Great Britain, but it would have to agree not to bring new ones from Africa. And Bunch had gotten Rhett to say that was impossible.

Chapter 25

A S HER MAJESTY'S CONSUL SAW Rhett to the door, Charleston was running on pure adrenaline. Secession was inevitable, and maybe war, although many hoped the confrontation would not come to that. But teetering on the edge of the unknown left people with the sensation that anything could happen at any moment. Bunch's friend, the old lawyer James Petigru, who seemed to be the last unrepentant Unionist in the state, called the legislature in Columbia an asylum "full of lunatics."

One evening Bunch followed a military band parading through the streets and saw it stop at the house of a young lawyer he considered a friend. The band struck up a tune and demanded the attorney come out and give a speech. "The amount of balderdash and rubbish which he evacuated about mounting the deadly breach, falling back into the arms of his comrades, and going off generally in a blaze of melodramatic fireworks, really made me so unhappy that I lost my night's rest," Bunch wrote in a private note.

In their moments of exaltation the secessionists saw themselves reliving the legendary American Revolution, when the colonies separated themselves from British tyranny. Apparently oblivious to the reaction of the allies they now needed badly, they reinstated "Evacuation Day," commemorating the date, December 14, when the British military had pulled out of Charleston seventy-eight years before. "The tea has been thrown overboard," exulted none other than Robert Barnwell Rhett; "The revolution of 1860 has been initiated."

All the while fear ran through the streets alongside triumphalism, especially the enduring fear of a "servile insurrection." Every black in Charleston came under suspicion, including the mulattoes, who'd enjoyed special standing, and free tradesmen, who now had to produce proof they were not slaves or risk becoming ones. Federal forts at the entrance to the harbor—Johnson, Moultrie, and

Sumter—loomed through the winter mists like specters of war. They must surrender, it was said, it was stated, it was shouted. A rumor started that the regular mail steamer from New York would bring six hundred Federal troops to shore up the bastions of Union authority. The news spread like wildfire, and volunteers scrambled to the port to load a few old guns onto a merchant ship. They figured they'd sail to the mouth of the harbor and stop the mail steamer there so it couldn't land any troops.

"Fortunately," Bunch wrote to Russell, "someone had sufficient sense to telegraph to the North for information." The rumor was nothing more than that. But if the story had been true, and if the Carolinians had tried to execute their impetuous plan, there wasn't much question that a war would have begun, no matter how much President Buchanan wanted to avoid one as he waited, with fearful impatience, for the end of his responsibilities. "I am disposed to contemplate any event as possible," said Bunch.

IN THE FOG before war, as Consul Bunch gathered intelligence, he looked to his most reliable sources for the kind of information that would help him feel his way forward. And among his many contacts in Charleston, he thought of the lawyer and historian William Henry Trescot as particularly interesting and, indeed, as a friend, even though he knew him to be a calculating secessionist. Trescot's arguments were meticulously reasoned and well informed; he was extraordinarily well connected; and this little man with intense, bright eyes was roaring good company. Mary Chesnut, wife of the senator, and private chronicler of the dawning Confederacy, loved to be scandalized by him. "I do not write to Trescot because he was too 'Frenchy' in some of his anecdotes to me," she told her diary.

Charleston was full of narrow-gauge ideologues like Rhett, but Trescot had one of the keenest minds in the country; he was the perfect exemplar of that very rare specimen, a true son of the South who truly was a man of the world. He was both a theorist and a practitioner of what later came to be called *realpolitik*. Trescot published two important histories about American diplomacy that were of special interest to those few Britons who read them. His interest was in the story of how diplomats might shape the fate of a nation or help create a new one altogether, as they'd done when they broke away from the Crown in the American Revolution and then shored up the structure of the young Republic. Armed and bloody confrontations were part of the process, and there was no use denying it. "No nation has ever yet matured its political growth without the stern and scarring experience of civil war," Trescot wrote in 1850. He did not see the United States of America as some divine invention, the self-acclaimed City on a Hill. He saw it as an experiment that had run its course, exhausted its potential. "It has achieved its destiny," wrote the secessionist intellectual, "let us achieve ours."

Yet a decade later, on the eve of the stern and scarring American Civil War, and as if out of the blue, Trescot suddenly was summoned to Washington to be second-in-command at the U.S. State Department.

The choice, on its face, was very strange. Secretary of State Lewis Cass was an ardent Unionist, ready to fight to hold the country together; Trescot was a fundamental believer in secession, ready to use any means at his disposal, especially diplomatic means, to take the country apart. But Cass was in his seventies. He was feeble, bloated, weary, and he was no favorite of Buchanan's.

Trescot wrote after the war that he did not know Buchanan or Cass personally at all, although he did have some "slight" familiarity with the power broker John Slidell. He claimed he got the appointment as assistant secretary of state because of the histories he'd written and his brief tenure in the American legation in London, but that was unlikely. Slidell and Buchanan wanted a go-between to help them deal with South Carolina, one way or the other. There was a Georgian in the cabinet, Buchanan's very close friend Howell

Cobb at Treasury, and a Virginian, Secretary of War John B. Floyd. Slidell, the power behind Buchanan's throne, could speak for Louisiana. But South Carolina was at the incendiary core of secession, and Buchanan wanted a direct line of communication. So, almost as soon as Trescot arrived in Washington in June, Buchanan made him acting secretary of state, and quickly brought him into his inner circle. Trescot then kept South Carolina's secessionists—and Robert Bunch—informed with his particular views of what went on in Buchanan's confused and divided cabinet.

On December 7, 1860, Trescot passed through Charleston for a few hours on his way from Columbia, where he'd been meeting with state officials, to Washington, where he was still a de facto member of the cabinet despite impending secession. While waiting for the steamer to take him north, he briefed Bunch on what was happening in both the state capital and the nation's capital. In Washington, Secretary of War Floyd "thought secession unwise and dissolution unnecessary." Floyd believed "the Black Republican triumph only temporary and that their success would be their destruction." But Floyd sympathized with the right of states to secede and agreed that they'd been provoked by the North. Buchanan himself agreed with Floyd that the Republicans had won a victory bigger than they could handle, but he didn't believe the South really wanted to divide the country, and he figured South Carolina would be left on its own. Based on this assumption, Buchanan had issued a long statement on December 3 in which he said, essentially, that he would not use force to hold the Union together. Trescot, who had spent the last six months working in close collaboration with Buchanan, told his friend Bunch—his friend the Queen's consul—that the president's address should be understood by other nations as "an official notification that the Union was dissolved and they might recognize [this] as soon as they pleased."

Trescot was playing Bunch, and Bunch listened patiently, weighing every word. He and Trescot had known each other for a long time. Trescot told Bunch that in his pocket he had his formal appointment as the commissioner of South Carolina to Washington who would bear official notification of secession, but he expected something more than that. Trescot told Bunch confidentially, of course, that he was considering a position as South Carolina's commissioner to England but that he was not interested in representing just one state and having Lord John Russell laugh at him. He wanted to go representing the whole Southern Confederacy.

Bunch let Trescot know he was impressed. Then he told him about his meeting with Rhett and, especially, their conversation about the revival of the African slave trade. Trescot said flatly that he thought "no Southern Confederacy would venture to propose its renewal." Trescot was playing him again.

Chapter 26

THOMAS SULLY'S PORTRAIT OF A beautiful eighteen-year-old Queen Victoria was simply extraordinary. Her crown was resplendent with diamonds, her earrings fraught with pearls, her ermine draped over her back in such a way that promised, if she were to turn, a vision of ample décolletage. But Victoria only half turned, gazing back over her bare shoulder at those beneath her as she walked lightly up a step toward her throne, almost as if toward her bed, at once beckoning and disdaining those who might follow her. Sully, who had grown up in Charleston, gave his personal copy of the full-length portrait to the Saint Andrew's Society in 1844, and his young Victoria had watched over countless balls and cotillions in St. Andrew's Hall ever since. But on December 20, 1860, it was the would-be revolutionaries of South Carolina at their momentous Secession Convention who settled into the velvet seats of the chaperone chairs and went on with their speechifying under the monarch's unsettling eyes.

The scholar-planter David Flavel Jamison, a tall, lanky figure who looked older and more distinguished than his forty-one years, brought the proceedings to order. The 169 Carolina grandees in front of him made up a venerable, dignified assembly. As class was measured in the South, they had a great deal of it: 90 percent of them owned slaves, and almost half of them owned more than fifty. But they'd had a hard time settling down to their work. First they'd met in Columbia in the city's First Baptist Church, but an outbreak of smallpox was spreading through the capital. (Rumor had it that Northern abolitionists had contaminated a box of rags to spread the disease.) So the delegates decamped to Charleston. The trip was long and dreary in midwinter. The trains rolled through pine forests and vast cotton fields, barren now except for black desiccated stalks and a few tattered bolls, before descending gently to the Low Country marshes and the Charleston peninsula. On the afternoon of the

second day, December 18, the delegates assembled in the same Institute Hall on Meeting Street where the Democratic convention
had come apart at the seams in the heat of early summer. But that
hall would not do, finally. It was too big and cavernous. The delegates were not welcoming the public or the press, especially not
the Northern press. (Rhett's son, Robert Barnwell Rhett Jr., the
editor of the *Charleston Mercury*, warned John Bigelow, the editor
of the pro-Republican *New-York Evening Post*, that he'd better not
think about sending a reporter. "No agent or representative of the
Evening Post would be safe in coming here," Rhett told Bigelow. "He
would come with his life in his hand and would probably be hung.")
So, with no crowds to cheer them on and no reporters to race to
the telegraph office with news of their deliberations, the secession
delegates decided to hold their closed-door sessions in St. Andrew's
Hall on Broad Street.

The city was in a state of febrile celebration, and Bunch watched
with cold contempt. "I think I can manage them unless they go
quite mad," he wrote to Lyons. "Their great aim is to be recognized
by Great Britain. They try to bluster about England wanting cotton
and being obliged to get it from them (that is, from a Southern Confederacy, for no one, I suppose, is ass enough to think that South
Carolina will form an independent empire for any great length of
time). But they are not quite as confident as they profess to be, and
I always tell them not to reckon too much upon their monopoly, as
the English are a determined and not a particularly stupid people,
and if they are put to it, will certainly grow plenty of cotton in India
or elsewhere and leave them out."

It wasn't clear what remnants of the Federal government would
continue to function after secession. Would the post office remain
open? Alfred Huger couldn't be sure. Customs clearance in the
port was going to be a real mess. And the flags of vessels sailing
from Charleston—the windblown insignias essential to distinguish
friend from foe, naval vessel from buccaneer, merchantman from
slaver—were liable to be completely improvised and of dubious

legality. British authorities should expect vessels registered in South Carolina to appear in British waters "decorated with palmettos, rattlesnakes, stars, or other ornaments not yet recognized by Great Britain except as growing, living, and being in the woods or the heavens," Bunch reported.

Bunch also wondered about his own future after secession. Where would Britain's representative in Charleston, accredited by the Federal government, fit into this farce? Maybe if the separation from the Union succeeded, he could become an ambassador to the Confederacy, for better or worse. Ever the careerist, Bunch did give that some thought. Or he might lose his position altogether. If South Carolina were allowed to secede quietly, as Trescot said might be the case, then Bunch would no longer have legal standing there. But if the Federal government refused to recognize secession, then Bunch's official accreditation, his exequatur, would remain in force: the United States would still claim authority even if it couldn't exercise it, and if the local powers he'd cultivated would tolerate his presence—perhaps even think it was useful—he could continue to report to his superiors in Washington and London.

Lyons told Bunch that in Washington many men hoped the departure of South Carolina from the Union could be carried out with dignity and discretion. Bunch said he had no expectation of either quality in that "incandescent body," the Secession Convention. Then Bunch reported on the state's newly elected governor, Francis Wilkinson Pickens, who was one of those thin-lipped, potbellied South Carolina politicians Bunch wrote about with utter and intemperate disdain. Bunch told Lyons that Pickens was "a noisy, vulgar beast," no matter that Pickens was a close friend of President Buchanan, who had appointed him minister to Saint Petersburg. His notorious wig, his blustery oratory, and his "absurd pomposity of manner" made him the object of ridicule. "There has not been time yet to get the secret history of his election," Bunch wrote to Lyons after the ballot in November, "but I suppose he has sold himself to the extremists."

That much was true. Pickens was new to his office and a new-comer to the cause of secession too, but his first public message as governor, delivered to the state legislature on the first day of the Secession Convention, left no room for compromise. He rehearsed all the old arguments about the North ignoring the Constitution and inciting a "servile insurrection," then drove home the point that Carolinians—white Carolinians, at any rate—expected their government to "become strongly military in character." The meaning was clear to Bunch: "Slavery can only be maintained at the point of the sword."

"Revolutions are the order of the day," Bunch told Lyons. The papers were full of long reports about Garibaldi's triumphant march north from Sicily to Naples to join up with King Victor Emmanuel II, and many an American noted that while the Union was coming apart, Italy was coming together. But this revolution in South Carolina was different from those in Europe in an even more fundamental respect. "Other nations, especially those enlightened and more old-fashioned in their notions, rebel, fight, and die for Liberty," wrote Bunch, while South Carolina "is prepared to do the same for slavery."

AT TWO O'CLOCK in the morning on December 21, Bunch was still writing. He had fired off three dispatches, he had telegraphed Lyons immediately after the Ordinance of Secession was passed at 1:15 the afternoon of the twentieth, and he had sent London a copy of the *Charleston Mercury* Extra with the enormous headline "The Union Is Dissolved!"

"My city is wild with excitement—bells ringing, guns firing, and scarcely one man in a thousand regrets the dissolution," he told Lyons in one of the letters he wrote that afternoon. The delegates had marched down Meeting Street to Institute Hall once more. They'd opened the doors to the public so everyone could witness the signing ceremony, and Bunch slipped in, standing to one side in the shadow of a pillar. The detestable Judge Magrath, who had decided importing slaves *from* Africa was no crime if they had been slaves *in* Africa, and who had done everything he could from the Federal bench to destroy Federal authority, was the first speaker at the signing ceremony. He entered stage right and walked slowly, deliberately, to the other side, where the document waited. "Fellow citizens," he said, "the time for deliberation has passed." He pulled his handkerchief out of his pocket, and he ran it through his hand as if he were about to perform a feat of magic or, perhaps, dry the sweat from his palm. Then, as he arrived at the document, stage left, he proclaimed, "The time for action has come!" The crowd exulted as if he'd divined the Second Coming.

For two hours the ceremony went on until, finally, when the last signature was scrawled on the document by former governor Manning, whom Bunch had once thought a reasonable man, the president of the convention waved the "cabalistic parchment" over his head shouting, "The Ordinance of Secession has been signed and ratified, and I now declare South Carolina to be a sovereign and independent commonwealth." Cheers erupted once more, hats were thrown into the air, handkerchiefs waved, and at 2:00 a.m., as Bunch tried to sum up his feelings at the end of that long day, the cannons were still blasting, and the firecrackers continued to explode.

At first almost unnoticed in the midst of the celebrations, the captured slave ship *Bonita* had arrived in Charleston Harbor. More than two months had passed since she was overtaken and boarded off the Congo by the U.S. Navy steamer *San Jacinto*, the most aggressive warship in the Africa Squadron. Her original crew and the slaves had been taken off. Only her ostensible captain and the U.S. Navy crew were on board. After many weeks at sea and in the middle of a ferocious winter storm, with her sails ripped, she was in danger of sinking as she finally pulled into Charleston in the new nation of South Carolina. "Owing to the late political events, there is no court of the United States here," Bunch informed Lord Russell. "There exist no means either for trying the captain (who is still here) or of condemning the vessel. The lieutenant in charge of the prize has written to Washington for instructions on the subject."

THE SECESSION CONVENTION'S final and authoritative statement, which it fashioned with many references to the Declaration of Independence and the Constitution of the United States, was published on Christmas Eve, 1860. It concerned itself entirely and exclusively with slavery. Secession, then, was not about tariffs, as some claimed before and long after the Civil War, and the issue of states' rights came down to the very specific right of white people in some states of the former United States to own slaves, to get them back if they ran away, and, by implication, to import them from Africa as they had been imported in the early years of the Republic. The Constitution had put a time limit of twenty years on that trade, but the Constitution, as the secessionists saw it, was a contract broken by the abolitionists that no longer applied to South Carolina or any other state that followed its lead.

Although Bunch had been predicting for many years the broad outline of the events that now surrounded him, to his own surprise he regretted the demise of the Union, and he said so in one letter after another. The United States had made itself "a great fact in the history of the world," he wrote, and had done credit to the Englishmen who founded the country. In Charleston, "Everybody wears a pleased expression, as if he or others had done something very clever without knowing exactly what it was," Bunch scrawled in those dark, early-morning hours on December 21. "But I much fear it will be 'he who laughs on Friday will cry on Sunday.' I am somehow sorry for the old Union, although he was a noisy old braggart. We have yet to see whether he will find any friends at the North to avenge his death."

ARLY ON CHRISTMAS EVE AFTERNOON, Robert Bunch received an unexpected visitor. A Mr. Thomas Butler Gunn from the *New-York Evening Post* was arriving too late for the Secession Convention's most dramatic act, but his editor, John Bigelow, had decided the story was too big to heed the warning of Robert Barnwell Rhett Jr. Gunn was taking his life in his hands, but he figured he'd have some added protection because he was, as many of his countrymen in America were inclined to say just then, "an Englishman thoroughly grateful for his British accent." Before Gunn left New York, he even went to the British consul there, the efficient Edward Mortimer Archibald, to get what he called "a quasi-passport to the South," and one of the first stops he made the day after he dropped his bags at the Charleston Hotel was down "on Meeting Street towards the Battery, the aristocratic end of it," to have that document countersigned "gratis" by Her Majesty's consul in South Carolina.

Bunch's home office was "an exceedingly British-looking apartment," Gunn wrote in his diary, "with portraits of the Queen, Prince Albert, the Prince of Wales, sketches of noble heads, and a large engraving of the coronation." About Bunch himself there was an air of inconspicuousness, even invisibility: he was "slim" and appeared "elderly," although he was only forty at the time. Gunn could not have known, of course, how difficult the last seven years had been. He saw Bunch as a "neatly shaved man attired in gray, with a tendency to baldness." When Gunn first entered, Bunch was "fussing about" trying to attach a little gilded version of the Prince of Wales crest, three feathers emerging from a coronet, above Bertie's portrait. Bunch said he'd gotten it in New York and mentioned that he'd been on the *Harriet Lane*, then gave up his fussing, put the crest away, and sat down to talk.

The two men quickly discovered that they enjoyed each other's company. Gunn found Bunch a "chatty, diplomatic, amusingly British person in manner, speech, and opinions." Bunch confided to Gunn, as the heir to the throne had, perhaps, confided to him, that Bertie might further his worldly education with a visit to the South and to the West Indies. (Bunch probably did not say how much that prospect horrified him.) The consul told tales of serving at several South American posts and regaled his new acquaintance with stories about his seven long years in South Carolina that left the reporter "half-laughing" for most of the time they were together.

For his part, Gunn had set out for Charleston on the side-wheeler *Marion*. His fellow passengers had included Southern medical students headed home to join regiments, an eccentric old sea captain who'd been to the Arctic and who now wrote pro-secession poetry, and an evil-looking dentist whose conversation Gunn summed up in a single sentence: "We have paid for our niggers, and we are going to keep 'em, by God!" It was a long trip.

"The first news that awaited us on landing was that we were 'out of the United States,'" Gunn told Bunch, who was slightly bemused. The reporter was not much impressed by what he saw of Charleston. "It looks like a small, old-fashioned New York," he said. Gunn had ridden on top of the coach taking him to the Charleston Hotel, and as he looked around on that Sunday afternoon, the little city was dead quiet.

For Gunn and for other British journalists from the North who had come down to cover secession, Her Majesty's man in South Carolina became a favorite source and an indispensable friend on the lonely and treacherous streets of Charleston. For Bunch, these visitors served several purposes and, in a few cases, posed serious risks. Some of them might have been spies, although for whom was never entirely clear. Some worked for publications that were rabidly hostile to the slaveholding South and reported under false names. Bunch entertained them, informed them; when possible he protected them. But he also used them. Through his journalist contacts and friends, he could filter out to the rest of the world his views of events in South Carolina and in the South that supported the private dispatches he was sending to Lyons and to London. Nothing amplified a diplomatic dispatch as much as a well-placed newspaper article. The only risk, and it was considerable, was that someone might reveal him as the source.

THREE DAYS AFTER Gunn's arrival, on the morning of December 27, 1860, Charleston woke to explosive news. The night before, Maj. Robert Anderson, the fifty-five-year-old commander of the Federal garrison, had transferred his entire unit out of the indefensible Fort Moultrie, moving his men in small boats so as not to attract attention, to the still-not-quite-finished Fort Sumter commanding the entrance to Charleston Harbor. Sumter was designed to be manned by more than six hundred officers and men. Anderson had only eighty-five soldiers, eight of whom were musicians. But the drums of war had picked up their pace.

At the Charleston Hotel, a blustery soldier of fortune with a wild-looking walrus mustache and a euphonious name, Maj. Roswell Ripley, hammered on the doors of anyone he could think to tell, bellowing, "By God, Bob's got 'em now. He's in Sumter, and all hell can't get him out!"

Ripley already had quite a reputation around town. He was born in Ohio, raised in New York, and his most recent employment had been in England, trying to sell Sharps rifles made in Connecticut to be used by British troops in the Crimea. But Ripley, who was graduated from West Point in 1843 and fought in most of the big battles of the Mexican War, was eager to get back into uniform. He figured, rightly, that he knew a whole lot more about soldiering, and especially about artillery, than these Carolina militia boys dressed up like French Zouaves and parading for their belles. So he'd fight and rise in rank and fight some more for Carolina or a new Confederacy. But he couldn't help admiring old Bob Anderson, the stern-looking Kentuckian who'd taught artillery at West Point and been wounded badly in the Mexican campaigns. The secret deployment to the nearly impregnable Fort Sumter was the right move—the only move—Anderson could make if he was going to hold out. He was now ensconced behind walls five feet thick with forty-two-pound guns at his disposal. All of Charleston understood the significance of his action. He did not intend to surrender peacefully. The annihilation Governor Gist had talked about might be closer than people thought.

Down on Meeting Street, meanwhile, Charleston's now-ex-member of Congress Laurence Massillon Keitt was in a state of apoplectic rage. Only a week had passed since Keitt's high spirits were on display in Washington. There he'd burst into a wedding reception attended by President Buchanan, brandishing a telegram announcing South Carolina's secession and shouting, "Thank God! Thank God!" (Buchanan thought at first there was a fire outside, and when his hostess brought him the actual news, he slumped back in his chair, and, clenching his hands on the arms, all he could think to say was, "Madam, might I beg you to have my carriage called?") Now Keitt stood outside the Mills House "blaspheming in a most energetic manner," Gunn reported.

Bunch and several of the semi-clandestine correspondents joined the crowds checking out the bulletins posted at the local newspaper offices, thereby gathering quantities of information and misinformation. Gunn dashed off a report claiming that the city was "frantic—the leading secessionists tearing their hair, and Major Anderson the hero of the occasion." (Whose hero, Gunn did not say.) Anderson had spiked the guns at Fort Moultrie, and wild rumors spread that they'd been booby-trapped to explode if anyone tried to render them serviceable again. (Untrue.) Anderson supposedly had taken "four hundred men" to Sumter (five times the number he had), with its guns that "command the harbor and the city."

Bunch had asked around about the range and the direction of Sumter's guns. He was worried for his house and his family. But Sumter was not built to attack the city; it was built to defend it and to dominate the entrance to the harbor. The effective range of its artillery was about two miles, so it wasn't likely its shells would rain down on Meeting Street; although from the top floor of Bunch's house it may have been possible to glimpse the hulking masonry of Sumter three and a half miles away and, were they to begin firing, the flash of its big guns.

For Bunch the most important news of the moment was that the secessionists were seizing all the Federal posts and property that they could. Bunch's first visit was to the U.S. Custom House, which he determined "no longer exists." The collector said henceforth all revenues would go to South Carolina. After initial hesitation, the South Carolina militias seized Fort Moultrie and, most important, the Charleston Arsenal, along with its twenty thousand firearms.

"The city is in a terrible state of excitement just now," Bunch told Lyons. If Anderson's move was "by order of the government, matters do not look pacific. It is possible, however, that the officer in command may have done it of his own accord, thinking Fort Moultrie untenable, as it certainly is. The news has only just come—the people are infuriated, and it is very likely that before this reaches Washington, Your Lordship may have heard by telegraph that an assault has been made."

In the meantime, the Secession Convention had picked three of its own grandees to go to Washington to present their terms to the Federal government. Bunch sent Lyons a quick sketch of each one: Robert W. Barnwell, "a planter of perfectly respectable character, but of no experience whatsoever in public affairs"; James L. Orr, "late speaker of the House of Representatives of the United States, a person well known at Washington, and possessed of some talent with conciliatory manners"; and "General J. H. Adams," whom Bunch had visited at Oak Hall Plantation and whom he knew all too well. Bunch described Adams without further elaboration as "late a Governor of South Carolina, a man of violent character and impulses, and an ardent advocate of the revival of the African Slave Trade."

President Buchanan agreed to meet with the three as private citizens and for two hours listened to their too-familiar justifications
for tearing the Union apart. This was an ultimatum, it seemed, not
a negotiation. But all Buchanan wanted to do at this point, and all
he could do, was leave the problem to his successor. The United
States might cease to be, but not on his watch. "You are pressing me
too importunately," said the weary president. "You don't give me
time to consider. You don't give me time to say my prayers. I always
say my prayers when required to act upon a great state affair." He
wished he could call a carriage that would take him away from all
this, but that would have to wait several more weeks until Lincoln's
inauguration put an end to his dreadful errand.

AT THE CHARLESTON HOTEL, things were getting ugly. Thomas
Butler Gunn's newfound friend Captain Colt, an agent for the
arms company that bore his family name, had a violent altercation
with one of his competitors in the business and feared that he, a
"damned Yankee," might be jumped by a mob or shot in the back.
Both Colt and Gunn started carrying pistols in their pockets (probably joking about each other's names), and they went looking for
advice to another new acquaintance, Charley Lamar, who was by
then famous far and wide as the man behind the *Wanderer*. Over
dinner and drinks in the hotel, Colt asked Lamar how he'd handle
the man threatening him. "If he gives you any trouble, call him out
and shoot him," Lamar said, as if that were the simplest thing in
the world. Such was the spirit of the times: a New York arms dealer
trying to peddle guns to the South consulting the most notorious
slaver in the country about how to confront the man who might
murder him.

"I must add here," Gunn wrote in his notes about the evening
with Lamar, "that the Charlestonians speak of the Slave Trade as
though it were an amiable weakness—a virtue pushed to excess."

. . .

JUDAH P. BENJAMIN stood to address the U.S. Senate on December 28, a cane on one side, a pistol on the other. He would sit in this chamber "now no more forever," he said, even as he rationalized with lawyerly rhetoric the position taken by the South. "We desire, we beseech you, let this parting be in peace," said Benjamin. "Indulge in no vain delusion that duty or conscience, interest or honor, imposes upon you the necessity of invading our States or shedding the blood of our people. You have no possible justification for it." Varina Davis, the wife of Jefferson Davis, remembered that Benjamin "held his audience spellbound for over an hour, and so still were they that a whisper could have been heard."

"The fortunes of war may be adverse to our arms," Benjamin declaimed, "you may carry desolation into our peaceful land, and with torch and fire you may set our cities in flame.... You may, under the protection of your advancing armies, give shelter to the furious fanatics who desire, and profess to desire, nothing more than to add all the horrors of a servile insurrection to the calamities of civil war; you may do all this—and more, too, if more there be—but you can never subjugate us."

What Benjamin did not say—publicly, at least—was that his fellow Southerners seemed intent on destroying themselves. The Buchanan government that he and Slidell had worked hard to shape was now falling apart in front of their eyes. Even before South Carolina seceded, Howell Cobb had resigned from Treasury and gone home to Georgia. General Cass tendered his resignation, then tried to withdraw it, only to have Buchanan accept it; Cass was furious that Buchanan failed to reinforce the forts in Charleston Harbor as Andrew Jackson had done three decades before. Then it was Slidell's turn to berate Buchanan: why hadn't the president said explicitly that he would *not* defend the forts? The weary head of state, his cabinet in chaos, his friends abandoning him, appeared to many a broken man.

The great irony of secession was that, if it were to be peaceful, it needed the cover given by a Federal government at least partly

sympathetic to its complaints. For all the romantic, fire-eating bellicosity of the would-be rebels, for all the martial traditions of their
slave-owning, slave-fearing society, and with all the guns they took
from Federal arsenals, they still were no match for the industrial
power of the North. Secession could be framed in the context of
war, but to succeed, it needed to be carried out in a context of complicity. A test of arms would be an invitation to disaster, and those
who knew something of the way the battlefield had changed over
the previous decade understood that perfectly well.

Benjamin was not a warrior, but he was as fascinated by tech-
nology as he was by many other subjects, and his frequent trips to
Europe gave him a chance to see just how fast the science of arma-
ments was progressing: the development of more accurate rifles firing the lethal Minié balls; the perfection of artillery with a range of
five miles or more. Benjamin understood the importance of capital
and steel when it came to winning a modern war, and the South did
not have enough of either. So his vision of the North bringing "torch
and fire" to the cities of the Confederacy was not mere rhetoric. If
the delicate process of secession went wrong, his prophecy would
become a virtual certainty.

"THINGS LOOK INDEED very serious in America," Lord Russell
wrote to Lord Lyons at the end of December in a note that betrayed
a certain lack of comprehension and a deep wish the problem would
just go away. Europe was in disarray, its delicate balances shifting.
War and rebellion swept Italy, and the French emperor kept moving his support from one contending party to another. Christians
were being massacred in Syria and Lebanon, and the only force
that would or could stand up to their Muslim attackers, strangely,
was the chivalrous old warrior from Algeria, Abd el-Kader, who'd
been exiled to Damascus by the French. The Second Opium War in
China had dragged on for four years. The Raj still suffered from the
traumas of the Sepoy Mutiny, and the Russian bear was lumbering,

as ever, toward India. The fact was, the British Empire was stretched thin, and this trouble in America was only one crisis among many.

"I don't see how the North is to bridle its tongue about slavery," Russell wrote, "but if the South does not wish secession, she may be content with a pledge that the president will not propose abolition." If Lord Russell had been reading the dispatches more closely, he'd have known that Lincoln *did not propose abolition*, and the South nonetheless *did want secession*. But he understood the bottom line in any case: "I fear there is no hope, or hardly any hope, of a compromise," said Lord Russell. "For ourselves, unless we are asked to mediate, I think we can do nothing more than deprecate collision. The South may have much to be thankful for that they have yet two months before they finally decide," that is, before Lincoln's inauguration on March 4, 1861. "I hope they will use them wisely."

Chapter 28

ROBERT BUNCH WAS IN THE eye of a storm that was about to shake the world like a Carolina hurricane. Her Britannic Majesty's consul in a small city in the American South, fighting to rectify a retrograde law that endangered a handful of black British citizens but enraged Her Majesty's government, had become the single most trustworthy source of information about a fast-approaching war with vast and as yet unimagined consequences.

He was worried for his family—probably he was terrified for them—but he also was exhilarated. He wanted to see everything. He wanted to know everything. And while he had never spent much time writing or thinking about the military, now he focused much of his attention on the deployments of the Federal Army and the soldiers of South Carolina.

Out at the entrance to Charleston Harbor, Tom Gunn's soldier-of-fortune friend Roswell Ripley now commanded some raw militias at Fort Moultrie, with his biggest guns trained on Bob Anderson at Sumter, and Anderson's bigger guns trained on him. Ripley did not give himself much chance of survival if Sumter opened up on him. "Perhaps a couple of hours, or he may blow us to hell in half that time," Ripley told Gunn.

For a few weeks the siege of Fort Sumter was oddly genteel. Charleston merchants kept the fort supplied with meat and rice, candles, oil, and other necessities. Robert and Henry Gourdin, from a prominent merchant family, kept up a running correspondence with their friend Maj. Anderson and helped him communicate with his wife and his brother. But the air of civility was deceptive. Each day held the potential for an explosion.

"Every one, old and young, is enrolled in some military company, and drilling is going on at all hours," Bunch wrote in an official dispatch to Lord Russell. "The public excitement is kept alive by the constant arrival of telegrams, many of the most absurd and mendacious character. Nothing is spoken of but bloodshed, and reasonable counsels are entirely disregarded."

On January 9, 1861, an unarmed ship sent by President Buchanan, the *Star of the West*, tried to resupply the garrison at Sumter. But in the blue-tinged light of early dawn, cadets from Charleston's famous military academy, the Citadel, spotted the ship and took a few shots with newly positioned guns on Morris Island. The *Star of the West* steamed ahead and ran up the Stars and Stripes. Then Roswell Ripley, who had been fortifying his position at Fort Moultrie, started firing on the ship. He hit it twice. The *Star of the West* retreated. No one was killed, and the guns of Sumter remained quiet—to the great disappointment of the crew aboard the *Star*, and to the considerable surprise and relief of Ripley. After that, Anderson sent an officer with a flag of truce to Governor Pickens to warn he'd prevent any ships from entering or leaving the harbor. The governor threatened to block any effort at all to resupply Sumter. The siege tightened.

"Our little teapot was ruffled yesterday by a tempestuous gale, but the wind has gone down today," Bunch wrote of the incident. "The *Star of the West* was fired into, and, very sensibly, 'turned off,' which I believe is the nautical term," he told Lord Lyons. "I consider that Major Anderson has behaved with the greatest prudence and humanity, as he would certainly have done a great—and what is more in this country, a *popular* thing—had he fired into the batteries which fired into his ship." By waiting and requesting further orders from Washington, he "gives the government another loophole of escape if they do not wish war," Bunch wrote. "But I fear that the popular feeling at the North is rising, and if General Scott 'goes to the country' with a 'cry' about the U.S. flag having been fired upon, I should fear the worst."

The *Star of the West* incident provoked a round of tense negotiations between Anderson and the new authorities in Charleston that went on for several days, and on January 13 Bunch wrote a cryptic note to Lyons. First, he wanted to let the minister in Washington know that he had mastered the new diplomatic cipher. Then he passed on an urgent, unencrypted bit of information: "I am assured . . . ," Bunch wrote, then crossed that out. "I am told," he continued, "by a person in authority that [Anderson] could not be got to fire a gun now even if ordered. Is he going to turn traitor?" Probably that bit of intelligence and speculation came from William Henry Trescot, who was proving a very dangerous sort of source: highly placed but, whether by accident or intent, very often very wrong.

Whom to trust? Where to turn? Where was the conflict headed? Bunch tried to stand back from his emotions. He had never had any sympathy with the secessionists, but now, as one state after another withdrew from the Union, its dissolution appeared a plain fact. "Each day brings us the intelligence of some secession to the Southern cause," Bunch wrote to Lord Russell. "Florida and Mississippi have certainly seceded, and I have no doubt that Alabama, Louisiana, Georgia, and North Carolina will follow." A new confederation was taking shape. It was almost impossible to imagine that Washington could recover all these territories. "Surely," Bunch wrote to Lyons, "it is madness to try to coerce the entire South."

As Robert Barnwell Rhett had foreseen, the claim that secession was done and irreversible eventually became the strongest argument the Southern states could make in the minds of Europe's leaders: they had created a fait accompli, and to try to force them back into a Union they utterly despised would be insane. But at the center of the secession, right from the beginning, the day-to-day bother of trying to do business under an erratic, cobbled-together coalition of ferociously independent states began to trivialize and undermine the ambitious project of the Confederacy.

In early January the lights in the lighthouses and the lamps in the buoys marking the channels into Charleston Harbor were extinguished to prevent hostile ships from entering at night. But, of course, all shipping was put at risk. The South Carolinians, ever fearful of invasion by the Union's Navy, kept claiming they'd sink hulks to block the passage, thus severing their own vital ties to the outside world.

As consul, one of Bunch's first responsibilities was to facilitate British trade, but commerce with the port of Charleston was just about dead. And while the military leadership of the South eventually proved impressive, the political leadership did not, especially in those early days. "Our governor, I regret to say, is a hopeless fool," Bunch wrote of Francis Wilkinson Pickens soon after the *Star of the West* skirmish. "People talk very seriously of impeaching him before the Legislatures. He is quite demented, everyone tells me— turns people out of his room by the shoulders, orders a thing at one minute and countermands it the next. It is not every one who can manage a revolution, even it if be in a teapot."

Bunch found himself, unpleasantly, dealing with Judge A. G. Magrath as South Carolina's new "secretary of state." Her Majesty's consul was careful not to use any formal title acknowledging Magrath's supposed authority, but he still had to talk to the man. After a discussion of his consular duties, as Bunch told Lyons, both Mr. Magrath and a Mr. Cilcott, the new secretary of war, "thanked me very much and expressed themselves sensible of my friendly endeavors." Bunch's "smile of indifference" must have become a rictus. "It will do no harm by and by to have been on good terms with them," wrote the ever-politic Bunch. "Secession is 'coming in so strong' that we must not be *too fond* of the U.S. government."

Mississippi, Florida, Alabama, and Georgia did, indeed, secede, and the Georgians, to the admiration of one and all in Charleston, were smart enough to take all the Federal forts before they pulled out of the Union. Louisiana seceded on January 26 and Texas on February 1. Plans were well under way for a congress to convene in Montgomery, the capital of Alabama, where a constitution would be written and a government chosen for the new Confederacy of slaveholding states.

Bunch the careerist wanted a piece of the diplomatic action. The British consul in Mobile, Charles Tulin, was a fool who spent almost no time in Alabama. His deputy, Charles Labuzan, had unvarnished slaveholding sympathies and was, thus, an unreliable reporter. Bunch may also have learned that his cousin and former boss in New York, Anthony Barclay, long since retired to a life of slaveholding leisure in Savannah, was angling to get back into diplomacy as Britain's envoy to the new Southern republic. So Bunch offered himself up to Lyons as an observer at the Montgomery convention, or, failing that, said he would send his deputy. But Lyons did not go for it. He did not suspect that Bunch had any sympathy with the South; that was never a question for him. But Bunch was such an irrepressible climber, perhaps Lyons did not want to encourage him. Or Lyons may have feared, knowing the tone of Bunch's letters, and never having seen Bunch in action in the South, that he might be indiscreet. The Charleston consul would report on the Montgomery convention from Charleston.

THE CHARLESTONIANS WERE closing ranks. News surged and then ebbed, and the out-of-town journalists in the city were beginning to feel real fear. In an anonymous dispatch to the *New-York Evening Post*, Bunch's new friend Tom Gunn wrote: "There is a system of espionage as complete as that organized by the first Napoleon. The gentlemanly stranger who, learning you are from the North, claims it as his own birthplace and sounds you with some mild Union sentiments, intimating his private conviction that 'we have gone too far here.' The barman who mixes your 'cocktail,' the colored waiter who attends assiduously upon our party at the hotel dinner and is much interested in the inevitable political conversations, the loungers in its hall or under its piazza—beware of each and all of them. Charleston is one vigilance committee."

As Gunn reported later, the more formal group of vigilantes

in Charleston included "men of all classes—planters, merchants, clerks, editors, gentlemen of independent fortunes, generally persons of standing and respectability, chosen by ballot." Different members had different functions in this "amateur detective organization" created to defend the interests of a slave-owning society. "Every Southerner believes that hired emissaries are employed by the abolitionists of the North to run off slaves, to tamper with them, to tempt them to commit murder, arson, and all conceivable atrocities," Gunn reported. More immediately relevant for him and his friends, many Southerners believed that Northern publications set out to instigate these crimes and that no pains or expenses were spared to circulate them in the South.

The vigilance committee in Charleston considered itself diligent in efforts to determine whether a suspect was accused falsely, but its operations were secret and silent. If a stranger was suspected, he was watched, and, if considered necessary, a professional detective, a Mr. Schuber, was put on his tail. Schuber would examine the suspect's baggage, question him, and then take him before members of the committee. The suspect could produce witnesses or other evidence attesting to his innocence, but if he failed to convince the committee, he'd be escorted by the detective to a railroad or steamboat, and his fare paid as far as the next stop, where "another vigilance committee, duly apprised by telegraph, is waiting for him," Gunn wrote. There, the treatment he received might not be so civilized.

When Gunn heard there was a rumor circulating in New York that he'd been tarred and feathered and ridden out of Charleston on a rail, he nearly panicked for fear someone would publish the bogus story and the people around him in Charleston, upon reading it, would make it come true. Bunch could commiserate: "A friend writes me from New York that *I* have been tarred and feathered."

If Bunch was joking, this was gallows humor.

The consul had grown increasingly worried about his basic communications with Washington and London and, more generally, the outside world. With the mails frequently disrupted, correspondence often had to be sent with informal messengers, but could they really be trusted? Many people asked or begged Bunch to find ways to get their letters out safely, most of the time for commercial reasons, and some volunteered to carry the diplomatic pouch themselves, but that was not usually an altruistic gesture. The satchel gave the bearer some authority passing through checkpoints, and often the bearer would take other bags of unofficial mail as well. It was an awkward and unreliable system. Anything could go wrong. But Bunch resorted to it time and again. He had little choice.

Chapter 29

SECESSION COINCIDED WITH THE HEIGHT of the social season in Charleston, and in 1861 the season culminated in February with the usual horse races, balls, and days and nights of carousing, just as it had every year since 1792. Normal business ceased during the Race Week celebrations, even with the threat of war hanging over the city, and there really was nothing else to do but follow the crowds to the Washington Race Course day after day.

Like any great saturnalia, the festivities of Race Week in Charleston brought together people from far and wide, from upstate and out of state; poor whites and ambitious slaves; chaste belles and beautiful harlots (as well as the not-so-chaste and the not-so-beautiful); apprentices and merchants; sailors and soldiers; planters and politicians. Attendees could see Frank Hampton, from one of the most famous families of South Carolina, riding against slave jockeys mounted on their owners' horses—may the best horses and the best jockeys win. The races were grueling and run in two, three, sometimes four successive one-mile heats. Exhausted horses got shaky. Winners suddenly became losers. The animals pulled up lame or stumbled, pitching their riders onto the turf and under the hooves of their rivals. The possibility that blood would be shed gave the races an edge of serious risk and extra excitement. Between heats, while grooms rubbed down the panting, sweating horses, the spectators placed their bets, ate and drank, drank some more, and searched for friends they might not have seen since the year before.

The Jockey Club erected a high fence around the track and charged admission, but it allowed friends of the members to come in for free. Others stayed outside and stood in their carriages to watch or looked down from the roofs of nearby houses that were turned into bars and gambling dens for the duration of the races. At the height of the festivities, thousands of people crowded inside the fence and around the perimeter, but the chosen few, including

Consul Bunch, joined the beauties and the matrons in what was called the Ladies' Clubhouse, a pavilion styled like the loggia of an Italian villa. Robert Bunch certainly seemed to be enjoying himself, but behind the scenes a serious problem fraught with very serious dangers had taken shape.

Bunch had been visited repeatedly at the consulate by a man named Russell Ramsay, an increasingly paranoid young Englishman working under ill-disguised cover for Horace Greeley's violently anti-Southern *New-York Tribune*. Ramsay, when challenged by people in Charleston, claimed to be a British businessman hoping to take advantage of South Carolina's pledge to reduce or abolish tariffs. He visited Bunch almost daily during Race Week, hoping to gather information, claiming to impart it, and just checking in. Thomas Butler Gunn had met Ramsay as well and thought him mendacious, callow, and indiscreet, a disaster waiting to happen. But in a city as small as Charleston, and in a press corps that was tiny and embattled, Gunn did not think it worth the effort to snub the young impostor.

On the Saturday of Race Week, Gunn and Ramsay planned to go out in a rented carriage. But when it came time to head to the track, Ramsay was nowhere to be seen, so Gunn went on without him. One of his acquaintances had given him the satin badge that let him inside the fence and even into the Ladies' Pavilion. Bunch was there already, with Emma and the Bunches' little girl, "looking and talking enormously British" but also seeming right at home. On occasions like this, Bunch relished his standing not only as Her Majesty's envoy, but as part of the extended family of Daniel Blake, owner of Board House and The Meadows. The aging planter and Emma's young sister, Helen, had just had their first child, the son christened Robert Bunch Blake.

But where was Ramsay? Bunch did not know. And the man never showed.

Gunn did not begin to sort out the mystery of Ramsay's whereabouts until that afternoon back at the hotel when he was taking a nap in his room. The young reporter masquerading as a merchant burst in on him, utterly frantic: "Tom, let's go to dinner, but I have to go up the street for about ten minutes. I'll be right back. Our friends mustn't wait for me," Ramsay declared. But he didn't come back. Gunn ran some errands, and when he went back upstairs, he noticed Ramsay's key in the door of his room. He knocked. He went inside. Nobody was there, and it looked as if Ramsay had been packing his trunk in considerable haste.

The next day Gunn was at the hotel bar when someone handed him a letter from Ramsay. "Don't mention this to anyone," it read. "Last night I got a notice that I had better go North." The vigilance committee was on Ramsay's case. He'd sent a letter to some English friends in Philadelphia to vouch for him, to say that he'd declined to write for the *Press*. (Deceptions on top of deceptions—he was writing for the *Tribune*.) Ramsay said that while he was waiting for those Philadelphia friends to get back to him, he had decided to go upstate to Columbia, the capital, and he'd already left.

Ramsay never did return to Charleston while Gunn was there, but he did slip back into town in early March. Eventually Gunn pieced together more of the young reporter's story, but the air of duplicity around him only deepened. His name apparently was not Ramsay but Buckstone, although Buckstone/Ramsay later met another Charleston acquaintance in Washington—the *New York Times* correspondent George H. C. Salter—and was introduced to him by yet another name.

"Salter thought there was a mystery about the fellow," Gunn wrote in his diary. Salter, who seems to have lived with Ramsay in a Charleston boardinghouse at one point, suspected Ramsay might be "a London detective," which was the euphemism of the time for a spy. Gunn said he thought Ramsay was an unlikely candidate. But, then again, there was the Bunch connection. Ramsay went to the consulate every day and seemed to have spent more time there than any of his colleagues. And when the vigilance committee caught up with Ramsay and had him thrown into jail, "Bunch freed him and got him off by sending him to Washington with a nominal dispatch to Lord Lyons," Gunn wrote, wondering "whether that amusing consul knew the nature of the enterprising young Britisher's employment."

Bunch certainly would have known as much about Ramsay as Gunn did—and probably much more. He gave Ramsay not just a nominal dispatch but a bag full of correspondence from British merchants in Charleston and sent him north with a letter of introduction to Lord Lyons:

"Mr. Ramsay has been the object of a good deal of suspicions here of late owing to some idea which has got abroad that he has corresponded with a New York newspaper," Bunch informed his superior, leaving out many details lest the letter be intercepted. "I have been compelled to interfere somewhat actively on his behalf with the authorities and have taken him into my house to prevent unpleasant consequences and a grave international question." Bunch said that he had managed to persuade Governor Pickens to guarantee Ramsay's safe passage without interference from the vigilance committee or the police.

This truly was above and beyond the call of duty, and extremely risky behavior. Bunch took Ramsay into his *house* because someone was on Ramsay's tail. He did so to prevent "a grave international question." He did this simply because Ramsay was a British citizen liable to be tarred and feathered for his activities. Or was there something else? Bunch raised the issue of Ramsay's safe passage out of Carolina with the governor of the state, thus identifying himself very closely and dangerously with this dubious young character, who did not seem to be a distinguished reporter at all.

None of Bunch's motives are elaborated in the letter introducing Ramsay to Lyons, but Bunch concluded with what sounded like a recommendation to Lyons to listen closely to what this man had to say, perhaps because he had, indeed, acquired some significant intelligence, or because Bunch had imparted some he wanted passed on: "Mr. Ramsay can give Your Lordship any information you may desire respecting matters here."

Chapter 30

WHILE CHARLESTONIANS PARTIED AND INTRIGUED, flirted and flaunted their finest during Race Week, delegates from the seven slave states that had already seceded called to order their convention in Montgomery, the dreary capital of Alabama. The delegates and those who wanted to meet them were packed into a filthy hotel called the Exchange, where they did much of their politicking and the informal part of their constitution writing at the bar.

They were hearing that some of the more sober voices in the South, realizing they were on the front line of a war to come, had begun to question and even to revile the fire-eaters who had brought this upon them. "Spratt wants the slave trade restored," marveled Alfred Huger, the Charleston postmaster, calling the mere idea "our degradation." "What an awful price to pay," he wrote to a friend, "even for liberty and for slavery!!! The South cannot have one without the other, but to fall back on barbarism and again undertake the taming of the cannibal is more than I am willing to bargain for!"

Certainly the message had reached Montgomery that talk of reopening the Atlantic slave trade would create problems with the British. Bunch had made sure of that in one conversation after another, first with Rhett and then with other delegates who went though Charleston, telling them they'd do better to ban the slave trade with Africa outright and "spontaneously" rather than "waiting for it to be demanded of the Confederacy, as it certainly would be, before its recognition by the Great Powers of Europe." In this, Bunch was going far beyond his brief. He seemed to be encouraging the Southerners to think recognition would be theirs for the asking if only they would make a few adjustments in their policies and pronouncements.

Yet Bunch knew that was not likely to be the case. He'd done just about everything he could over the previous five years to warn the Crown against recognizing these slaveholding, slave-trading republics under any circumstances. In fact, he was showing the skeptical Lord Russell, whom he informed of these conversations, that the Southerners were being given every chance to embrace policies Her Majesty's government might accept—knowing full well that even if they did ban the slave trade, it would be a deception. Russell, for his part, commended Bunch's discretion.

As with many diplomats and spies—who are also functionaries and bureaucrats—Robert Bunch had to try to protect his back as he moved through the maze of duplicity he'd constructed around himself. He did not report everything he did (even in his private letters to Lyons we do not hear much about his time spent with the pious slave-owning Blakes or the wily secessionist Trescot, when he must have dissembled endlessly even as he enjoyed the luxuries of their plantations), but he tried to report enough to cover himself if he was caught out. At the same time he constantly tried to read the winds of opinion among his superiors. If he had an inkling that, despite his best secret dispatches, London was inclined to go ahead with recognition of the Confederacy—and certainly such talk was in the air—then he needed to prepare the way for his future. Bunch had principles, but he had to remain in place if he was going to effect them.

At that critical moment, as the slaveholders rushed to create their Confederacy before Lincoln's inauguration, the Montgomery delegates around the bar at the Exchange Hotel had concerns about the African trade that were even more immediate than their worries about European recognition. The issue, they knew, was a potential political disaster for them. The Virginians were critically important. They had not yet decided to secede and they were absolutely and adamantly against the importation of cheap Africans that would undercut the value of the slaves they exported to the Deep South. Maryland was in play, as well, and had some of the same concerns. If the new Confederacy could bring those two states into its fold, Washington would be surrounded, and the war would be won before it was begun. If it could not get either of them to join, its credibility and its strategic position would be badly weakened. So, despite the continued opposition of fire-eaters such as Rhett, the majority of the delegates in Montgomery voted to outlaw the importation of slaves from Africa or, significantly, from any other state or region outside the borders of the new Confederacy—which, at that moment, meant Virginia and Maryland. If those two states wanted to keep their markets as slave sellers, they would have to join the new republic of slave buyers.

Bunch and Lyons understood all these political calculations. They considered the new Confederate constitution an utterly unreliable guide to the likely actions of the individual Confederate states and reported that to London. A republic based on the right of its members to secede would not have much authority to enforce its will on this question, especially if some of the most important states decided on their own to start importing Africans.

"Not much reliance can be placed upon the present proceedings," Lyons advised Lord Russell after publication of the Confederate constitution. "The acts of the Southern congress are now all directed toward producing immediate effects in the Border States and in the countries of Europe. Thus it has prohibited the Slave Trade, partly in deference to public opinion in Europe, but still more in order to conciliate Virginia and other states interested in the domestic Slave Trade. It has reserved to itself the power to prohibit the trade in Slaves with States not members of the new Confederacy, in order to alarm the breeders of Slaves in the states which have not yet seceded. The lever with which it hopes to move Great Britain and the other powers of Europe is of course Cotton."

Just how important that lever would be depended on the markets, however, and as it happened, there had been record crops and record exports in 1859 and 1860. The Southerners talked about the millions of British factory workers who could be put out of jobs with a cotton boycott or if the supply was cut off by a Union blockade. But Britain had a surplus of cotton warehoused. Its mills would not be in desperate need of new supplies for another year, if then. From the market's point of view, the whole crisis looked as if it might be over in plenty of time to keep the looms of Lancashire running.

The Montgomery delegates named Jefferson Davis president of the Confederacy and approved a new cabinet in late February. From Charleston, Bunch sent Lord Russell a long dispatch about those members he knew "personally or by their reputation." And as often as he could, Bunch hit buttons he knew would trigger concern in London, if not, indeed, alarm. He put the slave-trade issue to one side for the moment and shifted his focus to the question of the Confederacy's ambitions in the Caribbean and Central America.

Bunch wrote that Jefferson Davis's views throughout his time in public life had been "of the extremest Southern and Pro-Slavery character." He described him as "a firm believer in the 'manifest destiny' of the South to overrun and convert into Slave-holding states of a Southern Confederacy, Mexico, Central America, and Cuba." Such moves would put this new nation, if such it were, into direct conflict with Britain's interests and with Britain's navy. Davis "was a very warm advocate of the expeditions of López, Walker, and other Filibusters," and Bunch thought the main reason Davis was elected was because of his military reputation. The former U.S. secretary of war had a problematic penchant for the use of force and, Bunch suggested, was likely to use it if the South succeeded in establishing itself as an independent empire.

The rest of the new government was of less interest to Bunch. The vice president, Alexander Stephens of Georgia, was suspected of Unionist inclinations. The new Confederate secretary of state, Robert Toombs, also of Georgia, had been a U.S. senator and held other important posts, but he was no diplomat. Bunch called him "violent and impulsive" and "a secessionist of the worst kind." (Toombs had arrived in Montgomery expecting he'd be named president, but his volatile temperament and obvious drunkenness during dinners at the Exchange Hotel were part of the reason the convention passed him over.) As secretary of state, Toombs would control the Confederacy's foreign policy, Bunch noted, and "it is hoped that he will not hold that office long." As for the new attorney general of the Confederacy, Judah P. Benjamin, he was not someone whose career Bunch had followed closely, and the consul lumped him in with the other members of the cabinet as "the dead level of mediocrity."

Then, knowing full well he was overstepping the bounds of bureaucratic propriety (as he was always inclined to do), Bunch launched into a passionate denunciation of the Confederacy and everything it represented.

Bunch said he had the "firm conviction" that "the new Republic will never rise to eminence as a great power of the earth," and he was perfectly blunt about his reasons. "It is, in the first place, founded upon the possession of what may be called a monopoly of one single production—Cotton. So soon as that staple is subjected to competition (and may that day soon arrive), so soon as its cultivation is impeded or destroyed by causes either physical or political, so soon as some cheaper or more available fiber shall be substituted for it, from that moment does the importance of these Southern States diminish and their claim to consideration disappear." Bunch's point: there was no long-term benefit for Britain if it supported the breakaway states just to get their cotton. Then he hammered home his central argument, writing privately precisely the opposite of what he'd told Rhett and suggested to other delegates on their way to Montgomery: "This new Confederacy is based upon the preservation and extension of Negro slavery," Bunch said. "It seems, to my humble judgment, quite impossible that in the present age of the world, a government avowedly established for such purposes can meet with the sympathy and encouragement which are as necessary to Nations as to individuals."

Writing from the epicenter of secession and surrounded by ferocious partisans of the new Confederacy, Bunch wanted to go on record with London saying he didn't think the coalition of slave states could survive in "defiance of the sentiments of nature and of civilization." Then Bunch took a breath and added the predictable caveats. He was not calling for Britain to interfere with the way another country organized its labor force, but he believed that the Confederates would be ostracized by world opinion and regarded as little more than growers of cotton and rice. Implicit in Bunch's dispatch was the notion that if Britain sided with the South, even if the South won its gamble on secession, then Her Majesty's government would lose.

O N MARCH 4, ABRAHAM LINCOLN was to be inaugurated on a stage erected on the steps of the Capitol building, its dome still an ugly construction site that looked like the exposed skeleton of the Republic. Charles P. Stone, the just-promoted colonel charged with Lincoln's protection, had stationed sharpshooters the length of Pennsylvania Avenue with orders to kill anyone they suspected of trying to fire on the president, and he positioned more snipers in the wings of the Capitol, looking down on the stage where Lincoln would speak. The night before, the colonel learned of plans to put a bomb beneath the podium, so he stationed troops around the base, and he scattered plainclothes detectives throughout the crowd.

Lincoln and Buchanan rode in an open carriage from the Willard Hotel to the Capitol, with the crowd on Pennsylvania Avenue so thick in places that it forced the carriage to stop again and again. Before them went a float that was supposed to be the U.S. Constitution; on it sat thirty-four young girls, for the thirty-four states, dressed in virginal white. When the president's carriage reached a side entrance to the Capitol, the two men stepped down and walked to the Senate chambers arm in arm. Buchanan was "pale, sad, nervous," wrote a newspaperman on the scene. Lincoln's face was flushed, his lips "compressed." They waited while oaths were administered to two senators. "Mr. Buchanan sighed audibly and frequently," wrote the correspondent, "Mr. Lincoln was grave and impassive as an Indian martyr." Then they walked out into the daylight.

"We are not enemies, but friends," Lincoln told the South as he stood there in front of the Capitol. "We must not be enemies." He recognized the U.S. Constitution's guarantees for slave owners and would not interfere with them, he said, but no state or states had the right to destroy the Union. "Though passion may have strained, it must not break the bonds of affection. The mystic chords of memory, stretching from every battlefield and patriot grave to every living heart and hearthstone all over this broad land, will yet swell the chorus of the Union, when again touched, as surely they will be, by the better angels of our nature."

IN CHARLESTON, THOSE "better angels" were nowhere to be seen. Only the Southern version of the inauguration was allowed into print, and that mocked the whole affair, especially the security precautions. "Everything that appears here is dressed with secession sauce," Bunch wrote to Lyons.

As for Lincoln's speech, it was taken as a provocation and "little short of a declaration of war against the South," according to the *Charleston Courier*, which had once been the *Mercury*'s more sober counterpart but had now fallen into line with the secessionists. Bunch warned Lord Russell that military preparations in Charleston were being "pushed actively forward" under the command of "a Mr. Beauregard, previously a captain in the United States Engineers but now a *Brigadier General* in the service of the 'Confederate States,' who is said to be a very able officer and [was] the chief advisor of General Scott in the attack on the City of Mexico."

Pierre Gustave Toutant Beauregard, or P. G. T. Beauregard, as he was known, had his headquarters only a couple of blocks up Meeting Street from Bunch's house, and Bunch could hardly take a stroll toward the city center without passing young officers bustling in and out. If he turned in the other direction and walked down to the Battery, he saw across the gray waters of the bay the Carolinians building, day by day, an armor-plated floating gun platform with which to attack Maj. Anderson and his boys holed up in Fort Sumter. "I know nothing about the laws of war (or quasi-war)," Bunch wrote of this floating battery, "but the laws of common sense seem to dictate the propriety of [Anderson] blowing it out of the water." Yet day after day that did not happen, and tensions continued to grow. "My house is about three miles as the crow—or the shell—flies from Fort Sumter," Bunch told Lyons. "But unless the town is to be bombarded, I do not run much risk, as the attacking forts and batteries are seaward of me." Everybody in the city had begun to make such calculations about if or when the fighting might touch them.

Bunch had become Her Majesty's most important representative in the new Confederacy. He knew it, and he knew that Lord Lyons and Lord Russell knew it, and he would have liked a title to certify it somehow, and a raise in salary, of course. He dreamed of being a chargé d'affaires, a publicly acknowledged diplomat. But none of that led him to temper the contempt he expressed for just about everything the breakaway republic represented. The Charlestonians, he said, reminded him of a barnyard cock crowing defiance from atop a dunghill.

Bunch reported dutifully on the bait the Southerners were offering Britain in their attempt to gain quick recognition—the same basic incentives he and Rhett had talked about: low tariffs and a chance to do coastal trading. But he didn't believe there to be much substance behind those promises. Georgia would still want its industries protected, and Louisiana felt the same way about its sugar.

The South was sending commissioners to London to plead its cause, and Bunch said he hoped they would not be received at all or, if they were, not warmly. "They go believing in their inmost hearts that we cannot do without this confounded Cotton, and that we will do anything or yield anything to get it. This is not a flattering estimate of us, and I own that it galls me to think that we have allowed these slave-holders even this 'coign of vantage.'"

At the Confederacy's very first cabinet meeting in Montgomery the members had voted almost unanimously to support a cotton boycott to punish Great Britain until it agreed to support secession. Only Attorney General Judah P. Benjamin argued against such a move. He was a much wiser and more worldly man than Bunch had given him credit for. Probably he was the only man in the cabinet who fully understood the financial implications of what was coming. He argued that the South's cotton crop—its only significant source of cash—should be sold in Europe immediately for guns and gold in preparation for a long fight. But the others felt the whole affair would be over quickly. The new Confederate secretary of war, the intense and inept LeRoy Pope Walker of Alabama, had told his constituents that so little blood would be spilled, it could all be wiped up with a handkerchief.

Over the following weeks, the Confederate cabinet could not make out why the British were not racing to support the secessionist states that kept England's port of Liverpool and the vast mills in Manchester so busy. One obvious reason, widely reported, was the surplus from the previous year's record crop. If the war were short, the English mills wouldn't hurt, and, important, the value of the fiber already in the British warehouses was soaring. Another reason was natural caution about getting involved in another country's civil war and a reluctance to plunge into open armed conflict with the North. And then there was the problem of slavery and especially the slave trade with Africa, which, thanks to the reporting of Bunch and Lyons, remained an issue with British officials despite the official pronouncements in the new Confederate constitution. At one point Bunch's ostensible friend William Henry Trescot, who'd had to deal with the issue of the African slave trade as acting U.S. secretary of state under Buchanan, took it upon himself to say publicly that the British should mind their own business.

"That's not a reply at all," Bunch told him; "it's simply a growl." It's like a burglar telling a policeman to go walk his rounds and not to bother him, Bunch went on, but with a critical difference: the burglar didn't make a commitment not to steal spoons, while the U.S. government and now the Confederate government did claim they were committed not to steal people from Africa. As the British saw things, the question of the African slave trade was very much their business.

The cotton boycott was evolving. The Confederate government did not really have the authority to enforce it, but many planters felt it their patriotic duty to hold back their production. Then the Confederate cabinet, which always preached the gospel of free trade, convinced itself it could coerce the British by levying an export duty on cotton. Bunch was overjoyed. "Every farthing so imposed is a bounty to us to grow it elsewhere. If we do not stir ourselves to do so after this fright, Manchester and Liverpool deserve to be burned."

All this talk of boycotts and taxes was merely preliminary. It was obvious that when war came (there was now little question of "if"), the thunder on the American battlefields would echo around the world. It was also obvious that the first explosions would take place right there on the horizon, where the sky and the sea met at the edge of the Charleston Harbor, where more guns had now been positioned at Fort Moultrie to the north and on Morris Island to the south, ready and more than willing to open fire on Fort Sumter.

Part Four

First Shots

"OH, LORD WHY *did* I do it?" William Howard Russell asked himself on the morning of March 19, 1861. He had been in the United States for barely forty-eight hours, and already he was the subject of more stories than he had written. Arriving in New York aboard the Cunard steamer *Arabia* on March 16, he'd allowed himself to get swept up in the vast Saint Patrick's Day festivities on the seventeenth. Invited to "a little party" that night by his fellow Sons of Erin, he wound up among hundreds at the Astor House, where, well into his cups, he addressed the multitude. It seemed to him, he said, that the great contest taking shape was a test of republican institutions. Russell asked, in effect, whether a government of the people, by the people, and for the people could survive.

His bosses had warned him against making speeches. Horace Greeley's *New-York Tribune* quickly denounced Russell's remarks as a typical British misapprehension of a conflict that was really only about freedom versus slavery, and slavery was the aggressor. Russell read about himself in paper after paper as a vain, middle-aged man with a cocked nose, blue eyes, grizzled hair, and a double chin.

So began what probably was the unhappiest year in William Howard Russell's long career. His wife, Mary, had almost died in childbirth the previous autumn. He could not leave her and delayed his trip to America by several months until she seemed to be on the mend. The little boy she had borne was sickly and would die before Russell returned, and throughout his time in the United States Mary continued to suffer without him in England.

Russell's editors and his many admirers hungered for his coverage of battle, his dissection of strategy, his depiction, for better or worse, of the grim reality in camps and hospitals. But even apart from his concerns about the infirmity of his wife and child, he had been reluctant to depart for America. There were British interests in this fight, no doubt about it, but there were no British soldiers involved. Was this really his war to cover?

Finally John Delane, the editor of the *Times* of London, put up enough money to make the American war worth Russell's while. The correspondent would be paid £1,200 a year plus expenses, and since Russell already owed his wife's doctor £500, this was, Russell had to admit, "a lucky sort of intervention."

"You must go," said William Makepeace Thackeray, who lived near Russell's Sumner Place house in Kensington and often stopped by. "It will be a great opportunity."

Over the summer Thackeray, who had so many American friends, had introduced Russell to one named Samuel Cutler "Sam" Ward, a famous bon vivant who was quite extraordinary company. He came from what had been a prosperous family and remained a socially impressive one. His sister, Julia Ward, gained fame as a poet (she eventually wrote "The Battle Hymn of the Republic"), and her husband, Samuel Gridley Howe, had a reputation as a fighter for righteous causes ranging from Greek independence to the education of the deaf and blind to support for John Brown. Sam Ward seemed to know just about anyone that anybody had ever heard of in the northern United States: senators, poets, philanthropists, adventurers. And Russell could see why. He was "refined, philosophical, and cosmopolitan" in ways that Americans were not supposed to be. Ward was a risk taker and had one of those great magnetic personalities that got him into trouble almost as often as it got him out. He had already acquired and lost two fortunes before landing in Washington, where he later became not only a lobbyist but "The King of the Lobby," buttonholing and cajoling the men who made the laws. Ward promised to give Russell, if he came to the United States, a royal reception *à l'américaine*, and he kept his word. He and the increasingly influential *New-York Evening Post* editor, John Bigelow, another great friend of Russell's, had been there at the dock to receive him when he got off the boat.

William Howard Russell at that moment probably had greater

fame and influence than any journalist before or since. His dispatches from the Crimea—describing the by-then legendary Charge of the Light Brigade—and from India had been read around the world. Copyright laws were rare and their enforcement rarer, so articles in the *Times* of London showed up on broadsheets from Calcutta to Charleston, and Russell's stories, full of facts no one else had reported in narratives more compelling than anything anyone else was writing, were required reading by anyone who wanted to appear in the know about the greatest conflicts of the time.

During Russell's first weeks in the United States, his access to people in power amazed even him. All understood (as, indeed, Robert Bunch would come to understand) that if they could have Russell's ear, they could gain the world's attention. In Washington, Russell found himself dining with Sam Ward's good friend William Seward, now the U.S. secretary of state and the man who would handle the nation's delicate relations with the Crown. Seward had accepted the position as Lincoln's de facto number two, if not indeed the government's éminence grise, and he appeared a little more controlled in Washington than he had been at the drunken dinner with the Prince of Wales and the Duke of Newcastle a few months before. Seward encouraged Russell to drop by the secretary of state's office for a chat almost anytime he pleased, and when Russell had been in the capital for only two days, Seward took him to meet President Lincoln. The physically ungainly but utterly charming new head of state flattered Russell by telling him that "the London *Times* is one of the greatest powers in the world—in fact, I don't know anything that has much more power, except perhaps the Mississippi. I am glad to know you as its minister."

Russell met with everybody who was anybody, including the abolitionist firebrand Senator Charles Sumner, who was another close friend of Sam Ward. Dignitaries, members of Congress, and reporters flocked to meet Russell at the Willard Hotel, where he marveled, in passing, at the halls thick with office seekers and slick with spit from chewing tobacco.

One night the Lincolns invited Russell to dine at the White House along with Gen. Winfield Scott, now the commander of the Union Army, and several of the most important members of the cabinet. After dinner the men talked about the role of Britain in the crisis, hoping Russell would confirm their belief that "England was bound by her anti-slavery antecedents to discourage to the utmost any attempts by the South to establish its independence on a basis of slavery." Russell hoped that might be so but knew there were many considerations. The interests of commerce and morality did not always coincide. The statesmen of Britain might need to be reminded what it was that so appalled them about the Southerners and their servants, but at that moment and for more than a year to come the Union that Lincoln and Seward wanted to preserve was to be one where slavery continued to exist. The idea that war would be waged to preserve what Bunch would call that "great fact in the history of the world," the American experiment, was not nearly so compelling for the British public or its politicians.

Early on, Seward used Russell as a line of communication with the British public and with Her Majesty's government. The Lincoln administration had been in office less than a month when Seward gave the *Times* man a long interview at the State Department. Seward knew that London and Paris had watched one state after another secede and then assemble into what seemed a whole as the Confederacy. Fort Sumter was under siege. The Federal government appeared to be paralyzed. But what the Europeans had to understand, Seward said, was that for four long months, from Lincoln's election on November 6, 1860, to his inauguration on March 4, 1861, Southern sympathizers in the lame duck Buchanan administration had systematically laid traps for the incoming Republicans.

Seward was warming up to another of his bellicose threats. He wanted to make it clear to Britain and to Europe, through Russell's dispatches, what a disastrous situation the new administration had inherited, and how determined the administration was to set it straight. He told Russell that Buchanan's people had sent the U.S. Navy to far corners of the world and had stockpiled arms where Southern militias could seize them. They had stolen money from the national treasury. As Seward saw it, this was all part of a "deep conspiracy," and as soon as Lincoln was elected, the men engaged in it set out to destroy the Union.

Seward told Russell to make no mistake: the Republican administration would not give an inch, and the Union would hold. But it would take time, and "the danger was that foreign powers would be led to imagine the Federal government was too weak to defend its rights, and that the attempt to destroy the Union and to set up a Southern Confederacy was successful."

"In other words," Russell told his readers, Seward feared that "Great Britain may recognize the Government established at Montgomery." And then came the explicit challenge, so much like those Seward had made so many times before. He was ready, he said, "if needs be, to threaten Great Britain with war as the consequence of such recognition."

Russell, when he wrote this up, had to question Seward's grasp on reality. That same day Russell had watched newly enlisted Union troops parading around Washington with, as he saw it, precious little sign of military efficiency or fighting spirit. They were, he wrote, "starved, washed-out creatures." All things considered, Russell found it "a matter of wonderment" that the secretary of state of "a nation which was in such imminent danger in its very capital, and which, with its chief and his cabinet, was almost at the mercy of the enemy," had used such bellicose language in a report meant to be read by the most powerful governments in Europe. Yet, he concluded, "In all sincerity I think Mr. Seward meant it."

When Russell dined with the Southern commissioners in Washington a few nights later, they told him they regarded Lincoln with contempt. They saw Seward as "the ablest and most unscrupulous of their enemies." But in these early days of the war, before any shots had been fired, the Union secretary of state may have been outsmarting himself. His fear that Britain and other European nations might accept secession as a fait accompli was justified. But the great opponent of human bondage somehow failed to understand that the issue of slavery, and particularly the slave trade, was the most powerful tool he had to prevent British recognition of the South—if only he would use it. So sensitive was Seward to the risk that any talk of emancipation might inflame the critical slaveholding border states of Maryland, Kentucky, Missouri, and parts of Virginia that he issued orders to his envoys in Europe prohibiting them from discussing the issue of slavery at all. Seward did not raise the question of slavery with Russell even in passing. But in the weeks ahead, William Howard Russell would not leave it alone.

Chapter 33

I HAVE SENT MY WIFE AND child into the country for the month of April, not to avoid the shells from Fort Sumter, but to eat strawberries," Robert Bunch wrote to Lord Lyons. He was either joking or sending a guarded message or both. His situation in Charleston had, in fact, grown increasingly precarious. The omnipresent atmosphere of conspiracy and suspicion meant that people were more likely than before to look behind his "smile of indifference." Was he with them, or was he against them? And if he was with them, how could he prove it?

For some time, one of Bunch's tactics to shore up support among influential locals was to help Charleston's merchants and planters get their letters out to England. He preferred to use messengers with British backgrounds, even those like "Ramsay," the problematic newspaper correspondent (or spy). Importantly—indeed, vitally—each informal courier, even if he had been naturalized as an American citizen, would be given a British passport to help him travel between the Secession states and the Union states. But it was a risky strategy: the passports Bunch signed might suck him into the intrigues of those who carried them, and he might also find himself incriminated by the contents of the letters if they were opened. On the other hand, encrypted letters or telegraphs compounded the suspicions directed at the consul. At the height of tensions about Fort Sumter, Bunch had asked Lyons to send him a coded telegraph message to let him know what the hell was going on in Washington, but Lyons had decided not to, because he thought it would draw too much attention to the recipient.

Bunch not only worried about the risks to Emma and little Helen if war erupted, he worried about the risks to himself and his work if they stayed in the city. Now more than ever a wrong word uttered by his impassioned wife or even his six-year-old daughter could prove disastrous. If they went to stay with Emma's sister at Board House or The Meadows, whether they picked strawberries or not, they would be out of harm's way.

"Fort Sumter hangs in the balance, but we are promised action of some sort in a few days," Bunch wrote the afternoon of April 5, 1861. The Southern gunners were getting trigger-happy. Two nights before, they'd fired at a schooner full of nothing but ice that was bound from Boston to Savannah when it tried to pull into the harbor to escape bad weather. Their cannons had taken fifteen shots at her, Bunch noted, but only one of them scored, ripping through her mainsail.

"We are in the most frightful commotion imaginable," Bunch wrote on April 9. "It is fully believed that the U.S. government intends to reinforce Fort Sumter, and every man is under arms. If the news from Washington be true that reinforcements are on their way, there will be a desperate fight here before we are many days, perhaps hours, older." Bunch worried, half in jest, about the possibility that the "attached peasantry"—that is, the slaves—"may take advantage of everybody being away fighting the fort to start a little private war on their own account in the city." Bunch said he planned to be flying the Union Jack outside the consulate *en permanence.*

"Fort Sumter is perfectly surrounded by men—there are certainly between 6 and 7000 on the various islands," Bunch reported two days later. "My fear is that even if the U.S. supplies and reinforcement do not arrive, an attack will be made by the Southern troops. As the Irishman says, 'Everyone is *spoiling* for a fight.'

"I shall do my best to keep Your Lordship informed respecting the movements of the U.S. ships of war, but the information will not be easy to procure unless they fight their way into the harbor.

"Everything is upside now and cannot continue long in this state."

.   .   .

FEDERAL SHIPS WERE, indeed, on their way to resupply Fort Sumter. They arrived outside the harbor that same afternoon, and one of them was the same U.S. revenue cutter, the *Harriet Lane*, that had borne Crown Prince Bertie and Bunch and assorted dignitaries into New York City only a few months before. One of the sailors, Bradley Sillick Osbon, was an adventurer who'd also signed up as a correspondent for the *New York World*. He climbed up next to the coast pilot and looked at the harbor through his spyglass. There in the distance was Sumter with Old Glory still flying high above it. Gen. P. G. T. Beauregard had delivered an ultimatum to Maj. Anderson that very afternoon, demanding he surrender the fort. Anderson had refused.

ABNER DOUBLEDAY, ANDERSON'S second-in-command, was determined to get as much sleep as possible before the fighting began. He and the other officers had moved from their exposed quarters overlooking Fort Moultrie down into the powder magazines behind the thickest part of Sumter's walls. Then, around four in the morning on April 12, Doubleday heard someone groping around in the dark in his makeshift room and calling his name. It was Anderson. "I've just received a dispatch from Beauregard dated 3:20 a.m.," said the major. "They're going to open fire on us in an hour." Anderson, knowing his supply of ammunition was low, determined to hold his fire until after breakfast. So Doubleday stayed in bed. "We had no lights," he wrote later. "We could, in fact, do nothing before that time, except to wander around in darkness, and fire without an accurate view of the enemy's works."

As soon as the Confederate batteries could distinguish the outline of Sumter's walls in the first dim light before dawn, a little after 4:30 a.m., the firing began. Historical lore has it that the white-haired old secessionist Edmund Ruffin had the honor of firing the first shot from the batteries at Cummings Point on Morris Island.

Seconds later, at Fort Sumter, a round of shot buried itself in the wall just on the other side of Captain Doubleday's head, as he recalled, "in very unpleasant proximity to my right ear." Then "the firing burst forth in one continuous roar, and large patches of both the exterior and interior masonry began to crumble and fall in all directions."

Shortly after sunrise the soldiers in the Sumter garrison breakfasted on pork and water, then opened up with their own guns. But the fleet that had been sent to relieve them stayed outside the harbor.

BUNCH WATCHED THE fireworks from the roof of his house. All morning long the cannons continued to roar. Bunch reported that "the attacking batteries are eight in number, five at least of them firing shell," by which he meant exploding ordnance rather than solid cannonballs. "Major Anderson has no shell and from the small numbers of his men can only work four guns. Consequently not a single man has been hurt on the South Carolina side." The battle seemed very strange to Bunch, and, caught up in the moment, he was eager to get at least a little closer to the action.

In the early afternoon, a little skiff could be seen bobbing along the edge of the harbor with a slight, balding man, the British consul, aboard. For four and a half hours he and a South Carolina state senator visited the Confederate batteries. He said afterward that the Almighty must have deprived him of "all sense and intelligence" to make him do such a thing. "Of course, I really ran no risk except that of a shell falling short or taking a twist the wrong way," he said, and he "had a capital view of the firing on both sides but do not think that what I saw was sufficient to repay me for my trouble."

The shelling went on into the night, although Anderson's troops quit firing once it was dark. On the morning of April 13 they had more pork and water and then went back to their big guns. A sudden rainstorm brought a brief lull in the shelling, but at about eight o'clock Ripley began a concerted attack on the vulnerable officers' quarters using incendiary shells and cannonballs heated in Fort Moultrie's furnace. By a little after ten o'clock the whole wooden structure was ablaze, and a nearby magazine holding three hundred barrels of powder was in danger of exploding. The officers set to work with axes trying to tear away the wooden structures that might send sparks into the ventilators. The soldiers rolled the barrels out of the magazine to more sheltered locations. Maj. Ripley, when he saw the fire well under way, only increased the pace of his bombardment.

"By 11 a.m. the conflagration was terrible and disastrous," Captain Doubleday reported. "One-fifth of the fort was on fire, and the wind drove the smoke in dense masses into the angle where we had all taken refuge. It seemed impossible to escape suffocation. Some lay down close to the ground, with handkerchiefs over their mouths, and others posted themselves near the embrasures, where the smoke was somewhat lessened by the draught of air. Everyone suffered severely. I crawled out of one of these openings and sat on the outer edge; but Ripley made it lively for me there with his case-shot, which spattered all around. Had not a slight change of wind taken place, the result might have been fatal to most of us."

BUNCH REPORTED FORT SUMTER "badly on fire, blazing merrily" that morning. "In about 45 minutes, the conflagration abated. Subsequently, however, there have been two explosions in the Fort, one of which I saw. It looked very badly, but it is impossible to say what the damage has been. Anderson is evidently suffering today. There are vessels outside the Bar, which are believed to be U.S. Ships, but it is impossible to say. . . . I do not think that Anderson can hold out much longer unless he be reinforced. The odds are too great against him."

Bunch enclosed, for Lyons, a clipping from one of the Charleston papers describing the previous day's fighting. He appended a note in cipher. When decoded, it read, "A pack of horrid lies."

. . .

DOUBLEDAY ORDERED A few more rounds fired, to show the garrison wasn't dead yet. But "the scene at this time was really terrific," he wrote afterward. "The roaring and crackling of the flames, the dense masses of whirling smoke, the bursting of the enemy's shells, and our own which were exploding in the burning rooms, the crashing of the shot, and the sound of masonry falling in every direction, made the fort a pandemonium."

Suddenly a face appeared, looking in through one of the embrasures, or viewing slits, in the fortress wall. It was none other than Louis Wigfall, the former U.S. senator from Texas—he of the murderous reputation and the tiger eyes—who'd come over from Morris Island in a rowboat. Black oarsmen waited in the background, the water lapping against the gunwales of their little vessel as Wigfall, a bit out of breath and probably a trifle drunk, said he was speaking on behalf of Gen. Beauregard. He offered to let Anderson evacuate the fort with permission to salute the Federal flag—that is, to march out with the honors of war. They were the same terms offered by Beauregard three days before, when not a shot had been fired.

AT 2:30 P.M., Bunch wrote in his running account of the battle that "about an hour ago Fort Sumter's flagstaff was shot away. It remained down some time, but at last the flag appeared, seemingly hoisted on a chimney. After about 20 minutes, however, it came down, and a white flag was run up in its place. So we suppose Anderson has surrendered, but no particulars are known as yet." Then he could not help adding, "Of course, there is frightful excitement, and equally, of course, it is now quite evident that the Almighty is on our side, also that our cause is a just and holy one."

At 6:30 p.m., Bunch finished his last dispatch of the day to Lyons. "The fort has surrendered unconditionally, I believe. So far as I can learn, not one soul has been hurt on either side, which after 33 hours bombarding is a little curious. But we live in curious times."

The war had begun.

Chapter 34

Lyons warned bunch that William Howard Russell was on his way down to Charleston, but three days after Fort Sumter surrendered, the world's greatest war correspondent still had not arrived. Bunch said that in any case he was ready to help him in every possible way. "He will find four dinners a day if he can eat them, as the people are perfectly wild to make a favorable impression on him." Bunch insisted he was "not particularly" an admirer, but the attentions of such a famous journalist would be hard for him to resist, and Lyons, for his part, wanted to make sure that the opinionated consul got the right kind of messages across to this redoubtable newspaperman.

In Washington, Russell had won over Lyons immediately. "I was disposed to think kindly towards him," the minister admitted to Bunch, "because he spoke well and truly of my father [the admiral who commanded the Mediterranean Fleet] in his letters from the Crimea." Lyons, who did not want to see Her Majesty's government recognize the new Confederate States of America, knew that if William Seward followed through on his bluster about blockading Southern harbors or declaring them "no longer ports of entry," London would react strongly, and "I don't see how the question of recognition can be kept off." Lyons also told Bunch confidentially that the American envoy in London had been ordered to seek assurances that Britain would not recognize the Confederacy and came away with a very noncommittal answer. So it was imperative that Bunch say nothing to Russell that would encourage London to recognize the South.

"I shall be careful to conform my language to Your Lordship's wishes," Bunch assured him. "The information conveyed to me is indeed most important and shall be made a discreet use of." Then he added the obvious: "Late events will change the aspect of affairs very materially at home and abroad."

In the aftermath of Sumter, Lincoln was calling up 75,000 soldiers, provoking "sudden and immeasurable enthusiasm" in the North that surprised even its leaders. Two days later, Jefferson Davis issued a proclamation offering "letters of marque" to legalize privateers who attacked Federal ships. Lincoln responded by proclaiming a blockade of Confederate ports and declaring that Confederate privateers would be treated as pirates and hanged.

This was just what Lyons and Bunch had been dreading. Neither of them wanted to see the Crown throw its weight behind the South, which the blockade of Southern ports might provoke. But London hated privateers almost as much as it hated blockades, and that created some room for diplomatic maneuvering. "Privateers from the Confederacy will be, in plain language, pirates," said Bunch. There would be plenty to talk about with the man from the *Times*—discreetly, of course.

By the time W. H. Russell and Sam Ward finally arrived in Charleston, the air was full of that electric excitement that always marks the beginning of a long-anticipated war. And, thanks to the hospitality of Her Britannic Majesty's consul, Russell found himself almost as well connected in South Carolina as he had been in Washington. "Very civil and seems a very nice fellow," W. H. Russell jotted in his diary after his first meeting with Robert Bunch on that first day, and Bunch felt the same about Russell. "I like him very much and am much impressed by his powers of observation and conversation," Bunch wrote to Lyons.

As quickly as he could, Russell arranged to visit Fort Moultrie, where crates of Champagne and French paté were piled outside the tents, and Fort Sumter, where he ran into Louis Wigfall, the drunken, self-appointed Confederate colonel who'd brought the terms of surrender to Maj. Robert Anderson. The infamous duelist was dressed in a mix of military and civilian clothes—a blue frock coat with a red sash, a straight ceremonial sword at his belt, a loose silk handkerchief around his muscular neck, "and wild masses of black hair, tinged with gray" falling out from under his civilian hat.

A stubble of beard had grown across Wigfall's square jaw, and then there was the look in his eye: "flashing, fierce, yet calm—with a well of fire burning behind and spouting through it, an eye pitiless in anger, which now and then sought to conceal its expression beneath half-closed lids, and then burst out with an angry glare, as if disdaining concealment."

Russell came away deeply unimpressed with evidence of battle: "A very small affair, indeed, that shelling of Fort Sumter," he wrote. "Never did men plunge into unknown depth of peril and trouble more recklessly than these Carolinians."

As Russell and his group arrived back in Charleston after dusk, the city was a blaze of light, and the air was filled with the rolling of drums. Russell walked through the noisy streets toward the Mills House Hotel among droves of black men and women shuffling in haste to escape the last peal of the curfew bell and the patrols that followed it. "A squad of mounted horsemen, heavily armed, turned up a by-street, and with jingling spurs and sabers disappeared in the dust and darkness." The horse patrol of the City Guard. "They scour the country around the city," Russell was told, "and meet at certain places during the night to see if the niggers are all quiet."

The next day Russell took a long trip through the harbor in a small boat to further inspect the forts, accompanied by a Confederate officer who wanted to talk about nothing but his passion for Thackeray's novels. Then Russell went to dine with "our excellent Consul, Mr. Bunch, who had a small and very agreeable party to meet me." There were no Wigfalls in this group. They were "as distinguished a party as I could collect," Bunch told Lyons, "and a very fair showing of the best South Carolinians." Among them was the aged postmaster, Alfred Huger (pronounced *Hugee*, Russell noted), who was despondent over the coming of war. "I have lived too long," he said as tears rolled down his cheeks. "I should have died ere these evil days arrived." But he did not doubt that the South would emerge victorious.

"Only one of the company, a most lively, quaint, witty old

lawyer named Petigru, dissented from the doctrines of Secession," wrote Russell, "but he seems to be treated as an amiable, harmless person."

The dinner at Bunch's house began at five and lasted almost until midnight: a measure of its success. But genteel as the guests might have been, the discussion grew heated as the evening wore on, and Russell found it increasingly disagreeable to hear the Carolinians talk about England as if it had no interests that were not purely material. "Why, sir," boasted one of the guests, "we have only to shut off your supply of cotton for a few weeks, and we can create a revolution in Great Britain. There are four millions of your people depending on us for their bread, not to speak of the many millions of dollars. No, sir, we know that England must recognize us."

Toward the end of Bunch's dinner party, Russell took the consul aside to say he was fed up with the other guests. "If Great Britain is such a sham as they suppose, the sooner a hole is drilled in her and the whole empire sunk under water, the better."

Bunch laughed. "You won't mind it when you get as accustomed to this sort of thing as I am."

In the days that followed, Russell came to depend on Bunch as a touchstone of British common sense in a city of unruly passions, and also as a vital link for communications with the outside world. Russell, who worried that his wife would die in England or that some other family emergency might befall them while he was incommunicado, arranged to have any emergency telegrams sent to Charleston in care of Bunch. Meanwhile he sent his letters for the *Times* north to Washington or New York and on to London using Bunch's mailbag and his messengers. Often Russell ran so late writing his dispatches that he nearly missed the shipment. A couple of times Bunch had to stick the envelopes on the outside of bags that already were sealed and about to head on their way.

Soon the consul's frank opinions and analyses, so rarely heard by his circle of acquaintances in Charleston, started to make their way anonymously into Russell's copy—so much so that later, when

Russell's newspaper dispatches from South Carolina were questioned by some British officials, Bunch leapt to their defense. The second letter Russell filed from Charleston, for instance, talked about the way South Carolina aristocrats flirted with the idea of restoring the British monarchy, or some branch of it, in their Confederacy. The idea sounded absurd to many people, including Bunch's superiors. But Bunch wrote directly to Lord Russell in London and to Lyons in Washington to assure them that, strange as it might seem, W. H. Russell's reporting had been spot-on.

Bunch did not want the journalist's credibility to be doubted on any point, including even the royal fantasies of the Charleston aristocracy. It was more important still that Russell convey, convincingly, the quotidian barbarity of slavery and, if possible, present his readers in London with evidence that the African trade was no mirage. The consul had discovered in W. H. Russell a way to have his own views dramatized and amplified for a worldwide audience and, most especially, for the ministers who worked on Downing Street. They might ignore one or another of his dispatches (even though Lyons kept drawing their attention to them), but they could not entirely dismiss the *Times,* and when both lines of communication converged, the effect could be powerful, indeed. Or so Bunch hoped.

As Russell continued his travels through the South, his portraits of the people and their cause were his own, but clearly they were informed by what he had heard from the British consul. Bunch was "indiscreet" because when he spoke confidentially with the correspondent, the consul's views were obviously and thoroughly different from those of the people among whom he was posted. But Bunch's apparent indiscretions were, in fact, very much to the point. Nobody else Russell talked to could describe for him so vividly or so frankly the way the Southerners thought, the place that slavery occupied in their society, and the ends to which they were willing to go to build a new empire. Russell, throughout his travels, continued to write back and forth with Bunch, who continued to be a vital link for his communications with the outside world. Russell's letters to the *Times* from the South grew increasingly negative. He meditated on the evils of bondage as he saw them firsthand, and eventually he did, indeed, discover evidence of his own that the infamous slave trade with Africa was being revived.

WILLIAM HOWARD RUSSELL AND SAM WARD left Charleston at the end of April on an expedition to the plantation, deep in the Low Country among the rice fields near Beaufort, of William Henry Trescot. Trescot had not, in the end, become a Southern envoy to the Court of St. James's and had come back to the gloomy comforts of his estates among the slaves, the alligators, and the Spanish moss. Russell, on his way there, was more fascinated by the journey than by the destination. The roads were rudimentary, and part of the trip was in a slave-rowed skiff in the dark of night, the slaves singing mournfully about laying their bodies down and giving up their souls, while the stream "flowing between the silent, houseless, rugged banks ... put me in mind of the fancied voyage across the Styx." When, finally, they arrived at the plantation, Mrs. Trescot was just back from the slave quarters, where she had delivered a baby. "When people talk of my having so many slaves, I always tell them it is the slaves who own me," she said.

The daytime diversion organized for guests at Trescot's was angling for drum fish. But that wasn't really of much interest to Russell or, for that matter, to Trescot. They spent their time talking about their mutual friends at London clubs and, of course, about the war, until an old-timer from the marshes who'd come along on the trip told tales about harpooning the devilfish in those waters and nearly being carried away. When they got back to the plantation, they found that Edmund Rhett, another son of the fire-eater and brother of the editor of the *Mercury*, was paying a visit. He was "one of the most ultra and violent speakers against the Yankees I have yet heard," Russell remembered. Rhett declared confidently that Britain must recognize the South before the cotton harvest of October.

The deeper Russell and Ward got into Dixie, the more they heard the refrain about British dependence on slave-grown Southern cotton repeated ad nauseam; and the more they discovered the ways the Southerners rationalized their peculiar institution, the more Russell learned to hate slavery with a passion he hadn't felt before—the same passion that had arisen in the Charleston consul in the early days of his posting. "The misery and cruelty of the system," Russell wrote in one of his letters to the *Times*, "are established by the advertisements for runaway Negroes, and by the description of the stigmata on their persons—whippings and brandings, scars and cuts." (Very probably Bunch had shown him his collection of clippings.)

By the time Russell reached the Confederate capital, which was then still at Montgomery, Alabama, he could scarcely contain himself. He despised the city: "I have rarely seen a more dull, lifeless place; it looks like a small Russian town in the interior." He loathed his hotel, the Exchange, where five men were crowded into a room with three beds and mattresses on the floor: "Had it not been for the flies, the fleas would have been intolerable, but one nuisance neutralized the other." And the spectacle the next morning of a small-time slave trader auctioning off some field hands by a public fountain turned Russell's stomach.

The sheer banality of the scene made it all the more vile. A few bystanders and a couple of interested customers looked on while the auctioneer touted a slave's virtues as if he were a horse, then decided his fate for a fistful of dollars. "That nigger went cheap," said one of the spectators. "Yes, *sir*! Niggers is cheap now, that's a fact." But Russell made no observation on the sudden decline in the price of Negroes. What ate at him was the same sense of personal, national, and religious humiliation that Bunch wrote about so often when he considered that these Southern monsters claimed some link to British heritage. "The use of the English tongue in such a transaction, and the idea of it taking place among a civilized Christian people, produced in me a feeling of inexpressible loathing and indignation," wrote the man of the *Times*.

When Russell got to the faux Greek temple where the Confederate Congress met, he was brooding over what he'd just witnessed and just how much he detested the planter class he had come to know over the previous few weeks. "Assaulted by reason, by logic, argument, philanthropy, progress directed against his peculiar institutions, the Southerner at last is driven to a fanaticism—a sacred faith which is above all reason or logical attack in the propriety, righteousness, and divinity of slavery."

A few minutes after Russell arrived in the chamber of the Confederate Congress, the speaker called for the session to be held in secret, and Russell was about to leave. But Congressman Edmund Rhett, the same fire-eater's son he'd met on Trescot's plantation, asked Russell to stay. "If the *Times* will support the South, we'll accept you as a delegate," he said. Russell, so furious he was barely able to speak, left the chamber.

Russell paid a call on Jefferson Davis in Montgomery, in a makeshift office with a piece of paper reading "President" pinned to the door, and was not impressed, so he wandered down the hall to the office of Attorney General Judah P. Benjamin, who struck him immediately as "clever, keen and, well, *yes*!"

"Mr. Benjamin is the most open, frank, and cordial of the Confederates whom I have yet met," Russell wrote. "He is a short, stout man, with a full face, olive-colored and most decidedly Jewish features, with the brightest large black eyes." His manner was "brisk, lively, agreeable." Benjamin was ready to talk about all the issues of the day, and, like the renowned litigator—and card player—that he was, he intended to see how far he could push before someone pushed back.

The issue of the moment, as Bunch would have reminded Russell discreetly, was the authorization of privateers to fly the Confederate flag and pillage Yankee shipping. Russell said that when the North caught up with them, they'd be hanged as pirates.

"We have an easy remedy for that," said Benjamin. "For any man under our flag whom the authorities of the United States dare to execute, we shall hang two of their people."

Russell took this for the bluff that it was. But the larger question of how Europeans would handle those privateers, and whether the privateers would respect the British flag, was increasingly critical to London. For Great Britain, the basic purpose of the maritime power wielded by the Royal Navy was to assure the security of maritime commerce, and it worked hard to impose its vision of international law on all the seven seas. Britain's ferocious opposition to the slave trade was part of that picture: if it banned the commerce in humans, then so must everyone else.

In many other ways, as well, the question of what flags, what navies, what rules must be respected was critical to the way Britain organized its business and its Empire. Five years before, when Lord Clarendon had negotiated the end of the Crimean War, the leading powers of Europe had joined in the Declaration of Paris: no privateers, respect for neutral shipping, and no acceptance of blockades that were not actively enforced by naval power. It was a declaration plainly biased in favor of those nations such as Britain and France that had very large navies, could therefore enforce blockades, and had no need for privateers. At the time, the United States had refused to sign on, and the Confederacy, of course, had not existed.

The chances were just about nil that the Royal Navy would recognize the validity of the licenses being handed out by Jefferson Davis to would-be buccaneers, much less respect the protection they were supposed to gain from the Confederate ensign. So Russell put the question to the Confederate attorney general in the simplest terms: What if Britain refuses to recognize the Confederate flag?

"If England thinks fit to declare privateers under our flag pirates, it would be nothing more or less than a declaration of war against us," said Benjamin, "and we must meet it as best we can."

"So Great Britain is in a pleasant condition," Russell wrote afterward. "Mr. Seward is threatening us with war if we recognize the South, and the South declares that if we don't recognize their flag, they will take it as an act of hostility."

· · ·

AT MONTGOMERY, RUSSELL boarded the *Southern Republic* for the long voyage down the Alabama River to Mobile, and it was on that ship made of kindling that he saw firsthand the evidence he'd been looking for of the transatlantic slave trade: the survivors of the voyage of the *Clotilda* presented to him by the contemptuous Captain Meaher.

"Well, now, you think those niggers I have aboard came from Africa? I'll show you," Meaher had said, calling to a young boy with tribal scars and filed teeth. "What's your name?" the captain asked.

"Bully," said the boy.

"Where were you born?"

"Born in South Carolina, sir."

"There, you see," said the captain. "I've got a lot of these black South Carolina niggers aboard."

WILLIAM HOWARD RUSSELL went to Louisiana, Mississippi, and back into the North at Cairo, Illinois. He spent long hours with the British consuls he met along the way, and he met everybody who was anybody, including John Slidell, the puppet-master of the national Democratic convention in Charleston. There was no shortage of information, opinion, and gossip, and from it all Russell came away with two firm conclusions, which he repeatedly conveyed to his readers and which aligned directly with the analysis of Consul Bunch.

First, the Southerners would fight, and as hard and as long as they possibly could. Many Northerners, notably Seward, had tried to convince themselves otherwise. The Confederates, they said, were like wayward children who would come back to the family soon enough. But they were wrong. Russell figured that the secessionist Southerners—or "Seceshers," as he called them—would have to be defeated utterly and absolutely if the Confederate states were ever to be reunited with the North.

Second, the Southerners would cling to the institution of slavery, which Russell called "a cancer." He also believed that, whether in secret or in public, they would reopen the Middle Passage from Africa. Again he repeated a refrain that Bunch had made his own in confidential correspondence. "Of one thing there can be no doubt," Russell told his readers, "a slave state cannot long exist without a Slave Trade."

Chapter 36

ROBERT BUNCH WAS ABOUT TO undertake the most important diplomatic assignment of his career, but if it worked, nobody outside the Foreign Office and a handful of people directly involved would know what he had done. He would use third parties to keep his name and his government's role out of it, and he would use a lot of creative ambiguity—that tool of diplomacy and espionage that lets people understand what they want to understand without any express commitment—in order to get the job done.

The goal was nothing less than to define the rules of war and of commerce for Britain and other neutral powers at a time when both the South and the North had created a situation of dangerous, and potentially disastrous, confusion.

In April, in the aftermath of Sumter, Lincoln and Seward had declared a Federal blockade of Southern ports. This recognized the fact that Washington could not simply close them as if it were still in control, because it was not. But a blockade normally was an act carried out against a hostile power, not against one's own citizens. So the British government decided to clarify the matter by announcing in May that Great Britan recognized a state of belligerency between "the Government of the United States of America and certain states styling themselves the Confederate States of America."

This announcement, as Lord John Russell put it, was a matter "not of principle, but of fact," and carried with it limited, though important, consequences. Under international law at that time, belligerents had standing that rebels did not have. Belligerents could get loans abroad, they could buy military and naval supplies, they could visit foreign ports. Their revenue laws would be respected. Their flag would, indeed, be recognized. Belligerents were granted "a *quasi* political recognition."

Washington was furious, and Richmond, the new Confederate capital, was jubilant. But the measure did not open the way to the economic and military support for the South that William Seward desperately opposed, or that Jefferson Davis desperately wanted. In practical terms it was much more about definition than about recognition. Britain as well as France, which soon followed suit, wanted to be sure of their own national rights as neutrals in dealing with the two contending American governments and their armed forces. Britain and France were ready to go to war if they felt those rights were infringed, but they wanted to try a diplomatic route first, which is where Robert Bunch came in.

Under the 1856 Declaration of Paris that Clarendon had negotiated, neutral ships flying the flags of neutral nations had clearly defined rights: They could carry goods belonging to either of the belligerents without fear they'd be seized, as long as those goods were not "contraband of war," which was taken at that time to mean weapons. Neutral goods on the ships of belligerents would be immune from seizure by enemy ships, with the same caveat about contraband. And, finally, any blockade would have to be "maintained by a force sufficient really to prevent access to the coast of the enemy." It would not be enough for the Union simply to make a declaration saying that, for instance, Charleston was under blockade. The Union had to have warships in place to make that policy effective.

But there was one big problem with this tidy legalistic approach. Neither of the belligerents was a signatory to the Declaration of Paris, and neither was obliged to honor it.

In Washington, Lyons and the French minister, Count Henri Mercier, were working on Seward to try to get the U.S. government to sign on to the Declaration. The Confederates posed a more complicated challenge. London and Paris did not even want to acknowledge they were talking to them. The trick was to get them to act as if they'd voluntarily decided to embrace the neutrality and blockade provisions of the Declaration.

Lord Russell thought Consul Mure, in New Orleans, would be the man for the job, perhaps because he was older, perhaps because

Russell did not know how far New Orleans was from the new Confederate capital in Richmond, or perhaps because Russell had never been fond of Bunch's tone, his observations, or his presumptions in his dispatches. (Others, such as Permanent Undersecretary Edmund Hammond, had entirely lost their patience with Bunch.)

But Lord Lyons felt strongly that Her Majesty's man in Charleston, whom he had worked with so closely over the last year and felt he had gotten to know so well, would be just the diplomat for the job. Lyons had become Bunch's defender and promoter, protecting him from criticism and extolling the virtues of his reporting to London. Lyons never really had anyone else in mind. But, still, Lyons must have known that appointing Bunch to handle the most sensitive diplomatic initiative of the war up to that point was a very risky proposition. Already, ominously, there were signs that Seward's detectives—in effect, his secret police—had taken a decided interest in Bunch and his messengers.

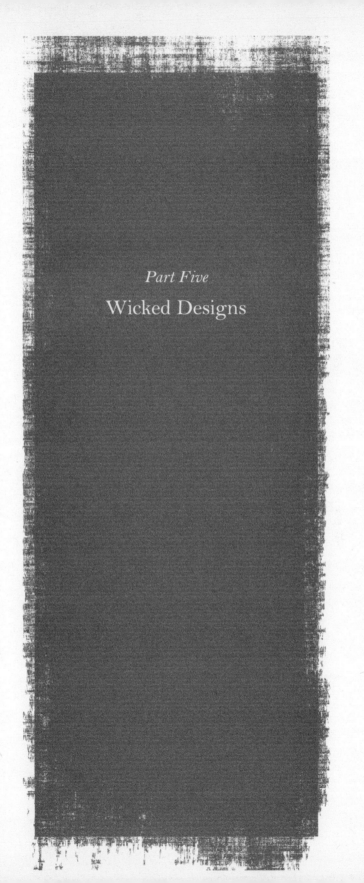

Part Five

Wicked Designs

THE JULY HEAT IN WASHINGTON was wet and stifling, and the slightest current of air was welcome, so Lord Lyons and his staff dined early at the legation, then sat out in the garden with William Howard Russell to hear about his travels through the South. While the correspondent had been away, the capital of the United States had become a precarious armed camp, with a restive Maryland at its back and a growing Confederate force in Virginia not far beyond the Potomac.

As fears in the U.S. capital rose, Seward's temper and his judgment seemed to fray. The more powerful the Confederates appeared, the more Seward "assumes higher ground, and becomes more exacting and defiant," Lyons said, and the more aggressive he became toward Britain. Lyons was disheartened by Seward's rants, and as W. H. Russell looked at the British minister in the fading light amid the infernal humidity of the garden, the reporter was struck by how "careworn and pale" Lord Lyons had become.

Seward was sending dispatches to his American envoys in London and Paris that "amounted to little less than a declaration of war against Great Britain," Lyons complained, and the letters were leaked to the American press before they'd made it halfway across the Atlantic. But those were nothing compared to the "violent language" that Seward used face-to-face.

It seemed impossible to believe that the U.S. secretary of state really wanted to plunge the country into a war with England and France. Either power alone would be far too much for the Union Navy; together they would be overwhelming. They could sweep aside the feeble blockade of the Southern ports; at the same time they could shut down the North's ports on the Atlantic and the Great Lakes—and that would be just the beginning. But Seward, cornered, seemed capable of anything. On June 6, Lyons had sent a telegram in cipher to Lord Russell. "No new event has occurred, but a sudden declaration of war by the United States against Great Britain appears to me to be by no means impossible, especially as long as Canada seems open to invasion."

ON THE FOURTH of July, the day the United States celebrated its independence from Great Britain, William Howard Russell went to the State Department to see William Seward for himself. The secretary looked much more haggard than he had three months before, and he made his bitterness perfectly clear.

"We are dealing with an insurrection within our own country, of our own people, and the Government of Great Britain have thought fit to recognize that insurrection before we were able to bring the strength of the Union to bear against it," Seward said. Then it was as if Seward just couldn't hold back anymore. "We have less to fear from a foreign war than any country in the world," he said. "If any European Power provokes a war, we shall not shrink from it. A contest between Great Britain and the United States would wrap the world in fire, and at the end it would not be the United States which would have to lament the results of the conflict."*

It was quite a show, and reflecting on it after he walked back onto the street full of July Fourth celebrations, Russell was bemused. "I could not but admire the confidence—may I say the coolness?—of the statesman who sat in his modest little room within the sound of the enemy's guns, in a capital menaced by their forces, who spoke so fearlessly of war with a power which should have blotted out the paper blockade of the Southern forts and coast in a few hours and, in conjunction with the Southern armies, have repeated the occu-

---

* Charles Francis Adams, writing fifty years later, would call Seward's remarks a "singularly visionary and delusive hallucination" but argue that Seward probably did believe that the United States, with its vast interior spaces, would have an advantage over the British with their far-flung colonies and extended supply lines.

pation and destruction of the capital." (Nobody had forgotten the destruction wrought by the British in the War of 1812.)

And yet, the Confederates were no longer so optimistic about their chances of winning the Crown's support. William Yancey, the great fire-eater who had ripped like a blazing comet through the Democratic Party's convention in Charleston, was now in Europe as the head of the Confederate commission seeking diplomatic recognition and material assistance. But he soon discovered that the oratory that had brought delegates and spectators to their feet in Charleston moved very few people on the far side of the Atlantic. His defenses of slavery and the slave trade fell on deaf ears, or very hostile ones. Indeed, he quit making them, and then he pretended he never had. In May, Yancey and the two other commissioners had an unofficial meeting with Lord Russell at his house in London, trying to persuade him that the main reason why the Southern states seceded was not slavery at all but the high Federal tariffs imposed on manufactured goods from abroad in order to protect the industries of the North. This rationale completely contradicted South Carolina's stated reasons for secession published fewer than five months before, but Russell did not debate; he just listened. And Russell did not ask the Confederate commissioners about the question of the slave trade to Africa. But then the Confederate delegates brought it up themselves. They knew how sensitive the issue was. They wanted to address it. They pointed out the article in their new constitution that made it illegal.

Lord Russell wondered about that. Since the commissioners had insisted on bringing up the matter, the Foreign Secretary said he'd heard that if the slave states found they could not compete successfully with the cotton of other countries, "they would revive the slave trade for the purpose of diminishing the cost of production." This was, in fact, part of the gospel in the pro-slavery crusade that Bunch had reported on since the mid-1850s; this was precisely the argument that Governor Adams had made in his stunning speech attacking Great Britain's use of "free slaves" to grow cotton in India and Egypt. But Yancey and his fellow commissioners insisted there was no proof to support such a notion, and, anyway, they insisted once more, their constitution forbade it. Lord Russell went back to listening and made no commitments whatsoever during this unofficial meeting with an unrecognized delegation.

Yancey was no fool. He knew his mission was failing. In June he wrote from Paris that "the government of England simply wants to see which shall prove strongest, and that it is sincere in its expressed design to be neutral." The Confederate commissioners concluded that their government had no chance of recognition and support unless and until their army had a major success on the battlefield.

All of the South was waiting as rumors circulated of the decisive fight about to begin, but then called off. "The long expected battle in Virginia seems to be deferred," Bunch wrote at the end of June. "Will not Congress do something to stop this wretched war?" But there was no turning back.

Chapter 38

W ILLIAM SEWARD SAW SPIES EVERYWHERE, and his spies
       were everywhere. His police, informants, and private de-
tectives kept a constant flow of information and allegations piling
onto his desk. Legal guarantees for suspected traitors and secret
agents were thrown out. When William Howard Russell met with
Seward in July, the reporter accused the secretary of running what
amounted to a police state, and Seward, for his part, was unapolo-
getic: "The government will not shrink from using all the means
which they consider necessary to restore the Union." But as word
got back to London of Seward's activities, Palmerston raged against
the effrontery of it all. "These North Americans," he said, "are following fast the example of the Spanish Americans and the Conti-
nental despots. They commit all sorts of violence without regard to
law, take up men and women and imprison them on mere suspicion,
and rule the land by spies and police and martial law."

Seward looked through the telegrams and dossiers. So many
traitors, so many conspiracies. And there was one name that kept
coming up again and again.

In June Seward got a report from John A. Kennedy, the superintendent of New York City's Metropolitan Police (the force aligned
with Seward and his Republican friends) stating unequivocally "the
British consul at Charleston, Mr. Bunch, is a notorious secessionist, and that he has used his position in every way he could since
the troubles began in aiding the secession movement." Kennedy's
letter complained that Bunch had issued passports to dubious characters, including one William Trappman, an American citizen who
had served as the Prussian consul in Charleston. It appears from
other correspondence that Trappman was involved in efforts to buy
arms for the Confederacy. He had nearly been arrested aboard a
steamer leaving Boston in mid-June but had said he was carrying
correspondence for Lord Lyons and presented a Bunch-issued travel

document. The Boston police allowed him to sail, only to discover a few hours later that Seward had ordered Trappman's arrest for treason.

It was not extraordinary that Britain's official consul would try to help out Prussia's honorary one, or that Bunch and Lyons used him to carry correspondence, but Seward's agents thought they now had Bunch dead to rights.

The police superintendent stated flatly that Bunch "used his office for facilitating the transmission of treasonable correspondence." The evidence was, to say the least, circumstantial. A Belgian merchant who was known to have secessionist sympathies and who might have left for Europe on a mission for the Confederacy "is in the habit of receiving letters from Charleston," which he would pick up at the office of Consul Archibald in New York, the police superintendent wrote. The police claimed that Archibald's deputy told them that before the mails from the South were stopped the New York consulate regularly received "packages of letters from Mr. Bunch for strange persons of whom they had no knowledge."

Seward's response was, for him, surprisingly measured. He decreed that all passports issued in the United States would have to be countersigned by him if they were to be valid. He sent a copy of the police report with a private note to Lord Lyons, and Lyons, apparently shocked, said Bunch must not have been aware of the courier's arms-buying activities.

Only a few weeks later, in July, the police picked up another suspect. Purcell M'Quillan, also written as Purcell M. Quillen, was an Irishman who'd been working as a clerk in a Charleston carpet warehouse. He had asked for a passport from Bunch so he could go visit his father in Baltimore. When he was arrested, manacled, and sent to the infamous prison at Fort Lafayette in New York Harbor, M'Quillan was, like many other suspected Southern agents and sympathizers, denied habeas corpus. The ostensible charges were spying for the rebels and trying to buy weapons, but M'Quillan was released after a few weeks following protests by Lord Lyons.

He may never have been involved in anything untoward, and it is plausible that the main reason the clerk was picked up was so Seward's men could gather more information on Robert Bunch.

The Charleston consul pretended to be unperturbed about all this. After all, M'Quillan was just one of so many messengers he'd sent northward. "I had some conversation with him when I gave him his passport (which I did after full inquiry, an examination on oath, etc.)," Bunch wrote to Lyons. "I asked him if he were going to Washington on his return to Charleston, and on his replying in the affirmative gave him a line to Your Lordship stating that he was a respectable young man and might be trusted with anything you might have for me. Of course, he may have been buying arms for the Southern Confederacy, but I really do not believe it."

Lyons was worried. The secret mission to Richmond to try to win Confederate compliance with the Declaration of Paris was approaching, and Bunch, the man he'd put in charge of it, already was under scrutiny. "Her Majesty's government does not wish for an *éclat* here, so be particularly careful to avoid bringing one on, either as respects yourself or me," Lyons warned Bunch. "They have already got stories about you and the persons to whom you have given passports to the North, which I shall do all I can to put straight. They make it necessary for you to be particularly cautious." At about the same time, Lyons wrote to Lord John Russell that he saw "symptoms of a determination here" to make Bunch "an object of attack." Lyons concluded by saying, "I have no doubt he will manage the negotiations about the Declaration of Paris as well and as prudently as any man." But the secrecy around the mission to Richmond was compromised before it ever started.

Hearing generally of Seward's concerns, Bunch could not figure out what was wrong: "The amusing part of all this to me is that the *U.S. government* should think, as it evidently does, that I have been working against *them*." The Confederates might accuse him of undermining their cause with good reason, he figured. But this was baffling. "I am perhaps wasting a good deal of indignation, as I do not know what is or is not alleged against me." He was just picking up signals from Lyons, Archibald, and one of the attachés in Washington, none of whom, it seems, had told him about the inquiries and allegations being made by the New York Metropolitan Police. "All allude to *something*, and I am really curious to know what it is."

Given all the pressure being put on them, Lyons and his consuls tried to find secure means of communications. More and more of their telegrams and letters were written in diplomatic cipher or admiralty cipher or whatever cipher they could find—for a while they were trading ciphers around like recipes for desserts. The mails were completely unreliable, and, as the Trappman and M'Quillan cases suggested, informal messengers might have—or might be alleged to have—dubious loyalties and connections. Eventually Lyons started dispatching Royal Navy cruisers to Charleston to pick up messages from Bunch. But in the meantime he used a company called Adams Express, a forerunner of today's parcel services, which managed to operate in both the South and the North. Probably it was not very safe, either. Its head of security was Allan Pinkerton, whose detective agency was a Seward favorite.

Chapter 39

THE TIME HAD COME FOR the mission to Richmond. Bunch made his way along Meeting Street, then down through the covered market, which was packed with people on a Friday afternoon. His old friend William Henry Trescot had an office nearby on East Bay Street. After the usual exchange of pleasantries and the offered drink, Bunch asked, "How well do you know Jefferson Davis?"

"Why, we have very cordial relations."

So Bunch went to the heart of the matter. He said that he and Monsieur de Belligny, the acting French consul in Charleston who had replaced the Count de Choiseul, had received dispatches that morning from their respective governments that were "of the most delicate and important character."

"We're instructed to make contact with the government in Richmond—but to do so through an intermediary," Bunch said. "I cannot explain more fully except in the presence of my French colleague, but we have agreed to meet you, to give you the instructions, and ask you to become the channel of communication between us and Richmond." According to Trescot's notes on the conversation, Bunch said this was a step of "great significance and importance."

That night, Trescot met with Bunch and de Belligny. Bunch read aloud the initial dispatch from Lord Russell sent in May, an official letter Lyons had sent him in early July, and a long private letter from Lyons as well, outlining the need to have the Confederate government sign on to the three key provisions in the Declaration of Paris. "And now you know all that I know myself," he said.

Trescot tested the consuls to see just how far they might go. "Are you prepared for the Confederate government to make an official declaration based on your request, thus giving it implied recognition in the eyes of the world?"

"No, no," said the consuls, almost in unison. "This has to be a spontaneous declaration," said Bunch.

"I don't see how you can ask that," replied Trescot. He also failed to see how the supposedly spontaneous commitment to the terms of an international treaty by an as yet unrecognized state would be binding. But the consuls were adamant about secrecy.

"If this becomes public, the United States government will revoke our exequaturs and will dismiss Lyons and Mercier from Washington," Bunch warned. The consuls might, as private citizens, say this was an important step toward recognition, but even assuming the aim of the British and French governments was to reach recognition, they wanted to do it so as not to provoke a break with Washington. Lyons had been perfectly explicit about that. "This indirect way is the only way," said Bunch.

Trescot didn't like the sound of it. "All this secrecy that you say is essential to the negotiations takes away from the Confederate government the very same incentive you say you're giving it."

"We can't make any commitments in that respect," said Bunch. "You will find the consequences most agreeable and beneficial to the Confederate government," de Belligny assured Trescot.

Finally Trescot agreed to accept the mission, but with an explicit understanding that when he met with Davis he would be free to advise him to accept the proposal or reject it, "as I think right."

The ball was now in play.

TWO DAYS LATER, on the morning of July 21, 1861, William Howard Russell was running late for a battle. Confederate troops under Gen. P. G. T. Beauregard, whom he knew from Charleston, and the Union Army under Gen. Irvin McDowell, whom he'd met several times, were massed around a little rivulet called Bull Run near the Manassas Gap Railroad junction. Everybody in Washington seemed to think this first major battle would be a Northern victory.

It might be the beginning of serious fighting. It might be the end of it. Whatever happened, there was no question, Russell had to be there to see it.

Since Russell's return from the South to the Federal capital, nothing had gone right for him. While he'd been away, and despite his reams of reporting, Delane and the other editors of the *Times* of London had taken a stand of clear sympathy with the secessionists. They reflected the interests of an elite with commercial concerns about cotton and contempt for the American notion of a republic. They also embraced the idea that, because Lincoln and Seward insisted this war was not about freeing the slaves, then truly that was the case. And for the masses, there was the appeal of the Southerners as underdogs struggling against the subjugation of Washington. The *Times* editors had become just the apostles of the fait accompli that Seward had feared. So even though the paper still ran Russell's articles about the inadequacies of the Southern military position, the arrogance of King Cotton, and the monstrosity of slavery, its editorials were such that Russell found the *Times* "assailed on all sides as a Secession organ, favorable to the rebels and exceedingly hostile to the Federal government and the cause of the Union." The net result for its correspondent was that he no longer had the kind of access to the Union military that he'd wanted and expected. Seward would still see him, but U.S. War Department passes were hard to come by, and on the eve of combat no one would give him the countersign so he could get through checkpoints to see the battle begin at dawn.

Not until midday did Russell finally get close enough to the fighting to hear "the thudding noise, like taps with a gentle hand upon a muffled drum" of artillery in action. Along with congressmen and other dignitaries, many of them accompanied by their wives, he watched from atop a hill above Centreville as distant wisps of smoke marked the opposing lines. He ate a sandwich. He drank some Bordeaux he'd packed in his case. By the time he drew closer to the fighting, the Union forces were pulling back; then, suddenly, they were fleeing in a rout so complete that he could hardly believe his eyes.

Russell was on a borrowed nag threading his way toward the action when he heard loud shouts ahead of him and saw several wagons coming from the direction of the battlefield. The drivers were trying to force their way past the ammunition carts coming up the narrow road. A thick cloud of dust rose behind them. Men were running beside the carts, between them. "Every moment the crowd increased, drivers and men cried out with the most vehement gestures, 'Turn back! Turn back! We are whipped.' They seized the heads of the horses and swore at the opposing drivers." A breathless officer with an empty scabbard dangling by his side got wedged for a second between a wagon and Russell's horse.

"What is the matter, sir?" Russell asked. "What is all this about?

"Why, it means we are pretty badly whipped," said the officer, "and that's the truth." Then he scrambled away.

The heat, the uproar, and the dust were "beyond description," Russell wrote afterward. And it all got worse when some cavalry soldiers, flourishing their sabers, tried to force their way through the mob, shouting, "Make way for the general!"

Russell made it to a white house where two field guns were positioned, when suddenly troops came pouring out of the nearby forest. The gunners were about to blast away when an officer or a sergeant shouted, "Stop! Stop! They are our own men." In a few minutes a whole battalion ran past in utter disorder. "We are pursued by their cavalry," one told Russell. "They have cut us all to pieces."

After a while there was nothing the world's greatest war correspondent could do but fall in with the tide of men fleeing the fighting. In all his battles, he had never seen anything like this: "Infantry soldiers on mules and draught horses, with the harness clinging to their heels, as much frightened as their riders; Negro servants on their masters' chargers; ambulances crowded with unwounded soldiers; wagons swarming with men who threw out the contents in the road to make room; grinding through a shouting, screaming mass of men on foot, who were literally yelling with rage at every halt and shrieking out, 'Here are the cavalry! Will you get on?'" They talked "prodigious nonsense," Russell said, "describing batteries tier over tier, and ambuscades, and blood running knee-deep." As he rode through the crowd, men grabbed at Russell's stirrups and saddle. He kept telling them over and over again not to be in such a hurry. "There's no enemy to pursue you. All the cavalry in the world could not get at you." But, as he soon realized, he "might as well have talked to the stones."

It was a long way back to Washington that day. But after several brushes with violent deserters, drunken soldiers, and more panic-stricken officers, Russell made his way in the moonlight to the Long Bridge across the Potomac and into the capital. He told anyone who asked him that the Union commander would regroup and resume the battle the next morning. But when he awoke in his boardinghouse on Pennsylvania Avenue, he found the city full of uniformed rabble. "The great Army of the Potomac," he wrote, "is in the streets of Washington instead of on its way to Richmond."

The Federal capital was essentially defenseless. "The inmates of the White House are in a state of the utmost trepidation," Russell wrote, "and Mr. Lincoln, who sat in the telegraph operator's room with General Scott and Mr. Seward, listening to the dispatches as they arrived from the scene of the action, left in despair when the fatal words tripped from the needle and the defeat was already revealed to him."

For the South, "here is a golden opportunity," said Russell. "If the Confederates do not grasp that which will never come again on such terms, it stamps them with mediocrity." But the rebels stayed where they were, and the fact that they did not march on Washington suggested this would be a long war.

As Russell studied the city, its politicians, and its dispositions in the aftermath of the battle, he did not agree with "many who think the contest is now over." He figured the Northerners had learned a lesson about "the nature of the conflict on which they have entered" and would be roused to action. But when the *Times* ran Russell's article on the battle, his balanced judgment about the lessons learned got no play. The whole effect of his account of the rout was to reinforce the editors' image of a South that not only would fight, but could fight better than the North and, therefore, should soon be free of it.

Obviously now the Palmerston government could recognize the Confederacy and would and should. And yet it did not.

Southerners, in full hubris, were continuing to withhold their cotton in order to inflict as much pain as possible on Britain for its evident reluctance to join their cause. Bunch sent a note to Lyons in cipher about these developments, then concluded, uncoded, with the ironic comment, "We are getting much 'riled' at not being recognized." Lyons labeled the letter in his file, *Wicked designs of the South.*

WHY DID BRITAIN hold back? William Seward's bluffs often are given credit, and, certainly, war with the Union was not something even Palmerston would embark on without some hesitation. But Seward's combative diplomacy might just as easily have brought the British into the fight. Seward's belligerence angered Palmerston and his cabinet much more than it awed them, especially after the Union's dismal performance at Manassas, and the applause for the embattled South in British newspapers was thunderous. To read the London press of that time is to marvel that the Crown did not embrace the Confederates as brothers in arms struggling against Yankee tyranny. Yet there was an arrogance about this new Confederacy and the pride it claimed to take in its peculiar institution that Palmerston found deeply distasteful. The "private" and "confidential" reporting he saw from his own men, Lord Lyons and Bunch, gave him a picture of the South very different from that put forth by the leader-writers in London. The minister and the consul told him what he needed to know, what he wanted to know, and, perhaps most important, what he did not want to know about the unforgivable inhumanity of slave owners and their ambitions to build an empire on the backs of Africans. These were the inconvenient but ineluctable truths Palmerston could not forget.

Even the Confederacy's most talented advocates in London had to recognize the deep British loathing for slavery and the trade. One of the best of them, James Spence, argued that secession was legal under the U.S. Constitution and, yes, a fait accompli and thus should be recognized, but he conceded to the British peers and public what he knew they already felt: slavery was "an evil in an economical sense, a wrong to humanity in a moral one," and he did not stop there. "No reasoning, no statistics, no profit, no philosophy, can reconcile us to that which our instinct repels," wrote Spence. Given this revulsion, Spence's strongest argument was that this vile institution had been supported by the very constitution that the Union forces claimed to defend, while Lincoln and Seward continued to say their war was not intended to free the slaves—no, not at all.

Palmerston often seemed to be drifting toward recognition of the South for practical commercial reasons and because he could not conceive how it could be forced to return to the Union. But he remained undecided. How could he forget the treatment of free black British sailors under the hideous Negro Seamen Act? How could he condone a new nation of filibusters out to conquer territories in Central America that the Crown was determined to protect? Palmerston truly could not imagine, moreover, that the British people would accept Southern insistence that fugitive slaves be returned to their owners once they had made it to free soil (the Southerners even tried to get them returned from the British Bahamas), and he could not stomach the idea that he, the leader of Christendom in its opposition to the slave trade, might be aiding or abetting its expansion.

If such concerns had not lingered like a sinister shadow in the background of all its discussions, the British cabinet might well have opted to recognize the Confederacy. It was a close—a very close—thing. And at just this moment of decision in the summer of 1861 Bunch was reporting from Charleston that the American squadron was being pulled back from African shores to build the Federal blockade along the Confederate coast. As a result, he said, slave traders flying the American flag would step up their traffic to Cuba. Lord Russell, acting on Bunch's note, demanded an explanation from Seward.

When Russell's instructions reached Lyons weeks later, and he went to see Seward, the response was not the truculent one that he expected. Seward said that, yes, warships such as the *San Jacinto* had been recalled from the African coast to patrol American shores, but he hoped he would be able to put them back on anti-slaving duty soon. Then Seward added, in what seemed on its face a stunning reversal of policy, that the Lincoln administration "had none of the squeamishness about allowing American vessels to be boarded and searched which had characterized their predecessors." Lyons, when he heard this, was stunned. He asked Seward to repeat what he'd just said. Seward told him that neither he nor anyone else in Lincoln's cabinet would object to the Royal Navy searching American-flagged vessels off the African coast if it was done in a proper manner and based on reasonable suspicion.

Was this the breakthrough in the fight against the slave trade that it seemed? Lyons advised Lord Russell not to trust Seward, who might make such vague, informal assurances in a conversation and reverse them the minute there was a sign the public disapproved.

In fact, Seward already was hell-bent on confrontation about another issue involving the activities of that British official he considered a dangerous partisan of the Southern cause: Her Majesty's consul in Charleston, South Carolina, Robert Bunch. The secret contacts with Richmond had been exposed.

Chapter 40

A T THE END OF JULY 1861, William Henry Trescot saw the train rolling into Gordonsville, Virginia, on its journey from the Battle of Bull Run back to Richmond. The wounded filled the cars, their groaning a chorus of pain. Some of them lingered on the verge of death. Many had died along the way. Any victory has its hideous faces, and these were some from the triumph at Manassas. Already there were recriminations about Beauregard's failure to advance on Washington after the battle, but, in truth, his forces were spent.

Trescot, following up on his conversation with Bunch and de Belligny, had traveled for two days from Charleston to Richmond, only to be told that Jefferson Davis, the man he had come to talk to, had gone to the battle. Trescot was on his way to find him there, when he learned at Gordonsville that Davis was on the train that had just passed by, accompanying the wounded. Trescot turned around and headed back.

When he finally caught up with the president of the Confederacy and presented the proposal given him by Consuls Bunch and de Belligny, Davis was suspicious. The first thing he wanted to know was why the British weren't raising this issue with his official representatives in London. Trescot reminded him that those commissioners had not yet been received officially. Seward had insisted that receiving them officially would be tantamount to recognition of the Confederacy, and recognition was the same as an alliance with the rebels, which would mean war between Britain and the United States—hence, this mission through back channels.

None of this did much to improve Davis's dim view of the affair. So Trescot suggested that Davis let it be known informally that he favored the proposal about maritime rights, and then his formal representatives in London could deliver the official word and be received, and that could set in motion the recognition and the alliance that the South so badly needed. Still, Davis was noncommittal, referring the matter to his cabinet and the Confederate Congress. It wasn't the solution Trescot had sought, which would, indeed, have opened negotiations between the Crown and the Confederacy. But from London's point of view, it worked.

The Confederate Congress approved the measures a couple of weeks later, recognizing three of the four key points in the 1856 Declaration of Paris. The South would *not* abolish privateering, but it would respect neutral flags, it would respect neutral goods, and it would recognize that a blockade, in order to be binding, must be maintained with sufficient force to prevent access to the coast.

CHARLESTON WAS HELL in August, but Robert Bunch was, more or less, in heaven. He had been entrusted with a hugely important diplomatic assignment, a secret one that had to be handled with enormous tact. For a man of such relentless ambition, this was a moment to be savored and exploited. Already he saw this as the ticket he needed to promotion, perhaps to his own legation. He had taken the initiatives that were needed and had ignored those that were not, fending off the foolish idea from London that he should make the idiot Governor Pickens his emissary. He had turned to his old friend William Henry Trescot, and Trescot had done a masterful job. Nobody who did not need to know would know about the mission, and those who did know would thank Bunch for it.

"We guarded as scrupulously as it was possible against the possibility of our action being traced," Bunch wrote to Lyons. Jefferson Davis had had to agree to keep the initiative under wraps before he was even allowed to know what it was. "We also made a positive stipulation that France and England were not to be alluded to," Bunch wrote. Lyons believed the job was well done.

· · ·

AS OCCASIONALLY HAPPENED, Lord Palmerston seemed to be thinking out loud in the House of Commons. On this particular day, July 26, 1861, Palmerston had been listening to a raucous debate about the slave trade around the world and what must be done to stop it. There was talk of Indian coolies smuggled by the French to the island of Réunion; there was talk about whether to pay to put a consul in Mozambique to try to keep the Portuguese in line; and there were many strong opinions, of course, about the impact of the widening "disruption of the American Republic" on the future of slavery and the slave trade.

The Radical UP William Edward Forster took a direct shot at the South and said that he would "look forward with great fear to the revival of the slave trade" if the Southern states should succeed in breaking away from the Union. He pointed to the fact that "Mr. Yancey, the leading Commissioner to Europe of the so-called Southern Confederacy," had proposed in years past to do away with the American laws against the slave trade.

Finally, Palmerston rose to speak, rambling on a bit about coolies, about France, and about Spain before finally turning his sights on America. He recited all the frustrations Britain had faced as slavers flew the American flag, the British were barred from searching them, and U.S. Navy cruisers failed to capture them.

"It was the spirit of the South which animated these expeditions," said Palmerston, and if the North should triumph, he had hopes that such a victory would end American involvement in the trade. But Palmerston added, "I do not believe that there is any real importation of slaves in the Southern States of America." It was clear he did not want to consider that possibility. "Cuba is now the only plague spot in the world," he said.

The reporting of Bunch, the reminders from Lyons, and the remonstrances of Radicals such as Forster seemed to have made little impression.

A day or so later William Howard Russell's account of the Battle of Manassas reached London, and Palmerston scrawled a note that was forwarded to Lyons. "The defeat at Bulls [*sic*] Run, or rather at Yankees [*sic*] Run, proves two things," he said. "First, that to bring together many thousand men and put uniforms on their backs and muskets in their hands is not to make an army. Disciplined, experienced officers and confidence in the steadiness of their comrades are necessary to make an army fight and stand. Secondly, that the unionist cause is not in the hearts of the mass of the population of the North."

"The Americans are not cowards," said Palmerston. Individually they were as brave as anyone, "and it is not easy to believe that if they had felt they were fighting for a great national interest, they would have run away as they did from the battle or that whole regiments would have quietly wandered away home just before the fight was to begin. The truth is, the North are fighting for an idea chiefly entertained by newspaper writers and by professional politicians, while the South are fighting for what they consider, rightly or wrongly, vital interests."

And yet, despite Palmerston's doubts about the slave trade to the Confederate states, and despite this lukewarm assessment of the Union fighting forces, Her Majesty's government was not going to give the South the support it needed unless insults and provocations by the North forced it to do so.

Acouple of weeks after bull run, a Unionist from Connecticut who would later be described as "a trustworthy gentleman" was signing the register at the Galt House Hotel in Louisville, Kentucky, when "a distinguished looking stranger entered the room and was immediately surrounded by a number of gentlemen of the secesh persuasion." Now that the fighting had begun in earnest, emotions were running high in the contested border state of Kentucky. Everybody was on edge, and the stranger's voice echoed through the reception area of the hotel. He told his new acquaintances that he was the British consul in Charleston, South Carolina, that he was an ardent sympathizer with secession, and that he expected soon to be appointed British minister to the Confederate government in Richmond. Everybody was listening. He said he was freshly arrived from the rebel capital with all the latest news. And his name, he said, was Robert Mure.

In fact, Mure was a bluff Scotsman who still spoke in Doric dialect after almost thirty years in South Carolina. He was a naturalized American citizen, and he had served in one of the Carolina militias (rumor had it he'd fought in the bloodless battle for Fort Sumter). Mure certainly was not the British consul in Charleston, but he had volunteered to serve as one of the many couriers used by the real consul, Robert Bunch. If he had not been such a braggart, he might well have gone about his business unmolested and, ultimately, with next to no impact from the widening American Civil War. But he just couldn't shut up.

Later that same day, the Unionist from Connecticut, who seems to have been a particularly diligent amateur spy, found himself sitting near Mure and another man in the hotel office as they were having a quiet but quite audible conversation over cigars. Mure said he had been closeted in Richmond with Jefferson Davis and members of his cabinet "for several days," and they had entrusted him with papers "which he believed would insure the recognition of the Confederacy by the Governments of Great Britain and France," along with financial documents "representing a large amount of money for the purchase of arms and munitions of war." Mure said he planned to leave Louisville on Sunday, August 11, heading for New York and Boston, where he would take the Cunard steamer for Liverpool under an assumed name.

The "trustworthy gentleman" from Connecticut followed Robert Mure to Cincinnati. Then he hurried to the telegraph office in the middle of the night to send a message to Seward. The operator was rousted out of bed and, as it happened, "possessed the Government cipher." He sent the following message, which landed like a bombshell in Seward's office the next morning:

CINCINNATI, August 12, 1861

WILLIAM H. SEWARD, Secretary of State, Washington, D.C.:

Robert Mure, an Englishman by birth but resident of Charleston, S.C., for the last thirty years, is to take the steamer at New York Wednesday for Europe. He has highly important dispatches from Confederate Congress very carefully concealed. Intercept dispatches and the Confederates will be in your power. Mr. Mure is cousin to British consul at New Orleans.

B. T. HENRY.

For the U.S. secretary of state and his spies, this bit of information seemed to pull everything into focus. For months, Seward's agents had been targeting Britain's consuls with a vengeance, and they had come across some incriminating information about the veteran William Mure in New Orleans. They claimed that he was working with his brothers in Canada on a blockade-running scheme and that he'd sent thousands of letters designed to help the Confederacy under the protection of the British seal.

If this Robert Mure was indeed a relative of the consul in New Orleans, that fact alone would raise suspicions. Mure's itinerary also was incriminating: he had traveled a circuitous route from South Carolina to Kentucky and Ohio in order to avoid Federal lines. And then there was the Charleston connection.

The same morning Seward got the message from "B. T. Henry," he sent a telegram of his own to Superintendent John A. Kennedy of the New York Metropolitan Police ordering Robert Mure's arrest. When the detectives tracked him the next day to the Brevoort House Hotel in Greenwich Village he immediately presented his documents, of course. The one authorizing him as an official courier of the diplomatic pouch was signed by Her Majesty's Consul Robert Bunch.

It seemed to Seward that he not only had the Confederates in his power, as the mysterious Mr. Henry had suggested, but Great Britain as well.

Two days after Mure's arrest, Seward called Lord Lyons to the State Department and showed him the haul that had been sent down from New York. Seward said he was sending the official dispatch bag, wrapped in brown paper, directly to London to be delivered in person to Lord John Russell. He also told Lyons that almost two hundred letters had been found among Mure's belongings that were not under seal. He had not read all of them yet, but he would.

Far to the South, Bunch was oblivious to the threat taking shape. Indeed, he remained almost euphoric. This was the first full summer he had spent in Charleston's pestilential climate, but the fevers of August had been mild, and he was feeling quite well—or better than well, because he saw himself as a survivor. How many times had he told the Foreign Office that to pass these summer months in Charleston was certain death for those who were not acclimated? And here he was, alive. And, yes, it would seem, very well acclimated.

On July 17, the same day that Lyons was writing up letters and dispatches about his unpleasant encounter with Seward and the captured documents that Bunch had entrusted to Mure, Bunch decided to press his case for a raise and for a promotion. He noted that George Mathew, then in Mexico, was making £1,000 a year as secretary of legation, almost twice his salary. Bunch thought that, given his stellar performance with the Trescot mission—the Confederate Congress had just accepted the neutrality provisions in the Declaration of Paris—maybe he could win an income and title similar to Mathew's, or maybe a better one, and maybe even in Richmond if at some point diplomatic representations there were upgraded. Bunch outlined his thoughts in a letter to Lyons, who had given him so many proofs of his friendly interest, and he enclosed a formal request to Lord Russell for a new position and a raise in salary.

In Washington, Seward and his men continued poring over every one of the letters Mure carried that was not in the diplomatic pouch. They were looking for something incriminating that they might include in a message to Lord Russell to accompany the unopened diplomatic bag. Seward had told Lyons he had no particular complaint about Bunch's conduct. But now he saw there was a great deal he could say about him. Many of the letters looked, to Seward, very treasonous, indeed, and some of them, certainly, praised Bunch as a friend of the South. After all, the merchants of Charleston were convinced this man was very much on their side. But among the papers spread across the tables at the State Department was one curious little note that seemed to be quite damning. It was not sealed in any way. It was not dated. It was not signed. But it said, in part:

> Mr. B., on oath of secrecy, communicated to me also that the first step to recognition was taken. He and Mr. Belligny together sent Mr. Trescot to Richmond yesterday, to ask Jeff. Davis, president, to [accept] the treaty of [commerce], to [accept] the neutral flag covering neutral goods to be respected. This is the first step of di-

rect treating with our government, so prepare for active business by January 1.

Less than one week after Mure's arrest, this mysterious, incendiary note was leaked to the *New-York Tribune*, presumably by William Seward, and with it the Union secretary of state began to whip up a crisis around Her Majesty's consul in South Carolina.

As usual, communications across the Atlantic moved slowly, but on September 3, Charles Francis Adams, the U.S. minister in Great Britain, was able to deliver the captured diplomatic pouch to Lord Russell along with Seward's demands that if any portion of the contents should prove treasonable to the United States, it should be turned over to the Americans, and Consul Bunch should promptly be made to feel "the severe displeasure" of his own government. In a separate note to Lord Russell that same day, Adams included an extract of the infamous unsigned letter and flatly demanded that Bunch be relieved of his duties.

When Bunch himself first learned of the mysterious note about his clandestine activities, he could hardly think what to say. He wrote to Lord Lyons in code: "Pray do not believe a word of the intercepted letters respecting my communication to the supposed writer. It is false and the work of a spy. The letter itself is absolute nonsense, as you must have seen. I am anxious to hear from you."

Lyons, increasingly paternal, wrote back, "I consider your negotiation to have been admirably managed," and, "I don't think the contretemps about Mr. Mure will signify." Lyons told Lord Russell he believed the "affair of Mr. Bunch's negotiation" would go away, and he thought it was "extremely well managed by Mr. Bunch and M. de Belligny." But Lyons did not forward Bunch's request for a promotion and a raise.

IF MURE AND the correspondence he carried had not been intercepted by Seward's agents, London's negotiation with the South might have ended there "without any drawback," as Lyons put it. The Crown's concerns about its shipping had been addressed. The Confederate delegation in London was still kept at arm's length. And Seward may have wanted to let the whole issue fade away, as Lyons believed. But Seward's initial reaction to the Bunch affair made that nearly impossible. In the heat of the moment after the Mure arrest he may really have believed that the diplomatic pouch was full of secret communications from the Confederate government to its agents in Europe. Then the leak to the *Tribune* had made the whole matter public and put Seward in a position from which it was very hard to back down. And eventually the passions aroused were such that Seward almost achieved for the Confederacy the recognition that Trescot's mission did not.

Seward focused the entire controversy on the fate of Robert Bunch, giving the impression that he himself had known nothing about what the British and French were up to with the Confederates. But Seward had known for months, in fact, since just after the recognition of the South's belligerent status. He had met with Lord Lyons and Count Mercier on May 18, and Mercier had shown him a letter from the French foreign minister that said plainly a communication with the Confederate government about the Declaration of Paris was in the works.

For that matter, as the crisis developed, Seward seemed to ignore completely the role of the French. He said nothing about de Belligny. His entire focus was on Bunch.

In fact, Seward wanted a scapegoat, and almost in the literal sense: he wanted all the sins of Britain laid upon it. And Bunch seemed such an easy target. He was just a consul. If Seward exerted enough pressure, surely London would sacrifice him.

Espionage is a profession full of ironies. Robert Bunch, who had worked so hard for so long for the "disentanglement" of Britain from the cotton-growing South, now suddenly became the symbol of secret and supposedly growing ties between the Confederacy and the Crown. But Lyons knew, and Lord Russell knew, and, indeed, Lord Palmerston knew that Bunch had been doing what they asked him to do, and much more than that. The greatest irony was that he had done his job too well, earning the trust of people he despised in order to report honestly and accurately to Her Majesty's government. But even his greatest defender, Lord Lyons, could not let that be known in Washington.

Bunch not only had convinced the people around him in Charleston that he accepted their ways and their world, he had also convinced Seward's spies. They had followed his couriers. They had read the mail he sent. And yet somehow they had missed his "private" and "confidential" letters, which, after all, were only rarely written in cipher. Did Seward never see Bunch's derisive portraits of the Confederate cabinet? Did he pay no attention to Bunch's damning appraisal of the Confederacy as an offense against the sensibilities of the civilized world?

At the Foreign Office not everyone took Bunch's side. Edmund Hammond, the Permanent Under-Secretary in London, told Lyons he was "thoroughly displeased" with Bunch. "He must have known the condition in which the consular correspondence is allowed to pass; if he is so obtuse as not to perceive that he was doing wrong in sending the numerous private letters . . . he is not fit for his post."

"Don't be hard upon Mr. Bunch until you get his full explanation," Lyons told Hammond. "He has been so entirely cut off from communication that he hardly knows what are the particular points which tell against him."

In truth, Lord Russell was not pleased with Bunch's efforts at a "full explanation," and even Lord Lyons was annoyed at what seemed rather futile hair-splitting. It turned out Bunch had not kept the Trescot mission entirely secret. He had consulted with two or three of his distinguished friends about it, one of whom might have written the incriminating unsigned note. And Bunch's formal denial of the charges leveled against him by Seward rested on three points: he doubted that Mure had carried any dispatches from the Confederate government outside the sealed pouch; "there was not one single paper in my bag that was not entirely and altogether on Her Majesty's service"; and the so-called passport he'd issued, to which Seward so objected, was really just a "certificate" to state that Mure was on official business. Bunch conceded he may have been stretching the point a bit on that document when he called Mure a "British merchant," given that he was long since a naturalized American citizen and no longer, therefore, a "British subject." Lyons curtly told Bunch he should quit the equivocating. It wasn't going to help.

Lyons had grown concerned about his man in Charleston, who seemed increasingly desperate, perhaps because of his disappointments—his secret diplomatic triumph had become a disaster—and very probably because of his fears for his safety. He had never spent so much time in Charleston without a break. From the beginning of his time there it had seemed a sort of luxurious prison full of cruel and capricious inmates who could turn on him at any moment. Now week after week Bunch watched as his lines of communication were threatened, and, worse than that, so were his lines of escape.

Bunch, as long as he retained his official credentials, was able to visit the Union ships blockading Charleston and talk with their commanders. He also tried to stay in very close touch with the British naval vessels patrolling off the coast. This was normal, since they had begun to carry important dispatches, but as the pressures on Bunch grew, his judgment seemed to wane. On his own initiative, Bunch sent a letter to one of the British naval officers whose ship was observing the blockade, suggesting he make a show of force to help free a couple of British merchantmen holed up in the port of Beaufort. Admiral Milne, the commander of the British fleet, was outraged: the Bunch note flatly contradicted his instructions to his captains to avoid any act "which might involve the two countries in war." Lyons scrambled to send a telegram stopping Milne from notifying London. "I was quite aghast," Lyons said, a word he rarely used. Explaining himself to Milne, Lyons said, "Mr. Bunch is so zealous and useful a public servant, and has hitherto been so discreet, that I was unwilling anything so likely to injure him should go home without his own explanation."

THE "BUNCH AFFAIR" was taking on a life of its own. The tone of the exchanges in dispatches from Seward and in the meetings that Adams had with Lord Russell in London grew so acerbic and belligerent that the crisis became "the great question" before the British government and grew "darker and darker every day," said Lord Russell. But the treatment of Robert Bunch, a representative of Her Majesty, was the sort of thing to be expected from "that singular mixture of the bully and coward" who held the position of U.S. secretary of state.

Palmerston's blood was up, and that was always dangerous. The United States was acting like a banana republic as far as he was concerned. He recalled his own glory days of gunboat diplomacy. South American governments had often tried to avoid responsibility for some affront to British interests by claiming that Britain's consuls should confine themselves to commercial functions and had no right to make demands, to which the response was usually that if the offending government did not want to hear from the consul, it would hear from a British admiral, "whose manner of dealing with such matters might be less agreeable."

Palmerston prepared to send a naval squadron and thousands of fresh troops to Canada in case this dispute over Bunch was used as a pretext for widening hostilities. "No man with half an eye in his head, or half an idea in his brain," he said, "could fail to perceive what a lowering of the position of England in the world would follow the conquest of our North American Provinces by the North Americans, especially after the Bull's [sic] Run races. We must defend Canada; and to defend it, we must have troops there."

Lord Russell joined the parade. "I quite agree with you about sending troops to Canada," he said. But cooler heads in the cabinet warned that if a large number of troops were sent to Canada with little or nothing to do, there would be a very big problem with desertions. That gave Palmerston pause. And Lord Russell decided that if Seward would accept his word that no recognition of the Confederacy was contemplated, the storm could blow over. "If they do not quarrel about Bunch," said Lord Russell, "we may rest on our oars for the winter." But the U.S. secretary of state would not leave the Bunch affair alone, picking at it like a wound that he did not really want to heal.

SEWARD DID NOT revoke Bunch's credentials right away, as he had threatened to do, and there were moments when he appeared to be softening. One day in mid-October he asked Lyons to stop by his office for a little chat. Seward had heard back from his envoy Charles Francis Adams in London. Lord John Russell had looked at the letters in the pouch. There was nothing in them treasonous or, indeed, of much interest—the usual missives from English governesses to their families and that sort of thing—certainly nothing that resembled incendiary communications from the inner circles around Jeff Davis. Seward had also gotten Lord Russell's response to the demand that Robert Bunch be removed. Russell had refused. Whatever reservations the Foreign Secretary might have had about Bunch's behavior, he had fully supported the mission to Richmond. Russell said flatly that Bunch was acting on instructions.

So Seward, watching the smoke from his cigar curl toward the ceiling, suggested it was time for the United States and Britain to put this "unfortunate affair of Mr. Bunch" behind them if they could. "I would like to find some way," he said, "to escape from this notion that Great Britain communicating with the Confederate States about maritime rights is an unfriendly act. Let's talk about this privately, shall we? And unofficially?"

Lyons, as usual, was happy to do so.

"Notwithstanding the language of the English press," said Seward, "I believe neither your government's ministers nor the leading members of their Liberal Party are unfriendly to the United States or have any desire to embarrass us in our operations against the South. . . . But this damn Bunch affair has brought about the exact state of things I wanted to avoid." He held up one of the dispatches from Adams. "Here is a plain official declaration to the United States minister in London, not only that your government recognized the Rebels as belligerents, but that it had entered into communication with the Rebel government. And you know it is extremely difficult, no, it is impossible for the United States to acquiesce in communications of this kind between foreign governments and the Rebels."

Lyons said little and studied Seward closely. The secretary of state seemed to be taxing his ingenuity, looking for a way to avoid a fight with Britain, for once, but at the same time he didn't want to lose his popularity among extremists in his party, and he didn't want the public thinking he'd pusillanimously retreated from the high-sounding positions he'd adopted in August.

Now Seward adopted a conspiratorial tone. "I need to gain time," he said. "In two months the whole business with the South will probably be finished. At any rate in two months the North will have possession of a cotton port, and we'll open it for exports, and this will change the views of the European powers."

Seward seemed to be very anxious. "It is all-important that I gain time," he said again.

. . .

TWO WEEKS LATER, Lyons reported that Seward had returned, suddenly, "to his old ways," and for no readily apparent reason. On October 26, Seward called Lyons to the State Department to inform him that he was withdrawing Bunch's exequatur and to read to him the official message he was sending to London. Seward said he flatly rejected Britain's claims that it had a right to communicate with Richmond as it had, and he wanted Bunch removed, he said, because of his known partisanship to the South.

"Never were serious charges brought upon a slighter foundation," Lyons wrote in his official dispatch to Lord Russell. "No one who has read Mr. Bunch's dispatches to Your Lordship and to me can consider him as in the least degree a partisan of the Southern cause." Clearly, "Mr. Bunch has merely been selected as a safer object of attack than the British or French Government."

"When Mr. Seward had finished reading the dispatch, I remained silent," Lyons wrote. "I allowed the pain which the contents of it had caused me to be apparent in my countenance, but I said nothing. From my knowledge of Mr. Seward's character, I was sure that at the moment nothing which I could say would make so much impression upon him as my maintaining an absolute silence. After a short pause, I took leave of him courteously, and withdrew."

Privately, Lyons wrote that if Seward remained "in his present mood," he would be glad to find a pretext for performing "other half-violent acts," and "if he finds these acts popular and not too dangerous as far as England is concerned, he will probably play out the play and send me my passports"—that is, expel Lyons—"on the plea of some consul's having communicated with the Southern government under instructions from me." This performance by Seward, as Lyons put it, was "one more proof that we cannot depend on his prudence or his moderation; that we must always be prepared for an attack."

The French were even more fed up than Lyons. Count Mercier was pressing for recognition of the Confederacy and the use of naval force to break the Federal blockade in order to get the cotton needed for French mills. Lyons pushed back. That sort of thing made no sense unless both countries were ready to go to war. He saw no alarm in England about cotton shortages. "On the contrary, men's thoughts appear to be turned hopefully towards new sources of supply," he told Mercier, "and there seems to be a very general opinion that if the momentary inconvenience is not very great indeed, it might be wise to endure it now, in order to be free in the future from the danger of depending so very much upon one country for an article of the greatest importance to us."

Lyons told Mercier, "I do not think that either the government or the people in England are prepared for such extreme measures as recognizing the Confederates and breaking up the blockade."

But if Seward continued his erratic, hostile behavior, that could change.

BUNCH, WITHOUT HIS exequatur and therefore without official standing as far as the Federal government was concerned, nonetheless remained in Charleston and continued to report, sometimes directly and sometimes over the signature of his deputy. But, really, nothing was the same. Even before his credentials were revoked, when a new diplomatic code was distributed, Hammond told Lyons that "Lord Russell will not give Bunch a cipher. The consul has done himself no good by the very lame explanation he has given respecting Mr. Mure; and you will see that he is now strictly prohibited from sending any private letter whatever under his official cover."

Lyons continued to defend Bunch and to try to reassure him. But Bunch found his depression hard to shake. His position was increasingly vulnerable in an increasingly vulnerable city. The Union Navy mounted an enormous expedition that took Beaufort, giving it a solid base from which to patrol the lower Atlantic coast. The blockade was tightening, and no one could say when Charleston would come under direct attack.

Whatever Lyons said, Bunch felt that the Foreign Secretary

wanted to be done with him, and he was right about that. When Lord Russell received word that Bunch's exequatur had been revoked, he told Palmerston not to worry too much about it: "It is the business of Seward to feed the mob with sacrifices every day, and we happen to be the most grateful food he can offer." In early December Russell told the American minister in London that he simply didn't want to talk about the Bunch case anymore; he "did not perceive that any advantage would be obtained by the continuance of this correspondence."

Seward and his agents, in their zeal to attack and neutralize Bunch, undermined everything he had done. They had had few better allies in the South, although they did not know it, and they had tried their best to destroy him. But Bunch's long record of dispatches about the Southerners, their politics, their key personalities and especially their craving for new slaves from Africa had slowed London's march toward recognition of the Confederacy. He had shaped and reinforced the skeptical reporting of William Howard Russell, which reflected so many of his own views, and he had provided a great deal of ammunition for Lyons to use in the continued fight to keep London neutral.

But the tensions raised by the "damn Bunch affair" did not subside. Seward's handling of the matter had made him, in the eyes of the British cabinet, "the very impersonation of all that is most violent and arrogant in the American character." And the possibility of war between the United States and the United Kingdom continued to loom like a thunderhead on the horizon. Any new incident could unleash the lightning.

Chapter 43

THE U.S. NAVY STEAMER *San Jacinto* was a good ship, and her officers and crew had done outstanding service off the African coast. They had run down the *Bonita* and the *Storm King*. They had seen hundreds upon hundreds of naked men, women, and children shackled belowdecks. They had seen them dying. They had witnessed with their own eyes the holocaust of the Middle Passage.

When sixty-three-year-old U.S. Navy captain Charles Wilkes got his assignment to the *San Jacinto* in the early summer of 1861, she was still stationed on the African slave coast, and officials in the Navy Department did not trust her captain, the Virginian Thomas Aloysius Dornin, to sail her back to American waters. They didn't want to run the risk that he'd hand her over to the Confederates. Apparently they did not share the same concern about Wilkes, but they made him travel, reluctantly and resentfully, all the way to Fernando Po, an island in the pestilential Bight of Benin, at the height of fever season to assume his new command.

Wilkes suspected that his superiors were trying to get rid of him—literally, to have him die. The motives of Secretary of the Navy Gideon Welles were "diabolical," he thought. West Africa truly was a fatal climate for white men. The famous British explorer Richard Francis Burton, who took over as British consul in Fernando Po that same year, reported that in a single epidemic 162 out of 278 Europeans on the island died. In the end, Wilkes did not get sick, but neither did he forget, and part of his search for glory in the months that followed was tied to his hope he could shame the men who'd sent him to Fernando Po.

Wilkes had once been very famous, but his days of reknown were decades behind him. As a young officer he had led the intrepid United States Exploring Expedition of surveyors and scientists who charted the waters around Antarctica and determined that it was, in fact, a huge continent. His chronicle of the adventure eventually became one of the most important scientific books of the time. (Bunch, whose mother's family was distantly connected to Wilkes, had made a special point to try to buy a copy of his magnum opus in the 1850s, until he discovered how expensive it was.)

In 1861, under Wilkes's command, the *San Jacinto*'s mission was to head back across the Atlantic to join the hunt for a Confederate commerce raider called *Sumter* that was capturing Union-flagged ships one after another in the waters around Cuba. But the *Sumter*'s captain, the increasingly famous Raphael Semmes, was a veteran of many commands in the U.S. Navy prior to secession, and he was far too smart for his pursuers.

By early November Wilkes had nothing to show for his months on patrol. But then he heard of another possible target—in some ways a very easy target—which he could not pass up.

The Confederate government had decided to upgrade its representation in Europe by sending two more of the South's most well-known politicians. James Mason, the former U.S. senator from Virginia who had co-chaired the U.S. Senate investigation into the John Brown affair with Jefferson Davis, would go to London. Former Louisiana senator John Slidell, the Democratic Party operative and former éminence grise of the Buchanan administration, was destined for Paris. In Washington, Seward had learned that his old Senate colleagues were on the notorious Confederate blockade runner and privateer the *Nashville* and had ordered it intercepted, but the ships that were sent missed their chance, and the envoys made it safely to Havana, the first stage of their trip to Europe.

Wilkes, just then, was on the other side of Cuba at the port of Cienfuegos, where he saw a newspaper report that Slidell and Mason had arrived on the island. From the U.S. consul in Havana, a former naval officer named Robert Wilson Shufedlt, Wilkes learned that the commissioners would be traveling on the next leg of their trip to England aboard the British packet steamer *Trent*.

Wilkes liked to say that he had at least a passing personal acquaintance with Mason and Slidell and their wives. He had spent so much time in Washington, moving in the outer orbits of its tight social circles, that he might have encountered them on many occasions. He claimed he found Mrs. Slidell, née Deslonde, a very impressive woman. "She was a refined and well educated lady from New Orleans," he recalled, and he liked to reminisce about passing "many pleasant evenings" at her home. But he was about to make their lives hell.

"It was a beautiful day and the sea quite smooth," Wilkes wrote afterward. He had positioned his ship in the Old Bahama Channel just east of Havana. Maybe he'd caused some comment when he loaded extra stores of whiskey for the men he planned to capture and fine "eatables" for the ladies he expected to accompany them. Wilkes, after all, fancied himself quite the gentleman as well as an officer. But he told not one man on board the *San Jacinto* what he planned to do. Only when the smoke from the *Trent* appeared in the distance did he call his officers together and suddenly order several of them arrested on suspicion of Confederate sympathies, including the head of the contingent of U.S. Marines that was aboard. Wilkes said he knew that "at heart" they were rebels. The rest, he believed, would obey his orders.

Now the *Trent* was drawing closer, coming into range. Without warning, Wilkes fired two shots across her bow. Immediately she stopped, and boats lowered from the *San Jacinto* rowed to meet her. There was no fight. But in later years Wilkes loved to tell the story that Slidell had slipped out a window onto the half deck and might have planned to make a stand but was caught before he could do so. Slidell's wife and daughters were beside themselves with rage. Amid the tears and screams one of them, a girl of sixteen, slapped First Lt. Donald McNeill Fairfax across the face. "Fairfax was a very good-looking fellow," Wilkes said, "and the girls being pretty, it was a fair reward for his trouble of making the search to have taken a kiss."

For two hours the boats conveyed the prisoners and their baggage from the *Trent* to the *San Jacinto*. But Mrs. Slidell and her children refused to go. The notes she wrote to her husband vented every French expletive that she could think of. Wilkes, making a show of his amusement, read them all and handed them to Slidell. Then Mason and Slidell and their secretaries proceeded to get drunk, according to the captain of the *San Jacinto*.

In Wilkes's long account of the incident, dictated many years later, he tried to settle scores after the fact. If he had known what "an ignorant John Bull" the captain of the *Trent* was, he would have "given him a lesson he would long have remembered." If he had had someone on board capable of commanding the vessel, he'd have taken the *Trent* as a prize. But he didn't. He took the two men, and he took them off a ship full of passengers flying the British flag. And for what?

This would have been a dangerous moment in any case, but coming on top of all the tension created by the Bunch affair, the *Trent* incident suddenly made war between the Union and the Crown seem not only possible but inevitable.

"IS IT TRUE that Mason and Slidell have been taken from a British packet ship?" a clerk asked Judah P. Benjamin at their offices in Richmond, where he was now Confederate secretary of war.

"Yes, it is," said Benjamin.

"Then, I am glad of it," said the clerk.

"Why is that?" Benjamin asked him, apparently surprised and perhaps thinking of the conditions under which his friend John Slidell would now be held.

"Because it will bring the Eagle cowering to the feet of the Lion."

Benjamin smiled. "Perhaps," he said. "Perhaps it is the best thing that could have happened."

·   ·   ·

IN WASHINGTON, THIS was a confrontation much closer to the brink than Seward—or Lincoln, certainly—had ever wanted. Lord Palmerston now readied British troops in Canada for war in earnest.

Madame Slidell, who had gone on to London after her husband was taken away, told the press and officials there that she believed Captain Wilkes had acted entirely on his own. But Palmerston was sure that this affront to the British flag was a calculated insult by the despised William Seward. He had Lord John Russell draft a note demanding an apology and the release of the diplomats. If no such action was taken within a week of receiving it, Britain would break off relations. The Queen's military commanders in Canada were told that the departure of the British minister from Washington would be the signal for war, beginning with the British seizure of Portland, Maine. War between the Union and the Crown appeared at that moment both inevitable and imminent.

Before the ultimatum could be sent, however, it had to be read and approved by the palace. On other occasions this might have been largely a formality, and, indeed, in this case Queen Victoria had other priorities. She was giving a dinner party and did not want it interrupted. But Prince Albert, her beloved consort, begged off from the dinner, saying he felt ill. Feverish with the first symptoms of the typhoid that would kill him a few days later, Albert sat down at his desk to look at the ultimatum, and he did not like what he saw. Palmerston and Russell were giving Lincoln and Seward no way out. They would have to bend to Britain's will, release Slidell and Mason, and apologize abjectly or face the greatest military power on earth.

For twenty years Albert had made the fight against slavery, and especially the slave trade, one of his important causes. He did not want to see the Crown tarnished by a war that might guarantee the continuation of slavery for generations to come. He deeply mistrusted Palmerston's bellicosity and thought of Russell as something of a lightweight. He wanted the harshness of the language in the official note to be softened: "Her Majesty's Government are unwilling to believe that the United States Government intended wantonly to put an insult upon this country. . . ." The new wording left a way open for Seward to explain the incident as an accident, if only he would take it.

O N THE NIGHT OF DECEMBER 11, as the Union and Great Britain waged their tense, slow-motion, diplomatic battle over the *Trent* Affair, and just as the first anniversary of South Carolina's secession approached, an enormous blaze cut a swath of destruction through the heart of Charleston. It started around ten o'clock in the evening, an hour after curfew, among some workshops and warehouses at the end of Hassell Street near the port. A stiff wind was coming in from the northeast, and the fire spread quickly, completely out of control, from one wood-frame building to another. All the militias and guards and fire companies that Charleston had organized to put out fires and put down rebellions (because the two were linked in the white Southerners' nightmare visions) proved powerless to arrest the spreading conflagration. At low tide—and this was at dead low tide—there was not enough water at hand to begin to douse the flames. Within less than an hour the blaze had reached Institute Hall on Meeting Street, scene of the fatal disintegration of the Democratic Party and the euphoric ratification of the Ordinance of Secession the year before. The stage where Yancey had once electrified the crowds, as well as the paintings of half-nude nymphs above it, succumbed to the flames. Fire engulfed the map of Africa and the bowie knife that pointed the way there.

The blaze destroyed the Charleston Hotel and threatened the Mills House Hotel, where guests, including the visiting Gen. Robert E. Lee, poured into the street, sure they were about to die. But the fast-moving fire was moving on, and St. Andrew's Hall on Broad Street was right in its path. Some brave Charlestonians—Britons, one assumes; royalists, without a doubt—rushed into the burning building to try to rescue the Sully portrait of the young Queen Victoria.

Perhaps Her Majesty's man in Charleston was among them. But he does not mention the fire at all in the private letters to Lord

Lyons that have survived. What we know is that Robert Bunch's home and office on Meeting Street near the Battery were spared, but they were only a few hundred yards from the inferno that filled the air with choking smoke and incandescent cinders. The Great Fire, as it came to be called, was so intense that it was visible to Union warships miles out at sea, and in that long night of the conflagration the streets were scenes of almost complete chaos.

At dawn, the fire spent, a third of the city smoldered in ruins, and even though the fire had started by accident, it gave people a sense of the horrors that the future might hold in store. Already the Federal forces that had taken Beaufort in the Battle of Port Royal a month before were pushing up the coast through Edisto Island and attacking Rockville, near Kiawah Island.

Robert Bunch must have felt, looking at the shattered city where he had spent almost a quarter of his life, that everything he had worked for was coming apart. He had never been so cut off and so alone. Three days before the fire he had written a long, plaintive letter to Lyons.

"I can see that the impression prevailing at the Foreign Office is that I as a consul am giving myself the style of a quasi-minister—writing freely, expressing opinions and the like. My dispatches containing information which no one else *could* give are left unnoticed—not even acknowledged. In fact, I am to consider myself 'snubbed'—if not worse."

Because other consuls either produced little or had taken leave, at the height of the crisis Bunch had been the only representative of Her Majesty's government in the whole of what he called "the Southern country." For months, since about the time of the attack on Fort Sumter, rabble-rousers had incited the Southern public against "the foreign consuls," who were seen as failing to recognize the independence of the Confederacy and perhaps as secret abolitionists as well.

"By ordinary management and common sense I have kept

things as they were," Bunch wrote to Lyons. "It is too long to explain how I have done this, but it has been in the main by conversation with influential persons and by representation of the impolicy of raising disagreeable questions." He confessed that he had corresponded with the "state department" in Richmond, quite apart from the Trescot visit, and he had tried to help British ships trapped in the harbor that wanted to escape the blockade, which Lyons, in November, had said should be observed. But what else could he do? In the process, he said, he had been able to protect many British citizens and keep them from being drafted into the Rebel Army.

Lyons did not forward Bunch's complaints to Lord Russell, and he warned Bunch that such letters would do him no good at the Foreign Office.

Still, Bunch remained in Charleston. He collected mail from other consuls as they resumed their posts, and he forwarded it on the British warships that now paid regular visits to pick up the correspondence. Bunch reported on the state of the harbor. Occasionally he even boarded British cruisers for a look at coastal operations and defenses and blockade operations. But his was no longer "a *political* office."

AT A CHRISTMAS ball in Washington, William Seward publicly told the Prince de Joinville, one of the French royals in town, that the effects of war between the United States and Great Britain would be terrible for everyone. William Howard Russell, who was there listening, heard Seward mouth the same threat he had made in one form or another many times before. "We will wrap the whole world in flame!" Seward said. There is "no power so remote that she will not feel the fire of our battle and be burned by our conflagration," Seward proclaimed.

But this time W. H. Russell was not impressed. He quoted someone else at the party saying that when Seward talked that way, he meant to back down. In fact, President Lincoln had made it clear that he did not want this fight and that they had come far too close to it. "One war at a time," he told his secretary of state.

The language offered by Prince Albert had left room for a face-saving response in Seward's reply: Charles Wilkes had not been acting under orders. Three days after Christmas the correspondence of Seward and the British and French foreign ministers was published, announcing the release of the Confederate emissaries.

"The bubble has burst," wrote William Howard Russell.

"Seward has cowered beneath the roar of the British lion and surrendered Mason and Slidell, who have been permitted to go on their errand to England."

In Richmond, Judah P. Benjamin's clerk wrote in his diary: "Now we must depend on our own strong arms and stout hearts for defense."

Chapter 45

M ORE THAN THREE YEARS OF war remained, but Britain
never again experienced a moment of crisis that brought it
so close to siding openly against the Union as the *Trent* Affair. One
reason, certainly, is that, even with Robert Bunch sidelined, Lord
Lyons would not let the slave-trade issue die. He continued to be the
bearer of the inconvenient truth about it, and with his guidance the
issue became, for the first time, a source of understanding instead
of anger between the Union and the Crown.

In early 1862, as Lyons understood, the Lincoln administration
needed to send some signals to a U.S. Congress increasingly dominated by radical abolitionists. The administration wanted to show it
was willing to change the old status quo of slavery, even if it was far
from ready to opt for emancipation, and the issue of the transatlantic trade was perfect for that purpose.

Already, months before, Seward had suggested the Federal
government would drop objections to British warships searching
suspected slavers flying the American flag. But Lyons had been
suspicious of Seward's commitment. Then, at the beginning of the
year, Nathaniel "Lucky Nat" Gordon was put on trial in New York.
The renegade sea captain from Maine who had narrowly evaded
capture by a British man-o'-war in 1850 off the coast of Brazil, and
who had lost 75 percent of his human cargo sailing to Cuba a decade later, had been captured on the *Erie* when it was intercepted
by the *Mohican* and the *San Jacinto* off the coast of Africa. The court
convicted Gordon of slaving, defined as piracy and a capital crime,
and President Lincoln rejected all calls for clemency. "Any man
who, for paltry gain and stimulated only by avarice, can rob Africa
of her children to sell them into interminable bondage, I will never
pardon," he declared. In February 1862, Gordon became the first
and the only American ship captain ever hanged for his crimes in
the Middle Passage.

Lyons had learned to read Seward's moods and his political needs, and after the *Trent* Affair he detected a certain sobering of the secretary's attitude toward the British. "He is not at all a cruel or vindictive man, but he likes all things which make him feel that he has power," Lyons told Lord John Russell. "I hope we may effect something practical as regards the Slave Trade while he is in the mood." When the British proposed a treaty calling for mutual "visit and search," which had always been the red line U.S. administrations refused to cross, Lincoln and Seward seized on it immediately. Their only caveat: they wanted to make it appear as if they had taken the initiative. In a matter of weeks Lyons reported that the treaty had a good chance of passing the Senate. "We are not likely to have so good a chance again," he reported to Russell on March 31. "I think therefore that I shall be doing what you wish if I sign it at once."

On April 25 Lyons wrote, "Yesterday was the anniversary of my arrival three years ago at Washington. I celebrated it by signing the Treaty for the Suppression of the Slave Trade." The American flag—at least, the Union flag—would no longer provide protection for traffickers in human flesh. A few days later Lyons was even more exultant. "The Slave Trade treaty has met with much more general approval than I expected," he said. "It has excited quite an enthusiasm among the anti-slavery party. I have never seen Mr. Seward apparently so much pleased. Mr. Sumner, who had had the management of it in the Senate, was moved to tears when he came to tell me that it had passed unanimously."

WHAT REMAINED TO be seen was how this new treaty would affect attitudes in the British cabinet. The Liberal MP William Edward Forster asked the government to state its view on the record for Parliament. The job was left to recently appointed Under-Secretary of State for Foreign Affairs Sir Austen Henry Layard. "The treaty is of a highly satisfactory nature," he said. "It gives the right of search to British cruisers, and there is every reason to hope that the Slave Trade, which has been carried on to so great an extent lately under the United States flag, will be suppressed."

Lord Palmerston, who was in Parliament that day, did not speak about the treaty. The county of Lancashire, at the heart of the British textile industry, was starting to feel the strain of cotton shortages. Moves to open up the Indian and Egyptian sources of fiber had not yet provided enough. The Confederate forces were continuing to rack up victories on the battlefield. Palmerston decided to reserve judgment.

The editorials in the London *Times* reflected these conflicting views and emotions. William Howard Russell's astute observations of the war had been cut short after less than a year on the ground in the Americas. He could no longer get permission to travel with the Union military after his account of the debacle at Bull Run. His name was touched by scandal when his friend and traveling companion through the South, Sam Ward, was said to have profited from information about the war that Russell had sent him. Russell's wife and children needed him desperately. And the editorial line taken by John Delane, editor of the *Times*, was so relentlessly pro-secession that it hardly seemed worth reporting contrary views. As early as September 1861, only eight weeks after Bull Run, Russell had written privately to Delane: "It is quite obvious, I think, that the North will succeed in reducing the South." But Delane was not going to publish anything like that. Now the *Times* cast the slave-trade treaty not as a triumph for British and Union diplomacy, but as "the first fruit of secession" and a victory over the North, thanks to the pressures of the rebellion.

Lord Russell, now Earl Russell, had made his views on the conflict increasingly clear. He wanted stability. He wanted an end to the war. If there were an end to the upstart, arrogant American Republic, that would suit him as well. He wished the whole problem would just go away so he could turn his attention fully to pressing issues in Europe and Asia.

Palmerston's position was much harder to figure.

In July, William Lindsay, one of the most strident pro-Confederate voices in Parliament, tried to push through a motion that called for Britain to "mediate" an end to a hopeless war. But Palmerston objected. He didn't like the grandstanding or, as he put it, the expressions of opinion at inopportune moments. The South had not yet established its independence, he said, and, therefore, it could not be recognized. The motion, if it carried, would put England on the side of the South and make any future effort (or pretense) at mediation that much harder. When he finished speaking, the motion was withdrawn.

Behind the scenes, Palmerston had let Earl Russell persuade him—or let Earl Russell believe he had persuaded him—that a plan for mediation must go ahead. It would not be for show, but would be a substantive initiative backed enthusiastically by the French and very probably by the other great European powers as well. Throughout September Russell and Palmerston seemed in perfect accord as they pulled together their coalition of mediators. Yet Palmerston still hesitated. What he wanted, in fact, was a battlefield victory by the Confederates so convincing that it would settle the problem for him. Gen. Robert E. Lee was pushing into Maryland, and that action could provide it. He might flank Washington and force a settlement. But on September 17 near Antietam Creek 26,000 men were killed, were wounded, or went missing in a single day of fighting, and Lee fell back into Virginia.

The factory workers and small merchants of Lancashire were now in desperate condition. Talk of pain had turned to talk of famine. Hundreds of thousands of people were out of work, and there was no hope that the winter would be anything but bleak.

The partisans of the South took encouragement from the much-quoted remarks of Chancellor of the Exchequer William Gladstone in October 1862: "There is no doubt that Jefferson Davis and other leaders of the South have made an Army; they are making, it appears, a Navy; and they have made—what is more than either—they have made a Nation." But Gladstone's speech did not start the wheels of industry rolling in Lancashire. It actually stopped those few that still were turning. Factory owners did not want to pay high prices for cotton, only to see the market open up suddenly, destroying their profits, which is what would happen in the short term if Britain declared for the Confederacy. So they waited, and more people lost their jobs. As Bunch and the other consuls were reporting, the unreliability of supplies was tied less to the Union blockade in the early years of the war, which was not very effective, than to the continuing embargo on cotton supported by Southern planters and politicians convinced they could squeeze Lancashire until London would bend to their will. This strategy did not endear them to the British government.

As the cabinet meeting to decide on mediation was postponed and then postponed again, even Earl Russell began to grow more cautious. The Confederates had created a nation, perhaps, but the chances that nation would get the alliance with Britain that it so desperately needed were dwindling rapidly.

Palmerston was listening to other voices now, among them that of Lord Lyons, who had finally taken a break from Washington and was in England dividing his time between London and Arundel Castle. Within the cabinet itself, Palmerston looked to Sir George Cornewall Lewis, the Secretary of War, as his commonsense anti-slavery conscience. And in that small circle of powerful men another figure loomed large, one who had not been in the cabinet for years but whose presence was felt by all: Lord Clarendon, who had worked so closely and so well for so long with Consul Bunch, and for longer still with Palmerston. It had been to Clarendon, in fact, that Bunch had addressed his Dispatch No. 10 in 1857 on the price of Negroes and the near certainty that Southern states would, if they could, reopen the slave trade with Africa. Clarendon and Secretary of War Cornewall Lewis were brothers-in-law, and very close friends, and they worked together in private to sway the government against intervention.

Palmerston, at just this moment, also turned to Clarendon to act as a critical go-between with the Earl of Derby, leader of the Conservatives in Parliament. Would they support British mediation? Clarendon came back with the message that Derby thought a British intervention of any sort in the American war "premature."

Clarendon could read Palmerston's moods like no one else. He knew that it would be fruitless to argue any case as a friend of the North. Seward, among others, had made that almost impossible. The debate would hinge on what made sense in Britain in domestic political terms, as well as what made sense economically. And in the background, always, would be the deep residual dislike, which did not need to be stated too crassly or too often, for the slave-owning and very probably the slave-trading South.

"Johnny [Russell] always loves to do something when to do nothing is prudent," Clarendon wrote to Lewis, congratulating him on making clear to the cabinet "the idiotic position" in which Britain would find itself when the North rejected the plan, as it certainly would, and when the British government showed that, really, it had no follow-up strategy short of starting a war it did not want to fight.

News had arrived of the preliminary Emancipation Proclamation announced on September 22, but at first it was not seen as a clear blow for freedom. Instead, it seemed a bid by the Yankees to provoke the dreaded "servile insurrection" in the South. The British might have come to this sinister conclusion on their own. After all, Palmerston had suggested that Great Britain could do precisely that as part of military strategy if it had gone to war against the United States in 1856, and Cornewall Lewis had held similar views back then. But in 1862 it was, once again, U.S. secretary of state William Seward who had undermined to the point of implosion any moral capital the Emancipation Proclamation might have had.

Seward had made the common American mistake of believing

that Her Majesty's government at all times and in all ways was focused on nothing but money and cotton. Over the summer Seward
had used emancipation not as a promise but as a threat, suggesting
that if the British tried to meddle in the war, Washington would
indeed incite the dread "servile insurrection," and then there would
be no cotton for British mills for a very long time. Seward occasionally even insisted he wanted to bring the South back into the
Union with its slaves still in bondage so they could produce cotton
for Britain, as if that would buy off British opinion. As a result, even
Lyons at first doubted the sincerity and the morality of the September Emancipation Proclamation. Within the cabinet, certainly, the
North gained no sympathy with its plans for emancipation in the
South.

But Secretary of War Cornewall Lewis, wisely, turned the issue
on its head. If a slave rebellion was, indeed, what the Union meant
to incite, then that showed the extreme bitterness that existed between North and South, which made impossible any "calm consideration" by the belligerents of Russell's plans for mediation or
armistice. Now Lewis had Palmerston's ear. If the North should
by some miracle concede the independence of the South, he said,
Great Britain would be midwife to a slaveholding republic. Therefore, the only policy that could be justified would be strict neutrality. Palmerston listened closely and told Russell he was inclined to
agree.

Palmerston was bothered by "the difficulty about slavery," he
wrote to Russell in early November. He recalled the way Southerners had demanded that slaves who landed on British territory—
whether Canada, the Bahamas, or elsewhere—must be returned to
their owners. There was no way the British people could ever support such a thing, Palmerston said. Lord Russell tried to make the
argument that if Britain did not take the lead on this mediation effort to end the war (in the Confederacy's favor), then France would
step forward. Palmerston said he was ready to let that happen. "The

French Government are more free from the shackles of principle and of right and wrong on these matters," said Palmerston, than his government was.

Finally, after almost two months of maneuvering, the cabinet met formally on November 11, and Earl Russell made his case for Britain to advocate a six-month armistice in the American conflict. When Palmerston spoke, he did so only briefly, talking mainly about his wish to alleviate the suffering of the people of Lancashire.

"The proposal was now thrown before the Cabinet, who proceeded to pick it to pieces," Cornewall Lewis wrote afterward. Except for Gladstone and a couple of others, "everybody present threw a stone at it of greater or less size." Since the proposed solution would have involved a lifting of the blockade, it was so obviously pro-Southern that it was never going to be accepted, at least not peacefully. "After a time, Palmerston saw that the general feeling of the cabinet was against being a party to the representation, and he capitulated. I do not think his support was very sincere. It certainly was not hearty." Palmerston's main motive, in Lewis's view, was "to seem to support" Russell.

There would be no mediation; there would be no armistice. There would be, almost certainly, no British intervention in the war.

THROUGH ALL THE weeks of diplomatic maneuvering in the fall of 1862, the specter of the Middle Passage and its millions of victims lingered in the background and could not be dispelled. The shackles of right and wrong held fast, and the message Bunch had pushed on Clarendon and Lyons—that the Confederates would reopen the Middle Passage with all its horrors no matter what they said officially or unofficially—had kept Britain chained to its principles.

At the same time, the Southerners behaved as if they were working from Robert Bunch's script for Confederate suicide.

Even the cosmopolitan Judah P. Benjamin refused to realize that his government's insistence not only on keeping slaves, but on keeping open the possibility of the slave trade with Africa, would cost the Confederacy everything.

One week before the final cabinet meeting about Russell's armistice proposal, the Confederate envoy to London, James Mason, wrote to Benjamin about what was to him a very disturbing conversation. He had dined with Lord Donoughmore, a Conservative whom he thought "a very intelligent gentleman, and a warm and earnest friend of the South." But Donoughmore had told Mason bluntly that if by some chance the Crown did move toward recognition of the Confederacy with the usual treaty of "amity and commerce," the government would "require as a *sine qua non* the introduction of a clause stipulating against the African slave trade."

One can imagine Mason, at that point, looking for someplace to spit out his tobacco. Because even Mason, who had been a potent symbol as a prisoner from the *Trent* but a disaster as a diplomat in London, was wise enough to see that Donoughmore was telling him something very important. And Donoughmore, lest Mason miss the point, was perfectly blunt: "Lord Palmerston will not enter into a treaty with you unless you agree in that treaty not to permit the African Slave Trade."

Mason knew the boilerplate response and gave it: the Confederate constitution banned the slave trade with Africa.

Donoughmore said that was all well and good, and everybody understood the official position, but it wasn't enough: "The sentiment of England on this subject is such that no minister could hold his place for a day if he negotiated a treaty without such a clause." As Bunch and Lyons had reported from the time the Confederate constitution was written, its guarantees against the African trade were legally ephemeral and at any rate unenforceable among such a loose agglomeration of sovereignties. If South Carolina or Louisiana or any other state wanted to reopen the gruesome trade with Congo, there would be very little that the Confederate government could or would do about it. So the British would accept nothing less than an explicit commitment to the Crown that no slaves would be imported, and even that might not be enough.

Donoughmore continued to be blunt: even if the Palmerston government fell, and the Tories went in, any treaty recognizing the Confederacy would have to have that unequivocal stipulation that the African trade would not be reopened.

Mason could not guarantee that his government would sign such a document. And Benjamin, who was now the Confederate secretary of state and still a bit too much the lawyer, would not budge on the point after he received Mason's letter. Benjamin declared that the South's position on the issue was clear enough in its constitution. To go beyond that, or reiterate it, was unconstitutional and unacceptable, and any further amendments would be for the individual member states of the Confederacy to decide. Benjamin could not have known about the dispatches from Charleston and Washington that had discredited that constitution even before it was written.

In South Carolina, Robert Bunch had no chance to celebrate his victory. Lincoln's announcement of emancipation had heightened the hysteria about a slave uprising. In the weeks that followed, people waited for the decree to take effect on January 1, 1863, as if Doomsday had been marked on the calendar. Were the ghosts of Saint-Domingue and of Denmark Vesey about to rage through the plantations of the South? Bunch did not think so. He wrote that he saw little possibility of an insurrection "in this neighborhood, at least," and he was soon proved right again. But Southerners were more riled than ever by Britain's refusal to recognize their cause, and Bunch had to work harder than ever to convince the good people of South Carolina that he remained a friend. British warships now paid frequent, seemingly friendly visits to the harbor to pick up dispatches. Bunch introduced the officers to Gen. Beauregard, Col. Ripley, and other stalwart defenders of the city. Occasionally Bunch traveled aboard the ships outside the harbor to look at the blockade, which he often found wanting. He shared that information with the people in Charleston who thought they knew him so well. And he knew, as everyone knew, that the Union would soon lay siege to the city. On the last day of 1862, in a letter to the commander of one of the British warships in the area, Bunch warned that the Royal Navy might soon be called upon to help evacuate British citizens before the Yankee attack began.

Chapter 46

I T WAS TIME FOR BUNCH to go. "The attack on Charleston is supposed to be imminent," Lyons wrote to Earl Russell on January 23, 1863. "It is, of course, possible that it may be delayed or that the design may be altogether abandoned. Nevertheless, I think it prudent to withdraw Mr. Bunch at once." Lyons did not want the Federal forces to find the consul there in "his present undefined position" without any recognized diplomatic cover, since his exequatur had been withdrawn more than a year before.

"I shall very much regret the loss of his valuable and interesting reports," wrote Lyons. "I need not remind Your Lordship that Mr. Bunch has remained at his post during the unhealthy as well as the healthy seasons, since the breaking out of the Civil War," Lyons said, making sure Earl Russell remembered that Bunch "has received Your Lordship's commendations for the zeal and ability which he has manifested on several occasions during this trying time."

On February 8, 1863, Robert Barnwell Rhett's newspaper, the *Charleston Mercury*, reported that Robert Bunch, the British consul, had sailed from Charleston the day before in the British steamer *Cadmus*.

"It is said that, under the prospect of a formidable attack on Charleston, it would not be proper to expose the obnoxious Mr. Bunch, deprived of his official position, to the hostility of the Yankee forces," the *Mercury* wrote, using the word *obnoxious* ironically. By then the paper had concluded that Robert Bunch was a true friend of the South. "It seems more probable, however, that the real motive of his withdrawal is a desire on the part of Lord Lyons and of the British Administration to gratify the United States Government in the removal of Mr. Bunch, *whose views and course have been more unprejudiced and just to the Confederate States than their own.*" The italics are the *Mercury*'s. "We throw out these views which occur to us for whatever they may be worth. Every one must judge for himself."

By early 1863 the North's war machine was so enormous that both the British and the French had given up any thought of challenging it directly. In July 1863, when the Confederacy lost the Siege of Vicksburg and the Battle of Gettysburg in the same week, the South's last, extremely faint hopes of winning European recognition and support were ended. The Lost Cause was lost for good.

The people who had known Consul Bunch in Charleston would never be aware of the role he had played in defeating their plans for a slaveholding empire. They just kept on fighting, holding out against the Union siege month after month for another two years after Bunch departed. Federal forces would make many attempts to take the harbor by sea and to attack the peninsula by land. The very center of the city came in range of Union guns. What the fire of 1861 had not destroyed, artillery began to pick apart. The glamorous racecourse became a fetid prisoner-of-war camp for captured Union soldiers, and then the site of a mass grave for some two hundred of them. The Confederate garrison in Fort Sumter held out, its walls reduced to rubble that was then reinforced with seawater-soaked cotton bales. It was not until early 1865, as the Union Army under Gen. William Tecumseh Sherman approached in its devastating "march to the sea," that the defenses of Charleston finally were abandoned.

Robert Bunch, for his part, had been reassigned to Cuba, where he sat on the joint commission adjudicating slave-trade cases. Subsequently he was posted to Bogotá, Colombia, where he became Her Majesty's minister plenipotentiary, the post he had wanted for many years.

Those who had fought long and hard for secession and the reopening of the slave trade with Africa brought the South nothing in the end but war, emancipation, economic ruination, and, finally, occupation by Northern troops. Some of them did not survive the fighting and others were broken along with their sinister dreams, but a few, arguably the most ruthless, managed to prosper and rebuild.

The Last Slavers

Timothy Meaher, who had constructed the *Southern Republic* to ply the waters of the Alabama River, and who had sent the *Clotilda* to bring the last cargo of African slaves known to land on the shores of the United States, concentrated on his lumber business after the end of the hostilities and amassed a sizable fortune before he died in 1892 at the age of eighty.

The people Meaher had imported to Alabama as slaves settled, after their emancipation, in a part of his estate just north of Mobile known ever since as Africatown. Several of them worked in Meaher's sawmill. One of them, Cudjo Lewis, lived until 1935, the last known witness to the horrors of the Middle Passage.

Charles A. L. Lamar, the young hothead behind the *Wanderer* expedition, did not fare so well. During the war he devoted most of his efforts to blockade running, and he thought that the *Wanderer*, which he had refurbished at considerable expense, would serve nicely to outrun the Yankee navy. But the same Lt. Tunis Augustus MacDonough Craven who had captured the *Wildfire* captured the *Wanderer* off the Florida Keys soon after fighting began, and it was incorporated eventually into the Union Navy.

Lamar had also bought the former slave ship *Bonita*, and he joined forces with none other than Lt. John Newland Maffitt, the former nemesis of slavers who had captured the *Echo*. Maffitt had resigned from the Union Navy and committed himself to the Confederacy, in whose service he became known as "the Prince of the Privateers."

Toward the end of the war, Lamar rejoined the land forces fighting last-ditch battles against the advancing Federal forces. Seven days after the surrender of Gen. Robert E. Lee at Appomattox Court House, Lamar was shot and killed during a small battle in Columbus, Georgia. He was one of the last men to die fighting in the Civil War.

The slaver *Echo,* also known as the *Putnam,* which Maffitt had captured and which anchored in Charleston Harbor in the summer of 1858, became the centerpiece of a minor epic. It was bought at auction a few months after its capture and then, when the war began, commissioned as the privateer *Jefferson Davis*. In July 1861 it captured a merchant ship called the *S. J. Waring* and put a prize crew aboard who set their course for South Carolina. They told the black twenty-seven-year-old steward and cook, William Tillman, that he was now the property of the Confederate Navy and he'd be sold as a slave when the ship reached port.

As the *Waring* neared Charleston, Tillman waited until the Confederate officers were asleep or dozing, then killed three of them with a hatchet and took command of the schooner. The two surviving members of the prize crew were freed to help sail it, and eventually it managed to make its way back to New York, where Tillman found himself feted as a hero. The showman P. T. Barnum put him on display, and several months later the courts awarded Tillman $6,000 in prize money (roughly $150,000 today) for recapturing his ship. The *Putnam/Echo/Jefferson Davis*, for its part, ran aground a few weeks later off the Florida coast and had to be abandoned.

The Fire-Eaters

Robert Barnwell Rhett never did live up to his pretensions. South Carolina had heeded his call to secession and war, but, that accomplished, the Confederacy had little place for him. He had imagined himself its president but never rose higher than a seat in the lower house. As the war wore on, he lambasted the leadership of Jefferson Davis, as many people did, but few would have preferred Rhett in the Confederate president's place.

Soon after the fighting began, people noticed what seemed at first merely an unsightly pimple on Rhett's nose. It grew over the course of the war, and by the end of the 1860s was devouring his face. Doctors operated on him repeatedly, with all the horrors that surgery entailed in the middle of the nineteenth century, but they could not stop the cancer's spread. By 1875, this man who had always been at once so plain-looking and yet so vain, considered himself too hideous to appear in public. He worked on a memoir, but it was never published in his lifetime. When the scholar William C. Davis was preparing the manuscript for academic publication 130 years later, he found a note that Rhett had scribbled down as a random thought: "In a strong man, Conceit is a weakness—in a weak man, strength." As Davis put it, Rhett "left the stamp of his strengths, his weaknesses, and his conceit on the blighted fortunes of his generation and his South."

Rhett died in 1876 at the age of seventy-five and was buried in what was at first an unmarked grave in Charleston's Magnolia Cemetery. His family could not afford a monument. Later one was erected nearby with the family name alone, "Rhett," the appellation that Mr. Smith had borrowed from his distant past, and that endures to the present.

Leonidas Spratt, forty-two years old when Sumter fell, was no longer quite the romantic young rabble-rouser he had been when Bunch first knew him and learned to loathe him. As war approached, Spratt had sold his newspaper, the *Charleston Standard*, to the Rhetts so he would have more time to give lectures, and when the fighting began, he became the *Mercury*'s correspondent on Virginia's battlefield. After the first Battle of Bull Run, Spratt wrote almost in passing in one of his articles that as South Carolina's Gen. Barnard Bee was trying desperately to rally his forces, he pointed to another officer and shouted at his terrified troops, "There is Jackson, standing like a stone-wall." And thus the flamboyant Spratt is said to have given the ascetic Gen. Thomas Jackson the name that will forever be associated with him.

By the end of 1861, Spratt had taken up arms himself and eventually rose to the rank of colonel. He spent much of his long life after the war living in Jacksonville, Florida, a state he had gone to as an envoy from South Carolina and had persuaded, finally, to join the Confederacy. In his dotage, Spratt wrote several tomes that tried to reconcile—sometimes in quite incomprehensible prose—the kingdom of God and the observable facts of the natural universe. When he died in 1903 at the age of eighty-five, brief notices appeared as far afield as the *Los Angeles Herald*. "He advocated secession most strenuously," read the obituary in California. There was no mention of the slave trade.

William Lowndes Yancey, who had electrified the Democratic convention in Charleston and played such an important role tearing down the party in order to tear apart the country, returned from his time as the Confederate envoy in Britain a bitterly disappointed man, and on a stop in New Orleans in March 1862 he shared his disillusionment with the public. "There was not a country in Europe which sympathized with us," he said. Southerners had miscalculated the power of cotton to force Britain and France into the fight. It was a factor in world commerce, but King Cotton did not have "absolute sway," Yancey told his audience. "We cannot look for any sympathy or help from abroad. We must rely on ourselves alone."

Judah P. Benjamin was never known as a "fire-eater." Indeed he was the most cultured and well-traveled man in the Confederate cabinet, the trusted right hand of Jefferson Davis, serving as secretary of state until the collapse of the rebel government. But Benjamin's legalistic view of the African slave trade, that it was banned in the Confederate constitution and that that was as far as the government need go, deeply undermined what faint hope the rebellion had of gaining formal British recognition.

After Richmond fell and the cabinet fled, Benjamin was the only member to escape capture and imprisonment. He made his way to Florida, and eventually to London. Because Benjamin had been born in what were then the British Virgin Islands, he was able quickly to reclaim his British nationality. In short order the famous international litigator became a London barrister and a Queen's Counsel and wrote important tomes on what would later be called corporate law. He had managed to preserve some of the fortune he had before the war, grew even richer afterward, and sent money to help support Varina Davis, a close friend and ally, while her husband, Jefferson Davis, was in Federal prison.

Benjamin never did return to the United States but divided his time between London and Paris, where his estranged wife and his grown daughter lived. He died in 1884, at age seventy-two, and is buried at Père Lachaise Cemetery in a well-tended grave that bears the medallion of the Confederate States of America.

Bunch's Circle

Among the people Bunch called the "better class" in Charleston, Alfred Huger was left broken by the war, in despair and in retreat until his death seven years later. The problematic William Henry Trescot, whose final allegiance was to the art of diplomacy, served on the staff of Col. Roswell Ripley in the brutal Virginia and Maryland campaigns of 1862, then in the South Carolina legislature while the war was winding down. And eventually Trescot went back to Washington. He was appointed to commissions negotiating with the Chinese and the Mexicans, served as the U.S. envoy to Chile, and was active almost until his death, at age seventy-five, in 1898.

The most important person by far for Bunch when he first moved to Charleston and long afterward was the distinguished lawyer and unrepentant Unionist James L. Petigru. But, as Thomas Butler Gunn learned when he visited him in 1861, even the paterfamilias of South Carolina's legal and political elite was on the defensive as the state became, in Petigru's famous phrase, a "lunatic asylum."

Petigru, born in 1789, died in March 1863, shortly after Bunch departed and long before the Civil War ended, but certainly not before he could see where it was leading. "It is an odd feeling to be in the midst of joy and congratulations that one does not feel," he said soon after the fighting started. "On the contrary, it is a feeling of deep sadness that settles on my mind. The universal applause that waits on secessionists and secession has not the slightest tendency to shake my conviction that we are on the road to ruin." When the war was well over, and all was lost, his friend the poet William Grayson wrote a verse dedicated to Petigru that conceded, more with affection than with bitterness, that Petigru had been right from the beginning to listen to his intellect and not to the clamor of public opinion:

> 'Tis for this we render honor—
> That he ranks among the few
> Who, amid a reign of Error,
> Dared sublimely to be true.

Petigru's house in town had burned in the fire of 1861, and before he died his home on Sullivan's Island was confiscated by the Confederate military fortifying Charleston Harbor. The epic defense of the city known as "the cradle of rebellion" was about to begin.

By the spring of 1863, the Union Navy had assembled the most powerful armada, in terms of raw firepower, that the world had ever seen. The British did not marshal as many guns and munitions at Sebastopol. But Charleston's defenses were under Gen. Beauregard, who had returned to the city that loved him so well, and he had made it almost impregnable. At Fort Sumter, at Fort Moultrie, beyond it on Sullivan's Island, and at other strategic sites around the harbor new batteries had been dug in. Mines were laid underwater, ropes were strung beneath the surface to snarl propellers, and the vaunted new ironclad navy of the Union, including seven ships modeled on the famous *Monitor*, soon discovered they were no match for the concentrated firepower of the Confederacy's land-based guns. The artillery duels lasted for almost two years and foreshadowed the stalemate on the Western Front in World War I.

In military terms, the defense of Charleston was both brilliant and heroic. But the special fabric of Charleston's society, its elegance and gentility, its pretensions and delusions, were frayed almost beyond recognition.

There was no general uprising of the slaves. Many were made to build the city's new defenses. Others continued to serve their masters obediently, quietly. After one dinner party, Mary Chesnut marveled at "those old grey-haired darkies and their automatic, noiseless perfection of training."

But there were many incidents, some of them spectacular, that deepened the fears of Charleston's white elite. In May 1862 a slave who served as a harbor pilot, Robert Smalls, sailed the steam-powered ship the *Planter* out of the harbor and into the hands of the blockading fleet. He put himself and the boat at the disposal of the Union Navy for the rest of the war.

Former slaves who had escaped to the North enlisted by the thousands in the ranks of specially formed Union regiments. Their first great test in battle came when they tried to storm the Wagner Battery on Morris Island just south of Sumter in July 1863. Six thousand men mounted the charge, and 1,500 died, including Union Col. Robert Gould Shaw, the white commander of the Massachusetts 54th, a black regiment. When the Union forces retreated, the Confederate officers, some of whom had known him personally, refused to return his body or treat it with any military honor. Shaw's corpse was stripped of its uniform and thrown into a ditch, as the Charleston press said, "with his niggers."

The vindictiveness of the battle for a city whose importance had become mainly symbolic did little credit to either side. The Confederate Army had been defeated already at Gettysburg and Vicksburg. New Orleans had long since fallen to Federal troops. Charleston Harbor was closed by a wall of Union warships. The city, cut off from the world, was dying from within. And yet, when the North managed to bring its artillery close enough to reach the southern part of Charleston—the elegant part where Bunch and all the "better class" had their homes, and where all the history of secession had been written—President Lincoln himself gave the order to bombard it with incendiary shells.

Still, the city held on.

Jefferson Davis visited Charleston in November 1863 and stood on the steps of City Hall amid buildings destroyed by fire and never rebuilt, looking out on homes deserted by their inhabitants and the steeple of St. Michael's Church, eventually painted black so it would be less useful for Yankee gunners setting their sights. He declared it would be better for the city to become a "heap of ruins" than for it to fall to the Yankees.

"Ruins!" the crowd answered back. "Ruins!"

By late 1864, with the defenses still holding out as if by miracle, but with the Union forces of Gen. William Tecumseh Sherman marching through Georgia to the sea, there had settled on Charleston a kind of *fin du monde* frenzy. Parties were thrown at which people sang psalms until midnight, then struck up a band and danced until dawn.

In the end, Sherman the ruthless realist decided the jewel of the South was not worth taking. "Charleston," he told Grant, "is now a mere desolated wreck, and it is hardly worth the time it would take to starve it out."

In early February 1865, just over two years after Bunch had left Charleston, Confederate troops abandoned the city. On February 18, occupying Federal forces, including black regiments, marched in. By April 14, five days after Lee's surrender at Appomattox and four years after Maj. Robert Anderson surrendered Fort Sumter, a great event was staged. Anderson, now a gray and weary colonel, once again raised the flag of the United States above Sumter's shattered walls. If he had had his wishes, he said, he would have done it in silence. Among the honored guests: the son of Denmark Vesey.

The feeling of jubilation in the North was short-lived. On that same night, President Lincoln was assassinated. But for the utterly defeated white elite of Charleston, who had thought they must start a war to escape Lincoln's rule, that was little consolation. Bunch's secret prediction six years before had come true: the prestige and power of these slaveholders was gone, never to return.

One of Charleston's distinguished matrons wrote years later that when she went into the heart of the city, which had become a lawless no-man's-land by 1865, roofs were shattered and chimneys crumbling, and no windows remained: "The streets looked as if piled with diamonds, the glass lay shivered so thick on the ground."

Bunch and the Ministers

Henry John Temple, 3rd Viscount Palmerston, lived to see the end of the American Civil War but not the definitive end of the slave trade. It endured in Africa and up into Arabia until 1877, officially, and along clandestine routes well into the twentieth century. In 1865, Palmerston was elected once again as Prime Minister, but he came down with a fever after contracting a chill in an open carriage. He was two days shy of his eighty-first birthday, and it is said, apocryphally but appropriately, that his last words were, "Die, my dear doctor? That is the last thing I shall do."

Earl Russell (formerly Lord John Russell) was there to take Palmerston's place but served for only eight months. Unable to hold his government together, he retired from his post and, to all intents and purposes, from public life.

Lord Clarendon returned as Foreign Secretary during Russell's brief tenure as Prime Minister, and then again from late 1868. When Clarendon died in the summer of 1870, it was said, he was still surrounded by dossiers from the far-flung corners of the world where Her Majesty had pressing interests.

Lord Lyons left Washington for good at the end of 1864 suffering from mental and physical exhaustion and, after a tour at the Divine Port overseeing Britain's relations with the Ottoman Empire, he was assigned to Paris as the ambassador. This was, from London's point of view, the most important diplomatic position in the Foreign Service. Lyons served there through twenty years of extraordinary tumult, weathering the Franco-Prussian War, the collapse of the French Empire, the rise of the Commune, its elimination, and the aftermath. While Lyons was ambassador, England and France had a ferocious falling-out over which country would dictate the future of Egypt. (The banks of the Nile had grown very rich growing cotton when the Confederacy's white gold was off the market; but the Egyptian rulers spent more than they earned, and the Europeans collected their debts.) Toward the end of Lyons's twenty years he was offered the position of Foreign Secretary. He was, he said, simply too tired to take it.

As for the last years of Robert Bunch spent in Colombia and Venezuela, they brought with them the coveted title of minister, but left him once again on the far fringes of London's field of vision.

As the interminable partisan wars of Latin America erupted, subsided, and erupted again, Bunch continued to try to travel throughout his area of responsibility, but he appears to have developed a condition, possibly prostate cancer, that made riding on horses or donkeys over long distances excruciatingly painful.

A smug official in the Foreign Office described Bunch as "a man spoilt by being raised beyond his proper sphere, and consequently too much impressed with a sense of his own dignity," but Bunch did his best to maintain his sense of justice and of irony right up until his death in 1881. Bunch had helped to change the course of history;

he had fought secretly but relentlessly against the cruel lunacy of slavery that surrounded him and that threatened to drag the wide world into America's war; he had defended the humanity of black men and women who were treated no better than animals. And yet he, Robert Bunch, had been forgotten. A little respect for his dignity did not seem, to him, too much to ask.

LETTERS AND DISPATCHES

Most of *Our Man in Charleston* was developed from the unpublished private correspondence of Robert Bunch with various ministers in Washington and foreign secretaries in London. These letters are in several different collections, which are organized in different ways.

The *official correspondence* is held at the British National Archives in Kew. Of particular importance are those dispatches and letters related to consular and diplomatic affairs in "America," which are filed under the heading FO5, and those related to "Slave Trade," which are filed under FO84. Numbers are then assigned to specific volumes. So, for instance, Bunch's rich correspondence in 1854 with Lord Clarendon, the foreign secretary, can be found under FO5/601. Bunch's dispatches and letters concerning the cases of the slave ships *Echo* and *Wanderer* in 1858 can be found in FO84/1059.

Generally speaking, the letters in these bound volumes at Kew begin with the responses of the foreign secretary and his office to various dispatches, arranged chronologically, then proceed with the dispatches from the various consulates, grouped by location and put into chronological order, and within that context they are most easily searched by date.

The *private correspondence* is in several different collections, most of which have not been catalogued in detail.

Bunch's correspondence with Sir Henry Bulwer, minister to Washington from 1849 to 1852, is held in the Norfolk Records Office, Norfolk, United Kingdom, as part of the Diplomatic Papers of William Henry Lytton Earle Bulwer, Baron Dalling and Bulwer, mostly under the filing code BUL 1.

Correspondence with Sir John Fiennes Crampton, secretary of legation at Washington from 1845 to 1852 and minister at Washington from 1852 to 1856, is held at Oxford University, Bodleian Library, Special Collections, much of it on microfilm.

Bunch's extensive private and confidential correspondence with Lord Lyons, the British minister at Washington from 1858 to 1864, is in the Duke of Norfolk Archives at Arundel Castle in Arundel, West Sussex, United Kingdom. This trove of documents, held in the castle's "Archive Tower," was essential to the research. It is organized by the writers of the letter and by date in little bundles tied with ribbons. Correspondence from Lyons to others is contained in Lyons's "Letter Books," arranged chronologically. In the endnotes to this volume, all relevant correspondence from the Duke of Norfolk's collection is cited as Lyons Papers.

Collections of *published correspondence* include:

Barnes, James J., and Patience P. Barnes. *The American Civil War Through British Eyes: Dispatches from British Diplomats.* 3 vols. Kent, OH: The Kent State University Press, 2003–2005. This is an indispensable reference work.

———. *Private and Confidential: Letters from British Ministers in Washington to the Foreign Secretaries in London, 1844–67.* Selinsgrove, PA: Susquehanna University Press, 1993. Not as complete as *British Eyes,* but the correspondence from the period when Lord Napier was minister to Washington was particularly useful.

The Executive Documents of the Senate of the United States for the First Session of the Forty-First Congress, 1869, "Claims Against Great Britain." Washington D.C.: Government Printing Office, 1870. This volume, published in various guises, has a wide range of correspondence to and from British officials.

Temperley, Harold, and Lillian M. Penson. *Foundations of British Foreign Policy from Pitt (1792) to Salisbury (1902), or Documents, Old and New.* Cambridge, UK: Cambridge University Press, 1938. Reproduces several gems.

The War of the Rebellion: A Compilation of the Official Records of the Union and Confederate Armies. U.S. War Department, Official Records, particularly Series II, Vol. II: "Treatment of Suspected and Disloyal Persons North and South." Washington, D.C.: Government Printing Office, 1897.

SELECTED BOOKS

There exist likely tens of thousands of books about the American Civil War, and hundreds were consulted in the research for *Our Man in Charleston.* A few of those that proved particularly helpful even when, in some cases, they came to conclusions different from mine were:

U.S.-U.K. Relations Before and During the American Civil War

Adams, Ephraim Douglass. *Great Britain and the American Civil War.* Charleston: Bibliobazaar, 2006. Reprint of the original 1925 Longmans, Green and Co. edition. This has long been the defining work on the subject.

Berwanger, Eugene H. *The British Foreign Service and the American Civil War.* Lexington: The University Press of Kentucky, 1994. Professor Berwanger is one of the very few scholars to have examined closely Robert

Bunch's private correspondence and to have understood how hostile to the South and slavery the consul really was.

Bonham, Milledge L., Jr., *The British Consuls in the Confederacy.* New York: Columbia University, 1911. This was accepted for many years as the definitive work on the subject. Unfortunately, Bonham does not appear to have had access to Bunch's private correspondence. As a result, even though this volume is cited frequently by other scholars, its interpretations can be misleading.

Crook, D. P. *The North, the South, and the Powers.* London: John Wiley & Sons, 1974.

De Leon, Edwin. *Secret History of Confederate Diplomacy Abroad.* Edited by William C. Davis. Lawrence: University Press of Kansas, 2005.

Ferris, Norman B. *Desperate Diplomacy: William H. Seward's Foreign Policy, 1861.* Knoxville: The University of Tennessee Press, 1976. Also see Ferris's, *The Trent Affair: A Diplomatic Crisis* (Knoxville: The University of Tennessee Press, 1977).

Foreman, Amanda. *A World on Fire: An Epic History of Two Nations Divided.* London: Allen Lane, an imprint of Penguin Books, 2010. Published in the United States as *A World on Fire: Britain's Crucial Role in the American Civil War.* A wonderfully detailed account focused on the war years.

Jenkins, Brian. *Britain and the War for the Union.* Vol. 1. Montreal: McGill-Queen's University Press, 1974.

Jones, Howard. *Blue and Gray Diplomacy: A History of Union and Confederate Foreign Relations.* Chapel Hill: The University of North Carolina Press, 2010. Also see Jones's earlier *Union in Peril: The Crisis over British Intervention in the Civil War* (Chapel Hill: The University of North Carolina Press, 1992).

Jordan, Donaldson, and Edwin J. Pratt. *Europe and the American Civil War.* Boston: Houghton Mifflin, 1931.

Mahin, Dean B. *One War at a Time: The International Dimensions of the American Civil War.* Washington, D.C.: Brassey's, 1999.

Myers, Phillip E. *Caution and Cooperation: The American Civil War in British-American Relations.* Kent, OH: The Kent State University Press, 2008.

Owsley, Frank Lawrence. *King Cotton Diplomacy.* Chicago: University of Chicago Press, 1959.

Antebellum Developments in Historical Perspective

Catton, Bruce. *The Coming Fury*. New York: Simon & Schuster/Pocket Books, 1961.

Egerton, Douglas R. *Year of Meteors: Stephen Douglas, Abraham Lincoln, and the Election That Brought On the Civil War*. New York: Bloomsbury Press, 2010.

Franklin, John Hope. *The Militant South: 1800–1861*. Urbana: University of Illinois Press, 2002. Originally published in 1956 by Belknap Press of Harvard University Press.

Freehling, William W. *The Road to Disunion*. Vol. 2, *Secessionists Triumphant, 1854–1861*. New York: Oxford University Press, 2007. Also see Freehling's *Prelude to Civil War: The Nullification Controversy in South Carolina 1816–1836* (Oxford, UK: Oxford University Press, 1966).

Goodheart, Adam. *1861: The Civil War Awakening*. New York: Vintage, 2011.

Holt, Michael F. *The Fate of Their Country: Politicians, Slavery Extension, and the Coming of the Civil War*. New York: Hill and Wang, 2004.

Klein, Maury. *Days of Defiance: Sumter, Secession, and the Coming of the Civil War*. New York: Knopf, 1997.

Oates, Stephen B. *The Approaching Fury: Voices of the Storm, 1820–1861*. New York: HarperCollins, 1997.

Parry, Albert. *Garrets and Pretenders: A History of Bohemianism in America*. Rev. ed. New York: Dover, 1960. Original published in 1933 by Covici, Friede.

Phillips, Ulrich Bonnell. *The Course of the South to Secession: An Interpretation*. Edited by E. Merton Coulter. New York: D. Appleton, 1939.

Potter, David M. *The Impending Crisis: 1848–1861*. Completed and edited by Don E. Fehrenbacher. New York: Harper, 1976.

Renehan, Edward J. *The Secret Six: The True Tale of the Men Who Conspired with John Brown*. Columbia: University of South Carolina Press, 1997.

Reynolds, David S. *Walt Whitman's America: A Cultural Biography*. New York: Knopf, 1995.

Antebellum Impressions by Contemporary Witnesses

Cairnes, John Elliott. *The Slave Power: Its Character, Career, and Probable Designs*. London: Parker, Son, and Bourn, 1862.

Mary Chesnut Diaries: Chesnut, Mary Boykin. *Mary Chesnut's Diary*. New York: Penguin Books, 2011; Daniels, Martha M., and Barbara E.

McCarthy. *Mary Chesnut's Illustrated Diary.* Gretna, LA: Pelican Publishing Company, 2011; Vann Woodward, C., ed. *Mary Chesnut's Civil War.* New Haven: Yale University Press, 1981; Vann Woodward, C., and Elisabeth Muhlenfeld, eds. *The Private Mary Chesnut: The Unpublished Civil War Diaries.* New York: Oxford University Press, 1984.

Dickens, Charles. *American Notes.* London: Chapman & Hall, 1913. Originally published in 1850 and currently available online as a Project Gutenberg eBook. The critique of slavery and its impact on American culture in the North as well as the South is angry and unrelenting, and many times in the Bunch correspondence the consul seems to be echoing Dickens.

Gunn, Thomas Butler. *Thomas Butler Gunn Diaries, 1849–1863.* 22 vols. St. Louis: State Historical Society of Missouri, 2013. A fascinating resource, available online at http://www.historyhappenshere.org/archives/7354.

Halstead, Murat B. *Caucuses of 1860: A History of the National Political Conventions of the Current Presidential Campaign.* Columbus, OH: Follett, Foster and Company, 1860.

Jones, J. B. *A Rebel War Clerk's Diary at the Confederate States Capital.* 2 vols. Philadelphia: J. B. Lippincott, 1866.

Malet, William Wyndham. *An Errand to the South in the Summer of 1862.* London: Richard Bentley, 1863.

Olmsted, Frederick Law. *The Cotton Kingdom: A Traveller's Observations on Cotton and Slavery in the American Slave States.* Edited by Arthur M. Schlesinger. New York: Knopf, 1962.

Ranken, George. *Canada and the Crimea, or Sketches of a Soldier's Life.* London: Longman, Green, Longman, Roberts & Green, 1863.

Thornbury, Walter. *Criss-Cross Journeys.* London: Hurst and Blackett, 1873. Reprint, Historical Collection from the British Library.

Turnbull, Jane M. E., and Marion Turnbull. *American Photographs.* London: T. C. Newby, 1859. Reprint, Historical Collection from the British Library.

Slavery and the Slave Trade

Bancroft, Frederic. *Slave Trading in the Old South.* Columbia: University of South Carolina Press, 1996. Originally published by J. H. Furst, 1931.

Brown, Christopher Leslie. *Moral Capital: Foundations of British Abolitionism.* Chapel Hill: The University of North Carolina Press, 2006.

Calonius, Erik. *The Wanderer: The Last American Slave Ship and the Conspiracy That Set Its Sails.* New York: St. Martin's Press, 2006.

Diouf, Sylviane A. *Dreams of Africa in Alabama: The Slave Ship* Clotilda *and the Story of the Last Africans Brought to America.* New York: Oxford University Press, 2007. Diouf was also kind enough to share with me some of her original documentation.

Drescher, Seymour. *Abolition: A History of Slavery and Antislavery.* Cambridge, UK: Cambridge University Press, 2009.

Fehrenbacher, Don E. *The Slaveholding Republic: An Account of the United States Government's Relations to Slavery.* Completed and edited by Ward M. McAfee. New York: Oxford University Press, 2001.

Huzzey, Richard. *Freedom Burning: Anti-Slavery and Empire in Victorian Britain.* Ithaca: Cornell University Press, 2012.

Joyner, Charles. *Down by the Riverside: A South Carolina Slave Community.* Urbana: University of Illinois Press, 1984.

Metaxas, Eric. *Amazing Grace: William Wilberforce and the Heroic Campaign to End Slavery.* San Francisco: HarperSanFrancisco, 2007.

Rediker, Marcus. *The Slave Ship: A Human History.* New York: Viking, 2007.

Rees, Siân. *Sweet Water and Bitter: The Ships That Stopped the Slave Trade.* London: Vintage, 2009.

Sinha, Manisha. *The Counter-Revolution of Slavery: Politics and Ideology in Antebellum South Carolina.* Chapel Hill: The University of North Carolina Press, 2000.

Soodalter, Ron. *Hanging Captain Gordon: The Life and Trial of an American Slave Trader.* New York: Washington Square Press, 2006.

Tadman, Michael. *Speculators and Slaves: Masters, Traders, and Slaves in the Old South.* Madison: University of Wisconsin Press, 1989.

Takaki, Ronald T. *A Pro-Slavery Crusade: The Agitation to Reopen the African Slave Trade.* New York: The Free Press, 1971. A very important and enlightening study.

Thomas, Hugh. *The Slave Trade: The Story of the Atlantic Slave Trade: 1440–1870.* New York: Simon & Schuster, 1997.

Wells, Tom Henderson. *The Slave Ship* Wanderer. Athens: University of Georgia Press, 1967.

BIOGRAPHIES BY SUBJECT

Prince Albert, Queen Victoria, and the Prince of Wales

Radforth, Ian. *Royal Spectacle: The 1860 Visit of the Prince of Wales to Canada and the United States.* Toronto: University of Toronto Press, 2004.

Ridley, Jane. *The Heir Apparent: A Life of Edward VII, the Playboy Prince.* New York: Random House, 2013.

Weintraub, Stanley. *Uncrowned King: The Life of Prince Albert.* New York: The Free Press, 1997.

Edward Archibald, Consul in New York

Archibald, Edith J. *Life and Letters of Sir Edward Mortimer Archibald: A Memoir of Fifty Years of Service.* Toronto: George N. Morang, 1924.

Judah P. Benjamin, Member of the Confederate Cabinet

Butler, Pierce. *Judah P. Benjamin.* Philadelphia: George W. Jacobs, 1906.

Evans, Eli N. *Judah P. Benjamin: The Jewish Confederate.* New York: The Free Press, 1988. An interesting look at Benjamin from a modern Jewish perspective.

Meade, Robert Douthat. *Judah P. Benjamin: Confederate Statesman.* Baton Rouge: Louisiana State University Press, 2001. Reprinted from the original 1943 Oxford University Press edition. I find this to be the most thorough and convincing of the biographies of Benjamin.

James Buchanan, U.S. President

Baker, Jean H. *James Buchanan.* New York: Henry Holt, 2004. Succinct and straightforward.

John Brown, Abolitionist and Insurgent

Horwitz, Tony. *Midnight Rising: John Brown and the Raid That Sparked the Civil War.* New York: Henry Holt, 2011. Of the many, many Brown biographies, this certainly is one of the most compelling.

Oates, Stephen B. *To Purge This Land with Blood: A Biography of John Brown.* Boston: University of Massachusetts Press, 1984.

Reynolds, David S. *John Brown, Abolitionist: The Man Who Killed Slavery, Sparked the Civil War, and Seeded Civil Rights.* New York: Vintage, 2006.

Jefferson Davis, President of the Confederacy, and His Wife, Varina Davis

Cashin, Joan E. *First Lady of the Confederacy: Varina Davis's Civil War.* Cambridge, MA: Belknap Press of Harvard University Press, 2006.

Davis, William C. *Jefferson Davis: The Man and His Hour.* Baton Rouge: Louisiana State University Press, 1991.

Andrew Jackson, President of the United States

Meacham, Jon. *American Lion: Andrew Jackson in the White House.* New York: Random House, 2008. Especially good on the Nullification Crisis of the early 1830s.

Abraham Lincoln, President of the United States

Goodwin, Doris Kearns. *Team of Rivals: The Political Genius of Abraham Lincoln.* New York: Simon & Schuster, 2005. This has become the reference point for most public discussion of the Lincoln administration.

Guelzo, Allen C. *Lincoln's Emancipation Proclamation: The End of Slavery in America.* New York: Simon & Schuster, 2004.

Holzer, Harold. *Lincoln at Cooper Union: The Speech That Made Abraham Lincoln President.* New York: Simon & Schuster, 2006. A particularly useful look at this pivotal address that defines so well the issues of slavery and the slave trade.

Lord Lyons, British Minister to Washington

Jenkins, Brian. *Lord Lyons: A Diplomat in an Age of Nationalism and War.* Montreal: McGill-Queen's University Press, 2014.

Newton, Lord. *Lord Lyons: A Record of British Diplomacy.* London: Edward Arnold, 1913.

Frederick Law Olmsted, Author and Landscape Architect

Rybczynski, Witold. *A Clearing in the Distance: Frederick Law Olmsted and America in the Nineteenth Century.* New York: Scribner, 1999.

Lord Palmerston, Foreign Secretary and Prime Minister of Great Britain

Ashley, Evelyn. *The Life and Correspondence of Henry John Temple Viscount Palmerston.* London: Richard Bentley & Son, 1879.

Brown, David. *Palmerston: A Biography.* New Haven: Yale University Press, 2010. The definitive work to date.

Robert Barnwell Rhett, Owner of the Charleston *Mercury* and Impassioned Secessionist

Davis, William C. *Rhett: The Turbulent Life and Times of a Fire-Eater.* Columbia: University of South Carolina Press, 2001.

————, ed. *A Fire-Eater Remembers: The Confederate Memoir of Robert Barnwell Rhett.* Columbia: University of South Carolina Press, 2000.

William Howard Russell, British War Correspondent

Crawford, Martin, ed. *William Howard Russell's Civil War: Private Diary and Letters, 1861–1862.* Athens: The University of Georgia Press, 1992.

Hankinson, Alan. *Man of Wars: William Howard Russell of the* Times. London: Heinemann, 1982.

Russell, William Howard. *My Diary North and South.* Boston: T. O. H. P. Burnham, 1863. Reprinted on demand in 2011 by Blackwell Books, London.

William Henry Seward, Secretary of State in the Lincoln Administration

Bancroft, Frederic. *The Life of William H. Seward.* New York: Harper & Brothers, 1900.

Hale, Edward Everett. *William H. Seward.* Philadelphia: George W. Jacobs & Company, 1910.

Seward, Olive Risley, ed. *William H. Seward's Travels Around the World.* New York: D. Appleton and Company, 1873.

Stahr, Walter. *Seward: Lincoln's Indispensable Man.* New York: Simon & Schuster, 2012.

Taylor, John M. *William Henry Seward: Lincoln's Right Hand.* New York: HarperCollins, 1991.

John Slidell, Louisiana Political Boss and Confederate Delegate to Paris

Willson, Beckles. *John Slidell and the Confederates in Paris (1862–65).* New York: Minton, Balch & Company, 1932. This little volume is highly readable but poorly sourced.

William Makepeace Thackeray, Famous Nineteenth-Century Novelist and Networker

Crowe, Eyre. *With Thackeray in America.* New York: Charles Scribner's Sons, 1893.

Monsarrat, Ann. *Thackeray: An Uneasy Victorian.* London: Cassell, 1980.

Denmark Vesey, Leader of a Planned Slave Rebellion in South Carolina in 1822

Robertson, David. *Denmark Vesey: The Buried History of America's Largest Slave Rebellion and the Man Who Led It.* New York: Knopf, 1999.

Charles Wilkes, the U.S. Naval Officer Who Nearly Started a War with the United Kingdom

Wilkes, Charles. *Autobiography of Rear Admiral Charles Wilkes, U.S. Navy, 1798–1877.* Edited by William James Morgan et al. Washington, D.C.: Naval History Division, Department of the Navy, 1978.

On Charleston and the South

McInnis, Maurie D. *The Politics of Taste in Antebellum Charleston.* Chapel Hill: The University of North Carolina Press, 2005.

Racine, Philip N., ed. *Gentlemen Merchants: A Charleston Family's Odyssey, 1828–1870.* Knoxville: The University of Tennessee Press, 2008. A compilation of letters that give a particularly vivid and personal picture of Charleston during the standoff over Fort Sumter.

Rosen, Robert N. *Confederate Charleston: An Illustrated History of the City and the People During the Civil War.* Columbia: University of South Carolina Press, 1994.

The South's Peculiar Manifest Destiny

Brown, Matthew. *Adventuring Through Spanish Colonies: Simón Bolívar, Foreign Mercenaries and the Birth of New Nations.* Liverpool, UK: Liverpool University Press, 2006.

Johnson, Walter. *River of Dark Dreams: Slavery and Empire in the Cotton Kingdom.* Cambridge, MA: Belknap Press of Harvard University Press, 2013.

May, Robert E. *Slavery, Race, and Conquest in the Tropics: Lincoln, Douglas, and the Future of Latin America.* Cambridge, UK: Cambridge University Press, 2013. Also see Robert E. May, *The Southern Dream of a Caribbean Empire, 1854–1861* (Gainesville: University of Florida Press, 2002; originally published in 1973 by Louisiana State University Press).

Notes

Many of the sources cited here are available online, but with a few exceptions I have left out the Internet addresses because, in my experience, those tend to become obsolete. Most of the extant material can be located quickly using the material from the citations in search engines.

PROLOGUE

1   **"before we will yield to the Yankees!"** William Howard Russell, *My Diary North and South* (Boston: T. O. H. P. Burnham, 1863), p. 185; reprinted on demand in 2011 by Blackwell Books, London. Note that the quotations here are reconstituted from paraphrasing, a technique I will use rarely and with full attribution throughout this book. There is no "imagined" dialogue, and settings are described only on the basis of documentary evidence.

1   **Slaughtered hundreds!** Sylviane A. Diouf, *Dreams of Africa in Alabama: The Slave Ship* Clotilda *and the Story of the Last Africans Brought to America* (New York: Oxford University Press, 2007), Kindle loc 141–148. Russell suggested he didn't think the captain expected to be believed, but the thrust of the story that the Indians were forced out certainly is true. In the 1830s, as Diouf notes, "'Alabama Fever' had spread throughout the South after the War of 1812 and brought white settlers by the tens of thousands. They entered the Alabama heartland, where they met fierce resistance from the Upper Creeks, who were then defeated during the Creek War of 1813–1814. More Indian land was lost as Choctaw, Chickasaw, and Cherokee (even though they had fought alongside the United States against the British) were also forced to relocate westward to Indian Territory after the Treaty of Dancing Rabbit Creek in 1830."

2   **"the air stinks of blood"** Alan Hankinson, *Man of Wars: William Howard Russell of the* Times (London: Heinemann, 1982), p. 127. Russell was writing to his wife about the aftermath of the Battle of Balaclava as Russian prisoners died around him.

2   **Russell went out on deck** Russell, *My Diary*, pp. 184–186.

3   **The boat was a pile of kindling** Ibid., p. 186; for further color, see T. C. DeLeon, *Four Years in Rebel Capitals: An Inside View of Life in the Southern Confederacy, from Birth to Death* (Mobile: The Gossip Printing Company, 1890), pp. 26–30.

5   **[Meaher] "kept the rest for himself"** Russell, *My Diary*, p. 187. The original entry in Russell's personal diary, now at the archives of the *Times* at News UK in Enfield, England, is partly written in

longhand, but the discussion about the boy with the filed teeth is in shorthand.

5   **The truth was well known** Diouf, *Dreams*, Kindle loc 1623.

5   **ritual scars in Africa** Ibid., Kindle loc 545: "Many deportees in Mobile had scarifications on the face and/or the body, and those who came from Atakora [a mountainous region of Benin] had gotten them in a particular manner. As they passed from one age class to the other their bodies indicated where they stood in the hierarchy. They received scarifications around the navel, then on the belly, and finally on the Chest. Those on the face, numerous and very fine, barely visible, had been done much earlier, when they were two or three years old. The teenagers also got their upper teeth filed with small stones in the form of spikes."

6   **[The British] still needed Southern cotton** Russell, *My Diary*, pp. 188–189. The dialogue here was partly written in Russell's interpretation of dialect. I have taken the liberty of modernizing some of the language to make it more readable.

PART ONE

Chapter 1

9   **enforce British interests** In 1848 Her Majesty's consul in Central America, Frederick Chatfield, had formed a ragtag army backed up by two Royal Navy warships that seized San Juan on the Caribbean coast of Nicaragua and renamed it Greytown. See Lester D. Langley, *America and the Americas: The United States in the Western Hemisphere* (Athens: University of Georgia Press, 2010), p. 58. A British consul in Havana was accused of fomenting a slave rebellion, and the consul in Canton played the pivotal role provoking what came to be called the Arrow War, or the Second Opium War, in 1856.

10   **"in a social sense, very unpleasant"** FO5/570 George Buckley Mathew letter, February 14, 1853. The small folio pages of the letter are inserted between pp. 148 and 151 of the larger dispatches and correspondence.

10   **"small fry"** FO5/579 Mathew to John Bidwell Jr., January 6, 1851.

10   **"a poor Peelite"** FO5/579 Mathew to John Bidwell Jr., January 6, 1851. Followers of Conservative leader and former Prime Minister Sir Robert Peel, who was a strong advocate of free trade. The Peelites eventually joined with Whigs and Radicals to form the Liberal Party (*liberal* being understood in the economic free-trade sense rather than the social sense employed in today's United States).

12   **insurrectionary plague that must be quarantined** Michael Alan Schoeppner, "Navigating the Dangerous Atlantic: Racial Quaran-

tines, Black Sailors and United States Constitutionalism" (Gainesville: University of Florida dissertation, 2010), passim.

12   **"deemed and taken as absolute slaves, and sold"** *The Statutes at Large of South Carolina*, p. 401, No. 2277, "An Act for the Better Regulation and Government of Free Negroes and Persons of Color; and for other purposes," Article III.

12   **Palmerston denounced the policy** Schoeppner, "Navigating," p. 269, citing FO5/579 Palmerston to Crampton, February 25, 1848, "Correspondence relative to the prohibition against the admission of free persons of colour into certain ports of the United States, 1823–1851."

13   **a growing sense of futility** For a very thorough treatment of the efforts to change South Carolina's law, see Philip M. Hamer, "British Consuls and the Negro Seamen Acts, 1850–1860," *The Journal of Southern History*, vol. 1, no. 2 (May 1935), pp. 138–168, passim; also James J. Barnes and Patience P. Barnes, *Private and Confidential: Letters from British Ministers in Washington to the Foreign Secretaries in London, 1844–67* (Selinsgrove, PA: Susquehanna University Press, 1993), pp. 70–71.

14   **refused to pay for his passage** FO5/570 Foreign Office to Mathew, June 13, 1853.

14   **an Englishman of the Americas** R. Burnham Moffat, *The Barclays of New York: Who They Are and Who They Are Not—and Some Other Barclays* (New York: Robert Grier Cooke, 1904).

15   **was then called Nueva Granada** José Asunción Suárez Niño, "La Legion Británica en la Época de la Independencia," published by the Academia Colombiana de Genealogía. What little has been written about Robert Henry Bunch Woodside, the consul's father, has appeared in Colombia, where he is known as the founder of the country's first ironworks and the father, with his second wife, of Doña Isabel Bunch Mutis, a well-known nineteenth-century poet who was the consul's half sister, albeit twenty-five years his junior.

According to this paper by Suárez Niño, Bunch's ancestors were close to the Stuart line of the British monarchy and departed Britain for the West Indies in the eighteenth century, settling in Jamaica, where they developed extensive banking and business interests with branches in New York, Philadelphia, and London. Consul Bunch's paternal grandfather supposedly was a baronet, Sir George Henry Bunch, while his grandmother was Charlotte Elizabeth Woodside, born in Nassau.

When Bolívar arrived in Jamaica in 1815, the young revolutionary so impressed R. H. Bunch that he decided to fund Bolívar's purchase of arms and provisions on his first campaign and afterward.

15   [would tell people in Charleston] that he went to Oxford This
        according to a letter from his daughter, Helen Bunch, written to the
        South Carolina Historical Society long after the consul's death and
        still in the society's files.

15   several delicate assignments Notes on Bunch's early adventures
        are drawn mainly from his correspondence in the Diplomatic Pa-
        pers of William Henry Lytton Earle Bulwer, Baron Dalling and
        Bulwer (1801–1872), held at the Norfolk Records Office, Norfolk,
        UK (not to be confused with the Duke of Norfolk Archives at
        Arundel Castle).
            Not all the assignments went well. In the summer of 1850,
        Bunch, with his fluent Spanish, escorted the Spanish Count-
        ess Alcoy through the hurly-burly of New York City. The British
        Crown had been meddling in Spanish politics for decades with
        several ends in mind, among them, importantly, the abolition of
        the vast slave trade that continued between Africa and the Spanish
        colony of Cuba. Now the British government was cultivating the
        countess's husband, Federico Roncali, who was then the governor-
        general of Cuba and soon to be, briefly, prime minister of Spain.
        All went well until the countess was about to leave New York, and
        her black twelve-year-old page was accompanying her baggage to
        the steamer. Out of nowhere, it would seem, an ardent abolition-
        ist spirited the boy away, intent on setting him free. Ironically, the
        page was not a slave, but, in any case, he was never seen again. An
        American judge, Commissioner George W. Morton, filed a report,
        which Bunch forwarded to then–Secretary of State Daniel Webster
        in Washington. Typically, Bunch appended a few deferential lines
        to Webster of his own. See Bunch to Bulwer, August 29, 1850, Nor-
        folk Record Office.

16   "zealots and helots" For a detailed history of the Slave Trade De-
        partment and its clerks, including the famous James Bandinel, who
        died in 1849, see Keith Hamilton, "Zealots and Helots: The Slave
        Trade Department of the Nineteenth-Century Foreign Office," in
        Keith Hamilton and Patrick Salmon, eds., *Slavery, Diplomacy and
        Empire: Britain and the Suppression of the Slave Trade, 1807–1975*
        (Eastbourne, UK: Sussex Academic Press, 2009), pp. 20–42.

17   "hankerings" Bunch to Crampton, March 26, March 28, April 1,
        May 24, 1853, Papers of Sir John Crampton, Bodleian Library, Ox-
        ford University, Oxford, UK.

Chapter 2

19   **"were it even threatened"** FO5/570 Bunch to Clarendon, November 29, 1853.

22   **an average of nearly 2 percent of the national income** Chaim D. Kaufman and Robert A. Pape, "Explaining Costly International Moral Action: Britain's Sixty-Year Campaign Against the Atlantic Slave Trade," *International Organization* (August 1999), vol. 53, no. 4, pp. 631–668.

24   **"Lord Cupid"** For the notes on Palmerston's love life, and much else about him, I am indebted to David Brown's superb *Palmerston: A Biography* (New Haven: Yale University Press, 2010), Kindle loc 250, 2125–2168. But this particularly succinct description of Palmerston as an old man comes from Christopher Hibbert writing for the BBC, February 17, 2011: http://www.bbc.co.uk/history/british/victorians/victoria_ministers_01.shtml.

24   **"delightful condition"** Brown, *Palmerston*, Kindle loc 3479.

25   **"never experienced before"** Richard Huzzey, *Freedom Burning: Anti-Slavery and Empire in Victorian Britain* (Ithaca: Cornell University Press, 2012), Kindle loc 3346.

25   **"repugnant to the spirit of Christianity"** Stanley Weintraub, *Uncrowned King: The Life of Prince Albert* (New York: The Free Press, 1997), pp. 104–105. Also see auction catalogue record of original notes from the speech: http://www.sophiedupre.com/stock_detail .php?stockid=14307.

27   **"in connection with this diabolical Slave Trade"** *Parliamentary Debates*, 3rd series, vol. 93, column 1076, July 16, 1844.

27   **He used Secret Service funds to bribe local politicians** Hugh Thomas, *The Slave Trade: The Story of the Atlantic Slave Trade: 1440–1870* (New York: Simon & Schuster, 1997), p. 740.

27   **the transatlantic slave trade with Brazil came to an end** See FO881/205 "Correspondence relative to the prohibition against the admission of free persons of colour into certain ports of the United States," Palmerston to Mathew, March 21, 1851. Also note that in February 1864 Palmerston wrote to Sir John Crampton, former chargé and later minister in Washington, that "the achievement which I look back on with the greatest and purest pleasure was forcing the Brazilians to give up their slave trade, by bringing into operation the Aberdeen Act of 1845." Cited originally in A. E. M. Ashley, *Life of Henry John Temple, Viscount Palmerston, 1846–1865* (London, 1876), pp. ii, 263–264, and referenced in "The Abolition of the Brazilian Slave Trade" by Leslie Bethell: http://tinyurl.com/ PalmerstonBrazil. The story of the *Camargo* is recounted in Ron

Soodalter, *Hanging Captain Gordon: The Life and Trial of an American Slave Trader* (New York: Washington Square Press, 2006), pp. 17–18.

29　**"The dates don't match"** David Steele, "Villiers, George William Frederick," *The Oxford Dictionary of National Biography*, online edition (Oxford, UK: Oxford University Press, 2009). The countess's remark is quoted in French, "*Les dates ne correspondent pas.*"

29　**"fiery little State"** FO5/570 Bunch to Clarendon, December 29, 1853.

Chapter 3

30　**British vessels in the port** Address of consular office was listed under "Matthews" in the Charleston City Directory.

31　**"called on to perform"** Eugene H. Berwanger, *The British Foreign Service and the American Civil War* (Lexington: The University Press of Kentucky, 1994), p. 4. Mathew also drew a salary from the Foreign Office and complained that he was only getting half of it over the many months that he was in England instead of Charleston.

32　**"looming in the future"** Bunch to Crampton, November 25, 1853, Papers of Sir John Crampton, Bodleian Library, Oxford University, Oxford, UK.

32　**"idle aristocracy"** William W. Freehling, *Prelude to Civil War: The Nullification Controversy in South Carolina 1816–1836* (Oxford, UK: Oxford University Press, 1966), p. 12.

33　**one proud matron** Mary Boykin Chesnut, *Mary Chesnut's Diary* (New York: Penguin Books, 2011), p. 33. Several of the Quinby photographs are available in Martha M. Daniels and Barbara E. McCarthy, *Mary Chesnut's Illustrated Diary* (Gretna, LA: Pelican Publishing Company, 2011).

35　**"in the back streets you see no one else"** George Ranken, *Canada and the Crimea, or Sketches of a Soldier's Life* (London: Longman, Green, Longman, Roberts & Green, 1863), p. 108.

36　**"showing what I felt"** Ibid., p. 115.

38　**"anxious for a change"** Bunch to Crampton, November 25, 1853, Crampton Papers.

38　**"too large for an insane asylum"** See, among other sources, Margaret Miner and Hugh Rawson, eds., *The Oxford Dictionary of American Quotations* (New York: Oxford University Press, 2006), p. 634. The published quote came out of a conversation with Robert Barnwell Rhett in 1860, but the question of secession had been raised on and off at least since the nullification crisis of 1832.

39　**"emancipation and abolitionism"** FO5/570 Bunch to Clarendon, November 29, 1853 (second of two dispatches on that date).

40   **changes to the law** FO5/570 Bunch to Clarendon, November 29, 1853.

40   **"a merry Xmas"** Bunch to Crampton, December 23, 1853, Crampton Papers.

Chapter 4

42   **"Race Week"** For a fascinating and detailed picture of South Carolina society in this period see Maurie D. McInnis, *The Politics of Taste in Antebellum Charleston* (Chapel Hill: The University of North Carolina Press, 2005). The descriptions of Race Week are on pp. 24–25.

43   **"no more to kill a slave than to shoot a dog"** FO84/948 Bunch to J. B. Bergue, January 11, 1854. Part of this letter was quoted in Laura White, "The South in the 1850's as Seen by British Consuls," *The Journal of Southern History*, vol. 1, no. 1 (February 1935), pp. 29–48, which has been cited in many other books and papers. But White, perhaps out of prudery, omitted the part about making the slaves strip and touching them.

44   **"indiscreet zeal of Her Majesty's Consul"** FO5/601. The account of the apprentice John Hayes and the wreck of the *Charlotte* is to be found in Bunch to Clarendon, January 27, 1854; Clarendon to Bunch, February 25, 1854.

Chapter 5

45   **"literary emporium"** John Russell's Book Store had two different locations on King Street in the 1850s according to its advertisements in the *Courier*. One of them is now occupied by Victoria's Secret; the other, at 251 King Street, is a women and girls' clothing store, Palm Avenue, which has maintained the configuration of the old façade from the original building with "its ample entrance and handsome plate-glass windows."

For further background see Richard J. Calhoun, "The Ante-Bellum Literary Twilight: *Russell's Magazine*," *The Southern Literary Journal*, vol. 3, no. 1 (Fall 1970), pp. 89–110; and Michael O'Brien, *Conjectures of Order: Intellectual Life and the American South, 1810–1860*, vol. 2 (Chapel Hill: University of North Carolina Press, 2004), p. 481, which mentions the description of the entrance and windows.

46   **let them buy them!** William Grayson, *"The Hireling and the Slave"* (Charleston: John Russell, 1855), passim.

46   **"to blunt a man's moral sense"** Bunch to Crampton, March 10, 1852, Papers of Sir John Crampton, Bodleian Library, Oxford University, Oxford, UK.

46   "a little eccentric" Bunch to Lyons, May 26, 1860, Lyons Papers.

46   [met] Macaulay and interviewed Prince Albert O'Brien, *Conjectures*, p. 323.

48   "lone star of disunion" William C. Davis, *Rhett: The Turbulent Life and Times of a Fire-Eater* (Columbia: University of South Carolina Press, 2001), p. 215.

49   the city's very existence Ibid., p. 264.

49   [Spratt] to buy the struggling *Charleston Standard* William W. Freehling, *The Road to Disunion*, vol. 2—*Secessionists Triumphant, 1854–1861* (New York: Oxford University Press, 2007), p. 169. Freehling gives a very lively portrait of Spratt in his excellent chapter on the efforts to revive the slave trade, pp. 168–183.

50   the importation of slaves from Africa See especially Ronald T. Takaki, *A Pro-Slavery Crusade: The Agitation to Reopen the African Slave Trade* (New York: The Free Press, 1971), passim. Freehling's note on Takaki in *Disunion*, p. 554, is spot-on: "The movement to reopen the African slave trade almost always receives short shrift in accounts of the coming of the Civil War. The reason: The radicalism never captured anything close to a southern majority and thus allegedly must be considered an antebellum sideshow. But by that reasoning, secessionism, also never commanding a majority until Lincoln 'coerced' the disunionists, also must be considered a sideshow. The point is that a disunionist minority ultimately made majoritarian history (as minorities often do). . . . Thus the reopening campaign offers the best window into the (minority) mentality that would ultimately make a revolution. Something so analytically valuable deserves central consideration." Freehling recommends Takaki's as the best book on the subject. For a very interesting interpretation of the phenomenon in a Marxist context, see Manisha Sinha, *The Counter-Revolution of Slavery: Politics and Ideology in Antebellum South Carolina* (Chapel Hill: The University of North Carolina Press, 2000).

50   Spratt's notoriety began to spread "The African Slave-Trade to Be Revived," *New York Times*, July 29, 1854; and "The Slave Trade," *New York Times*, August 26, 1854.

51   "editorially" a jackass Bunch to Crampton, February 14, 1856, Crampton Papers.

Chapter 6

52   "the most splendid of the season" Kevin Eberle, *A History of Charleston's Hampton Park* (Charleston: The History Press, 2012), p. 35.

52   **"disregard my recommendations"** FO5/601 Bunch to Clarendon, February 15, 1854. Some of the formal locutions in this quotation have been modernized.

53   **"desire to see the law repealed"** FO5/601 Bunch to Clarendon, February 15, 1854.

53   **"in perfect harmony"** FO5/601 Bunch to Clarendon, March 22, 1854.

54   **"annoyance of our common enemy"** FO5/601 Bunch to Clarendon, March 22, 1854.

55   **"fifty-two pirates too delicious"** FO5/601 Bunch to Crampton, August 23, 1851, Papers of Sir John Crampton, Bodleian Library, Oxford University, Oxford, UK.

55   **"acquisition of the Island of Cuba"** FO5/601 Bunch to Clarendon, April 19, 1854.

56   **such measures would end the slave trade** C. Stanley Urban, "The Africanization of Cuba Scare, 1853–1855," *The Hispanic American Historical Review*, vol. 37, no. 1 (February 1957), pp. 29–45.

56   **Judah P. Benjamin, introduced similar resolutions** Robert Douthat Meade, *Judah P. Benjamin: Confederate Statesman* (Baton Rouge: Louisiana State University Press, 2001), p. 92; reprinted from the original 1943 Oxford University Press edition.

57   **"outrage connected with Slavery"** FO5/601 Bunch to Clarendon, June 8, 1854.

58   **"I mean, Public Opinion"** FO5/601 Bunch to Clarendon, June 8, 1854."

58   **"a proposal for change"** FO5/601 Bunch to Clarendon, June 18, 1854.

58   **"remonstrances and interventions"** FO5/601 Clarendon to Bunch, June 30, 1854.

58   **actually have to comply** Urban, "Africanization," pp. 41–42.

60   **"endeavored to gain"** FO5/601 Bunch to Clarendon, November 28, 1854.

60   **"any other section of the civilized world"** FO5/601 Bunch to Clarendon, December 22, 1854.

61   **"confer a blessing upon the African Race"** FO84/948 Bunch to Clarendon, December 28, 1854, with enclosure. Freehling is very good on the question of the border states drifting away from the South.

Chapter 7

62   **"Muscovite guns"** As quoted in Alan Hankinson, *Man of Wars William Howard Russell of the* Times (London: Heinemann, 1982), pp. 73–74.

62   **"proven the present system to be futile"** Crampton to Bunch, June 25, 1854, enclosure, Papers of Sir John Crampton, Bodleian Library, Oxford University, Oxford, UK.

63   **"the moment of its completion"** FO84/948 Crawford to Crampton, October 11, 1854.

63   **"that prostitution of their flag"** "The Slave-Trade; Remarks of Lord Palmerston in the House of Commons," *New York Times*, August 10, 1861.

63   **lodge diplomatic protests** Bunch to Crampton, January 31, 1855, Crampton Papers.

64   **volunteer for service in the Crimea** James J. Barnes and Patience P. Barnes, *Private and Confidential: Letters from British Ministers in Washington to the Foreign Secretaries in London, 1844–67* (Selinsgrove, PA: Susquehanna University Press, 1993), p. 118.

65   **"tearing the vitals of the Union"** Crampton to Clarendon, January 13, 1856, cited in Barnes and Barnes, *Private and Confidential*, pp. 145–146.

65   **"the smile of indifference"** Bunch to Crampton, December 8, 1855, Crampton Papers.

66   **"shake the Union to its base"** Harold Temperley and Lillian M. Penson, *Foundations of British Foreign Policy from Pitt (1792) to Salisbury (1902), or Documents, Old and New* (Cambridge, UK: Cambridge University Press, 1938), Document 106, p. 295, cited as from the Private Clarendon Papers, in Palmerston's hand, but unsigned and apparently of the year 1855.

67   **Helen remained an outspoken Unionist** William Wyndham Malet, *An Errand to the South in the Summer of 1862* (London: Richard Bentley, 1863), p. 243.

68   **"sufficient proof to convict any white person"** Bunch to Crampton, November 15, 1855, with enclosure, Crampton Papers. There are many allusions to the works of Charles Dickens, directly and indirectly, in Bunch's letters. The great British novelist had used the notices for absconded slaves to devastating effect in the closing chapters of his *American Notes*, about his travels through the United States on a reading tour in 1842. The runaways are described by their owners as wearing iron collars around their necks, iron bars on their legs, suffering from gunshot wounds, identifiable by severed fingers, notched ears, marks of lashings, broken limbs, and

burns. "Ran away, a negro woman and two children," reads one of the items placed in a newspaper by an owner who clearly was as shameless as he was cruel: "A few days before she went off, I burnt her with a hot iron, on the left side of her face. I tried to make the letter M." Dickens believed this license to torture, maim, and kill corrupted the whole of society with its violence, even in states where slavery was banned. In a country where men "learn to write with pens of red-hot iron on the human face" they grow to be bullies and, "carrying cowards' weapons, hidden in their breast [that is, concealed weapons], will shoot men down and stab them" when they quarrel.

68   **Manning had approved** FO5/601 Bunch to Clarendon, December 28, 1854.

69   **"fully impressed with the importance of the subject"** FO5/626 Bunch to Clarendon, February 9, 1855.

69   **"information and guidance"** FO5/626 Bunch to Clarendon, June 30, 1855.

69   **a "triumph"** FO5/626 Bunch to Clarendon, June 30, 1855.

70   **"impossibility in fact"** Bunch to Crampton, January 20, 1856, Crampton Papers.

71   **"Clarendon is pettifogging"** Bunch to Crampton, January 20, 1856, Crampton Papers.

72   **"M is a touchy sort of customer"** Bunch to Crampton, January 29, 1856, Crampton Papers.

72   **"useless to strive"** Bunch to Mure, January 27, 1856, Crampton Papers.

Chapter 8

73   **off the coast of Angola** "Slave-Trade Treaties," *New York Times*, June 26, 1858, pp. 4–5.

74   **shattered the cane** Much has been written about the Sumner-Brooks affair, but few accounts are as sharp and succinct as that on the website of the U.S. Senate itself: http://www.senate.gov/artandhistory/history/minute/The_Crime_Against_Kansas.htm.

74   *"Vive la république!"* **Bunch concluded** Bunch to Crampton, May 29, 1856, Papers of Sir John Crampton, Bodleian Library, Oxford University, Oxford, UK.

74   **"all matters of interest"** FO5/649 Foreign Office to Bunch, July 3, 1856.

75   **"anxious to fight"** FO5/649 Bunch to Clarendon, June 13, 1856. Typically, Bunch began filing these dispatches updating the Foreign

Office on events throughout the United States before he actually received formal permission to do so.

Chapter 9

76 **commodity for speculation** Frederic Bancroft, *Slave Trading in the Old South* (Columbia: University of South Carolina Press, 1996), p. 340; originally published by J. H. Furst, 1931.

76 **"the strength and security of it"** Ibid., p. 339.

77 **"the disease it seeks to cure"** FO5/626 Bunch to Clarendon, November 28, 1855, enclosure of the Adams speech.

77 **"a natural condition of the Negro"** FO5/626 Bunch to Clarendon, December 21, 1855, enclosure from the *Charleston Standard* dated December 3, 1855.

78 **"by re-opening the African slave trade"** FO5/649 Bunch to Clarendon, November 29, 1856, enclosure of the Adams speech.

79 **"limits of the state"** FO5/649 Bunch to Clarendon, December 26, 1856.

79 **"no veto power in this State"** FO5/649 Bunch to Clarendon, December 26, 1856.

PART TWO

Chapter 10

83 **"the evil which is rapidly developing"** FO5/677 Bunch to Clarendon, March 4, 1857.

84 **"probably of the West Indies"** FO5/677 Bunch to Clarendon, March 4, 1857.

85 **"a bubble market in human beings"** Frederic Bancroft, *Slave Trading in the Old South*, "The 'Negro Fever,'" (Columbia: University of South Carolina Press, 1996), pp. 339–364, passim; originally published by J. H. Furst, 1931.

85 **"all our mountain streams"** Ronald T. Takaki, *A Pro-Slavery Crusade: The Agitation to Reopen the African Slave Trade* (New York: The Free Press, 1971), p. 39.

86 **"a set of Red Republicans"** William Howard Russell, *My Diary North and South* (Boston: T. O. H. P. Burnham, 1863), p. 185, p. 211; reprinted on demand in 2011 by Blackwell Books, London.

86 **"comparatively worthless"** James McPherson, *Battle Cry of Freedom: The Civil War Era* (New York: Oxford University Press, 1988), Kindle loc 4093.

87   **"slave trade shall be attended to"** Napier to Clarendon, May 26, 1857, Clarendon Papers, Bodleian Library, Oxford University Oxford, UK.

88   **the slightest hint of a provocation** Harral E. Landry, "Slavery and the Slave Trade in Atlantic Diplomacy, 1850–1861," *The Journal of Southern History*, vol. 27, no. 2 (May 1961), pp. 184–207.

88   **"existing political structure can last long"** Napier to Clarendon, March 8, 1858, cited in James J. Barnes and Patience P. Barnes, *Private and Confidential: Letters from British Ministers in Washington to the Foreign Secretaries in London, 1844–67* (Selinsgrove, PA: Susquehanna University Press, 1993), pp. 195–196.

Chapter 11

90   **"stolid Charlestonians"** Ronald T. Takaki, *A Pro-Slavery Crusade: The Agitation to Reopen the African Slave Trade* (New York: The Free Press, 1971), p. 213.

91   **150 miles east of Havana** "The Cruise of the *Dolphin*," *Charleston Daily Courier*, August 31, 1858, p. 3.

91   **twenty years before** Dictionary of American Naval Fighting Ships: http://www.history.navy.mil/danfs/d5/dolphin-iii.htm.

92   **threw them into the sea** Douglas A. Levien, *The Case of the Slaver* Echo: *History of the Proceedings* (Albany, NY: Weed, Parsons & Company, 1859), pp. 3–5.

92   **"mere skeletons"** "The Cruise of the *Dolphin*," *Charleston Daily Courier*, August 31, 1858, p. 2.

92   **was from Boston** One of the ironies of this case in retrospect is that the captain of the slaver was from New England, and the commander of the *Dolphin*, John Maffitt, was a Southerner who resigned his commission when war broke out and later became one of Charleston's prominent blockade runners. Philip N. Racine, ed., *Gentlemen Merchants: A Charleston Family's Odyssey, 1828–1870* (Knoxville: The University of Tennessee Press, 2008), p. 471, note p. 857.

92   **"the shark of the Atlantic"** The *Liverpool Mercury*, reprinted in the *Charleston Daily Courier*, October 1, 1858.

93   **Federal government would never allow it** "A Slaver in the Bay," *Charleston Daily Courier*, August 28, 1858, p. 1.

94   **"health of the gang has much improved"** "The Slave Ship and Slave Cargo at Charleston," from the *Charleston Mercury*, September 1, 1858, reprinted in the *New York Times*, September 6, 1858. Also note the discourse on the meaning of such dances in Silviane A. Diouf,

Dreams of Africa in Alabama: The Slave Ship Clotilda *and the Story of the Last Africans Brought to America* (New York: Oxford University Press, 2007), Kindle loc 1664: "Dancing has never been just entertainment in Africa, where people accompany every event, including the most dreadful, with dance and music. Dance is life, and like life, it is joy and pain. What the passengers observed on the steamboats were Africans and African Americans who had regained possession of their bodies. They used them to express themselves openly, something they were forbidden to do in any other manner and circumstance; and they externalized their feelings, including anger, contempt, and derision for the spectators in ways that were not decipherable by outsiders."

94   **"sad and distressed condition"** "The *Niagara* and the Africans," *Charleston Daily Courier*, November 24, 1858, p. 2.

95   **"the flag of the South"** "The Revival of the Slave Trade," *Charleston Daily Courier*, September 4, 1858, p. 2.

95   **"I can never forget it"** Takaki, *Crusade*, p. 226.

Chapter 12

96   **under the American flag** Ronald T. Takaki, *A Pro-Slavery Crusade: The Agitation to Reopen the African Slave Trade* (New York: The Free Press, 1971), p. 224.

96   **"bent upon her destruction"** Ibid., p. 221. Also see FO5/601 Bunch to Clarendon, June 8, 1854: The cry of self-preservation "is always on the lips of a Carolinian when he is about to justify an outrage connected with slavery."

96   **"done daily in our streets"** "The Captured Slavers," *Charleston Daily Courier*, September 1, 1858, p. 1.

97   **"respect for the Law"** FO84/1059 Bunch to Malmesbury, September 14, 1858.

97   **"swinging them up to the yard-arm"** "The *Niagara* and the Africans," *Charleston Daily Courier*, November 24, 1858, p. 2; eventually it was reported that seventy-one Africans had died on the voyage, "The Cruise of the *Niagara*," *Charleston Daily Courier*, December 15, 1858, p. 2.

98   **"allow a trial to take place"** FO84/1059, Bunch to Malmesbury, December 13, 1858.

98   **"emboldened to offer a few remarks"** FO84/1059, Bunch to Malmesbury, December 16, 1858.

99   **well established as part of Savannah's elite** Lyons wrote in 1861 that Molyneux's income was £200,000 a year. That would com-

pare to about £500 for Bunch on a government salary. Lyons Letter Book, April 12, 1861.

99   **pestilential heat on the coast** Both Molyneux and Bunch's brother-in-law Daniel Blake had large estates near Asheville, North Carolina, and there is an interesting nexus in the genealogical records: one of Blake's sons by his first wife was named Edmund Molyneux Blake; one of his sons by his second wife (Bunch's cousin as well as his sister-in-law) was Robert Bunch Blake. "Blake of South Carolina," *The Southern Historical and Genealogical Magazine*, vol. 1, no. 2 (April 1900), pp. 153–166.

100   **"Slave Trading or any other villainy"** FO84/1059 Bunch to Malmesbury, December 16, 1858. What Bunch did not say in this dispatch and did not reveal in private to Lord Lyons in Washington until late the following year—and might never have revealed to the Foreign Office—was that he left Charleston on July 1, 1858, when the *Wanderer* was still in the harbor, and two days later his vice consul, H. Pinckney Walker, at William Corrie's request, issued travel documents to three members of the *Wanderer*'s crew: Egbert Farnum, Brent, and Dennis. Technically they were not so much passports as attestations, since the men in question were not British subjects, but Walker recorded them in the consular diary as passports. In a private letter to Lyons on November 19, 1859, Bunch said that he, for one, had never doubted that the *Wanderer* was a slaver. It had been under suspicion as such since it left New York, even though it had passed customs there and had been visited by Federal officials in Charleston Harbor as well, with no suggestion it would be stopped. (I find no evidence that if Bunch believed this, he bothered to report it before the scandal broke at the end of 1858.) Bunch finally told Lyons about this when the Federal prosecutor who was trying the *Wanderer* cases in Savannah summoned Walker to testify. The "passports" had been found aboard the *Wanderer* after it offloaded its slaves. Bunch said the worst that could be said of Walker was that Corrie "humbugged" him like so many others. "It is evident that the infernal blackguard Corrie wished to have evidence of the respectability of his friends (!) in order to blind Her Majesty's officer on the Coast of Africa." Bunch followed up with another letter and a brief newspaper clipping about Walker's testimony in Savannah. Lyons agreed that it was best not to inform the Foreign Office unless it seemed likely the matter would be picked up in the English press. See Bunch-Lyons correspondence, November 1859, Duke of Norfolk Archives, Arundel Castle.

102   **"a few additional regiments"** Takaki, *Crusade*, p. 209; also see Tom Henderson Wells, *The Slave Ship* Wanderer (Athens: University

of Georgia Press, 1967), and Erik Calonius, *The* Wanderer: *The Last American Slave Ship and the Conspiracy That Set Its Sails* (New York: St. Martin's Press, 2006), passim.

102   **"prestige and power of Slave holders"** FO5/720 Bunch to Russell, January 6, 1859.

103   **"felt so sure with Lord Clarendon"** David Steele, "Villiers, George William Frederick," *The Oxford Dictionary of National Biography*, online edition (Oxford, UK: Oxford Universtiy Press, 2009).

103   **"claims of public duty"** Stuart J. Reid, *Lord John Russell* (London: Sampson Low, Marston, 1895), Kindle loc 1901.

Chapter 13

105   **"old-fashioned sailing vessels"** Napier to Malmesbury, January 10, 1859, cited in James J. Barnes and Patience P. Barnes, *Private and Confidential: Letters from British Ministers in Washington to the Foreign Secretaries in London, 1844–67* (Selinsgrove, PA: Susquehanna University Press, 1993), p. 209.

106   **an isolated incident** Robert Ralph Davis Jr., "Buchanan Espionage: A Report on Illegal Slave Trading in the South in 1859," *The Journal of Southern History*, vol. 37. no. 2 (May 1971), pp. 271–278.

107   **"nor courteous to me"** Lyons Letter Book, to Consul Bunch, October 9, 1859, Duke of Norfolk Archives, Arundel Castle.

107   **"mortified at the rebuke"** Bunch to Lyons, October 10, 1859, Duke of Norfolk Archives, Arundel Castle.

108   **Lord Lyons in the late spring of 1859** Nicomede Bianchi, *Storia documentata della diplomazia europea in Italia*, vol. 6, pp. 408–409; Raymond A. Jones, *The British Diplomatic Service, 1815–1914* (Waterloo, ON, Canada: Wilfrid Laurier Universtiy Press, 1983), pp. 126–127; *Rassegna storica del Risorgimento*, "England, Piedmont, and the *Cagliari* Affair," 1998, p. 147; Amanda Foreman, *A World on Fire: An Epic History of Two Nations Divided* (London: Allen Lane, an imprint of Penguin Books, 2010), published in the United States as *A World on Fire: Britain's Crucial Role in the American Civil War*, Kindle loc 804; "Lyons, Richard Bickerton Pemell," *The Oxford Dictionary of National Biography*, online edition (Oxford, UK: Oxford University Press, 2009); Brian Jenkins, *Lord Lyons: A Diplomat in an Age of Nationalism and War* (Montreal: McGill-Queen's University Press, 2014), passim.

108   **"whose character is known to this country"** Brian Jenkins, *Britain and the War for the Union*, vol. I (Montreal: McGill-Queen's University Press, 1974). p. 44.

109   **risk upsetting his valet** Foreman, *Fire*, Kindle loc 802.

109   **Or so he said.** Bunch to Lyons, October 11, 1859, Lyons Papers, Duke of Norfolk Archives, Arundel Castle.

109   **"independent of the Federal Government"** Lyons to Bunch, October 13, 1859, Lyons Letter Book, Duke of Norfolk Archives, Arundel Castle.

110   **"to say nothing of baggage"** Bunch to Lyons, October 16, 1859, Duke of Norfolk Archives, Arundel Castle.

Chapter 14

111   **"absurd enough"** Lyons to Consul Moore (Richmond), October 23, 1859, Lyons Letter Book, Duke of Norfolk Archives, Arundel Castle.

111   **"trouble brewing for us all"** Bunch to Lyons, October 16, 1859, Duke of Norfolk Archives, Arundel Castle.

112   **"I believe a conspiracy has been formed"** William C. Davis, *Jefferson Davis: The Man and His Hour* (Baton Rouge: Louisiana State University Press, 1991), pp. 276–278; also see Congressional Gazette, 36th Congress, 1st Sess. (1859–1860), I:62.

112   **"what is called 'an original'"** George Macaulay Trevelyan, *Garibaldi's Defence of the Roman Republic* (London: Longman's, Green, and Co., 1912), p. 351. Trevelyan was given access to Forbes's papers by Forbes's daughter between the first and second editions of his book and thus provides by far the most complete portrait of the soldier of fortune in his Italian years.

112   **"most courageous and honorable soldier."** Ibid., pp. 252–253.

113   **a practical guide to insurgency** Hugh Forbes, *Manual for the Patriotic Volunteer on Active Service in Regular and Irregular War: Being the Art and Science of Obtaining and Maintaining Liberty and Independence*, 2 vols. (New York: W. H. Tinson, 1855). The book may not have made money, but it did have a certain following. The well-known writer, traveler, and landscape architect Frederick Law Olmsted not only bought arms for free-soil settlers in Kansas, he forwarded them a copy of Forbes's *Manual* "with relevant sections underscored in ink," according to Witold Rybczynski, *A Clearing in the Distance: Frederick Law Olmsted and America in the 19th Century* (New York: Scribner, 1999), Kindle loc 2165.

113   **whorehouse on Delancey Street** Edward J. Renehan, *The Secret Six: The True Tale of the Men Who Conspired with John Brown* (Columbia: University of South Carolina Press, 1997).

114   **"the craftiness of partial insanity"** "The Life of Osawatomie Brown," *Emporia News*, Emporia, Kansas, November 12, 1859, p. 3.

114   **"cannot be constantly depended upon"** Forbes, *Manual*, p. 10.

115   **God knew better** Mark A. Lause, *Race and Radicalism in the Union Army* (Chicago: University of Illinois Press, 2009), pp. 29–31.

116   **"keen eyes were seeking for an adversary"** William Howard Russell, *My Diary North and South* (Boston: T. O. H. P. Burnham, 1863), pp. 185, p. 50; reprinted on demand in 2011 by Blackwell Books, London.

116   **"getting up military revolutions"** *Report of the Select Committee of the Senate Appointed to Inquire into the Late Invasion and Seizure of the Public Property at Harper's Ferry*, pp. 253–255.

116   **"the whole matter in all its bearings"** Walter Stahr, *Seward: Lincoln's Indispensable Man* (New York: Simon & Schuster, 2012), p. 180.

117   **"strewn with documents"** "More of the Forbes Correspondence: Report to the British Anti-Slavery Society on American Politics Generally and Abolitionism Particularly, Etc.," *New York Herald*, October 28, 1859.

117   **"communicate the papers to Your Lordship"** Bunch to Lyons, October 31, 1859, Lyons Papers, Duke of Norfolk Archives, Arundel Castle.

120   **the Barbary Coast** Richard Huzzey, *Freedom Burning: Anti-Slavery and Empire in Victorian Britain* (Ithaca: Cornell University Press, 2012), Kindle loc 1268.

PART THREE
Chapter 15

125   **"terror in this community and state"** FO5/720 Bunch to Russell, November 24, 1859.

125   **"leaving in great numbers"** FO5/720 Bunch to Russell, December 9, 1859.

125   **"revolver pistols"** FO5/720 Bunch to Russell, November 24, 1859.

126   **"abolition tendencies"** James J. Barnes and Patience P. Barnes, *Private and Confidential: Letters from British Ministers in Washington to the Foreign Secretaries in London, 1844–67* (Selinsgrove, PA: Susquehanna University Press, 1993), pp. 220–221; FO5/716, folio pp. 348–349.

126   **"the [powder] magazine here is guarded."** Bunch to Lyons, December 24, 1859, Lyons Papers, Duke of Norfolk Archives, Arundel Castle.

126   **a riot or an uprising** FO5/720 Bunch to Lyons, November 24, 1859.

126   **"Comité de Salut Publique"** FO5/720 Bunch to Russell, December 31, 1859. Note that Dickens had just published *A Tale of Two Cities*

in 1859, and it was being serialized in the American press, so references to The Terror were particularly fashionable.

128   **stay in force** Barnes and Barnes, *Private and Confidential*, p. 221; Bunch to Lyons, December 24, 1859, Lyons Papers, Duke of Norfolk Archives, Arundel Castle.

129   **"where will the practice stop?"** Bunch to Lyons, December 10, 1859, Lyons Papers, Duke of Norfolk Archives, Arundel Castle.

Chapter 16

130   **"a free-labor nation"** Walter Stahr, *Seward: Lincoln's Indispensable Man* (New York: Simon & Schuster, 2012), p. 174.

131   **The New York crowd, of course, went wild.** "Departure of Senator Seward for Europe," *New-York Tribune*, May 9, 1859, p. 5, writing about Seward's departure on Saturday, May 7.

132   **Pembroke Lodge** John M. Taylor, *William Henry Seward: Lincoln's Right-Hand Man* (New York: HarperCollins), p. 113.

132   **"I could not be a plebeian"** Frederick William Seward, *Seward: Senator and Secretary of State* (Auburn, NY.: Derby and Miller, 1891), p. 390.

132   **"aghast"** Amanda Foreman, *A World on Fire: An Epic History of Two Nations Divided* (London: Allen Lane, an imprint of Penguin Books, 2010), Kindle loc 1447, published in the United States as *A World on Fire: Britain's Crucial Role in the American Civil War*, p. 45, citing Deborah Logan, ed., *The Collected Letters of Harriet Martineau*, 5 vols. (London, 2007), vol. 4, p. 180.

132   **"vaporing, blustering, ignorant man"** Foreman, *Fire*, pp. 45–46, Kindle loc 1447.

133   **"pretty much finished"** Stahr, *Indispensable*, p. 177.

134   **"might have critical ones"** Frederick W. Seward, *Reminiscences of a War-Time Statesman and Diplomat, 1830–1915* (New York: G. P. Putnam's Sons, 1916) p. 129.

Chapter 17

135   **"send into those states"** Lyons to Russell, March 5, 1860, Lyons Letter Book, Duke of Norfolk Archives, Arundel Castle. The words I have here as "superiority" and "happy" are not clear in the manuscript copy.

135   **supply the *Wanderer*** Tom Henderson Wells, *The Slave Ship Wanderer* (Athens: University of Georgia Press, 1967), p. 13.

135   **the slave deck was laid** The *Jehossee* owner claimed, of course, that it was not in the least equipped to carry slaves. See Bunch to Lyons,

June 4, 1860, Lyons Papers, Duke of Norfolk Archives, Arundel Castle.

136   *"Insulted Flag"* Ron Soodalter, *Hanging Captain Gordon: The Life and Trial of an American Slave Tradeer* (New York: Washington Square Press, 2006), p. 40, citing "Squadron Letters" M-89, Roll III.

136   **"Slave Trading impudence"** Bunch to Lyons, April 3, 1860, Lyons Papers, Duke of Norfolk Archives, Arundel Castle.

138   **"amicable settlement"** Lyons to Russell, April 10, 1860, cited in James J. Barnes and Patience P. Barnes, *Private and Confidential: Letters from British Ministers in Washington to the Foreign Secretaries in London, 1844–67* (Selinsgrove, PA; Susquehanna University Press, 1993), p. 231.

138   **payroll as a secret agent** FO84/1086 Archibald to Russell, May 7, 1859.

139   **"fabric manufacturing industry"** Bunch to Lyons, May 24, 1860 (Queen's birthday), clipping from *Evening News* of May 23 enclosed, Lyons Papers, Duke of Norfolk Archives, Arundel Castle.

140   **"killed a man named Bird in cold blood"** Bunch to Lyons with enclosure, April 12, 1860, and Lyons Letter Book, to L. T. Wigfall, April 11, 1860. Wigfall subsequently apologized, and Lyons accepted his apology. Lyons Papers, Duke of Norfolk Archives, Arundel Castle.

Chapter 18

142   **"very improperly dressed females"** Murat B. Halstead, *Caucuses of 1860: A History of the National Political Conventions of the Current Presidential Campaign* (Columbus, OH: Follett, Foster and Company, 1860), p. 5.

142   **"battle, murder, and certain death"** Bunch to Lyons, March 22, 1860, Lyons Papers, Duke of Norfolk Archives, Arundel Castle. The prizefight rhetoric was inspired, no doubt, by the vaulting passions and voluminous press coverage that surrounded the world's first great international prizefight on April 17, 1860, between Tom Sayers, the English champion, and John Carmel Heenan, "the Benicia Boy" from San Francisco. The fight at Farnborough, England, lasted forty-two blood-soaked rounds over two and a half hours and was declared, in the end, a draw.

143   **"generally and individually"** Bunch to Lyons, April 23, 1860, Lyons Papers, Duke of Norfolk Archives, Arundel Castle.

143   **"making night hideous"** Halstead, *Caucuses*, p. 13.

144   **"pluck to make its points"** Ibid., pp. 5–6.

144   **"uppermost in their minds"** Ibid., p. 13.

144   **"war to the knife"** Ibid., p. 7.

146   **"a very pretty quarrel"** Bunch to Lyons, April 27, 1860, Lyons Papers, Duke of Norfolk Archives, Arundel Castle.

146   **"feathers are drooping"** Halstead, *Caucuses*, p. 47.

149   **"frightful fiasco"** Bunch to Lyons, May 1, 1860, Lyons Papers, Duke of Norfolk Archives, Arundel Castle.

Chapter 19

150   **"there be anything to get, which I doubt"** Bunch to Lyons, May 3, 1860, Lyons Papers, Duke of Norfolk Archives, Arundel Castle.

150   **"a free man when he was so kidnapped!"** FO84/1112 Bunch to Lord John Russell, May 3, 1860.

151   **vindicate our honor by a war** FO5/745 Bunch to Lord John Russell, May 3, 1860.

151   **hoped Lyons agreed with him** Bunch to Lyons, May 4, 1860, Lyons Papers, Duke of Norfolk Archives, Arundel Castle.

152   **"all I love and respect"** Bunch to Lyons, May 7, 1860, Lyons Papers, Duke of Norfolk Archives, Arundel Castle.

Chapter 20

154   **"appear to be children"** FO84/1112 Mure to Lord John Russell, May 18, 1860.

154   **"scarcely space to die in"** Craven to Toucey, June 8, 1860, quoted in Warren S. Howard, *American Slavers and the Federal Law, 1837–1862* (Berkeley: University of California Press, 1963), pp. 124–126. Also see the excellent, detailed account of the *Wildfire*'s history by Ted Maris-Wolf of Washington College in his video lecture "Blood and Treasure": http://youtube/S2uKjdVKZQM.
       Note that Lt. Tunis Augustus MacDonough Craven, who was in the first class of midshipmen at the U.S. Naval Academy in 1852 went on to command the ironclad *Tecumseh* in the Union Navy. "Every American would learn that when the *Tecumseh* was torpedoed and sunk by the Confederates at Mobile Bay, Admiral Farragut cried, 'Damn the torpedoes! Full speed ahead.' But we Cravens know that the crew and the pilot escaped while Tunis Augustus went down with the ship, saying, tradition has it, 'After you, Pilot.' " John Piña Craven, *The Silent War: The Cold War Battle Beneath the Sea* (New York: Simon & Schuster, 2001), p. 179.

155   **"on the soil for generations"** James Buchanan, "Third Annual Message to Congress," *The Works of James Buchanan*, ed. John Bassett Moore, vol. 10, *1856–1860* (Philadelphia: J. B. Lippincott, 1910).

156   **"execrable traffic"** Republican Party platform of 1860, published on the website of the American Presidency Project: http://www .presidency.ucsb.edu/ws/?pid=29620.

Chapter 21

157   **healthier place than Charleston** Bunch's father's mother's family were Woodsides, one of the old families of the Bahamas.

157   **not understood at all** "Report of the Committee of the City Council of Charleston upon the Epidemic Yellow Fever of 1858," Walker, Evans & Co.'s Steam Power Presses, 1859, passim, sent as enclosure in FO5/720 Bunch to Russell, August 28, 1859. Also see Bunch to Lyons, May 29, 1860, Lyons Papers, Duke of Norfolk Archives, Arundel Castle.

158   **smeared by smashed bugs** Bunch to Lyons, May 29, 2013, Lyons Papers, Duke of Norfolk Archives, Arundel Castle.

160   **every feeling of humanity** FO84/1112 Lousada to Lord Russell, July 28, 1860, and Russell note on same dated August 23, in folio pp. 46–49.

162   **legend of the *Clotilda* began to grow** Copies of the original accounts of this voyage were shared with me by Sylviane A. Diouf, who used them in her *Dreams of Africa in Alabama: The Slave Ship* Clotilda *and the Story of the Last Africans Brought to America* (New York: Oxford University Press, 2007).

164   **it was just business** Ron Soodalter, *Hanging Captain Gordon: The Life and Trial of an American Slave Trader* (New York: Washington Square Press, 2006), pp. 58–59.

165   **what sort of ship this *Storm King* was** "The Case of the Slaver Storm King," *Richmond Dispatch*, February 7, 1861.

Chapter 22

167   **impression of Southern behavior remained** "The Falsely Alleged Insult to the Prince of Wales," *Richmond Dispatch*, November 13, 1860.

169   **"*very great lengths*" to remedy them** Bunch to Lyons, February 2, 1860. The first couple of sentences in this quotation were paraphrased in the original letter, but most of it is Bunch quoting himself as accurately as he can (or so he says). It is clear that Bunch felt he had to inform Lyons of this incident, since Corcoran, the influential Washington banker, was among the dinner guests and was very "perturbed." Bunch wanted to make sure Lyons saw his version of the event first, before he heard it from someone else.

169   **"simply the act of lawless ruffians"** "Senate Select Committee Report on the Harper's Ferry Invasion," 36th Congress, 1st Sess., Senate, Rep. Com. No. 278, June 15, 1860.

169   **"monarch in ancient or modern times"** "The Prince in New-York," dateline October 12, 1860, for the *Times* of London, reprinted in the *New York Times*, November 8, 1860.

170   **infamous mobs run wild** Herbert Asbury, *The Gangs of New York: An Informal History of the Underworld* (New York: Thunder's Mouth Press, 1990), pp. 92–107; originally published by Alfred Knopf, 1927.

171   **"clamber into the carriage at once"** N. A. Woods, *The Prince of Wales in Canada and the United States* (London: Bradbury & Evans, 1861), p. 374. Woods was the special correspondent of the *Times*.

171   **"doing so would be in bad taste"** Thomas Butler Gunn, *Thomas Butler Gunn Diaries, vol. 14, September 23, 1860, to December 31, 1860* (St. Louis: State Historical Society of Missouri, 2013), p. 40.

171   **"hoarse, undulating roar"** Woods, *Prince*, p. 377.

172   **on its way to Africa** "The Slave Trade in New-York: Rearrest of John A. Machado," *New York Times*, September 21, 1862; "The Slaver *Mary Francis*: United States Commissioner's Office," *New York Times*, September 13, 1861.

Chapter 23

176   **"increase day by day in intensity"** FO5/745 Bunch to Lord John Russell, November 13, 1860.

176   **"enlightenment of the Free States"** FO5/745 Bunch to Lord John Russell, November 29, 1860.

176   **"pledged to their destruction"** FO5/745 Bunch to Lord John Russell, November 29, 1860.

177   **"ability, industry, or good conduct"** FO5/745 Bunch to Lord John Russell, November 27, 1860, with copy of Governor Gist speech enclosed.

Chapter 24

183   **"a system of labor appointed of God"** FO5/745 Bunch to Lord John Russell, December 5, 1860. The dialogue between Bunch and Rhett is paraphrased in the original dispatch.

184   **"the maintenance of slavery within the territory of a state"** FO5/745 Note signed "P," date unclear, but the reference to Rhett means it must refer to the December 5 dispatch, folio p. 207.

Chapter 25

185   **an asylum "full of lunatics"** Robert N. Rosen, *Confederate Charleston: An Illustrated History of the City and the People During the Civil War* (Columbia: University of South Carolina Press, 1994), p. 42.

185   **"I lost my night's rest"** Bunch to Lyons, December 14, 1860, Lyons Papers, Duke of Norfolk Archives, Arundel Castle.

185   **"tea has been thrown overboard"** William C. Davis, *Rhett: The Turbulent Life and Times of a Fire-Eater* (Columbia: University of South Carolina Press, 2001), p. 375.

186   **"any event as possible"** FO5/745 Bunch to Lord Russell, November 29, 1860.

186   **"too 'Frenchy' in some of his anecdotes to me"** Martha M. Daniels and Barbara E. McCarthy, *Mary Chesnut's Illustrated Diary* (Gretna, LA: Pelican Publishing Company, 2011), p. 375.

187   **"let us achieve ours"** Michael O'Brien, *Conjectures of Order: Intellectual Life and the American South*, vol. 2 (Chapel Hill: University of North Carolina Press, 2004), p. 327.

189   **"no Southern Confederacy would venture to propose its renewal"** When Bunch put pen to paper the next day, he outlined the conversation with Trescot in a private note to Lyons, but when he wrote about it in a formal dispatch to Lord Russell, he left out altogether Trescot's doubts about the South reopening the Middle Passage. Bunch thought he knew better, and he was not going to confuse London with conflicting opinions on such a critical issue. See Bunch to Lyons, December 8, 1860, 3:00 p.m., Lyons Papers, Duke of Norfolk Archives, Arundel Castle.

Chapter 26

190   **Rumor had it** Jamie Malanowski, "The Government Disintegrates as the Union Dissolves," *New York Times* (blog), December 19, 2010: http://opinionator.blogs.nytimes.com/2010/12/19/the-government-disintegrates-as-the-union-dissolves/.

191   **"He would come with"** Robert N. Rosen, *Confederate Charleston: An Illustrated History of the City and the People During the Civil War* (Columbia: University of South Carolina Press, 1994), p. 42.

192   **"There has not been time"** Bunch to Lyons, December 15, 1860. Lyons Papers, Duke of Norfolk Archives, Arundel Castle.

193   **"the point of the sword"** FO5/745 Bunch to Russell, December 19, 1860.

194   **"Owing to the late political"** FO84/1112 Bunch to Russell, December 22, 1860; *New York Times*, December 26, 1860, reprint of

Charleston Courier, December 22, 1860. *Courier* says *Bonita* arrived on Tuesday, which would have been December 18, 1860.

195 **The Constitution had put** "South Carolina Declaration of the Causes of Secession," in Brooks D. Simpson, Stephen W. Sears, and Aaron Sheehan-Dean, eds., *The Civil War: The First Year Told by Those Who Lived It* (Washington, D.C.: The Library of America, 2011), pp. 149–155.

Chapter 27

196 **Gunn was taking his life in his hands** "The Vault at Pfaff's: An Archive of Art and Literature by New York City's Nineteenth-Century Bohemians," a website that can be found at http://digital.lib.lehigh.edu/pfaffs/people/individuals/109/.

196 **Her Majesty's consul in South Carolina** Thomas Butler Gunn, *Thomas Butler Gunn Diaries*, vol. 15, *January 1, 1861, to February 28, 1861* (St. Louis: State Historical Society of Missouri, 2013), p. 166. The document countersigned by Bunch is reproduced between pages 152 and 153.

197 **for most of the time** Ibid., p. 166.

199 **Buchanan thought at first** Bruce Catton, *The Coming Fury* (New York: Simon & Schuster/Pocket Books, 1961), p. 140.

Chapter 28

205 **communicate with his wife** Philip N. Racine, ed., *Gentlemen Merchants: A Charleston Family's Odyssey, 1828–1870* (Knoxville: The University of Tennessee Press, 2008), pp. 415–451.

206 **"reasonable counsels are entirely disregarded"** FO5/780 Bunch to Lord Russell, January 4, 1861.

207 **Bunch wrote to Lord Russell** FO5/780 Bunch to Lord Russell, January 11, 1861.

209 **Britain's envoy to the new** Anthony Barclay to Sir Henry Bulwer, January 26, 1861, Norfolk Records Office, Norfolk, UK.

209 **In an anonymous dispatch** Thomas Butler Gunn, *Thomas Butler Gunn Diaries*, vol. 15, *January 1, 1861, to February 28, 1861* (St. Louis: State Historical Society of Missouri, 2013), p. 49.

210 **the treatment he received** Ibid., stamped page 183.

Chapter 29

212 **Between heats, while grooms** There's an excellent sketch of the Washington Course, as the race track was called, and its long

history on the website of the Preservation Society of Charleston: http://www.halseymap.com/Flash/window.asp?HMID=29; also see John B. Irving, *The South Carolina Jockey Club* (Charleston: Russell & Jones, 1857).

214   **"I had better go North"** Thomas Butler Gunn, *Thomas Butler Gunn Diaries*, vol. 15, *January 1, 1861, to February 28,m 1861* (St. Louis: State Historical Society of Missouri, 2013), pp. 141–142, 185–186.

214   **Committee caught up** Ibid., pp. 56–57.

215   **Bunch concluded with what** Bunch to Lyons, April 15, 1861, Lyons Papers, Duke of Norfolk Archives, Arundel Castle.

Chapter 30

216   **they did much of their politicking** William Howard Russell, *My Diary North and South* (Boston: T. O. H. P. Burnham, 1863), p. 165; reprinted on demand in 2011 by Blackwell Books, London.

216   **"What an awful price"** Philip N. Racine, ed., *Gentlemen Merchants: A Charleston Family's Odyssey, 1828–1870* (Knoxville: The University of Tennessee Press, 2008), p. 442.

216   **Bunch had made sure** FO5/780 Bunch to Russell, February 12, 1861.

218   **It has reserved** Lyons to Russell, February 26, 1861, cited in James J. Barnes and Patience P. Barnes, *The American Civil War Through British Eyes: Dispatches from British Diplomats,* vol. 1: *November 1860–April 1862* (Kent, OH: The Kent State University Press, 2003), p. 34. In March 1861, as if to confirm British suspicions that the Confederate constitution's prohibition of the African slave trade was insincere, Confederate secretary of state Robert Toombs instructed his envoys to Europe to offer to assume all obligations in treaties between the United States and Britain—except for those connected with the suppression of the slave trade.

220   **"the sentiments of nature and of civilization"** FO5/780, Bunch to Russell, February 28, 1861.

Chapter 31

222   **The night before** Charles P. Stone, "Washington on the Eve of War," *Century Magazine*, July 1883, pp. 458–466; also see this account, interesting as much for its publisher as for its content, on the Central Intelligence Agency website: https://www.cia.gov/library/publications/additional-publications/civil-war/SML.htm.

222   **Then they walked out into the daylight** *New York Times*, March 5, 1861.

223 **Bunch warned Lord Russell** FO5/780 Bunch to Russell, March 8, 1861.

223 **Bunch wrote of this floating** Bunch to Lyons, February 16, 1861, Lyons Papers, Duke of Norfolk Archives, Arundel Castle.

223 **"My house is about three miles"** Bunch to Lyons, March 9, 1861, Lyons Papers, Duke of Norfolk Archives, Arundel Castle.

224 **atop a dunghill** Bunch to Lyons, March 21, 1861, Lyons Papers, Duke of Norfolk Archives, Arundel Castle.

225 **As the British saw things** Bunch to Lyons, March 21, 1861, Lyons Papers, Duke of Norfolk Archives, Arundel Castle; also see as background "General Telegraphic News: The Slave and Coolie Trade, Official Correspondence with the British Government," *New York Times*, August 20, 1860.

226 **Bunch was overjoyed** Bunch to Lyons, March 4, 1861, Lyons Papers, Duke of Norfolk Archives, Arundel Castle.

PART FOUR

Chapter 32

229 **"Oh, Lord why *did* I do it?"** Martin Crawford, ed., *William Howard Russell's Civil War: Private Diary and Letters, 1861–1862*, (Athens: University of Georgia Press, 1992), p. 17.

229 **Horace Greeley's *New-York Tribune*,** March 20, 1861, in Howard Cecil Perkins, ed., *Northern Editorials on Secession*, 2 vols. (New York: The American Historical Association, 1942), 2:939; also see "Our Own," *Harper's Weekly*, April 13, 1861, p. 227.

229 **The little boy** Russell's personal diary entry, November 9, 1861. Spelling and punctuation changed to modern usage. Crawford, *Private Diary*, p. 169.

230 **"You must go"** Alan Hankinson, *Man of Wars: William Howard Russell of the* Times (London: Heinemann, 1982), p. 152.

231 **Ward promised to give Russell** Ibid., p. 150.

231 **When Russell had been** Ibid., p. 158.

233 **He was ready** William Howard Russell, *My Diary North and South* (Boston: T. O. H. P. Burnham, 1863), pp. 60–61; reprinted on demand in 2011 by Blackwell Books, London.

234 **So sensitive was Seward** Frederic Bancroft, *The Life of William H. Seward* (New York: Harper & Brothers, 1900), p. 317; also see pp. 328–330 for a very good discussion of how the North overestimated anti-slavery sentiment in Europe while the South grossly underestimated it.

Chapter 33

235   **And if he was with them** Bunch to Lyons, April 5, 1861, Lyons Papers, Duke of Norfolk Archives, Arundel Castle.

235   **Bunch had asked Lyons** Lyons Letter Book, to Bunch, April 13, 1861, Lyons Papers, Duke of Norfolk Archives, Arundel Castle.

236   **Bunch said he planned** Bunch to Lyons, April 9, 1861; note that "attached peasantry," often used to describe feudal estates in Europe and in Ireland, was used by Lyons on occasion when discussing the slaves in the United States. See James J. Barnes and Patience P. Barnes, *Private and Confidential: Letters from British Ministers in Washington to the Foreign Secretaries in London, 1844–67* (Selinsgrove, PA: Susquehanna University Press, 1993), p. 220.

237   **Gen. P. G. T. Beauregard had delivered** J. Cutler Andrews, *The North Reports the Civil War* (Pittsburgh: University of Pittsburgh Press, 1985), p. 1.

237   **"We had no lights"** Abner Doubleday, *Reminiscences of Forts Sumter and Moultrie in 1860–61* (New York: Harper & Brothers, 1876), p. 142.

240   **"But we live in curious times"** Running account of the battle of Fort Sumter, in Bunch to Lyons, April 13, 1860, Lyons Papers, Duke of Norfolk Archives, Arundel Castle.

Chapter 34

241   **"He will find four dinners"** Bunch to Lyons, April 16, 1861, Lyons Papers, Duke of Norfolk Archives, Arundel Castle.

242   **In the aftermath** Frederic Bancroft, *The Life of William H. Seward* (New York: Harper & Brothers, 1900), p. 163.

242   **"Privateers from the Confederacy"** Bunch to Lyons, April 24, 1861, Lyons Papers, Duke of Norfolk Archives, Arundel Castle.

242   **"seems a very nice fellow"** Martin Crawford, ed., *William Howard Russell's Civil War: Private Diary and Letters, 1861–1862* (Athens: University of Georgia Press, 1992), p. 39.

242   **"impressed by his powers of observation"** Bunch to Lyons, April 17, 1861, Lyons Papers, Duke of Norfolk Archives, Arundel Castle.

243   **A stubble of beard** William Howard Russell, *My Diary North and South* (Boston: T. O. H. P. Burnham, 1863), pp. 106–107; reprinted on demand in 2011 by Blackwell Books, London.

243   **Russell came away** Ibid., pp. 108–109.

243   **"Only one of the company"** Ibid., p. 117.

244   **"You won't mind it"** Ibid., p. 118.

244   **A couple of times Bunch** Bunch to Lyons, April 29, 1861, Lyons Papers, Duke of Norfolk Archives, Arundel Castle.

245   **But Bunch wrote directly** Copy of Bunch to Lord Russell in Lyons Papers dated June 20, 1861, Duke of Norfolk Archives, Arundel Castle.

Chapter 35

248   **"The misery and cruelty"** William Howard Russell, *My Diary North and South* (Boston: T. O. H. P. Burnham, 1863), p. 170; reprinted on demand in 2011 by Blackwell Books, London.

248   **He despised the city** Ibid., p. 165.

248   **He loathed his hotel** Ibid., p. 164.

248   **What ate at him** Ibid., p. 169.

249   **a sacred faith which is** Ibid., p. 168.

249   **Russell, so furious he** Ibid., p. 168.

250   **"If England thinks fit"** Ibid., pp. 175–176.

252   **"Of one thing there"** Ibid., p. 293.

Chapter 36

254   **In Washington, Lyons and the French minister** Charles Francis Adams, *Seward and the Declaration of Paris: A Forgotten Diplomatic Episode, April–August 1861* (Boston: Massachusetts Historical Society, 1912), p. 31.

PART FIVE

Chapter 37

259   **The more powerful the Confederates** See William Howard Russell, *My Diary North and South* (Boston: T. O. H. P. Burnham, 1863), p. 377 (reprinted on demand in 2011 by Blackwell Books, London), about his conversation with Lyons, much of which echoes Lyons to Russell, May 20, 1861, cited in James J. Barnes and Patience P. Barnes, *Private and Confidential: Letters from British Ministers in Washington to the Foreign Secretaries in London, 1844–67* (Selinsgrove, PA: Susquehanna University Press, 1993), pp. 85–88.

259   **On June 6** James J. Barnes and Patience P. Barnes, *The American Civil War Through British Eyes: Dispatches from British Diplomats*, vol. 1, *November 1860–April 1862* (Kent, OH: The Kent State University Press, 2003), p. 110.

262   **there was no proof** Robin W. Winks, *Civil War Years: Canada and the United States* (Montreal: McGill-Queen's University Press, 1999), pp. 47–48.

262   **The Confederate commissioners** Frederic Bancroft, *The Life of William H. Seward* (New York: Harper & Brothers, 1900), p. 184.

Chapter 38

264   **He sent a copy** Norman B. Ferris, *Desperate Diplomacy: William H. Seward's Foreign Policy, 1861* (Knoxville: the University of Tennessee Press, 1976), p. 98.

265   **He may never have been involved** See detailed correspondence on the case in *The War of the Rebellion: A Compilation of the Official Records of the Union and Confederate Army*, Series II, Vol. II, "Treatment of Suspected and Disloyal Persons North and South," Case of Purcell M. Quillen (Washington, D.C.: Government Printing Office, 1891), pp. 415–424. Also see Milledge L. Bonham Jr., *The British Consuls in the Confederacy* (New York: Columbia University, 1911), p. 26; James J. Barnes and Patience P. Barnes, *The American Civil War Through British Eyes: Dispatches from British Diplomats*, vol. 1, *November 1860–April 1862* (Kent, OH: The Kent State University Press, 2003), p. 216, note 27; *Illustrated London News*, vol. 39, no. 1103, p. 153, August 17, 1861 (dispatch sent August 3, 1861), and *Illustrated London News*, vol. 39, no. 1105, pp. 208–209, August 31, 1861 (dispatch sent August 17, 1861): "Purcell M'Quillan, the incarcerated British subject, whom the Commander of Fort Lafayette refused to bring into court on a writ of habeas corpus, has been released by the Secretary of War in consequence of the intervention of Lord Lyons."

265   **"I really do not believe it"** Bunch to Lyons, July 8, 1861, Lyons Papers, Duke of Norfolk Archives, Arundel Castle.

265   **"particularly cautious"** Lyons to Bunch, July 6, 1861, Lyons Letter Book, Lyons Papers, Duke of Norfolk Archives, Arundel Castle.

265   **"as prudently as any man."** Lyons Letter Book, to Lord Russell, Private, July 8, 1861, Lyons Papers, Duke of Norfolk Archives, Arundel Castle.

Chapter 39

268   **"as I think right"** I have taken some liberties with the dialogue adapted from paraphrasing, including some of the attributions, which were to both consuls together but which I have assigned either to Bunch or to de Belligny. The text of the original Trescot memorandum was published by Edward A. Trescot, William H. Trescot's son, in "The Confederacy and the Declaration of Paris," *American Historical Review*, vol. 23, no. 4 (July 1918).

269   **"the cause of the Union"** William Howard Russell, *My Diary North and South* (Boston: T. O. H. P. Burnham, 1863), p. 440; reprinted on demand in 2011 by Blackwell Books, London.

269   **"muffled drum"** Ibid., p. 444.

271   **"might as well have talked to the stones"** Ibid., p. 454.

272   *Wicked designs* **of the South** Bunch to Lyons, July 8, 1861, Lyons Papers, Duke of Norfolk Archives, Arundel Castle. Also see Phillip E. Myers, *Caution and Cooperation: The American Civil War in British-American Relations* (Kent, OH: The Kent State University Press, 2008), p. 210; Colin Frank Baxter, *Admiralty Problems During the Second Palmerston Administration, 1859–1865* (Athens: University of Georgia, 1965), pp. 166–171; Brian Jenkins, *Britain and the War for the Union*, vol. I (Montreal: McGill-Queen's University Press, 1974), p. 249.

273   **free the slaves—no, not at all** John Bigelow, "The Confederate Diplomatists and Their Shirt of Nessus," *Century Magazine*, May 1891, pp. 122–123; James Spence, *The American Union; Its Effect on National Character and Policy, with an Inquiry into Secession as a Constitutional Right and the Causes of Disruption* (London: Richard Bentley, 1862), p. 131.

274   **step up their traffic to Cuba** FO84/1137 Lyons to Russell, September 10, 1861, Lyons Papers, Duke of Norfolk Archives, Arundel Castle.

274   **"characterized their predecessors"** Jenkins, *War*, pp. 249–250, citing FO84/1137 Lyons to Russell, September 10, 1861.

Chapter 40

276   **"France and England were not to be alluded to"** Bunch to Lyons, August 16, 1861, Lyons Papers, Duke of Norfolk Archives, Arundel Castle.

277   **American laws against the slave trade** The entire debate is published in *Hansard's Parliamentary Debates: Third Series*, 1861, vol. 164, pp. 164–165.

278   **"rightly or wrongly, vital interests"** Palmerston note enclosed in Earl Russell's private letter to Lord Lyons, August 16, 1861, signed "P 15/8-61," Lyons Papers, Duke of Norfolk Archives, Arundel Castle.

Chapter 41

280   **"possessed the Government cipher."** See "A Scrap of War History: How a Secret Scheme for Securing Recognition of the Southern Confederacy Was Averted," *New York Times*, August 9, 1875, p. 3. This account, alluded to by Milledge L. Bonham Jr. in *The British Consuls in the Confederacy* (New York: Columbia University, 1911), p. 31, was published long after the event and is full of obvious inaccuracies. Most conspicuously, in the actual telegram sent to Seward, Mure's first name is given, correctly, as Robert, while in the article reprinted by the *Times* from the *Hartford Courant* the boastful courier is identified incorrectly as William Mure.

The extent to which the pseudonymous Mr. B. T. Henry turned himself into a spy on the spot that day in Louisville remains an open question, as does his identity. He says in the published account that he wanted to preserve his anonymity even in 1875 because "certain members of his family were on terms of intimate friendship with the Mure family." There is no indication of what business "B. T. Henry" had in Louisville to begin with, and the speed with which he found not only a telegraph operator but the government code and managed to get a message directly to Seward suggests he was not such an amateur as he professed.

280 **pull everything into focus** Extensive correspondence about the case, including the B. T. Henry message, can be found in *The War of the Rebellion: A Compilation of the Official Records of the Union and Confederate Army*, Series II, Vol. II, "Treatment of Suspected and Disloyal Persons North and South," Case of Robert Mure (Washington, D.C.: Government Printing Office, 1897), pp. 643–665.

281 **protection of the British seal** Norman B. Ferris, *Desperate Diplomacy: William H. Seward's Foreign Policy, 1861* (Knoxville: The University of Tennessee Press, 1976), p. 98.

282 **new position and a raise in salary** Bunch to Lyons, August 17, 1861, Lyons Papers, Duke of Norfolk Archives, Arundel Castle.

282 **Bunch's conduct** Lyons to Bunch, August 17, 1861, Lyons Letter Book, Lyons Papers, Duke of Norfolk Archives, Arundel Castle.

283 **"active business by January 1"** This is the extract of the letter contained in the official correspondence between U.S. minister Charles F. Adams and Lord Russell. As Eugene H. Berwanger points out in Berwanger, *The British Foreign Service and the American Civil War* (Lexington: The University Press of Kentucky, 1994), p. 42, the original copy that actually was confiscated left three spaces blank, and when the *Tribune* published the letter, it filled those in. Those words appear here in brackets. See *New-York Tribune*, August 21, 1861, and *War of the Rebellion* documents, p. 651. In that edition "Mr. B" becomes "Mr. Bunch":

DEPARTMENT OF STATE, Washington, August 17, 1861.
CHARLES FRANCIS ADAMS, &c.

SIR: Among the letters found on the person of Robert Mure mentioned in my dispatch of this date there are many which more or less directly implicate Mr. Robert Bunch, the British consul at Charleston, as a conspirator against the Government of the United States. The following is an extract from one of them:

Mr. Bunch on oath of secrecy communicated to me also that the first step to recognition was taken. He and Mr. Belligny together sent Mr. Trescot to Richmond yesterday to ask Jeff. Davis, President, to   the treaty of   to   the neutral flag covering neutral goods to be respected. This is the first step of direct treating with our Government. So prepare for active business by January 1.

You will submit this information to the British Government and request that Mr. Bunch may be removed from his office, saying that this Government will grant an exequatur to any person who may be appointed to fill it who will not pervert his functions to hostilities against the United States.

I am, sir, respectfully, your obedient servant,

WILLIAM H. SEWARD.

283 **"anxious to hear from you"** The date on this deciphered message, August 31, 1861, appears to be anomalous. Bunch first learned of Mure's arrest on August 18. He immediately sent an official note saying that the "passport" Mure carried really was only a certificate to help him move through the lines. In a long private note the same day, August 18, Bunch devoted several pages to his recent visit to the Union blockading ship *Roanoke* and his conversations with the captain, as well as his growing problems finding messengers. He deals with the portentous arrest up North only in passing: "Mr. Mure's case seems a very hard one and a most arbitrary act." The *New-York Tribune* published the infamous anonymous letter about Mr. B and "the first step to recognition" on August 21, and it is certain that Bunch or his friends such as Yeadon at the *Courier* would have heard about it by telegraph that same day. The desperate note quoted here, found among the Lyons Papers at Arundel Castle, is headed "Decypher Private" without the encrypted text attached, which probably means it was sent as a telegram rather than a letter, and from the tone it would seem to have been sent immediately on August 21, not August 31.

284 **focus was on Bunch** Berwanger, *British Foreign Service*, pp. 48–49.

Chapter 42

285 **"he is not fit for his post"** Hammond to Lyons, November 30, 1861, Lyons Papers, Duke of Norfolk Archives, Arundel Castle.

286 **it wasn't going to help** Ephraim Douglass Adams, *Great Britain and the American Civil War* (Charleston: Bibliobazaar, 2006), p. 176; reprint of the original 1925 Longmans, Green and Co. edition.

286 **"involve the two countries in war"** Brian Jenkins, *Lord Lyons: A Diplomat in an Age of Nationalism and War* (Montreal: McGill-Queen's University Press, 2014), Kindle loc 2944.

286   **"home without his own explanation"** Lyons to Admiral Milne, October 28, 1861, Lyons Papers, Duke of Norfolk Archives, Arundel Castle.

286   **"darker and darker every day"** Russell to Cowley, the British ambassador in Paris, cited by Norman B. Ferris, *Desperate Diplomacy: William H. Seward's Foreign Policy, 1861* (Knoxville: The University of Tennessee Press, 1976), p. 102, and Amanda Foreman, *A World on Fire: An Epic History of Two Nations Divided* (London: Allen Lane, an imprint of Penguin Books, 2010), published in the United States as *A World on Fire: Britain's Crucial Role in the American Civil War*, p. 98.

286   **"singular mixture of the bully and coward"** Russell to Palmerston, cited by Ferris, *Desperate*, p. 111; Adams, *Great Britain*, p. 185, note 383.

286   **"less agreeable"** Ferris, *Desperate*, p. 114. Note that the British consul in Canton, China, one Harry Parkes, ordered the bombardment of that city in 1856 after a perceived insult to the British flag, thus setting into motion the events that led to the Second Opium War.

286   **"must have troops there"** Howard Jones, *Blue and Gray Diplomacy: A History of Union and Confederate Foreign Relations* (Chapel Hill: The University of North Carolina Press, 2010), p. 67.

288   **"rest on our oars for the winter"** Adams, *Great Britain*, p. 175, citing Russell to Palmerston, September 19, 1861.

289   **"and unofficially?"** This dialogue is reconstructed from the paraphrases of a conversation between Seward and Lyons that took place on October 12, 1861. Lyons to Russell, October 14, 1861, Lyons Papers, Duke of Norfolk Archives, Arundel Castle.

289   **"all-important that I gain time"** Continuation of dialogue adapted from Lyons to Russell, October 14, 1861.

290   **"and withdrew"** FO5/773 Lyons to Russell, October 28, 1861.

290   **"prepared for an attack"** FO5/773 Lyons to Russell, October 28, 1861.

291   **"breaking up the blockade"** Lyons to Russell, October 28, 1861, Lyons Papers.

291   **"under his official cover"** Hammond to Lyons, October 24, 1861, Lyons Papers.

292   **"arrogant in the American character"** Martin Duberman, *Charles Francis Adams, 1807–1886* (Boston: Houghton Mifflin, 1960), p. 267.

Chapter 43

293   **278 Europeans on the island died** Charles Wilkes, *Autobiography of Rear Admiral Charles Wilkes, U.S. Navy, 1798–1877*, ed. William James Morgan et al. (Washington, D.C.: Naval History Division, Department of the Navy, 1978), p. 907; Mary S. Lovell, *A Rage to Live: A Biography of Richard and Isabel Burton* (New York: Norton, 2000), p. 390.

293   **sent him to Fernando Po** Wilkes, *Autobiography*, p. 907.

294   **discovered how expensive it was** Wilkes's mother, Mary Seton, was the sister of William Seton, who married Bunch's mother's half sister, Elizabeth Ann Bayley Seton. Wilkes's mother died soon after he was born, and for a time he was raised by his aunt, Mrs. Seton, before she went to Italy with her fatally ill husband, converted to Catholicism, and founded a religious order. See Wilkes, *Autobiography*, p. 2.

295   **The rest, he believed, would obey his orders** Wilkes, *Autobiography*, pp. 767–773.

296   **"best thing that could have happened"** J. B. Jones, *A Rebel War Clerk's Diary at the Confederate States Capital*, vol. 1 (Philadelphia: J. B. Lippincott, 1866), p. 93. Paraphrases have been turned to full quotations here.

Chapter 44

297   **portrait of the young Queen Victoria** Several of the details here were compiled in Brian Hicks, "Charleston at War: Charleston Beaten Down by Great Fire," *The Post and Courier*, January 30, 2011.

300   **" 'snubbed' "—if not worse** Bunch to Lyons, December 8, 1861, Lyons Papers, Duke of Norfolk Archives, Arundel Castle.

301   **drafted into the Rebel Army** Bunch to Lyons, December 8, 1861, Lyons Papers, Duke of Norfolk Archives, Arundel Castle.

302   **"stout hearts for defense"** J. B. Jones, *A Rebel War Clerk's Diary at the Confederate States Capital*, vol. 1 (Philadelphia: J. B. Lippincott, 1866), p. 103.

Chapter 45

303   **crimes in the Middle Passage** Ron Soodalter, *Hanging Captain Gordon: The Life and Trial of an American Slave Trader* (New York: Washington Square Press, 2006), pp. 184–189.

304   **"while he is in the mood"** James J. Barnes and Patience P. Barnes, *Private and Confidential: Letters from British Ministers in Washington*

to the Foreign Secretaries in London, 1844–67 (Selinsgrove, PA: Susquehanna University Press, 1993), p. 280.

304   **"Suppression of the Slave Trade"** Ibid., p. 282.

305   **"will be suppressed"** "Great Britain," *New York Times*, May 21, 1862.

305   **"reducing the South"** Ephraim Douglass Adams, *Great Britain and the American Civil War* (Charleston: Bibliobazaar, 2006), p. 168; reprint of the original 1925 Longmans, Green and Co. edition.

305   **thanks to the pressures of the rebellion** "Great Britain," *New York Times*, May 21, 1862.

307   **London would bend to their will** Frank Lawrence Owsley, *King Cotton Diplomacy* (Chicago: University of Chicago Press, 1959), pp. 24–39.

308   **a war it did not want to fight** Adams, *Great Britain*, p. 329.

309   **that would buy off British opinion** Ibid., p. 365.

310   **his government was not** Ibid., p. 331.

310   **"to seem to support" Russell** Ibid., p. 335.

312   **the African trade would not be reopened** John Bigelow, "The Confederate Diplomatists and Their Shirt of Nessus," *Century Magazine*, May 1891, pp. 115–116. The dialogue here is reconstructed slightly from paraphrases.

312   **the Confederacy to decide** Frederic Bancroft, *The Life of William H. Seward* (New York: Harper & Brothers, 1900), pp. 331–332.

313   **before the Yankee attack began** James J. Barnes and Patience P. Barnes, *The American Civil War Through British Eyes: Dispatches from British Diplomats*, vol. 2, *April 1862–February 1863* (Kent, OH: The Kent State University Press, 2005), p. 312.

Chapter 46

314   **several occasions during this trying time** James J. Barnes and Patience P. Barnes, *The American Civil War Through British Eyes: Dispatches from British Diplomats*, vol. 2, *April 1862–February 1863* (Kent, OH: The Kent State University Press, 2005), pp. 304–305.

315   **Every one must judge for himself** "Important from the South," *New York Times*, February 12, 1863.

EPILOGUE

317   **the last known witness** Sylviane A. Diouf, *Dreams of Africa in Alabama: The Slave Ship* Clotilda *and the Story of the Last Africans*

Brought to America (New York: Oxford University Press, 2007), Kindle loc 2231 and 3933.

318   **killed three of them with a hatchet** "The Schooner *S. J. Waring*," *Harper's Weekly*, August 3, 1861; Rick Beard, "'The Lion of the Day,'" *New York Times*, August 4, 2011.

319   **endures to the present** William C. Davis, ed., *A Fire-Eater Remembers: The Confederate Memoir of Robert Barnwell Rhett* (Columbia: University of South Carolina Press, 2000), pp. xviii–xx.

320   **"standing like a stone-wall"** Patricia G. McNeely, Debra Reddin van Tuyll, and Henry H. Schulte, eds., *Knights of the Quill: Confederate Correspondents and Their Civil War Reporting* (West Lafayette, IN: Purdue University Press, 2010), p. 20.

320   **"advocated secession most strenuously"** "Deaths of the Day," *Los Angeles Herald*, October 5, 1903, p. 3.

320   **"We must rely on ourselves alone"** Eric H. Walther, *William Lowndes Yancey and the Coming of the Civil War* (Chapel Hill: The University of North Carolina Press, 2006), p. 335.

322   **"Dared sublimely to be true"** Cited by Greg Hambrick, "James Petigru Dared to Challenge Confederacy," *Charleston City Paper*, April 6, 2011.

323   **"noiseless perfection of training"** Cited by Robert N. Rosen in *Confederate Charleston: An Illustrated History of the City and the People During the Civil War* (Columbia: University of South Carolina Press, 1994), p. 130. Rosen's book is much more than a handsome decoration for coffee tables; it tells as well as anyone has the story of the city in the war years. I have drawn on it for several details here.

323   **black regiment** These events were popularized by Hollywood in the 1989 film *Glory*.

324   **incendiary shells** Rosen, *Confederate Charleston*, p. 119.

324   **"Ruins!"** Ibid., p. 127.

324   **"starve it out"** Ibid., p. 132.

325   **"so thick on the ground"** Ibid., p. 142.

326   **"a sense of his own dignity"** Joseph Smith, *Illusions of Conflict: Anglo-American Diplomacy Toward Latin America, 1865–1896* (Pittsburgh: University of Pittsburgh Press, 1979), p. 15.

Acknowledgments

Our Man in Charleston, which was very long in contemplation, research, and writing, would never have been finished were it not for Kevin Doughten, my truly extraordinary editor at Crown. When we began working together in late 2013, the narrative—indeed, the narratives—were spread all over the map from Alabama to Boston to the Bight of Benin. Her Majesty's Consul Robert Bunch was the central figure, to be sure, but he was lost in a crowd of fascinating characters.

Kevin, who looked up every footnote, read deeply into the published materials, and carefully considered every comma in the manuscript again and again (with the able and amiable assistance of Claire Potter) knew that we could pare away much of the supporting cast and bring the spotlight to bear much more sharply on the character of Bunch, with his great mission and also his many foibles. I can't really say Kevin is the Max Perkins of his generation (I certainly am not the Thomas Wolfe or Ernest Hemingway of mine), but I do think he is one of the last really great book editors in the business.

As I say, *Our Man in Charleston* was a long time coming, and proper acknowledgment of the many people who contributed to it in many different ways requires a note about its genesis and gestation.

I first got interested in the period and its personalities back in 1991 when I read a biography of the great British explorer Sir Richard Francis Burton, whose extraordinarily well-documented life has one great lacuna, in the summer of 1860 when he traveled to the United States and disappeared for several weeks in the South. Probably he was drinking a lot. Even more probably, he was gathering intelligence for some of his powerful friends in Britain. This was, after all, the eve of the American Civil War, and much of the British economy depended on Southern cotton.

As I pondered all this, I took on many other unrelated projects. I wrote a memoir about my father and two novels about jihadist terrorism. The attacks on September 11 happened, and I wrote another book about the New York City Police Department. I kept on picking up this manuscript and putting it down year after year, sometimes trying the story out as fiction, sometimes as nonfiction, until I realized there was no solid information about what Burton was doing, and, making the work more difficult still, the better I got to know him, the less I liked him.

When I looked at whom he met, or might have met, however, the other historical characters fascinated me and, slowly, the picture of Bunch began to emerge at the center of the intrigue about cotton and the slave trade in the early days of the war that had such fateful results by the end.

My agent, Kathy Robbins, was marvelously patient and constructive all this time. Her husband, British editor and author (and fencer) Richard Cohen, also took a great interest. My good friend and longtime editor Alice Mayhew, who has a passion for the Civil War, frequently helped me think through bits and pieces of the developing story.

Work on the present book finally began in earnest in 2010, when John Glusman acquired the project for Crown. We had a good understanding of where we might go with it, but John left a year later, and upheavals in the news business as I moved from weekly journalism to daily and sometimes hourly reporting at *The Daily Beast* kept me tied up for much of the following two years. Through that time, Sean Desmond kindly shepherded the project at Crown. Then came Kevin Doughten and the rest, one might say, is this history.

Research for this book was done at several different institutions. In the United States, the Library of Congress and the National Archives in Washington, D.C., were particularly important, of course, and Eddie Becker, a legendary researcher, was helpful by introducing me to the right corners of those vast collections. At the New York Public Library I, like many others, benefitted greatly from the knowledge and consideration of David Smith, once profiled as "Librarian to the Stars," and a great help, in fact, to any serious researcher.

I spent many fascinating days poring over 160-year-old newspapers and other documents at the Charleston Library Society, often with the help of my wife, Carol, who is, in addition to her many other impressive and endearing attributes, a very determined researcher. In addition to Executive Director Anne Cleveland, I would like to thank some members of the Library Society staff who helped me in years past, including Carol Jones, Debbie Fenn, and Robert Salvo.

I would also like to thank Stephen J. White Sr., a devoted scholar and the director of the Charleston Historical Society. Stephen introduced me to David T. Gleason at Northumbria University, and our correspondence about the Irish role in the antebellum South was especially useful. Stephen also introduced me to Nic Butler, the City Historian for Charleston, who clarified several vital details.

Faye Jensen and her staff at the South Carolina Historical Society were gracious and helpful. Their file on Robert Bunch was invaluable, and they have the only known photograph of "our man in Charleston." When I could not go there myself, I was helped tremendously by Hannah Neff, then a student at the Savannah College of Art and Design, who did some great digging and turned up some real treasures.

In Britain, the staff at the British Library in London and the National Archives at Kew were always very professional and helpful, not only when I appeared in person but when we corresponded by e-mail.

At Oxford's Bodleian Library, I am thankful to Colin Harris, superintendent of the Special Collections Reading Rooms, for his help and the assistance of his gracious staff in the course of several visits as I went through Bunch's private correspondence with the British chargé d'affaires and later minister in Washington, John Crampton.

At the Norfolk Records Office in Norfolk, United Kingdom, my special thanks to Rachel Farmer, who made it possible for me to get copies of several important documents from the papers of Henry Lytton Earle Bulwer.

The greatest treasure trove of Bunch correspondence, however, is in the Duke of Norfolk's Archives at Arundel Castle in West Sussex, which houses the Lyons Papers. When some of them were stored, previously, at the West Sussex Records Office in Chichester in 2012, my journalist colleague Mairi Mackay was kind enough to go down from London, like a Sherpa amid the mountain of papers, and scout out some of the most interesting documents, including some of those written in code.

I subsequently went to Arundel Castle, where the entire collection of Lyons Papers is now, and where archivist Rebecca Hughes and archive assistant Craig Irving gave me every possible assistance. I like to think they also shared in some of the excitement as we discovered one little revelation after another, including many more letters written partially or entirely in cipher. From the documents there emerged the important nuances of the Bunch-Lyons relationship.

Several individuals encouraged me and helped me frame my thoughts along the way, including, over a lunch one day, Amanda Foreman, author of the epic *A World on Fire*, and Sylviane Diouf, author of *Dreams of Africa in Alabama*, who was kind enough to share with me some of her original documentation about the voyage of the *Clotilda*.

My correspondence with Ted Maris-Wolf, now at Brown University's Center for the Study of Slavery and Justice, was very useful as I tried to gain a deeper understanding of the Buchanan administration's shifting, and shifty, policy toward the African slave trade. My journalistic colleague Will Cathcart, who is descended from a distinguished Charleston family, has provided very useful advice about the city and its people.

David Laven at the University of Nottingham in the United Kingdom helped me delve into the story of Hugh Forbes and Garibaldi, a bit of history virtually unknown to American readers.

My research into the Bunch family's important Colombian connections would not have been possible without the help of Adrianne Foglia, a fine journalist and a friend for more years than either of us would count, who was formerly the spokesperson for the Colombian embassy in London. Adrianne dug quickly and deeply into the mystery of Robert Bunch's Latin American connections, and we discovered just what an extraordinary background he had.

In my *Newsweek* days, my editors Mark Whitaker, Jon Meacham, and Tina Brown all encouraged my research. In my Paris office, Ginny Power was a constant support, and Florence Villeminot was a brilliant, diligent researcher.

At *The Daily Beast* there are some interesting Southerners who have shared their thoughts about the Civil War then and the culture wars now. Editor in Chief John Avlon (from Charleston) and Malcolm Jones, editor of the book section, helped me think about the narrative of the 1850s as it relates to contemporary politics.

Finally, I would like to thank some personal friends and family not only for their encouragement but also for helping me escape my daily routine every so often by putting me up in some lovely contemplative hideaways: John Henry Whitmire offered refuge any number of times in South Carolina, and one day in London in 2009, as I was trying to explain my research into Burton and how I'd learned to dislike the man, John Henry helped me to understand that Bunch was the key to this story. Alice Cathrall offered Carol and me her warm Southern hospitality in her beautiful home in Wilmington, North Carolina. Gina and Courtlandt Miller gave us solitude high above the sea in Cap Ferrat, and Laura Paglieri handed over the keys to her getaway apartment near Courmayeur, at the foot of Mont Blanc, where nature puts everything into perspective.